Egyptian Colloquial Arabic

FRANTIŠEK ONDRÁŠ

SET OUT

This book has been published with the support of the Ministry of Education Grant Nr. LN00A064 (The Czech National Centre for Egyptology) and the entire edition costs have been covered by UNIS, Ltd.

ISBN 80-86277-42-9

Acknowledgements

This book would not have been possible without the help of many people, who supported me with their advice or practical help. I would like to express my sincere thanks especially to my dear wife, Ḥosna ʿAbd as-Samīʿ Maḥmūd, without whose continuous understanding and support this book would never have seen the light of day. I appreciate the openness with which my parents accepted my work and would like to express my gratitude to them here as well.

The assistance and grant for my work was provided by the Czech National Centre for Egyptology, Charles University Prague, and my earnest thanks belong to this institution as well.

Contents

Preface

This book is conceived as a help to all those interested in Egyptian Colloquial Arabic, students of Arabic language, Egyptology, and the general public with interest in the Arab world and culture.

The textbook is divided into 20 lessons, which provide a systematic explanation of the grammar of the Egyptian Colloquial Arabic followed by a corresponding set of exercises for practical introduction to the language. An integral part of each lesson is formed by a compound of phrases for everyday use.

Each lesson consists of a text, illustrating the grammar, and introducing the reader to a particular conversation situation, which the visitor of Egypt may encounter during his/her stay. Their sequence is conceived as a "Language guide" to Egypt beginning with *The Airport, Taking the taxi, Checking in a hotel, At the market, A museum visit, In a coffeehouse, Train station, An official reception…*

Illustrative anecdotes, taken from original Egyptian sources and giving a hint of the Arabic sense of humor and comic situations, accompany each topic. Practical information is given in addition along the texts and phrases, which form an inseparable part of the knowledge of Egyptian Arabic.

Although this is not a phrasebook, that would claim to include all possible conversational moments, which can be met when communicating with native speakers, it should provide the reader with adequate knowledge of the language to be able to communicate with the Arabic speakers in general, i. e. Egyptians or non-Egyptians, in Egypt or elsewhere.

The student should make use of the exercises, consisting of questions related to each text. The reader should practice his abilities in conversation related to the topic of the text. The key to each exercise is given in the appendix. The individual lessons are accompanied by vocabularies, arranged according to the English alphabet. It is necessary to point out a few remarks regarding the position of words that include some particular Arabic consonants.

Words beginning with ***ʿ* (*ʿayin*)** are arranged according to the consonant that follows the ***ʿ* (*ʿayin*)**. The consonant ***q* (*qāf*)** is most commonly pronounced as the so-called ***hamza* - *ʾ***. Words beginning with this consonant are positioned as if they would begin with ***q***. If ***ʾ* (*hamza*)** does not represent a pronunciation form of ***qāf***, the words are treated as if they were without this consonant.

Lessons 1 to 20 use the transcription of Arabic script, which should enable the student an easier start with the grammar of Egyptian Colloquial Arabic. Lesson 21 provides basic information about the Arabic script, which is the only way that native speakers of Arabic use to render their mother tongue in a written form.

The student should find considerable help in the audio CD, which accompanies this textbook.

How to use this book?

The book should be useful for all interested students of Egyptian Colloquial Arabic, regardless their previous knowledge of the Standard or Classical Arabic. Good pronunciation is more easily obtained with the help of a teacher, but the students can help themselves by carefully reading aloud the texts and vary the sentences in exercises, texts etc. By a continuous reading and pronunciation exercise the students should be able to master the language.

The knowledge of Arabic script enables better communication, better understanding of Arabic art and culture, and helps in the orientation in the Arabic countries, which makes every sojourn easier, more enjoyable and more engaging.

The recommended system how to use the textbook is as follows:

a) Read the grammar of each lesson
b) Listen to the text on the CD
c) Read the text
d) Study the vocabulary
e) Read the questions and answer them
f) Translate the text
g) Study the grammar
h) Do the exercises
i) Repeat the vocabulary
j) Read the anecdote

Note: The transcription of Arabic names used in maps and plans follows the conventional transcription used in the most of published maps of Egypt. The transcription in this book is therefore different.

Introduction

Egyptian Colloquial Arabic is a mother tongue to 70 millions of Egyptians and a means of communication to millions of people living in the Arab world. Egyptian Arabic is one of the numerous colloquial forms of the Arab language, spoken all over the Arab world. In Egypt herself, Egyptian colloquial Arabic in the variant, to which this textbook is dedicated, is spoken mainly in Cairo and its surroundings. In addition, the language possesses many subdialects in the provinces.

Despite its original limitation to Egypt and the concentration of most of its speakers around the country's capital, Egyptian Colloquial Arabic became one of the forms of Arabic, which are widespread throughout the Arab world as a sort of *lingua franca*. This is chiefly due to the fact, that a number of Egyptians with higher education and skills work nowadays in other Arab countries all over the Middle East. And secondly, the overwhelming Egyptian television, film and music production entered the mass media markets of the Middle East, and has won a renowned position. It can be said, with a certain caution, that Cairo maintains its position of the cultural capital of the Arab world.

The cultural and religious coherence of the Arab world is borne by Standard Arabic, the language of the Qur'an, which is strictly codified and united for all Arab-speaking countries, and even the whole Muslim world, for which Standard Arabic represents the untouchable language of the Scripture. Standard Arabic is the language used in science, literature, newspapers, all official documents, television and broadcast. It is taught in schools, and the level of mastering it depends on the level of education of each individual.

Colloquial Arabic represents the means of everyday communication. Colloquial Arabic can be divided geographically, according to the area where each dialect is spoken. There are a few closely related groups of colloquial languages. Moroccan, Algerian and Tunisian Arabic are close to each other. On the other hand, Libyan Arabic is distinct. Sudanese Arabic is related to the Egyptian colloquial language. Common features characterize Jordanian, Palestinian, Lebanese and Syrian Colloquial Arabic. Iraqi and Kuwaiti Arabic form another group. The spoken languages of Saudi Arabia, the countries of the Gulf, and of Yemen are close relatives as well.

It has to be said that the term Egyptian, Syrian or Moroccan Colloquial Arabic usually refers to the language spoken in the capital and its neighbourhood. The other parts of the countries have their own subdialects.

In the everyday use, regardless of their educational or social status, all Egyptians use Egyptian Colloquial Arabic. The language is not a monolith with a unified lexicon of Arabic origin only. Coptic, Turkish, Persian and Greek have influenced it. The last two centuries brought a lot of words of Italian, French and English origin. English influence is still the dominant one, providing new enrichments to the Egyptian thesaurus. It is often due to the fact that some of the technical expressions and appliance names are English and are used in slightly Arabised form.

Egyptian Colloquial Arabic is used in television, radio broadcasting and film production for audience in all Arab countries. Numerous prosaic, as well as poetic works, plays, folk tales, proverbs and short stories are conceived in Egyptian Colloquial Arabic. It should not be forgotten, that newspaper and magazine advertisements and various leaflets use colloquial Arabic too.

The most widespread dialect of Egyptian Colloquial Arabic is the dialect of Cairo, spoken not only by the inhabitants of the capital and its environs, but by all the people, who have been studying, working or living in Cairo. Another remarkable subdialect is the Alexandrine one, spoken by the citizens of this great Mediterranean harbour. The people of bigger harbour and fishermen's cities of the Delta, Damietta and Port Said (*Dumyāṭ, Būr Saʿīd*) also have subdialects of their own. Furthermore, rural areas of the Delta have their own subdialects, showing different pronunciation and some peculiar morphological traits. These last features plus some syntactical changes are characteristic mainly of the easternmost part of the Nile delta (*Sharʾīya*).

Upper Egypt – *iṣ-Ṣaʿīd* – has a specific dialect of its own, showing distinguished lexical traits and having its own pronunciation rules, entirely different from the Cairene dialect. Similar features are present in the subdialects of the Western Desert Oases and the Sinai, furthermore showing morphological and syntactical changes, which in the first group are near to Libyan Arabic and in the second one have a lot in common with Bedouin Arabic dialects of the neighbouring Asian areas.

The phonetic, morphological and other peculiarities and variants proper to Egyptian Colloquial Arabic are the result of geographic as well as of sociocultural differentiation. University graduates have different speech nuances than people without higher education, people of position express themselves differently than those who belong to the worker class. Even the speech of women has its own attributes in phonetics and lexicon, compared to that of men. The lexical usage of Egyptian Arabic enables to determine, whether the speaker is a Christian or a Muslim, as both religious communities have a vocabulary of their own, related to their religious practices as well.

Selected bibliography:

1. Arnaudies, A. – Boutros, W., *Lexique pratique des chantiers de fouilles et de restauration* {Français – Egyptien / Egyptien – Français}, Institut Français dʾArchéologie Orientale – Bibliothèque generale. XV, 1996. Le Caire.
2. Badawi, S. – Hinds, M., *A Dictionary of Egyptian Arabic* {Arabic – English}, Beirut, Libraire du Liban. 1986.
3. Boutros, W., *Lexique franco-egyptien – le parler du Caire*. Institut Français dʾArchéologie Orientale. Bibliothèque generale 21 – 2000.
4. Mitchell, T. F., *An Introduction to Egyptian Colloquial Arabic*, London. Oxford University Press. 1960.
5. Boutros, W., *Ahlan wa sahlan, methode dʾ arabe egyptien du Caire*. Editions Dar el-Nashr Hatier, Le Caire. 1993.

Pronunciation

Arabic consonants

Egyptian Colloquial Arabic has 26 consonants, which are encoded by 28 graphemes in the Arabic script.

ʾ (hamza – the glottal stop)
- this consonant sounds as the English "bottle" pronounced with a cockney accent, dropping the double "t". In Arabic: *ʾabadan* (not at all), *saʾal* (he asked), *ʾimḍā* (signature)
- note the words beginning with a vowel, but not with hamza: *istirkhā* (relaxation), *iftakar* (he thought)
- ***hamza*** is consistently written instead of the ***i***- of the definite article (***il***-), which is omitted when the definite article follows a word ending in a vowel: *bi ʾl-ʿarabī* (Arabic). The general rule is: when the first of two adjoining words ends in a vowel and the second one begins with it, the final vowel of the first word is omitted and ***ʾ*** (***hamza***) is written instead of it.

b (bāʾ)
- this consonant is pronounced as in English: bat, bottle, bench – *balad* (country, countryside), *gabal* (mountain), *ʾab* (father)

t (tāʾ)
- this consonant is pronounced as in English: tick, tap – *tarabēza* (table), *iktishāf* (discovery), *tābūt* (coffin)

g (gīm)
- this consonant is pronounced as in English: gum, bug – *ganb* (side), *magalla* (magazine), *ʾintāg* (production)

ḥ (ḥāʾ)
- this consonant is pronounced as a deep, breathy h. The mouth is slightly open and the tongue is arched against the back of the throat: *ḥabīb* (beloved), *baḥr* (sea), *sāyiḥ* (tourist)

kh (khāʾ)
- this consonant is pronounced as "ch" in Scottish "loch" – *khōf* (fear), *ʾakhīr* (the last), *khōkh* (peaches)

d (dāl)
- this consonant is pronounced as in English: dig, down – *durg* (drawer), *khidma* (service), *gild* (skin)

r (rāʾ)
- this consonant is pronounced as rolled "r": Spanish "arriva" - *rās* (head), *sharāb* (socks), *sūr* (wall)

z (zāy)
- this consonant is pronounced as in English: zoom, zombie – *zbūn* (customer, client), *tazkara* (ticket), *butagāz* (gas oven)

s (sīn)
- this consonant is pronounced as in English: set, boss - *sifāra* (embassy), *garson* (waiter), *dars* (lesson, course unit)

sh (shīn)
- this consonant is pronounced as "sh" in English: shore, shawl – *shahr* (month), *bāsha* (sir), *mafrash* (tablecloth)

ṣ (ṣād)
- this consonant is pronounced as emphatic s. The tongue is arched against the back of the throat and the consonant gets a dark tone: *ṣūra* (photograph, picture), *Maṣr* (Egypt), *rkhīṣ* (cheap)

ḍ (ḍād)
- this consonant is pronounced as emphatic d. The tip of the tongue leans against the upper teeth and its body against the gums, the root of the tongue is arched against the back of the throat and the consonant gets a dark tone: *ḍahr* (back), *ʾōḍa* (room), *maraḍ* (illness)

ṭ (ṭāʾ)
- this consonant is pronounced as emphatic t. The tip of the tongue leans againt the upper row of the teeth and its body against the gums, the root of the tongue is arched against the back of the throat and the consonant gets a dark tone: *ṭālib* (student), *baṭāṭis* (potatoes), *khallāṭ* (mixer)

ẓ (ẓāʾ)
- this consonant is pronounced as emphatic z. The tip of the tongue leans against the upper row of the teeth and its root is arched against the back of the throat, thus the consonant gets a dark tone: *ẓābiṭ* (officer), *maẓbūṭ* (precise, precisely), *lafẓ* (word, expression)

ʿ (ʿēn)
- this consonant is pronounced as a guttural stop. The mouth is slightly opened, the tongue is arched against the back of the throat (the sound is created by pronouncing an "ah" sound and simultaneously pressing against the throat above the Adam's apple): *ʿēn* (eye), *maṭʿam* (restaurant), *rugūʿ* (return)

gh (ghēn)
- is pronounced as a velar stop. The sound is similar to French "r": *ghada* (lunch), *lugha* (language), *bulūgh* (maturity)

f (fāʾ)
- this consonant is pronounced as in English: fox, often – *fikra* (thought, idea), *sofra* (dining room), *ẓarf* (envelope)

q (qāf)
- this consonant is pronounced as hamza: *ʾ/qamar* (moon), *maʾ/qlī* (fried), *ṭabaʾ/q* (plate)
- words coming from the context of standard Arabic form an exception. Here, q is pronounced as an uvular stop k: *il-Qāhira* (Cairo), *saqāfa* (culture), *mulḥaq* (attaché)
- in Upper Egypt, this consonant is pronounced as **g**: *g/ʾahwa* (coffee), *mag/ʾfūl* (closed), *shōg/ʾ* (desire)

k (kāf)
- this consonant is pronounced as in English: kettle, poke – *kursī* (chair), *maktab* (office), *mabrūk* (blessed)
l (lām)
- this consonant is pronounced as in English: love, blank – *laban* (milk), *salaṭa* (salad), *fūl* (beans)
m (mīm)
- this consonant is pronounced as in English: mother, symbol – *makān* (place), *samak* (fish), *nōm* (sleep)
n (nūn)
- this consonantis pronounced as in English: name, month – *nūr* (light), *manga* (mango), *lamūn* (lemon)
h (hā')
- this consonant is pronounced as in English: head, hide – *haram* (pyramid), *sahl* (easy), *'Allāh* (Allah, God)
w (wāw)
- this consonant is pronounced bilabially as the English w: well, power – *ward* (rose), *mahwūs* (possessed), *gauw* (weather, air, atmosphere). After a word-final consonant, it is pronounced as English u: put, took – *ḥelu* (nice, sweet)
y (yā')
- this consonant is pronounced as the English y: you, beyond – *yōm* (day), *malyān* (full), *mashy* (walk)

Double consonants are pronounced as a single prolonged one, not as two adjoining consonants: *maḥaṭṭa* (stop), *radd* (answer, reaction), *mayya* (water), *muhimm* (important), *lammā* (when), *ḥall* (solution), *ṣaḥḥ* (correct), *iḥmarr* (he became red)

Words of foreign origin contain also the consonants **v** and **j**: *villa* (villa), *jaket* (jacket), *jelatti* (ice-cream)

Arabic vowels
Short: **a, e, i, o, u**
Long: **ā, ē, ī, ō, ū**

a - ā:
- next to emphatic consonants, both ***a*** and ***ā*** are pronounced somewhat deeper and closer to ***o***: *ṣabr* (patience), *ṣāyim* (fasting), *ḍaghṭ* (pressure), *ḍāmin* (granting), *ṭalab* (request), *ṭāliʿ* (rising), *ẓālim* (unjust, unfair)
- next to other vowels, ***a*** is pronounced as an open ***a***: *kharag* (he went out), *ʿamalit* (she made), ***ā*** is close to an open ***ē***: *sāfir* (he travelled), *kānit* (she was)

e - ē:
- **e** is pronounced as English **e** in bet, ***ē*** is somewhat more closed: *lē(h)* (why), *zēt* (oil)

i - ī:
- next to emphatic consonants, both ***i*** and ***ī*** are pronounced somewhat deeper: *wiṣil* (he arrived), *ʾaṣīl* (original), *nḍīf* (pure), *laṭīf* (nice, kind), *ṭinn* (tonne)

o - ō:
- these vowels are pronounced as the English ***o***: shot, and ***aw***: shawl, dawn – *lo* (to him), *ṣōt* (voice), *fōʾ* (over), *ṣaḥbo* (his friend)

u - ū:
- these vowels are pronounced as the English ***u***: put and ***oo***: food, tool – *shuf*! (look), *humma* (they), *gūʿ* (hunger), *nūr* (light), *katabū* (they wrote)

Diphthongs
au:
lau (if), *mauhūb* (talented), *faraula* (strawberries), *mirauwaḥ* (going home)
ay:
zay (as), *gay* (coming), *dayman* (always), *mayyit* (dead)

Note:
- if a group of three consonants appears, the vowel ***e*** is inserted in front of the last one: *ma gibt(e)lūsh* (I did not bring to him)
- if two consonants stand at the end of the word, they take the vowel ***i***: *ma katabsh(i)* (he did not write)
- vowels, that stand word-medially in brackets, may, but need not be read: *k(i)fāya*, *kh(u)sāra*
- short vowels standing at the end of the word are prolonged, if the word takes on a pronominal suffix: *yikhalli – yikhallīk*, *shayfa - shayfāk*
- imperfect vowels of words with the second consonant ***w*** or ***y*** are shortened in negative forms: *shāf – mashafsh(i)*, *yigīb – mayigibsh(i)*

Stress
The following rules guide the placement of stress:
- the word-initial closed syllable bears the stress:
a) the syllable may be long – *mak**tūb*** (written), *mar**sūm*** (drawn)
b) the syllable may be short and closed by two consonants – *kha**ragt*** (I went out)
- when the last syllable is open (long or short) or closed with a short syllable, the stress moves to the last-but-one long or closed syllable: *kha**rag**na* (we went out), ***shuf**tū* (you [pl.] saw), *muta**shak**kir* (thanking), *muta**sā**miḥ* (tolerant)
- when the last syllable is open (long or short) or closed with a short vowel, and if the last-but-one syllable is open and short and if the third syllable from the end is closed, the stress stays on the last-but-one vowel: *mudar**ri**sī* (my teacher), *tukh**ru**gū* (you go out [pl.]), *mak**ta**ba* (library), *ʿan**di**na* (by us, we have), *ʿan**du**hum* (by them, they have)
- when the last-but-one syllable is open and short and so is the third syllable from the end, the stress lies on the latter: ***ṭa**laba* (students), ***da**rasit* (she studied), ***kha**ragū* (they went out)

1

Id-dars il-ʾauwalānī/Lesson 1

Fi ʾl-maṭār

- Is-salāmu ʿalēku!
- Wi ʿalēkum is-salām! Ḥaḍretak mnēn?
- ʾAna min ʾIngilterra.
- Mnēn fi ʾIngilterra?
- Min London.
- London madīna gamīla?
- ʾA(h), hiya madīna gamīla giddan.
- Wi ʾl-gauw fī London di ʾl-waʾti ḥelu?
- Il-ḥamdu li ʾllāh, il-gauw kwayyis hnāk.
- Ḥaḍretak sāyiḥ walla ṭālib?
- ʾAna lissa ṭālib.
- Fēn il-basbōr, min faḍlak?
- Itfaḍḍal, ḥadretak, ʾaho.
- Il-basbōr gdīd khāliṣ, wi fēn il-fīza ʾl-maṣrīya?
- Hena, mi ʾs-sifāra ʾl-maṣrīya fī London.
- Ish-shanṭa kbīra wi tiʾīla.
- Ṣaḥḥ, hiya malyāna shwayya.
- Itfaḍḍal, ʾiqāma saʿīda fī Maṣr!

Fatḥit il-gallābīya min wara?
Di ʾākhir mōḍa fī ʾŪrubbā.
What, a gallabiya with a neckline at the back? That's the latest European fashion.

I. ʾAsʾila (Comprehension Questions):

1. Iṭ-ṭālib mnēn?
2. Il-gauw fī London ḥelu walla wiḥish?
3. Il-basbōr gdīd walla ʾadīm?
4. Iṭ-ṭālib ʾinglīzī walla maṣrī?
5. Ish-shanṭa khafīfa?

II. Qawāʿid (Grammar):

1. The Article

The definite article: ***il*** is used for both the singular and plural of masculine and feminine nouns. It precedes the noun and also the adjective qualifying this noun:

il-bēt il-kbīr - the house the big = the big house, *il-warda ʾl-gamīla* = the beautiful rose, *il-ʾaṭfāl il-ḥelwīn* = the nice children

use of the definite article: for nouns (adjectives) denoting known, aforementioned or defined objects.

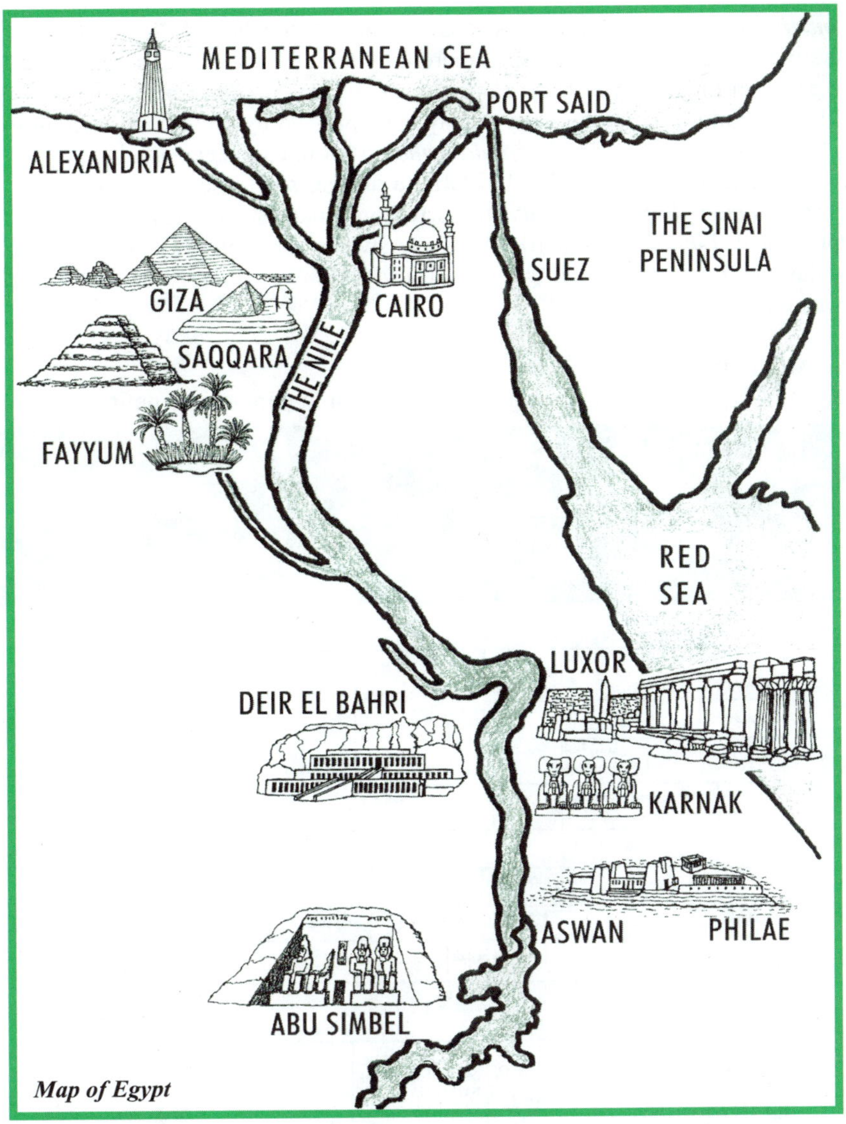

Map of Egypt

If the definite article follows a word ending in a vowel, the ***i*** of ***il*** is omitted: *il-ʿarabīya ʾg-gdīda* (the new car) – in pronunciation, the last syllable of the noun is bound to the ***–l*** of the definite article: *il-ʿarabīyag-gdīda*.

If the definite article precedes a noun (adjective) beginning with the consonants *t, d, ṭ, ḍ, s, z, ṣ, ẓ, sh, n, r*, or occasionally *g* and *k*, the ***–l*** of the definite article assimilates these consonants: *it-tarabēza* (the table), *id-dolāb* (the case), *iṭ-ṭabīb* (the physician), *iḍ-ḍalma* (the darkness), *is-samak* (the fish), *iz-zbūn* (the customer), *iṣ-ṣūra* (the picture), *iẓ-ẓābiṭ* (the officer), *ish-shams* (the sun), *in-nūr* (the light), *ir-rās* (the head), *ik-kitāb* (the book), *ig-gawāb* (the letter).

The indefinite article: There is no special morpheme for the indefinite article in Arabic, the indefinite article is expressed merely by the absence of the definite article (as in the plural in English): *bēt kbīr* (a big house), *warda gamīla* (a beautiful rose), *ʾaṭfāl ḥelwīn* (nice children); occasionally it may be expressed by the numeral *wāḥid/waḥda* (one): *wāḥid muwaẓẓaf* (a clerk), *waḥda muhandisa* (an engineer – f.).
Many proper names do not take the definite article, since they are defined on their own: *Muḥammad, Buṭrus, Yaḥya*; similarly some names of cities and states: *Maṣr* (Egypt, Cairo), *Libnān* (Lebanon), *ʾAswān* (Aswan); some proper names appear only with the definite article: *il-Qāhira* (Cairo), *in-Nīl* (the Nile), *il-ʾIskindirēya* (Alexandria).

2. The Attribute

The attribute stands after the noun and agrees with it in number and definiteness:

masculine:	*maṭār gdīd*	- a new airport
	il-maṭār ig-gdīd	- the new airport
feminine:	*ʾahwa tiʾīla*	- strong coffee
	il-ʾahwa it-tiʾīla	- the strong coffee

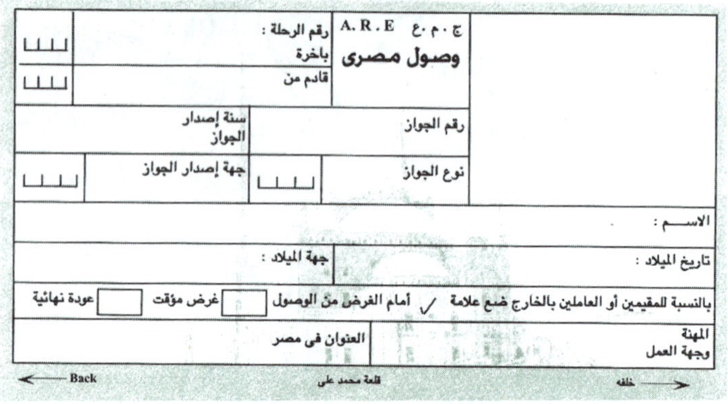
A. R. E ج ٠ م ٠ ع
وصول مصرى
رقم الرحلة :
باخرة
قادم من
رقم الجواز
سنة إصدار الجواز
نوع الجواز
جهة إصدار الجواز
الاســـم :
تاريخ الميلاد :
جهة الميلاد :
بالنسبة للمقيمين أو العاملين بالخارج ضع علامة ✓ أمام الغرض من الوصول
غرض مؤقت
عودة نهائية
المهنة
وجهة العمل
العنوان فى مصر
Back
قلعة محمد على
خلفه

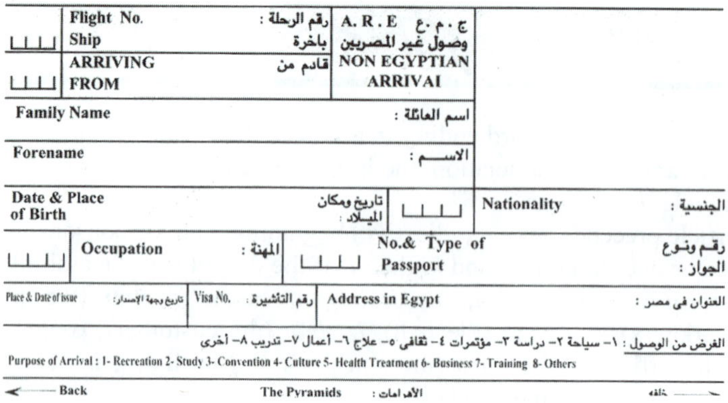
A. R. E ج ٠ م ٠ ع
وصول غير المصريين
NON EGYPTIAN ARRIVAI
Flight No. رقم الرحلة :
Ship باخرة
ARRIVING FROM قادم من
Family Name اسم العائلة :
Forename الاســـم :
Date & Place of Birth تاريخ ومكان الميلاد :
Nationality الجنسية :
Occupation المهنة :
No.& Type of Passport رقم ونوع الجواز :
Place & Date of issue تاريخ وجهة الإصدار:
Visa No. رقم التأشيرة :
Address in Egypt العنوان فى مصر :
الغرض من الوصول : ١– سياحة ٢– دراسة ٣– مؤتمرات ٤– ثقافى ٥– علاج ٦– أعمال ٧– تدريب ٨– أخرى
Purpose of Arrival : 1- Recreation 2- Study 3- Convention 4- Culture 5- Health Treatment 6- Business 7- Training 8- Others
Back
The Pyramids الأهرامات :
خلفه

Arrival card for the Arab Republic of Egypt (from the Cairo International Airport)

3. Nominal Predicate. Nominal Sentence

When the noun and adjective do not agree in definiteness, they form a nominal sentence and the adjective becomes a nominal predicate in the relative present tense. It does not require any copula, such as the verb "to be": *Il-maṭār gdīd.* – The airport is new. *Il-ʾahwa tiʾīla.* – The coffee is strong. *Yaḥya ṭālib maṣrī.* – Yahya is an Egyptian student.

4. Personal pronouns

	singular		plural	
1st pers.	*ʾana*	- I	*ʾeḥna*	- we
2nd pers. m.	*ʾenta*	- you		
2nd pers. f.	*ʾenti*	- you	*ʾentū*	- you
3rd pers. m.	*huwa*	- he		
3rd pers. f.	*hiya*	- she	*hum/humma*	- they

They never take the definite article.

III. Tadrībāt (Exercises):

Targama (Translation)

The student is an Egyptian. Where is the old airport? Here is the strong coffee. The weather in Cairo is beautiful. Where is the British passport? Where is the new doctor from? Where is the big bag? The rose is very beautiful.

Kammil! (Complete!)

Is-ṣūra ... ʾl-kitāb. Il-muwaẓẓaf ... ʾs-sifāra ʾl-maṣrīya. Is-sāyiḥ ... ʾl-ʾahwa ʾg-gamīla. Iẓ-zābit ... ʾl-matār. London ... ʾIngilterra.

IV. Mufradāt (Vocabulary):

ʾā(h)	yes; but yes; of course
ʾaho	here, look!
ʿarabīya	car
ʾAswān	Aswan
basbōr	passport
bēt	house, home
brīṭānī	British
ḍalma	darkness
dolāb	case
fēn?	where?; where to?
fī	in, on, at
fīza	visa
gauw	weather, atmosphere
gamīl, gamīla	beautiful

gawāb	letter
gdīd, gdīda	new
giddan	very
ḥelu, ḥelwa (pl. ḥelwīn)	beautiful, nice
hena	here
hnāk	there
khafīf, khafīfa	light
khāliṣ	totally, completely, absolutely
ʾIngilterra	England
ʾinglīzī, ʾinglīzīya	English
ʾiqāma	stay
il-ʾIskindirēya	Alexandria
kbīr, kbīra	great, big, large
kitāb	book
kwayyis, kwayyisa	good
lē(h)?	why?
Libnān	Lebanon
lissa	(not) yet, just
madīna	town
malyān, malyāna	full
Maṣr	Egypt
maṣrī, maṣrīya	Egyptian
maṭār	airport
min	from (shortened to mi- before the definite article: mi ʾl- ...)
mnēn	where from?
muhandis, muhandisa	engineer
muwaẓẓaf, muwaẓẓafa	clerk
in-Nīl	the Nile
nūr	light
ʾadīm, ʾadīma	old
il-Qāhira	Cairo
ʾahwa	coffee, café
ʾawi	very, too (much)
rās	head
ṣaḥḥ	right, correct
sāyiḥ, sāy(i)ḥa	tourist
samak	fish
saʿīd, saʿīda	happy
sifāra	embassy
ṣūra	picture, photograph
shams	sun
shanṭa	bag
shwayya	some, several, a few
ṭabīb, ṭabība	physician, doctor

ṭālib, ṭāl(i)ba	student
tarabēza	table
ṭifl, ṭifla (plural ʾaṭfāl)	child
tiʾīl, tiʾīla	heavy, strong (drink)
wāḥid, wāḥ(i)da	one
walla	or
warda	rose, flower
wi, u	and, also
ẓābiṭ, ẓābiṭa	officer
zbūn, zbūna	Customer

V. Taʿbīrāt (Phraseology):

Ḥaḍretak!	Sir! Dear Sir! (polite form of masculine singular)
Ḥaḍretik!	Madam! Dear Madam! (polite form of f. singular)
Ḥaḍarātku!	Ladies and Gentlemen!, Dear Sirs!, Dear Madams! (polite form of masculine, feminine plural)
Il-ḥamd(u) li ʾallāh!	Thank God!
Is-salām(u) ʿalēku!	Peace with you! (the most common Muslim greeting)
Wi ʿalēkum is-salām.	Answer to the preceding sentence
Itfaḍḍal!	Please! (there you go – invitation; masculine singular)
Itfaḍḍalī!	Please! (there you go – invitation; feminine singular)
Itfaḍḍalū!	Please! (there you go – invitation; m. and f. plural)
Min faḍlak!	Please, (polite request masculine singular)
Min faḍlik!	Please, (polite request feminine singular)
Min faḍluku!	Please, (polite request masculine and feminine plural)

2

Id - Dars it-tānī/Lesson 2

it-Taks(i)

- ʾAywa, yā ʾ(u)sṭa, fāḍī?
- ʾĀ(h), itfaḍḍal, rāyiḥ fēn?
- ʾAna rāyiḥ funduʾ in-Nīl, wusṭ il-balad, bas mish fākir ism ish-shāriʿ.
- Diʾīʾa waḥda, ḥaḍretak shāyif kharīṭit il-Qāhira? Huwa hena ʿala ʾl-kornīsh.
- Il-masāfa ṭwīla?
- La, ʾuṣayyara.
- ʾEnta rākin il-ʿarabīya ganb maḥaṭṭit il-ʾotobīs lē(h)?
- Il-makān kwayyis ʾawi, huwa ʾuddām ṣālit il-maṭār ʿala ṭūl.
- W ʾenta sākin ʾurayyib min wusṭ il-balad?
- La, ʾana sākin biʿīd, fī Ḥelwān.
- Yā ʾ(u)sṭa, sāmiʿ iṣ-ṣōt ig-gamīl?
- Ṭabʿan, ʾana fātiḥ ir-rad(i)yō, ḥaḍretak mish ʿārif "is-Sitt", il-muṭriba ʾl-maṣrīya ʾl-mashhūra ʾUmm Kulsūm?
- Ṣaḥīḥ, ʾana fākir il-ism. Il-funduʾ ʿa ʾl-yimīn. ʾAna nāzil. Itfaḍḍal il-flūs.
- Yā bē(h), ʾana ʿāwiz fakka!
- Ṭayyib, ʾenta rāgiʿ il-maṭār di ʾl-waʾti?
- La, khalāṣ, ʾana wākhid il-ʾagāza mi ʾn-nahār da.

Ibʾa ilbis banṭalōn ʿashān mish ʿārif ʾashūf mi ʾl-gallabīya.

You'd better wear trousers, no one can see over the gallabiya.

I. ʾAsʾila:

1. Iṭ-ṭālib fākir ism il-funduʾ?
2. Sawwāʾ it-taks rākin fēn?
3. Iṭ-ṭālib sāmiʿ ʾē(h)?
4. Is-sawwāʾ rāgiʿ il-maṭār?
5. Iṭ-ṭālib il-inglīzī sākin fī Ḥelwān?
6. Huwa ʿārif ʾUmm Kulsūm?
7. Is-sawwāʾ wākhid il-ʾagāza min ʾemta?
8. Mīn ʿāwiz fakka?

II. Qawāʿid:

1. The active participle

The active participle is formed according to the paradigm of ***F ā H i M***, i.e. the first consonant of the root is followed by the vowel ***ā***, the second by the vowel ***i***; for example the root FHM (to understand) forms the active participle ***FāHiM*** (understanding).

the root NZL (to descend, to get off) — ***NāZiL*** (descending)
the root RKB (to take [a means of transport]) — ***RāKiB*** (going by)
the root KTB (to write) — ***KāTiB*** (writing)
the root KhRG (to sort) — ***KhāRiG*** (sorting)
the root SKN (to live, to dwell) — ***SāKiN*** (living)
the root RGʿ (to return, go back) — ***RāGiʿ*** (returning)
the root ʿML (to do) — ***ʿāMiL*** (doing).

Verbs with the second consonant ***w*** or ***y*** form the active participle according to the pattern RWḤ (to go, to leave) – the active participle ***RāYiḤ*** (going, leaving).

the root NWM (to sleep) — ***NāYiM*** (sleeping)
the root ʿWZ (to want) — ***ʿāWiZ*** (or ***ʿāYiZ***) (wanting)
the root ShYF (to see) — ***ShāYiF*** (seeing)
the root GYB (to bring) — ***GāYiB*** (bringing).

Verbs with the third consonant ***w*** or ***y*** form the active participle according to the following pattern: the root MShY (to go, to stride) – the active participle ***MāShī*** (going, striding).

the root NSY (to forget) — ***NāSī*** (forgetting)
the root FḌY (to be free, vacant) — ***FāḌī*** (free, vacant)
the root ʿLW (to be high) — ***ʿāLī*** (high).

Verbs that have the hamza (ʾ) as the first consonant in the standard language form the active participle according to the pattern:

the root ʾKhD (to take) – the active participle ***WāKhiD*** (taking).
the root ʾKL (to eat) — ***WāKiL*** (eating).

Feminine active participles are formed by adding the suffix ***–a*** to the masculine form. The first vowel is shortened (from ***-ā-*** to ***-a-***) and the second vowel (***-i-***) is eliminated.

FāHiM+a	***FaHMa***	***NāZiL+a***	***NaZLa***		***RāKiB+a***	***RaKBa***
KāTiB+a	***KaTBa***	***KhāRiG+a***	***KhaRGa***		***SāKiN+a***	***SaKNa***
RāGiʿ+a	***RaGʿa***	***ʿāMiL+a***	***ʿaMLa***		***RāYiḤ+a***	***RaYḤa***
NaYiM+a	***NaYMa***	***ʿāWiZ+a***	***ʿaWZa***	*or*	***ʿāYiZ+a***	***ʿaYZa***
ShāYiF+a	***SHaYFa***	***GāYiB+a***	***GaYBa***		***MāShiY+a***	***MaShYa***
NāSiY+a	***NaSYa***	***FāḌiY+a***	***FāḌYa***		***āLiY+a***	***ʿaLYa***
WāKhiD+a	***WaKhDa***	***WāKiL+a***	***WaKLa***			

Both masculine and feminine plural forms are formed by adding the suffix **-īn** to the singular masculine participle. The first vowel (***-ā-***) is shortened and the second vowel (***-i-***) is eliminated.

FāHiM+īN FaHMīN	***NaZLīn***		***RaKBīn***
KaTBīn	***KhaRGīn***		***SaKNīn***
RaGʿīn	***ʿaMLīn***		***RaYḤīn***
NaYMīn	***ʿaWZīn***	*or*	***ʿaYZīn***
ShaYFīn	***GaYBīn***		***MaShYīn***
NaSYīn	***FaḌYīn***		***ʿaLYīn***
WaKhDīn	***WaKLīn***		

The passive participle
The passive participle is formed by prefixing the morpheme ***ma-*** to the first consonant of the root, which lacks a vowel between the first and second consonant and takes the vowel **ū** between the second and third consonant: KTB – ***maKTūB*** (written).

maFHūM (understood, comprehended) ***maDRūS*** (studied)
maRSūM (drawn) ***maRKūN*** (left, parked)

Uses of the participles:
1. To express the present simple tense: *Huwa nāzil hena.* – He takes off here. *Hiya ʿayza ʾl-kharīṭa.* – She wants the map. *ʾEntū rakbīn il-ʾotobīs?* – Do you go by bus? *Hum saknīn fī Brāg.* – They live in Prague.
2. To serve as an attribute: *il-mudarris il-kātib* (the writing teacher), *gawāb maktūb* (a written letter).
3. To express a nominal predicate. In this use, the active participle coresponds in meaning to the English present continuous, and the passive participle to the English present perfect: *Ir-rākib nāyim.* – The traveller is sleeping. *Iṭ-ṭalba rayḥa Maṣr.* – The student is going to Egypt. *Il-muwaẓẓafīn mashyīn.* – The clerks are leaving. *Il-gawāb lissa mish maktūb.* – The letter has not yet been written.

2. The particle "*mish*" ("*mush*")
This particle stands between the subject and the nominal predicate and serves as a negative copula: *ʾAna mish murshid.* – I am not a guide. *Hiya mish tshīkīya.* – She is not Czech. *Huwa mush nāzil hena.* – He does not take off here. *ʾEḥna mish rakbīn il-ʾotobīs.* – We are not taking the bus.

As in English, there is only one negation in an Arabic sentence:
ʾAna mish ʿāwiz ḥāga. – I don't want anything. (lit.: I don't want a thing.)

3. Feminine gender
Arabic nouns and adjectives are either masculine or feminine in gender, feminine nouns or adjectives usually end in ***–a***: *murshida* (a [female]) guide), (*twīla*) (long [f.]). Some masculine nouns, too, end in ***–a***: *ʿomda* (mayor), *khalīfa* (khalif); or in ***–ī***: *makwagī* (laundryman, ironer), *kumsarī* (conductor).

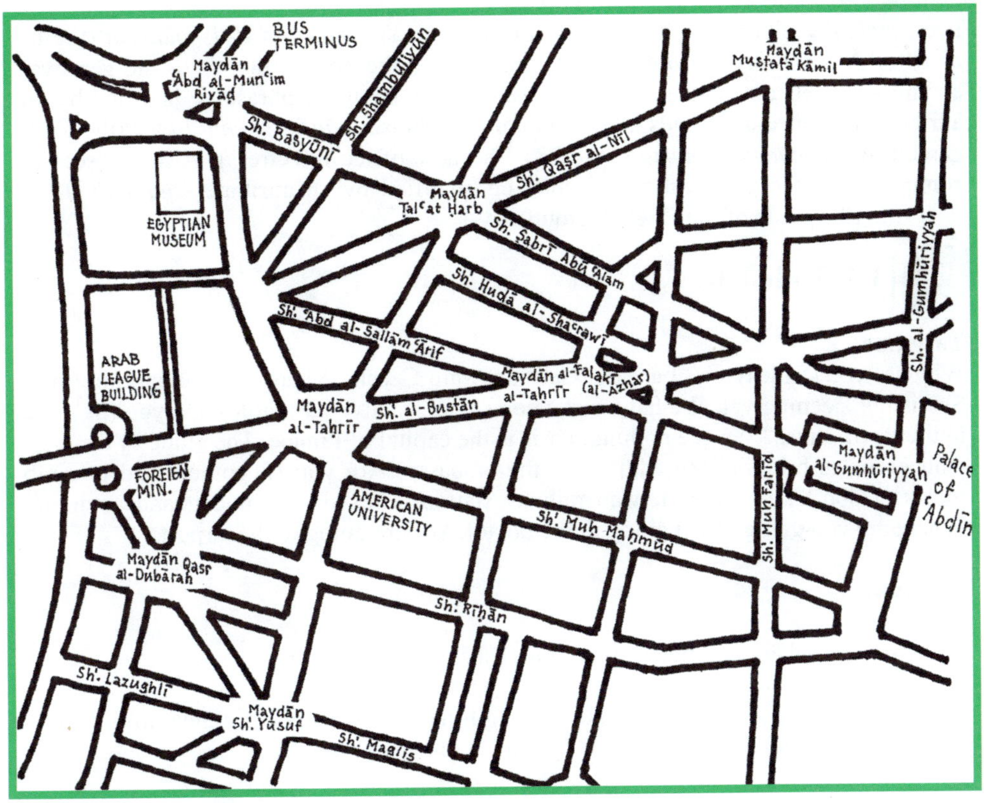

Map of the centre of Cairo

Some feminine nouns end in a consonant; these have a natural feminine gender: *ʾumm* (mother), *ʾukht* (sister), *bint* (daughter, girl); or they are names of countries: *Maṣr*, *Tūnis*, *il-Fayyūm*, *Dumyāṭ*; cosmic bodies: *shams* (the sun), *sama* (the sky); of natural phenomena and conflicts: *nār* (fire), *ḥarb* (war); and parts of the human body: *rās* (head), *ʿēn* (eye), *widn* (ear), *manakhīr* (nose), *ʾīd* (hand), *rigl* (leg), *baṭn* (belly), *dimāgh* (head, brain).

4. The genitive (or possessive case)

The genitival phrase is used to express the appositional adjunct and may be formed out of two or more components. The second component is determined by the definite article or by the pronominal suffix and determines the first component: *bāb il-bēt* (the door of the house; the house door), *yōm il-wuṣūl* (the day of arrival), *ẓābit ig-gumruk* (customs officer), *shāṭiʾ il-baḥr* (seaside).

If the first component of the genitival phrase is formed by a feminine noun ending in ***–a***, this suffix changes to ***–it***: *sifāra* (embassy) + *Maṣr* (Egypt) = *sifārit Maṣr* (the Embassy of Egypt), *gnēna* (garden) + *ʾAswān* = *gnēnit ʾAswān* (the garden of Aswan); *mudīra* (directress) + *il-maktab* (office) = *mudīrit il-maktab* (the directress of the office); *maktaba* (library) + *il-ʾIskindirīya* (Alexandria) = *maktabt il-ʾIskindirīya* (the library of Alexandria). Before a noun with the definite article, the ***-i-*** of the genitival ending ***-it*** is left out. If the first component of the genitival phrase is qualified by an attribute, this attribute stands after the genitival phrase: *bāb ig-gnēna ʾl-kbīr* (the great garden gate), *mudirt il-maktab ig-gdīda* (the new office directress). Also the second component of the genitival phrase may be qualified by an attribute: *murshidt il-fōg il-ʾinglīzī* (the guide of the English group).

III. Tadrībāt:

Targama

Why are you (f.) leaving? I am not German, I am Czech. Where are you parking (m.)? She is not sleeping yet. We have just eaten (*lissa* + active participle). Do you (pl.) live in the town centre? We see nothing. Paris is the capital of France. The guide of the German group is bringing the address of the embassy. Are you (f. polite) used to Arab meals? I don't know the Helwan railway station. They do not understand anything. Where are you going? I am going to the doctor. We are going to the airport.

Kammil!

a) rāyiḥ b) in-nahār da c) maṭār d) rakbīn e) shāṭiʾ f) sākin

1. ʾAna mish fākir ... il-Qāhira. 2. Huwa ... fi ʾl-madīna ʾl-gamʿīya. 3. ʾEḥna mish ragʿīn... 4. Ḥaḍretak ... fēn? 5. ʾEntū ... ʿē(h)? 6. Hum ʾaʿdīn ʿala ... il-baḥr.

Kornish – the waterfront of the Nile with the hotels Semiramis, Shepheard and il-Borg

IV. Mufradāt

ʾagāza	holiday
ʾaywa	yes
ʾakl	food
ʿala	on, at (shortened to ʿa- before the definite article)
ʿala-ṭūl	right, straight, immediately
ʿa ʾl-yimīn	to the right
ʿālī	tall, high
ʾalmānī, almānīya	German
ʾAlmāniyā	Germany
ʿāmil	working, worker
ʿārif	knowing
ʿāṣima	capital
ʿāwiz / ʿāyiz	wanting
bāb	door, gate
baḥr	sea
balad	country, village, countryside
Bārīs	Paris
bas	only; but
baṭn	belly
Brāg	Prague
bē(h)	sir (title, address)
bint	girl, daughter
biʿīd	far, distant
biʿīd min	far from
diʾīʾa	minute
di ʾl-waʾti	now
dimāgh	head, brain
ʾeḥna	we
ʾemta	when?
ʿēn	eye
fāḍī	free, empty
fāhim	understanding
fakka	change (money)
fākir	remembering
Faransā	France
fātiḥ	opening
flūs	money
fōg	tourist group
funduʾ	hotel
gāyib	bringing
ganb	next to
gnēna	garden

gumruk	customs
ḥāga	thing, something, anything
ḥarb	war
Ḥelwān	Helwan
khalāṣ	end, finished
khārig	leaving, sorting
kharīṭa	map
ʾīd	hand
la, laʾ	no
li	to, for (dative)
kātib	writing
kornīsh	shore, bank
madīna gamʿīya	university college or campus
madrūs	studied
maḥaṭṭa	station
makān	place, room
maktab	office, writing table
maktaba	library
maktūb	written
manakhīr	nose
markūn	parked, left behind
marsūm	drawn
masāfa	distance
mashhūr	famous
māshī	striding, going
mīn	who?
mudarris	teacher
mudīr	director
murshid	tourist guide
muṭrib	singer
nāyim	sleeping
nār	fire
nāsī	forgetting
nāzil	leaving, accommodating, descending
in-nahār da	today
ʾotobīs	bus
ʾāʿid	sitting
ʾuddām	in front of
ʾurayyib	close, soon
ʾurayyib min	close to
ʾuṣayyar	short
rad(i)yō	radio
rāgiʿ	returning

rāyiḥ	going, leaving – without preposition = to a place – with the preposition li = to a person
rākib	travelling
rākin	parking
rigl	leg
ṣaḥīḥ	yes, sure, right
sākin	living
ṣāla	hall
sama	heaven, sky
sāmiᶜ	hearing
sawwāᵓ	driver
sitt	madam (friendly address)

is-Sitt	epithet of the Egyptian singer ʾUmm Kulsūm
ṣōt	voice, sound
shāyif	seeing
shāriʿ	street
shāṭiʾ	bank
ṭabʿan	of course
ṭayyib	good, kind
taks(i)	taxi
tshīkī	Czech
ṭwīl	long
ʾukht	sister
ʾumm	mother
ʿunwān	address
ʾusṭa	Master, chief (to address artisans, taxi drivers, etc.)
wākil	eating
wākhid	taking
wākhid	to be used to *(ʿala)*
widn	ear
wusṭ	center, middle
wuṣūl	Arrival

V. Taʿbīrāt:

ʿĀmil ʾē(h)?	How are you? (m.)
Ḥaḍretak ʿāmil ʾē(h)?	How are you? (polite m.)
ʿAmla ʾē(h)?	How are you? (f.)
Ḥaḍretik ʿamla ʾē(h)?	How are you? (polite f.)
ʿAmlīn ʾē(h)?	How are you? (pl.)
Ḥaḍarātku ʿamlīn ʾē(h)?	How are you? (polite pl.)

Id - Dars it-tālit/Lesson 3

Fi ʾl-funduʾ

- Masāʾ il-khēr!
- Masāʾ in-nūr! ʾAyyi khidma!
- Fī ʿanduku ʿōḍa faḍya bi srīr wi balakōna?
- Lahẓa, li ʾl-asaf, di ʾl-waʾti mafīsh ʿandina ʾōḍa bi srīr wi balakōna, fī ʾōḍa min ghēr balakōna bas.
- Fīhā ḥammām?
- ʾĀ(h), fīhā ḥammām, tallāga wi telefiziyōn. Mish ḥaḍretak kunt ʿandina ʾabli keda?
- Maẓbūt, maʿāya kart il-funduʾ wi ʾismī maktūb ʿalēh.
- Ḥaḍretak kunt mabsūṭ hena?
- ʾAwi. Il-funduʾ ʿāgibnī giddan. Barḍo ṣaḥbitī kānit mabsūṭa ʿanduku khāliṣ.
- ʾAna farḥān bi-kalāmak ig-gamīl. Iṭfaḍḍal, miftāḥ il-ʾōḍa!
- Maʿalesh, fēn shanṭitī?
- Ganb(i) bāb ʾoḍtak.
- Mā shāʾallāh! Khidmitku mumtāza!
- Ḥaḍretak fī bētak. ʿAlā fikra, ʾiqamtak ʿandina bi ʾl-fiṭār.
- ʾAlf shukr! ʿAndī suʾāl.
- Iṭfaḍḍal!
- Fī min hena ʾotobīs li-ghāyit il-Gīza?
- ʾAywa, fī. Il-maḥaṭṭa ʿa ʾn-naṣya ʾusād il-funduʾ.
- Min faḍlak, il-ʾasansēr nāzil walla ṭāliʿ?
- Nāzil.
- Ṭayyib, shukran wi maʿa ʾs-salāma!

Gōz ḥaḍretik bāʿit lik il-hadīya di wi bi-yiʾūl lik mish ʿāyiz yishūf wishshik tānī.

Your husband is sending you this present and says he doesn't want to see you any more.

I. ʾAsʾila:

1. Fī fi ʾl-funduʾ ʾōḍa faḍya bi ʾl-balakōna?
2. Wi ʾt-tallāga kānit fi ʾl-ʾōḍa?
3. Iḍ-ḍēf kān mabsūṭ fi ʾl-funduʾ ʾabli keda?
4. ʾIsmo maktūb fēn?
5. Il-funduʾ ʿāg(i)bo?
6. Mīn kān farḥān bi-kalāmo ʾl-gamīl?
7. Shanṭito kānit fn fi ʾl-funduʾ?
8. ʾIqamto fi ʾl-funduʾ kānit bi ʾl-fiṭār?

II. Qawāʿid:

1. Pronominal suffixes (possessive pronouns)
Pronominal suffixes can qualify nouns, adjectives, verbs, prepositions and particles. Following nouns, they express the English possessive pronouns.

a) Pronominal suffixes after consonants:

bēt + **ī**	= *bētī*	(my house)
bēt + **ak**	= *bētak*	(your house – m.)
bēt + **ik**	= *bētik*	(your house – f.)
bēt + **o**	= *bēto*	(his house)
bēt + **hā**	= *bēthā*	(her house)
bēt + **na**	= *bētna*	(our house)
bēt + **ku**	= *bētku*	(your house – pl.)
bēt + **hum**	= *bēthum*	(their house)

b) Pronominal suffixes after long vowels:

ʾakhū + **ya**	= *ʾakhūya*	(my brother)
ʾakhū + **k**	= *ʾakhūk*	(your brother – m.)
ʾakhū + **ki**	= *ʾakhūki*	(your brother – f.)
ʾakhū + **h**	=*ʾakhūh*	(his brother)
ʾakhū + **hā**	=*ʾakhūhā*	(her brother)
ʾakhū + **na**	=*ʾakhūna*	(our brother)
ʾakhū + **ku**	=*ʾakhūku*	(your brother – pl.)
ʾakhū + **hum**	=*ʾakhūhum*	(their brother)

c) Pronominal suffixes after nouns ending in *-a*:

Before a suffix pronoun, the ending *–a* changes to *–it* (if a vowel follows this ending, *-i-* is left out): *maktaba* + *ī* > *maktabit* + *ī* = *maktabtī* (my bookcase, my library) *maktabtak, maktabtik, maktabto, maktabithā, maktabitna, maktabitku, maktabithum.*

d) The 1st person singular pronominal suffix takes the form **–nī** when attached to a verb or active participle: *Huwa shāyifnī* – He sees me. *ʾEnta fākirnī*? – Do you remember me?

e) The final -*a* of the feminine active participle is lengthened before the pronominal suffix, and it takes on the accent: *Hiya shayf**ā**nī* – She sees me. – *ʾEnti fakr**ā**h*? – Do you remember him? *Hiya mish samʿ**ā**na* – She does not hear us.

f) The pronominal suffix determines the noun like the definite article or the second member of a genitival phrase: *maktabtī ʾl-kbīra* – my large bookcase, but: *Maktabtī kbīra*. – My bookcase is large.

NIle island il-Gezira in the centre of Cairo

2. Prepositions with pronominal suffixes:

fī (in, on, at):	*fīyya* (in me), *fīk* (in you – m.), *fīki* (in you - f.), *fīh* (in him (m.), *fīhā* (in her), *fīna* (in us), *fīku* (in you – pl.), *fīhum* (in them)
min (out of, from):	*minnī* (from me), *minnak, minnik, minno, minhā, minnina/minna, minku, minhum*
ʿala (on, at):	*ʿalayya* (on me), *ʿalēk, ʿalēki, ʿalēh, ʿalēhā, ʿalēna, ʿalēku, ʿalēhum*
maʿa (with, together with):	*maʿāna* (with me), *maʿāk, maʿāki, maʿāh, maʿāhā, maʿāna, maʿāku, maʿāhum*

wayya (with, together with): *wayyāya* (with me),
wayyāk, wayyāki, wayyāh, wayyāhā, wayyāna, wayyāku, wayyāhum

li (to, for, dative): *lī/līya* (for me),
lak/līk, līki, lo, lahā, lina, luku, luhum

ʿand (at, by): *ʿandī* (by me),
ʿandak, ʿandik, ʿando, ʿandahā, ʿandina, ʿanduku, ʿanduhum

ʿan (about): *ʿannī* (about me),
ʿannak, ʿannik, ʿanno, ʿanhā/ʿannahā, ʿanna/ʿannina, ʿanku/ʿannuku,ʿanhum/ʿannuhum

ʿashān (because of, for): *ʿashānī* (for me, because of me),
ʿashānak, ʿashānik, ʿashāno, ʿashānhā, ʿashānna, ʿashānku, ʿashānhum

min ghēr (without): *min ghērī* (without me),
min ghērak, min ghērik, min ghēro, min ghērhā, min ghērna, min ghērku, min ghērhum

ḥasab (after, according to): *ḥasabī* (according to me),
ḥasabak, ḥasabik, ḥasabo, ḥasab(a)hā, ḥasabna, ḥasabku, ḥasabhum

ḥawālī (around): *ḥawālēya* (around me),
ḥawālēk, ḥawālēki, ḥawālēh, ḥawālēhā, ḥawālēna, ḥawālēku, ḥawālēhum

fōʾ (above, over): *fōʾī* (over me),
fōʾak, fōʾik, fōʾo, fōʾahā, fōʾ(a)na, fōʾuku, fōʾ(u)hum

taḥt (under): *taḥtī* (under me),
taḥtak, taḥtik, taḥto, taḥtahā, taḥtina, taḥtuku, taḥtuhum

bēn (between): *bēnī* (between me),
bēnak, bēnik, bēno, bēnhā, benna, benku, benhum

ḍidd (opposite): *ḍiddī* (opposite me),
ḍiddak, ḍiddik, ḍiddo, ḍiddahā, ḍiddina, ḍidduku, ḍidduhum

bi faḍl (thanks to): *bi faḍlī* (thanks to me),
bi faḍlak, bi faḍlik, bi faḍlo, bi faḍlahā, bi faḍlina, bi faḍluku, bi faḍluhum

ʾuṣād (opposite): *ʾuṣādī* (opposite me),
ʾuṣādak, ʾuṣādik, ʾuṣādo, ʾuṣādhā, ʾuṣādna, ʾuṣādku, ʾuṣādhum

ganb (next to): *ganbī* (next to me),
ganbak, ganbik, ganbo, ganbahā, ganbina, ganbuku, ganbuhum

ʾabl (before): *ʾablī* (before me),
ʾablak, ʾablik, ʾablo, ʾablahā, ʾablina, ʾabluku, ʾabluhum

baʿd (after): *baʿdī* (after me),
baʿdak, baʿdik, baʿdo, baʿdahā, baʿdina, baʿduku, baʿduhum

ʾuddām (in front of): *ʾuddāmī* (in front of me),
ʾuddāmak, ʾuddāmik, ʾuddāmo, ʾuddāmhā, ʾuddāmna, ʾuddāmku, ʾuddāmhum

wara (behind): *warāya* (behind me),
warāk, warāki, warāh, warāhā, warāna, warāku, warāhum

3. The Perfect

Arabic has two basic verbal forms – the perfect and the imperfect. Both originally expressed aspect rather than tense. The perfect expressed the perfective aspect, above all in the past, but it was also used in the present (for example in oaths) or in the future (for example in optative sentences). The imperfect expressed the imperfective aspect, above all in the present and future, but also a repeated action in the past. This original aspectual distinction still applies in some cases; it may, however, be stated that in general the perfect now expresses the past tense and the imperfect the present or future tense.

In terms of the verbal root, verbs may be divided into strong and weak verbs. Strong verbs are formed by consonants (radicals), which are not subject to change with inflection. The first, second or third radical of weak verbs is ***w*** or ***y***. These consonants are in certain cases reduced, and/or merge with the preceding vowel or else assimilate.

The perfective of the verb "to be":

Singular		**Plural**
3. m.	*kān* (he was)	**3.** *kān-**ū*** (they were)
3. f.	*kān-**it*** (she was)	
2. m.	*kun-**t*** (you were)	**2.** *kun-**tū*** (you were)
2. f.	*kun-**ti*** (you were)	
1. m. +f.	*kun-**t*** (I was)	**1.** *kun-**na*** (we were)

Depending on the context, the perfect can be translated as the English past simple or past perfect.
There is no infinitive in Arabic, its function is fulfilled by the perfect 3rd person masculine singular: *kān*.

Negative forms are made by adding the particle ***ma-*** before the verbal form, and the particle ***–sh(i)*** at the end of the form:
makansh(i) (he was not)*, makanitsh(i), makuntish, makuntīsh,*
makuntish, makānūsh, makuntūsh, makunnāsh. In the 3rd person m. and f. sg., the vowel *-**ā**-* is reduced to ***-a-.***

4. "To have"

The possessive verb is usually expressed by the preposition ***ʿand, maʿa, wayya,*** or ***li***.
The most common preposition used is ***ʿand :*** *ʿAndī fikra kwayyisa* – I have a good idea.
ʿAnduhum bēt kbīr. – They have a big house. *ʿAndak waʾt*? – Have you got a moment?

Negative forms: *maʿandīsh* (I have not), *maʿandaksh, maʿandikīsh, maʿandūsh, maʿandahāsh, maʿandināsh, maʿandukūsh, maʿanduhumsh(i).*
Maʿandīsh fikra kwayyisa. Maʿanduhumsh(i) bēt kbīr. Maʿandaksh(i) waʾt?

The prepositions ***maʿa*** and ***wayya*** express "to have something on oneself, with oneself": – *Maʿāya flūs.* - I have money on me. *Maʿāh il-miftāḥ.* – He's got the key on him.

Negative forms – *maʿīsh* (I haven't got on me), *maʿaksh, maʿakīsh, maʿūsh, maʿahāsh, maʿanāsh, maʿakūsh, maʿahumsh.*
Maʿīsh flūs. Maʿūsh il-miftāh.

The preposition ***wayya*** is negated by means of the particle ***mish/mush***:
Mish wayyāk karnē(h)? – Haven't you got the card with you?

The preposition ***li*** is used to express interpersonal relations: *Līya ʾakh ṣghayyar.* – I have a small brother. *Lo ṣaḥba gamīla.* – He has a beautiful fiancée.
The corresponding negative forms are *malīsh, malaksh, malīsh, malūsh, malhāsh, malnāsh, malkūsh, malhumsh.*
Malīsh ʾukht ṣ(u)ghayyara.

The past tense of possessive phrases is formed by means of *kān*: *Kān ʿandī fikra kwayyisa.* – I had a good idea. *Kān ʿanduhum bēt kbīr.* – They had a big house. *Kān ʿandak waʾt?* – Did you have time? *Makansh(i) maʿāya flūs.* I did not have money on me. *Makansh(i) līya ʾukht ṣ(u)ghayyara.* – I did not have a small sister.

5. Particles "*fī*" and "*mafīsh*"
The particles express existence and non-existence respectively; they correspond to the English verb "to be" in the 3rd person m. and f., both sg. and pl. present tense. Often they express the English "there is (not)," "there are (not)."
Fī ʿēsh baladī? – Do you have country bread? *ʾAywa, fī.* – Yes, we have.
Fī mayya sokhna? – Is there hot water? *La, mafīsh.* – No, there is not.
Fī ʿanduku laban ṭāze? – Do you have fresh milk?
La, mafīsh ʿandina laban ṭāze. – No, we have not.

III. Tadrībât:

Targama
Did you visit ("were you by") your sister yesterday? I did not have my passport on me. Do you have change please? We have not yet been to our hotel. Why have you been there without us? He has neither father nor mother. Her bag was very heavy. Who was here before us? Have you got the key of your car? Their picture was in the newspaper. Our stay in Aswan was short. Do you (f.) hear me well? When were you at the Ramses Railway Station? We were there an hour ago.

Kammil!
a) ʾakhūya b) ʾāʿid c) makansh(i) d) ʿāgibna e) malūsh f) ʿandak

1. ... ʿandī ʿunwāno. 2. Hiya ʿarfa ... 3. ... waʾt in-nahār da? 4. Zmīlī ... ganbak. 5. ... ʾakh. 6. Il-fundu' ... ʾawi.

IV. Mufradāt

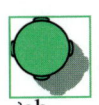

ʾab	father (before the genitive and pronominal suffixes ʾabū)
ʿāgib	being liked (by someone); followed by a pronominal suffix or noun without preposition
ʾakh	brother (before the genitive and pronominal suffixes ʾakhū)
ʾalf	thousand
ʾayy(i)	whatever, whichever
ʿan	about
ʿand	at, by
ʾasansēr	lift
ʿashān	because of, for
baʿd	in, after
baladī	home, local
balakōna	balcony
barḍo	also, too
bēn	between, among
bi	with
bi-faḍl	thanks to
biṭāʾa	ID card
ḍidd	opposite
ʾembāreḥ	yesterday
ʿēsh	bread
farḥān	being happy
fikra	thought, idea
fiṭār	breakfast
fōʾ	above
gurnān	newspaper
ḥammām	bath, toilet
ḥasab	according to
ḥawālī	around, ca., approximately
ʾism (ʾasmāʾ)	name
khidma	service
kalām	speech, utterance
kān	to be
karnē(h)	ID card
kart	card, business card, postcard
laban	milk
laḥẓa	moment
li-ghāyit	until, toward
maʿa	with, together with

mabsūṭ	satisfied
mayya	water
maẓbūṭ	precise, precisely
miftāḥ	key
min ghēr	without
mumtāz	excellent
mūsīqā	music
naṣya	corner
ʾōḍa	room
ʾabl	before
ʾablina, ʾabl(i) sāʿa	before us, an hour ago
ʾabl(i) keda	before (adverb)
ʾuṣād	opposite
sāʿa	hour, watch
sāḥib	friend
ṣ(u)ghayyar	small
sokhn	warm
srīr	bed
suʾāl	question
shukr	thanks
taḥt	under, below
tāliʿ	rising
tallāga	refrigerator
ṭāze	fresh
telefiz(i)yōn	TV set
waʾt	time
wayya	with, together
walā	nor
wara	behind
zmīl (zamāyil)	colleague, co-worker

V. Taʿbīrāt:

Masāʾ il-khēr!	Good evening! (lit. An evening of good!)
Masāʾ in-nūr!	Answer to the above (lit. An evening of light!)
Maʿa ʾs-salāma!	Good-bye!
ʾAyyi khidma!	At your service!
Li ʾl-ʾasaf.	Unfortunately.
Maʿalesh.	Nothing happened. There's nothing we can do. Sorry.
Mā shāʾallāh!	That's great, wonderful, admirable!
ʿAla fikra.	By the way.
Shukran!	Thank you!
ʾAlf shukr!	Thanks a lot!
Bēnī bēnak.	Between us.
Malīsh fi ʾl-mūsīqā.	I am not good at music. I do not understand music.
Ṭayyib.	All right.

4

Id - Dars ir-rābiʾ /Lesson 4

Fi ʾs-sūʾ

Yā khabar ʾabyaḍ, ʾana mish fākir, kīlo laḥma bi kām?

Oops, I don't remember; how much are two pounds of meat?

ʾAsḥābī ʾl-maṣrīyīn ʿazamūnī ʾembāreḥ li-ziyārithum fi ʾl-balad. Il-ʾauwil n(i)zilt maʿāhum sūʾ is-Sayyida. Makuntish ʿārif sikkito wi ʿashān keda ṭalabt minhum musāʿada. R(i)kibna ʾl- ʾotobīs min ʾuddām il-funduʾ wi baʿdēn il-metro min mīdān it-Taḥrīr. Nzilna fī maḥaṭṭit is-Sayyida Zēnab. Dakhalna ʾs-sūʾ, kān fīh ḥagāt ktīr ʾawi. Saʾalna wāḥid mi ʾl-bayyāʿīn ʿala fakha gamīla wi ḥaẓẓina kān gamīl ʾawi. Ir-rāgel kān ʿando fakha ḥelwa khāliṣ. Wazan lina khamsa kīlo burtuʾāl, ʾarbaʿa kīlo yūs(t) ʾefendi wi talāta kīlo mōz. Baʿdi keda dakhalna maḥall il-gazzār, dabaḥ lina farkhitēn kubār wi ʾaṭaʿ lina itnēn kīlo laḥmit bitello. Il-gazzār ʿamal lina siʿr kwayyis. Kharagna mi ʾs-sūʾ ... bas fēn il-khuḍār? Rigiʿna wi ʿala ṭūl naṣaḥūna ʿinn il-khudār it-ṭāze wi ʾr-rkhīs ʿand sitt fallāḥa ʾaʿda ganb(i) maḥall is-samak. Is-sitt wazanit lina itnēn kīlo ṭamāṭim, talāta kīlo khiyār, nuṣṣ(i) kīlo filfil rūmī wi sitta kīlo baṭāṭis. Dafaʿna ʾl-flūs, shakarna ʾl-bayyāʿa, msikna shunaṭna wi kharagna mabsūṭīn ʿa ʾl-ākhir. ʾAʿdna shwayya ʾuddām kushk il-garanīn wi sh(i)ribna ʾizāz(i)t il-mayya ʾl-maʿdanīya. Bi-ṣarāḥa, kunna ʿaṭshānīn wi taʿbānīn khāliṣ.

I. ʾAsʾila:

1. Mīn nizil sūʾ is-Sayyida ʾembāreḥ?
2. Iṭ-ṭālib ṭalab minhum musāʿada lē(h)?
3. Rikbū ʾē(h)?
4. Saʿalū mīn ʿala fakha gamīla?
5. Ir-rāgel wazan luhum kam kīlo tuffāḥ?
6. Mīn ʿamal luhum siʿr kwayyis?
7. Shakarū ʾs-sitt il-fallāḥa ʿala ʾē(h)?

II. Qawāʿid:

1. Plural

A) The suffixed plural

The suffixed plural is formed by means of the following endings:

-īn: for masculine nouns denoting an action like *shayyāl* (bearer) – *shayyālīn*, *fallāḥ* (peasant) – *fallāḥīn*, *ṭabbākh* (cook) – *ṭabbākhīn*;

for masculine active participles: *shāyif* (seeing) – *shayfīn*, *rāyiḥ* (going) - *rayḥīn*, *sāmiʿ* (hearing) – *samiʿīn*;

for masculine passive participles: *mabsūṭ* (satisfied, contented) – *mabsūṭīn*, *mahwūs* (enchanted, fascinated) – *mahwūsīn*;

for masculine adjectives: *ṭayyib* (good-hearted) – *ṭayyibīn*, *kwayyis* (good, good-quality) – *kwayyisīn*;

Masculine adjectives ending in *–ī* add a **-y-** before the **–īn** ending: *maṣrī* (Egyptian) – *maṣriyīn*, *libnānī* (Lebanese) – *libnāniyīn*.

-āt: for feminine nouns ending in *–a*: *ṭāliba* (student; f.) – *ṭālibāt*, *murshida* (guide; f.) – *murshidāt*, *muṭriba* (singer; f.) – *muṭribāt*;

for masculine nouns of foreign origin: *ʾotobīs* (bus) – *ʾotobisāt*, *telefiziyōn* (television) – *telefiziyōnāt*;

words of foreign origin ending in **o/ē** have an **-h-** before the ending **-āt**: *rad(i)yo* (radio) – *rad(i)yohāt*, *balṭo* (overcoat, coat) – *balṭohāt*, *karnē* (card) – *karnēhāt*;

with inanimate nouns: *gawāb* (letter) – *gawabāt*, *sharāb* (pair of socks) – *sharabāt*, *milaff* (file) – *milaffāt*.

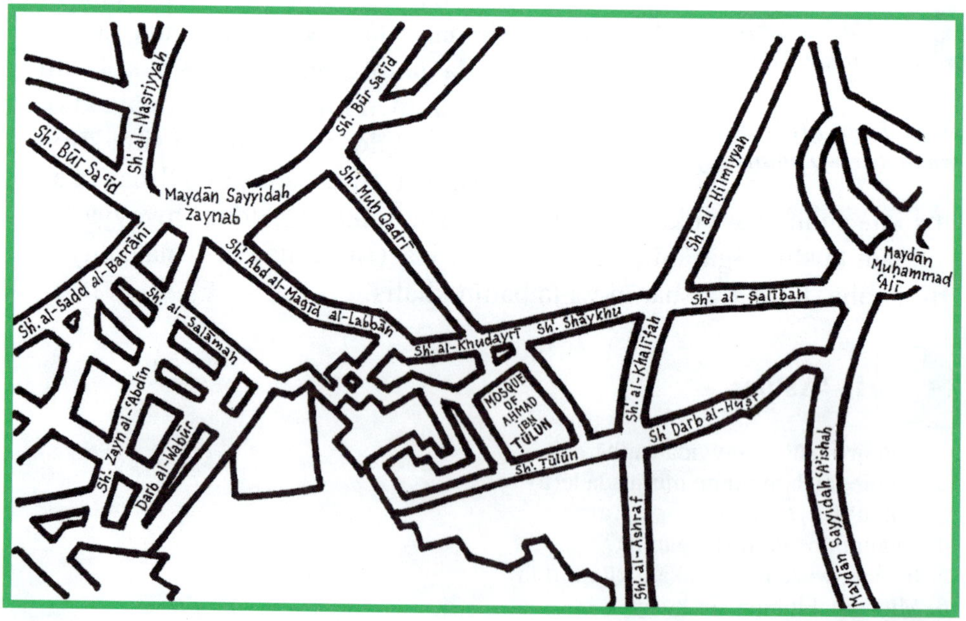

Map of the is-Sayyida Zēnab quarter

-īya: for masculine nouns denoting occupations and ending in *–ī*: *kumsarī* (conductor) – *kumsarīya*, *gazmagī* (shoemaker) – *gazmagīya.*

B) Broken plural

The broken plural is formed from masculine and feminine nouns and adjectives according to various patterns:

- *BēT* (house) – *BuYūT*, *ZēT* (oil) – *ZuYūT*, *ʿēN* (eye) – *ʿuYūN*
- *KāTiB* (writer) – *KuTTāB*, *SāYiḤ* (tourist) – *SuYYāḤ*, *RāKiB* (passenger) – *RuKKāB*, *SāKiN* – *SuKKāN*
- *NaHR* (river) - *ʾaNHāR*, *KhaBaR* (report, information) – *ʾaKHBāR*, *LōN* (colour) - *ʾaLWāN*
- *GuRNāN* (newspaper) – *GaRaNīN*, *FuSTāN* (dress – usually women's) – *FaSaTīN*
- *ShāRiʿ* (street) – *ShaWāRiʿ*, *ṬāBiʿ* (postal stamp) – *ṬāWāBiʿ*, *ḌāFiR* (nail) – *ḌaWāFiR*, *GāMiʿ* (mosque) – *GaWāMiʿ*
- *ʿaMīṢ* (shirt) - *ʿuMṢāN*, *GhaṬa* (lid, cap, cover) – *GhuṬYān*, *ṢaBī* (apprentice) – *ṢuBYāN*
- *ShiBBāK* (window) – *ShaBaBīK*, *MiFTāḤ* (key) – *MaFaTīḤ*, *MaNDīL* (handkerchief, napkin) – *MaNaDīL*, *ʾuNBūBa* (pipe, pipeline) – *ʾaNaBīB*
- *KuRSī* (chair) –*KaRāSī*, *LēL* (night) – *LaYāLī*, *MaBNa* (building) – *MaBāNī*
- *MuDīR* (director) – *MuDaRa*, *WaZīR* (minister) – *WuZaRa*
- *RaṢīF* (platform, pavement) - *ʿaRṢiFa*, *LiḤāF* (blanket) - *ʾaLḤiFa*
- *MaKTaB* (office, writing table) – *MaKāTiB*, *MaRKiB* (vessel) – *MaRāKiB*, *MuʿGaM* (dictionary) – *MaʿāGiM*, *MaSGiD* (mosque) – *MaSāGiD*
- *GDīD* (new) – *GuDāD*, *KBīR* (big, great) – *KuBāR*, *ṬWīL* (long) – *ṬuWāL*, *LaṬīF* (kind, gracious) – *LuṬāF*

Plural nouns that do not denote human beings are treated as feminine singular nouns, adjectives in the role of their attributes or nominal predicates take feminine singular forms: *ʾalwān gamīla* (nice colours), *ig-garanīn il-maṣrīya* (the Egyptian newspapers), *Il-makātib kbīra.* (The offices are large.)

In case of **plural nouns denoting human beings,** adjectives used as attributes and predicates ***agree with their nouns in number*** – *suyyāḥ gudād* – new tourists, *banāt ḥelwīn* – beautiful girls; *Il-murshidāt luṭāf.* – The guides are kind.
But: *Sittāt maṣrīyāt* (Egyptian women) – since here the adjective expresses nationality, thus it agrees with its noun in both number and gender, similarly also *Il-banāt inglīzīyāt.* – These girls are English.

2. The dual

The dual is formed by means of the ending ***-ēn***, suffixed to the singular noun; masculine nouns: *bēt* + *ēn* = *bētēn* (two houses), *ṭabīb* + *ēn* = *ṭabībēn* (two doctors), *gawāb* + *ēn* = *gawābēn* (two letters);
In case of feminine nouns, the ending ***–a*** is transformed into ***–it*** and the dual ending *–ēn*

A sample of Egyptian banknotes

is attached to the resulting form: *warda – warditēn* (two roses), *ṭāl(i)ba – ṭālibtēn* (two female students). Feminine nouns ending in a consonant make use of the ending ***–ēn*** like masculine nouns: *ʾukht – ʾukhtēn* (two sisters), *bint – bintēn* (two daughters), *ḥarb – ḥarbēn* (two wars).
Adjectives qualifying dual nouns as attributes or nominal predicates are plural in form: *bētēn kubār* (two large houses), *bintēn ḥelwīn* (two nice girls).

Use of dual forms
Most usually, the dual is used when one refers to the pairs of parts of the body
– such as, the arms, the legs, the eyes etc.
ʿēnēn, widnēn, ʾīdnēn, riglēn
– or, if one refers to double time periods, such as
yōm – yōmēn (two days), *ʾusbūʿ* (week) *– ʾusbūʿēn* (two weeks), *shahr* (month) *– shahrēn* (two months), *sana* (year) *– sanitēn* (two years), *ʿām* (year) *– ʿāmēn* (two years), *ʾarn* (century) *– ʾarnēn* (two centuries), *ʾalf* (thousand) *– ʾalfēn* (two thousand), *milyōn – milyōnēn* (two million);
Attention – the numeral *mīya* (hundred) *– mitēn* (two hundred)!
Two objects are usually expressed by means of the numeral two – *itnēn*, standing before singular or plural nouns – *itnēn shāy* (two cups of tea), *itnēn muwaẓẓafīn* (two clerks).

3. Cardinal numerals

	Masculine	**Feminine**
1	wāḥid	waḥda
2	itnēn	itnēn
3	talāt	talāta
4	ʾarbaʿ	ʾarbaʿa
5	khamas	khamsa
6	sitt	sitta
7	sabʿ	sabʿa
8	taman	tamanya
9	tisʿ	tisʿa
10	ʿashar	ʿashara

Use: when counting, the numerals 1 and 2 take the masculine form, 3–10 are feminine. The numeral *wāḥid/waḥda* is placed after the counted object for emphasis: *mudarris wāḥid* (one teacher), *shanṭa waḥda* (one bag). The numeral stands before a plural noun (in case of nouns denoting persons): *itnēn mudarrisīn* (two teachers), *itnēn rukkāb* (two passengers); other nouns usually assume the dual form, but substance nouns, like sugar, salt, wheat etc., are in the singular.
The numerals 3 – 10 stand in front of the noun, which then assumes a plural form; the numerals are masculine in gender and take the ending ***-t*** when standing before a noun with an initial vowel (not the numerals ending in *-t*): *ʾarbaʿ tazākir* (four tickets), *khamas kutub* (five books), *talāt ʾuwaḍ* (three rooms), *sitt ʾasabīʿ* (six weeks);
but *ʾarbaʿ(i)t ʾaflām* (four films), *khamast ʾirghifa* (five bread cakes), *sabʿ(i)t ʾiyyām* (seven days), *tisʿit ʾumṣān* (nine shirts), *ʿash(a)rit ʾasabīʿ* (ten weeks).
When the noun concerned denotes money, measures or weights, the numeral assumes the feminine form and the noun concerned is in the singular: *talāta ginē* (three pounds), *khamsa kīlo* (five kilograms), *sabʿa santi* (seven centimetres).

4. The perfect of regular verbs

The basic form, the simple perfect stem of the verb, usually consists of three consonants and vowels **-a-** or **-i-**. Endings are attached to this basic form.
Root K T B ("to write") – perfect stem K a T a B (he wrote/has written = "to write").

singular			**plural**	
3rd person m.	K a T a B	*he wrote*	K a T a B-**ū**	*they wrote*
f.	K a T a B-**it**	*she wrote*		
2nd pers. m.	K a T a B-**t**	*you wrote*	K a T a B-**tū**	*you wrote*
f.	K a T a B-**ti**	*you wrote*		
1st person	K a T a B-**t**	*I wrote*	K a T a B-**na**	*we wrote*

Verbal forms ending in a vowel take the ending ***-h*** instead of the pronominal suffix ***-o***, the short vowel is lengthened and the stress lies on the last syllable:

KaTaB-ti	**+** h	=	KaTaBtīh	(you have written it)
KaTaB-ū	+ h	=	KaTaBūh	(they have written it)
KaTaB-tū	+ h	=	KaTaBtūh	(you have written it)
KaTaB-na	+ h	=	KaTaBnāh	(we have written it)

If both vowels of the verb stem are ***-i-***, the first is left out in forms with endings beginning in a consonant.

ShiRiB (to drink) – *ShRiBt* (I drank)
SiMiʿ (to hear) – *SMiʿna* (we heard)
RiGiʿ (to return) – *RGiʿt* (you returned)
NiZiL (to get off) – *NZiLti* (you got off)

If a verbal stem with two vowels ***-i-*** is followed by an ending with ***-ū-***, the vowel ***-i-*** between the second and third consonant of the root is left out.

ShiRBū (they drank)
SiMʿū (they heard)
RiGʿū (they returned)
NiZLū (they got off)

Negative forms make use of the particle ***ma-*** standing before the verb form, and the particle ***–sh(i)*** affixed behind the verb form.

ma-KaTaB-sh(i) (he has not written) *ma-KaTaBū-sh* (they have not written)
ma-KaTaBit-sh(i) (she has not written)
ma-KaTaBt-(i)sh (you have not written) *ma-KaTaBtū-sh* (you have not written)
ma-KaTaBtī-sh (you have not written)
ma-KaTaBt-(i)sh (I have not written) *ma-KaTaBnā-sh* (we have not written)

1. If the affixing of the particle ***–sh*** creates a group of three consonants *ma K a T a B t sh*, an auxiliary vowel ***-i-*** is inserted between the negative particle ***–sh*** and the verbal stem: *ma K a T a B t **i** sh* (I/you have not written).

2. If a pronominal suffix is attached to the verbal stem, the negative particle ***–sh*** is affixed only behind this suffix:

ma D a R a S na hā sh (we have not studied it)
ma ʿ a Z a M ū nī sh (they did not invite me)
ma S i M i ʿ it nī sh (she did not hear me).

3. If the pronominal suffix follows a preposition, the negative particle follows this entire form:

ma K a T a B lī sh (he has not written to me)
ma K a T a B it lukū sh (she has not written to you)
ma K a T a B ū lnā sh (they have not written to us).

4. The pronominal suffix of the 3rd person masculine singular ***–o*** changes to ***–ū*** before the negative particle ***–sh***:

KaTaBt o (I have written it) >
ma Ka T a B tū sh (I have not written it)
KaTaBt(e) lo (I have written to him) >
ma K a T a B t(e) lūsh (I haven't written to him).

5. If the pronominal suffix of the 3rd person masculine **singular** follows a long vowel, ***–h*** changes to ***–hū*** before the negative particle ***–sh***, and the vowel of the perfect ending is shortened:

KaTaBūh (they have written it) – *ma K a T a B u hū sh* (they have not written it)
KaTaBnāh (we have written it) – *ma K a T a B na hū sh* (we have not written it)
KaTaBtūh (you have written it) – *ma K a T a B tu hū sh* (you have not written it)
– *ma K a T a B tu hū l(i)nā sh* (you have not written it to us)

The negative particle "**mish**" and its use with the perfect verbal form

m(a)	PERFECT STEM					SUFFIX	DIRECT OBJECT	INDIRECT OBJECT	sh
ma	K	a	T	a	B				sh(i)
ma	K	a	T	a	B		hā		sh
ma	K	a	T	a	B		hā	lī	sh
ma	K	a	T	a	B	t	ū / uhū		sh
ma	K	a	T	a	B	na	hū		sh
ma	K	a	T	a	B	ū	hū	l(i)nā	sh

The English "**anything**" is expressed by the Arabic *ḥāga* (a thing): *Ma darastish ḥāga.* I have not studied anything. *Maḥaddish katab lina ḥāga.* Nobody wrote anything to us.

Use of the perfect:
The Arabic perfect expresses both the perfective and imperfective aspects of the past tense, corresponding to the English past simple and past perfect:
Nizlū fī maḥattit Ramsīs. – They got off at Ramsis station. *Dakhalna ʾl-maṭʿam.* – We entered the restaurant. *ʾAfalt il-bāb lē(h)?* Why did you close the door?
ʾAʿadtū fēn? Where did you sit down?

III. Tadrībāt:

Targama
She made me three bread cakes with cheese. Five passengers got off at the Main Station. The rooms with a balcony were occupied. I have not yet written to you my address in Cairo. Why haven't you invited him? When did you hear the voices? She has two little sisters. The historical mosques are right in front of you. The doors were not shut. Why didn't you sit at the window? Did you weigh also the apples for me? The film has not ended yet. Her last letters were very long. We did not ask anyone about anything. They did not order anything from us.

Kammil!
fanādiʾ ... (gamīl), muwaẓẓafīn ... (gdīd), yōmēn ... (ḥelu), ʾakhbār ... (kwayyis), fasatīn ... (ṭwīl), muṭribāt ... (maṣrī), mafatīḥ ... (ʾadīm), balṭohāt ... (tiʾīl)

A subway station in Cairo

IV. Mufradāt

ʾakhīr	the last
ʿa(la) ʾl-ʾākhir	completely, totally, absolutely
ʿām (ʾaʿwām)	year
ʿamal (i)	to do
ʿaṭshān	thirsty
il-ʾawwil	at first
ʿazam (i)	to invite
baʿadēn	after, then
baʿdi keda	thereafter
bayyāʿ, -īn	salesman
balṭo (balṭohāt)	coat
baṭāṭis	potatoes
bi-ṣarāḥa	honestly
bitello	veal
burtuʾāl	oranges
dabaḥ	to kill/slaughter (an animal)
dafaʿ (a)	to pay
dakhal (u)	to enter
ḍāfir (ḍawāfir)	nail
fakha	fruit
fallāḥ, -īn	peasant, farmer
farkha (frākh)	chicken, poultry
filfil rūmī	pepper
film (ʾaflām)	film
fustān (fasatīn)	dress (ladies')
gāmiʿ (gawāmiʿ)	mosque (the place of Friday's congregational prayer)
gazmagī, -ya	shoe seller, shoemaker
gazzār, -īn	butcher
ghaṭa (ghuṭyān)	lid, cap, stopper
gibna (giban)	cheese
ginē(h), -āt	pound
gurnān (garanīn)	newspaper
ḥad	someone
ḥaẓẓ (ḥuẓūẓ)	luck
khabar (ʾakhbār)	message, news
kharag (u)	to sort
khiyār	cucumbers
khiliṣ (a)	to end, finish
khuḍār	vegetables
ʾinn	that
yūs(t) ʾeffendi	mandarins

katab (i)	to write
kīlo	kilogram, kilometre
ktīr	a lot, much, often
kumsarī, -ya	conductor
kursī (karāsī)	chair
kushk (ʾakshāk)	kiosk, stand
laḥma (luḥūm)	meat
laṭīf (luṭāf)	kind, nice
lēl (layālī)	night
libnānī, -īyīn	Lebanese
liḥāf (ʾalḥifa)	blanket
lōn (ʾalwān)	colour
mabna (mabānī)	building
maʿdanī	mineral
maʾfūl	closed
maḥaddish	nobody
maḥall, -āt	shop
maḥwūs	enchanted, fascinated, possessed by some thing
mandīl (manadīl)	handkerchief, scarf
markib (marākib)	boat, ship
masgid (masāgid)	mosque (the place of worship in general)
mashghūl	busy
maṭʿam (maṭāʿim)	restaurant
metro	subway, tube
mīdān (mayadīn)	square
mīya (miʾāt)	hundred
milaff, -āt	file
milyōn (malayīn)	million
misik (i)	to take, to grasp
mōz	bananas
muʿgam (maʿāgim)	dictionary
musāʿada	help
nahr (ʾanhār, ʾanhur)	river
naṣaḥ (a)	to counsel someone something *(bi)*
nizil	to get off, descend, accommodate oneself
nuṣṣ (ʾanṣāṣ)	half
ʾōḍa (ʾuwaḍ)	room
ʾaʿad (u)	to sit, sit down
ʾafal (i)	to close, shut
ʾamīṣ (ʾumṣān)	shirt
ʾarn (ʾurūn)	century
ʾaṭaʿ (a)	to cut
ʾizāza (ʾazāyiz)	bottle
rāgel (riggāla)	man

rāʾīsī	main
raṣīf (ʾarṣifa)	pavement, traffic island
rghīf (ʾarghifa)	cake, slice (of bread)
rkhīs	cheap
rigiʿ(a)	to return
rikib (a)	to go by, take something
saʾal (a)	to ask
ṣabī (ṣubyān)	boy, apprentice
ṣafḥa, -āt	page
ṣāḥib (ʾaṣḥāb)	friend
is-Sayyida	is-Sayyida Zēnab, Lady Zēnab's mosque
sana (sinīn, sanawāt)	year
santi	centimetre
sikka (sikak)	road, way, path
simiʿ (a)	to hear, listen
siʿr (ʾasʿār)	price
sitt, -āt	woman, Mrs.
sūʾ (ʾaswāʾ)	market, marketplace
shahr (shuhūr, ʾashhur)	month
shāy	tea
shayyāl, -īn	bearer
shakar (u)	to thank someone (without preposition) for something *(ʿala)*
shanṭa (shunaṭ)	bag
sharāb, -āt	socks
shibbāk (shababīk)	window
shirib (a)	to drink
taʿbān, -īn	tired
ṭabbākh, -īn	cook
ṭābiʿ (ṭawābiʿ)	stamp (postal)
it-Taḥrīr	Taḥrīr (main Cairo square)
ṭalab (u)	to ask for, order something
ṭamāṭim	tomatoes
tārīkhī	historical
tazkara (tazākir)	ticket
tuffāḥ	apples
ʾunbūba (ʾanabīb)	pipe, pipeline
ʾusbūʿ (ʾasabīʿ)	week
wazan (i)	weigh
wazīr (wuzara)	minister
zēt (zuyūt)	oil
ziyāra	visit

Note: Brackets behind the verbs contain imperfect vowels (cf. Lesson 5).

V. Taʿbīrāt:

ʾAywa, bi ʾẓ-ẓabṭ!	Yes, precisely!
Bas(i) keda?!	No more? Enough so?
Bi-balāsh!	For free!
Bi-kam?	How much is it?
Khallīhā keda!	Leave it so! (amount)
Kifāya?	Enough?
ʾaddi ʾē(h)?	How many?

5

Id - Dars il-khāmis /Lesson 5

il-Maṭʿam

-Ḥa-nuʾ ʿud fēn?
-It-tarabēza di faḍya. Itfaḍḍalū uʾ ʿudū hena!
-Il-ʾawwil ʿawzīn nishrab ḥāga sāʾ(i)ʿa wi baʿdēn ḥa-nuṭlub il-ʾakl.
-Fī maṭʿamna bi-nuṭbukh ʾakl sharʾī wi gharbī.
-Bi-tikhbizū ʿēsh baladī barḍo?
- ʾAywa, wi bi-niʾmil sandawichāt fūl ʾu ṭaʿmēya.
-Ṭayyib, mumkin nuṭlub salaṭit khuḍār wi salaṭit ṭ(i)ḥīna wi shurbit ʿads wi wāḥid samak mashwī wi wāḥid maʾlī wi ṭabaʾēn ruzz bi ʾsh-shiʿrīya wi ʾl-ḥelu – jelatti.
-Ma tuṭlub līsh jelatti, ʾana ʿāwiz baṭṭīkh.
-Ḥa-tishrabū ʾē(h) baʿd il-ʾakl?
-Lissa mish ʿarfīn, ḥaḍretak mumkin tisʾalna baʿd(i) shwayya?

Taman kull(i) lōḥa ḥasab siʿr il-laḥma fi ʾs-sūʾ.

The price of each picture is corresponding to the market price of meat.

-Ḥāḍir, taḥt ʾamruku.
-Baʿd ʾiznak, mumkin ʾadkhul il-ḥammām, ʿāwiz ʾaghsil ʾīdayya.
-Itfaḍḍal, fī wishshak ʿala ṭūl.
- ʾAllāh! Il-ʾakl da gamīl ʾawi wi ʾs-salaṭāt di ma ḥaṣalitsh(i). Tislam ʾīdēk!
-Tislam.
-Mumkin nisʾal ḥaḍretak ʿala ḥāga?
- ʾAwi, ʾawi.
- ʾEḥna ʿawzīn niʿzim zmīlna wi niʿmil lo ʿanduku iḥtifāl bi-munasbit ʿīd mīlādo. Lāzim niḥgiz il-makān min di ʾl-waʾti?
-La, mish lāzim. Ibʿatū lna ʾṭ-ṭalab bi-yōm il-ḥafla wi ʿadad iḍ-ḍuyūf.
-Ḥa-nidfaʿ ʿarbūn?
-La, mish ḍarūrī, ḥa-tidfaʿū ḥisābku baʿd il-ḥafla. ʾIn shāʾ allāh.

I. ʾAsʾila:

1. Iḍ-ḍuyūf dōl kānū ʿawzīn yishrabū ʾē(h) il-ʾawwil?
2. Il-maṭʿam da bi-yikhbiz ʿēsh baladī?
3. Il-maṭʿam da bi-yiʿmil salaṭāt mumtāza?
4. Mīn kān ʿāwiz jighsil ʾīdēh?
5. Iḍ-ḍuyūf saʾalū ʾl-garsōn ʿala ʾē(h)?
6. Kān lāzim yiḥgizū ʾl-makān ʿala ṭūl?
7. Kān lāzim yibʿatū ṭalabhum li mīn?
8. ʾEmta ḥa-yidfaʿū ḥisābhum?

The menu of the restaurant Radwan on the Cairo Dokki square

II. Qawāʿid:

1. Demonstrative pronouns

	this:	that:	very close object:	
m.	da	dukha	ʾaho/ʾahūwad	this very
f.	di	dikha	ʾahi/ʾahīyad	this very
pl.	dōl	dukhum	ʾahum	these very

Use of the demonstrative pronouns:
When used ***as attributes***, demonstrative pronouns follow the determined noun or adjective, or its attribute, and they agree with it in gender: *il-bēt da* (this house), *ig-gnēna di* (this garden), *il-muwaẓẓafīn ig-gudād dōl* (these new clerks); plural inanimate nouns are treated as feminine singular nouns – the demonstrative pronoun assumes either feminine singular, or plural form: *il-ʾumṣān di* / *il-ʾumṣān dōl* (these shirts), *il-ʾayyām di* (these days), *il-yōmēn dōl* (these days – dual).
When used as subjects, demonstrative pronouns stand before the defined or undefined noun: *da bēt* (this is a house.), *da bēthum* (this is their house), *di madīnitna* (this is our town), *da ʾl-matḥaf il-maṣrī* (this is the Egyptian Museum), *dikha ʿarabīyto ʾg-gdīda* (that is his new car), *dōl ṭullābhā* (these are her students), *dōl ʾaṣḥāb ʾakhūya* (these are friends of my brother).

2. The imperfect of regular verbs

The imperfect is formed by prefixes, suffixes, and vowel changes within the verbal stem. There is no vowel after the first consonant. There is a vowel *-a-*, *-i-* or *-u-* after the second consonant. After the third consonant, there is no vowel in forms without suffixes. Forms with suffixes have a vowel. Each verb must be learned together with its imperfect vowel, i.e. the particular vowel after the second consonant.

Paradigms:

Verbs with imperfect vowel *–i-*:

	singular:	**negative forms:**
3rd pers. m.	*yi KTiB* – he writes	*ma yi KTiBsh(i)* – he doesn't write
3rd pers. f.	*ti KTiB* – she writes	*ma ti KtiBsh(i)* – she doesn't write
2nd pers. m.	*ti KTiB* – you write	*ma ti KtiBsh(i)* – you don't write
2nd pers. f.	*ti KTiBī* – you write	*ma ti KTiB īsh* – you don't write
1st pers.	*a KTiB* – I write	*ma KTiB sh(i)* – I don't write

	plural:	**negative forms:**
3rd person	*yi KTiBū* – they write	*ma yi KTiB ūsh* – they don't write
2nd person	*ti KTiBū* – you write	*ma ti KTiB ūsh* – you don't write
1st person	*ni KTiB* – we write	*ma ni KTiB sh(i)* – we don't write

Verbs with imperfect vowel *–a-*:

	singular:	**negative forms:**
3rd pers. m.	*yi FHaM* - he understands	*ma yi FhaM sh(i)* – he doesn't understand
3rd pers. f.	*ti FHaM* – she understands	*ma ti FhaM sh(i)* – she doesn't understand
2nd pers. m.	*ti FHaM* – you understand	*ma ti FhaM sh(i)* – you don't understand
2nd pers. f.	*ti FHaMī* – you understand	*ma ti FHaM īsh* – you don't understand
1st pers.	*a FHaM* – I understand	*ma FHaM sh(i)* – I don't understand

	plural:	**negative forms:**
3rd person	*yi FHaMū* – they understand	*ma yi FHaM ūsh* – they don't understand
2nd person	*ti FHaMū* – you understand	*ma ti FHaM ūsh* – you don't understand
1st person	*ni FHaM* – we understand	*ma ni FHaM sh(i)* – we don't understand

Verbs with imperfect vowel *–u-*:

	singular:	**negative forms:**
3rd pers. m.	*yu KhRug* – he goes out	*ma yu KhRuGsh(i)* – he doesn't go out
3rd pers. f.	*tu KhRug* – she goes out	*ma tu KhRuGsh(i)* – she doesn't go out
2nd pers. m.	*tu KhRuG* – you go out	*ma tu KhRuG sh(i)* – you don't go out
2nd pers. f.	*tu KhRuGī* – you go out	*ma tu KhRuGīsh* – you don't go out
1st pers.	*a KhRuG* – I go out	*ma KhRuG sh(i)* – I don't go out

	plural:	**negative forms:**
3rd person	*yu KhRuGū* – they go out	*ma yu KhRuGūsh* – they don't go out
2nd person	*tu KhRuGū* – you go out	*ma tu KhRuGūsh* – you don't go out
1st person	*nu KhRuG* – we go out	*ma nu KhRuGsh(i)* – we don't go out

Use of the imperfect:
a) To express the **present** tense, mainly corresponding to the English present simple. Imperfect forms expressing the meaning of present simple and present continuous use the particle ***bi***- (with the imperfect prefix of 1st person singular, the particle combines to ***ba***-): *bi-yiktib* (he writes), *bi-yifhamū* (they understand), *bi-nukhrug* (we are going out), *baktib gawābāt* (I write, am writing letters), *baktibhā* (I write them), *bakhrug kulli yōm* (we go out every day), *basmaʿ ʿanno* (I hear about him).

Negative forms: *ma bi-yiktibsh(i), ma bi-yifhamūsh, ma bi-nukhrugsh(i), ma baktibsh(i), ma baktibhāsh, ma bakhrugsh(i), ma basmaʿsh(i)*

b) To express the **future** tense. Imperfect forms expressing the future tense use the particle ***ḥa***- (before the 1st person singular imperfect prefix shortened to ***ḥ***-: *ḥa-yiktib* (he will write), *ḥa-yifhamū* (they will understand), *ḥa-nukhrug* (we will go out), *ḥaktib* (I will write), *ḥakhrug* (I will go out), *ḥasmaʿ* (I will hear).
To **negate the future tense**, the particle ***mush/mish*** is used. It stands before the future verb form: *mish ḥa-yiktib* (he will not write), *mish ḥa-yifhamū* (they will not understand), *mish ḥa-nukhrug* (we will not go out), *mish ḥaktib* (I will not write), *mish ḥakhrug* (I will not go out), *mish ḥasmaʿ* (I will not hear).

c) To express the **subjunctive after modal verbs** (corresponding to the use of the English infinitive): *ʿĀwiz ʾaktib ig-gawāb.* – I want to write the letter. *ʿAyzīn yinzilū hena.* – They want to get off here. *Mumkin nirkab it-taks.* We can take a taxi. *Lāzim tismaʿū ʾl-ʾakhbār.* – You (pl.) have to listen to the news.

3. The imperative
The imperative is formed from 2nd person forms of the imperfect by replacing the prefix ***ti***- by ***i***- (in case of verbs with imperfect vowel -***i***- or -***a***-), or ***u***- (in case of verbs with imperfect vowel -***u***-).:

Impf. vowel	***-i-***	***-a-***	***-u-***
2nd pers. m.	*iKTiB!*	*iFHaM!*	*uKhRuG!*
2nd pers. f.	*iKTiBī!*	*iFHaMī!*	*uKhRuGī!*
2nd pers. pl.	*iKTiBū!*	*iFHaMū!*	*uKhRuGū!*

The negative imperative is formed from the negative form of the 2nd person imperfect – the negative particle ***mush/mish*** is split into two parts, ***m(a)-,*** standing before the verb form, and ***-sh(i)***, standing after the verb form: *matiKTiBsh(i)!* – Do not write! (m.), *matiKTiBīsh!* – Do not write! (f.), *matiKTiBūsh!* – Do not write! (pl.), *matuKhRuGsh(i)* – Do not go out! (m.), *matiSMaʿūhāsh!* – Do not listen (pl.) to her!

4. Modal verbs "must", "can/may", want"
"**Must**" is expressed by the immutable impersonal form ***lāzim*** (it is necessary, desirable): *Lāzim ʾakhrug shwayya.* – I must walk a little. *Lāzim yinzil hena.* – He must get off here. *Lāzim nifhamo kwayyis.* – We must understand him well.
Negative form: *Mish lāzim tirkabū ʾt-taks(i).* – You needn't take a taxi.

"Can/may" is expressed by the immutable impersonal form ***mumkin*** (it is possible): *Mumkin nuʾʿud fēn?* – Where can we sit? *Mumkin tiktibū ig-gawāb da bi ʾl-ʿarabī?* – Can you write the letter in Arabic? *Mumkin ʾashrab shāy?* – May I have tea?

Negative form: *Mish mumkin yisʾalūhum?* - Can't they ask them?

"**Want**" is expressed by the active participle ***ʿāwiz/ʿāyiz***, which agrees in number and gender with the subject: *ʾAna ʿāwiz ʾargaʿ ʿala ṭūl.* – I want to return right away. *ʾEḥna ʿayzīn nisʾalhum.* – We want to ask them. *ʾEntū ʿawzīn tishrabū ʾē(h)?* – What do you want to drink?

Negative form: *Huwa mish ʿāwiz yuʾʿud barra.* – He doesn't want to sit outside.

The **past and future tense** of "must", "can/may" and "want" is formed by the past and future tense of the verb ***kān*** (cf. Lesson 6 – imperfect of the verb ***kān***), which stands before the forms *lāzim*, *mumkin*, and *ʿāwiz / ʿāyiz*. With impersonal forms, ***kān*** assumes the 3rd person masculine singular form, with *ʿāwiz / ʿāyiz*, the verb *kān* agrees in number and gender with the subject.

III. Tadrībāt:

Targama

Don't you (pl.) want to sit down at the window? Can you (f.) make roasted fish for us? We must order something to eat. The English tourists return by the hotel bus. I hear this news very often. She will not take a taxi. I must wash my hands. Do not (m.) get off at this station! Take (f.) something else! Please, pay your bill today! He wants to invite us to his birthday party. They will not like this film. They will not understand us. We must ask you for the address of this restaurant. The waiter wants to know the number of guests. These problems do not happen in our company. Why will you not drink anything? We can't book the theatre tickets for him. Send us your request this week!

Kammil!

da / di / dōl

a) *ʾasḥābna* ... b) *ḍēfna ʾl-ʾagnabī* ... c) *il-buyūt ig-gamīla* ... d) *il-munasba ʾl-ḥelwa* ...
e) *ʾaʿyādna* ... f) *ir-ruzz* ... g) *iṭ-ṭabbākhīn il-mumtāzīn* ... h) *il-mudun it-tārīkhīya* ...

IV. Mufradāt

ʿadad (ʾaʿdād)	number
ʿads	lentils
ʿagab (i)	to be liked by someone
ʾagnabī (ʾagānib)	foreign, foreigner
ʿarbūn	deposit
baʿat (a)	to send
baʿdi shwayya	in a while
barra	outside, out, abroad
baṭṭīkh	melon
ḍarūrī	necessary, inevitable, it is necessary
ḍēf (ḍuyūf)	guest
fihim	to understand
fūl	beans
garson	waiter
gharbī	western, European
ghasal (i)	to wash
ḥafla (-āt)	party, celebration, concert, performance
ḥagaz	to reserve, book, order
ḥaṣal	to happen

Shawerma – a favourite fast food

Maharagān il-Āys krīm, ice-cream festival: weeks of ice-cream treats in Egyptian sweet shops

ḥelu	dessert, sweet
ḥisāb, -āt	bill
khabaz (i)	to bake
ʿīd (ʾaʿyād)	festive day, festival
ʿīd il-mīlād	birthday
iḥtifāl	party, celebration
ʿirif (a)	to know
madīna (mudun)	city, town
maʾlī	fried
masraḥ (masāriḥ)	theatre
mashwī	roast (meat)
matḥaf (matāḥif)	museum
mīlād	birth
mumkin	it is possible
munasba, -āt	occasion
ruzz	rice
sāʾiʿ	cold, cooled
sāyiḥ (suyyāḥ)	tourist
salaṭa, -āt	salad
sandawīch, -āt	sandwich
sharʾī	eastern, Oriental
shiʿrīya	noodles
shirka (shirkāt)	firm, company
shurba	soup

ṭabaʾ (ʾaṭbāʾ)	plate
ṭabakh (u)	to cook, prepare a meal
ṭalab, -āt	request
ṭaʿmēya	fried burgers of beans, vegetables and spices (vegetable patties)
tānī	again, once again, second, another
ṭ(i)ḥīna	tahīna (sesame paste)
wishsh (wushūsh)	face
jelatti	ice-cream

V. Taʿbīrāt:

ʾAllāh!	Great! Wonderful!
Baʿd ʾiznak (ʾiznik, ʾiznuku)	Excuse me! I am sorry!
Fī wishshak!	Right in front of you!
Ḥādir!	At your service!
Il-ʾakl ma ḥaṣalsh(i).	The food is excellent! (lit.: didn't happen)
Il-yōmēn dōl.	Now. Nowadays.
ʾIn shāʾallāh!	If God will. Maybe. Let's hope.
ʾAwi, ʾawi!	With pleasure!
Taḥt ʾamruku!	At your service! Please!

6

Id - Dars is-sādis /Lesson 6

Ziyārt il-matḥaf

Da faks ḥagarī gay min ʿand ʾabūk fi ʾl-Matḥaf il-brīṭānī baʿdima ʾtsaraʾ min hena wi bi-yiʾūl ʾinno mabsūṭ wi farḥānīn bīh il-ʾInglīz wi bi-yiʿām(i)lūh kwayyis ʾawi wi bi-yiʾūl ʿoʾbālku lamma ʾtitsirʾū wi as-salām li ʾl-gamīʿ.

This is a stone fax, which came from your father from the British museum, where he was stolen from here. He says that he is satisfied, the English are happy about him and treat him very well. He wishes you the same destiny. Best regards to all!

Min ʾusbūʿ ruḥt il-Qāhira, ʿashān ʾazūr il-Matḥaf il-maṣrī. Zamaylī min Maʿhad il-ʾāsār il-maṣrīya ʾl-ʾadīma ʾālū lī ʾinn lāzim ʾashūf ʾasār Maṣr il-firʿaunīya.
- ʾEmta ʿāwiz tirūḥ il-Matḥaf il-masrī?
- Bukra, yā baʿdo. Mumkin ʾasīb lak khabar ʿashān tirūḥ maʿāya?
-Ṭabʿan, bas sib lī risāla ʿala ʾl-maḥmūl, ʿashān mish ḥabāt fī bētī il-lēla di.
- ʾAlō, mumkin tifūt ʿalayya bukra ʾiṣ-ṣubḥ ʿashān nirūḥ il-Matḥaf il-maṣrī?
Iṣ-ṣubḥ ʾumt badri. Zmīlī fāt ʿalayya fi ʾl-maʿād. Rikibna ʿarabīyito, kān bi-yisūʾhā kwayyis ʾawi. Fi ʾl-matḥaf ʾāl lī ẓābiṭ shurṭit is-siyāḥa ʾinno ʿāwiz jishūf shanṭitī. Fataḥt(a)hā lo. Kunt shāyil fīhā kamerit fīdyo.
ʾUlt(e) lo ʾinnī ḥasībhā maʿa ḥaras il-matḥaf. Zmīlī ṭalab minnī biṭāʾ(i)tī id-daulīya ʿashān yigīb lina tazākir li ʾṭ-ṭalaba.
ʾUddām il-matḥaf shufna rāgel ʿagūz, kān bi-yibīʿ il-bardīyāt. Wi gouwa ʾl-matḥaf tuhna shwayya wusṭ it-tamasīl il-kbīra. Shufna hnāk ʾasariyīn maṣriyīn, kānū bi-yiʾīsū ʾt-tawabīt il-khashabīya mi ʾd-Daula ʾl-ḥadīsa. Ṣaḥīḥ, ʾinn ʾaṣḥāb it-tuḥaf il-maʿrūda hena mātū min zamān, bas rūḥ ḥaḍārithum il-ʿazīma bi-tiʿīsh li-ghāyit ʿaṣrina ʾl-ḥāḍir.

I. ʼAsʼila:

1. Mīn ʼāl lī ʼinn lāzim ʼashūf ʼāsār Maṣr il-firʻaunīya?
2. Kunt ʻāwiz ʼasīb khabar li zmīlī ʻashān ʼē(h)?
3. ʼUlt(e) lo ʼē(h) fi ʼl-maḥmūl?
4. Kunt shāyil ʼē(h) fī shanṭitī?
5. Zmīlī ṭalab minnī biṭāʼ(i)tī ʼd-daulīya lē(h)?
6. Mīn kān bi-yibīʻ il-bardīyāt ʼuddām il-matḥaf?
7. ʼEzzāy tuhna gouwa ʼl-matḥaf?

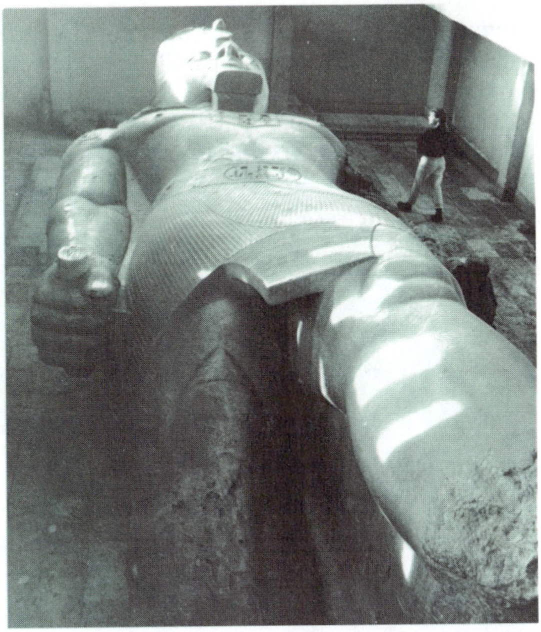

Ramesses II in Memphis

II. Qawāʻid:

1. Verbs with the second consonant *w* or *y*

Many common Arabic verbs replace the second consonant of the 3rd person singular and plural perfect forms with the long vowel **ā**. This **ā** was originally a ***w*** or ***y***, which is still found in other perfect forms as ***u*** or ***i***, and in the imperfect and the imperative as **ū**, **ī**, or **ā**.

a) Verbs with ū (*w*) in imperfect forms:

ShĀF (to see)

perfect:

	singular:	negative:	plural:	negative:
3rd pers. m.	***ShāF***	***ma ShaFsh(i)***	***ShāF-ū***	***maShāF-ūsh***
3rd pers. f.	***ShāF-it***	***ma ShāFitsh(i)***		
2nd pers. m.	***ShuF-t***	***ma ShuFtish***	***ShuF-tū***	***maShuF-tūsh***
2nd pers. f.	***ShuF-ti***	***ma ShuFtīsh***		
1st pers.	***ShuF-t***	***ma ShuFtish***	***ShuF-na***	***maShuF-nāsh***

imperfect:

	singular:	negative:	plural:	negative:
3rd pers. m.	***yi-ShūF***	***ma yi-ShuFsh(i)***	***yi-ShūF-ū***	***ma yi-ShūF-ūsh***
3rd pers. f.	***ti-ShūF***	***ma ti-ShuFsh(i)***		
2nd pers. m.	***ti-ShūF***	***ma ti-ShuFsh(i)***	***ti-ShūF-ū***	***ma ti-ShūF-ūsh***
2nd pers. f.	***ti-ShūFī***	***ma ti-ShūFī(sh)***		
1st pers.	***a-ShūF***	***ma-ShuFsh(i)***	***ni-ShūF***	***ma ni-ShuFsh(i)***

Imperative: *ShuF!* (m.), *ShūFī!* (f.), *ShūFū!* (pl.).
Negative imperative: *ma tShuFsh(i)!* (m.), *ma tShūFīsh!* (f.), *ma tShūFūsh!* (pl.).
– the *-i-* of the prefix ***ti-*** is left out.

Active participle: *ShāYiF* (m.), *ShaYFa* (f.), *ShaYFīn* (pl.).
- Other verbs following this paradigm: *KāN (yi-KūN)* – to be, *RāḤ (yi-RūḤ)* – to go, to go by, *ʾāL (yi-ʾūL)* – to say, *ZāR (yi-ZūR)* – to visit, *ʾāM (yi-ʾūM)* – to stand up, to stand, *MāT (yi-MūT)* – to die, *BāS (yi-BūS)* – to kiss, *FāT (yi-FūT)* – to come by, come for something, to pass, *DāS (yi-DūS)* – to stand, step on something, *Dāʾ (yi-Dūʾ)* – to taste.

imperfect of the verb KāN:

	singular:	negative:	plural:	negative:
3rd pers. m.	***yi-KūN***	***ma yi-KuNsh(i)***	***yi-KūN-ū***	***ma yi-KūN-ūsh***
3rd pers. f.	***ti-KūN***	***ma ti-KuNsh(i)***		
2nd pers. m.	***ti-KūN***	***ma ti-KuNsh(i)***	***ti-KūN-ū***	***ma ti-KūN-ūsh***
2nd pers. f.	***ti-KūNī***	***ma ti-KūNī(sh)***		
1st pers.	***a-KūN***	***ma-KuNsh(i)***	***ni-KūN***	***ma ni-KuNsh(i)***

Imperative: *KuN!* (m.), *KūNī!* (f.), *KūNū!* (pl.).
Negative imperative: *ma tKuNsh(i)!* (m.), *ma tKūNīsh!* (f.), *ma tKūNūsh!* (pl.).

b) Verbs with *ī* (*y*) in imperfect forms:

GĀB (to bring)
perfect:

	singular:	negative:	plural:	negative:
3rd pers. m.	***GāB***	***ma GaBsh(i)***	***GāB-ū***	***maGāB-ūsh***
3rd pers. f.	***GāB-it***	***ma GāBitsh(i)***		
2nd pers. m.	***GiB-t***	***ma GiBtish***	***GiB-tū***	***maGiB-tūsh***
2nd pers. f.	***GiB-ti***	***ma GiBtīsh***		
1st pers.	***GiB-t***	***ma GiBtish***	***GiB-na***	***maGiB-nāsh***

imperfect:

	singular:	negative:	plural:	negative:
3rd pers. m.	***yi-GīB***	***ma yi-GiBsh(i)***	***yi-GīB-ū***	***ma yi-GīB-ūsh***
3rd pers. f.	***ti-GīB***	***ma ti-GiBsh(i)***		
2nd pers. m.	***ti-GīB***	***ma ti-GiBsh(i)***	***ti-GīB-ū***	***ma ti-GīB-ūsh***
2nd pers. f.	***ti-GīBī***	***ma ti-GīBī(sh)***		
1st pers.	***a-GīB***	***ma-GiBsh(i)***	***ni-GīB***	***ma ni-GiB-sh(i)***

Imperative: *gib!* (m.), *gībī!* (f.), *gībū!* (pl.).
Negative imperative: *ma tgibsh(i)!* (m.), *ma tgībīsh!* (f.), *ma tgībūsh!* (pl.). – the –***i***- of the prefix ***ti***- is left out.

Active participle: *GāYiB* (m.), *GaYBa* (f.), *GayBīn* (pl.).
- Other verbs belonging to this group: *ShāL (yi-ShīL)* – to carry, carry away, dispose of, *SāB (yi-SīB)* – to let, to let go, to leave, *GhāB (yi-GhīB)* – to be missing, *ʿāSh (yi-ʿīSh)* – to live, *Bāʿ (yi-Bīʿ)* – to sell.

c) Verbs with ā (*w*) in imperfect forms:

NĀM (to sleep)
perfect:

	singular:	negative:	plural:	negative:
3rd pers. m.	***NāM***	***ma NaMsh(i)***	***NāM-ū***	***ma NāM-ūsh***
3rd pers. f.	***NāM-it***	***ma NāMitsh(i)***		
2nd pers. m.	***NiM-t***	***ma NiMtish***	***NiM-tū***	***ma NiM-tūsh***
2nd pers. f.	***NiM-ti***	***ma NiMtīsh***		
1st pers.	***NiM-t***	***ma NiMtish***	***NiM-na***	***ma NiM-nāsh***

imperfect:

	singular:	negative:	plural:	negative:
3rd pers. m.	***yi-NāM***	***ma yi-NaMsh(i)***	***yi-NāM-ū***	***ma yi-NāM-ūsh***
3rd pers. f.	***ti-NāM***	***ma ti-NaMsh(i)***		
2nd pers. m.	***ti-NāM***	***ma ti-NaMsh(i)***	***ti-NāM-ū***	***ma ti-NāM-ūsh***
2nd pers. f.	***ti-NāMī***	***ma ti-NāMī(sh)***		
1st pers.	***a-NāM***	***ma-NaMsh(i)***	***ni-NāM***	***ma ni-NaM-sh(i)***

Imperative: *nam!* (m.), *nāmī!* (f.), *nāmū!* (pl.).
Negative imperative: *ma tnamsh(i)!* (m.), *ma tnāmīsh!* (f.), *ma tnāmūsh!* (pl.).
– the ***-i-*** of the prefix ***ti-*** is left out.

Active participiple: *NāYiM* (m.), *NaYMa* (f.), *NaYMīn* (pl.).
– Other verbs following this paradigm: *KhāF (yi-KhāF)* – to be afraid, *BāT (yi-BāT)* – to spend the night.

2. Clauses of purpose and cause

The conjunction ***ʿashān / ʿalashān*** (so that, in order to) indicates clauses of purpose. The verb of the purpose clause always assumes the imperfect form, irrespective of the tense of the main sentence: *Ruḥt il-Qāhira ʿashān ʾazūr il-Mathaf il-maṣrī.* – I went to Cairo in order to visit the Egyptian museum. *Ḥa-nuʾʿud hena ʿashān nismaʿ kwayyis.* – We will sit here, so that we hear well. *Kān lāzim yiʾūmū ʿashān yishūfūh.* – They had to stand up in order to see him. *ʿĀwiz ʾaktib lo ʾl-khabar da ʿashān ma tifūtūsh furṣit il-ʿumr.* – I want to write him a message, so that he doesn't miss the occasion of his life.

The conjunction ***ʿashān/ʿalashān*** introduces also clauses of cause. The verb of such a clause may assume any tense: *Shakarnāhā ʿashān ʿamalit lina siʿr mumtāz.* – We thanked her, because she made us a good price. *Saʾalit ʿalēh ʿashān(o) lissa ma rigiʿsh(i).* She asked about him, because he hadn't returned yet. *Ḥasīb luhum ʿanduku ʿunwānī ʿashān mish ḥashūfhum tānī ʾabl(i) safarhum.* – I will leave my address for them with you, since I will not see them before my departure.

3. Future tense of "must", "may" and "want"

The future tense of phrases meaning "**must**", "**may**" and "**want"** is formed by means of the future tense of the verb ***kān***, placed before the words ***lāzim***, ***mumkin***, and ***ʿāwiz*** or ***ʿāyiz***. When placed in front of impersonal forms, the verb ***kān*** always assumes

The Egyptian Museum in Cairo

the 3rd person masculine singular form, in the case of the verb "to want", the verb ***kān*** agrees with the subject in number and gender: *Ḥa-yikūn lāzim yirgaʿū ʾn-nahār da.* – They will have to return today. *Mish ḥa-yikūn mumkin yisʾalo.* – He will not be able to ask him. *Ḥa-tikūn ʿawza tighsil ʾīdēhā.* – She will want to wash her hands. *Mish ḥa-yikūnū ʿawzīn yuṭlubū ḥāga.* – They will not want to order anything.

The future (and past) tense of "to want" can also be expressed by means of the verb ***ʿāz (yiʿūz)*** – to wish, to want: *Ḥa-tiʿūz tighsil ʾīdēhā.* She will want to wash her hands. *Mish ḥa-yiʿūzū yuṭlubū ḥāga.* – They will not want to order anything. *ʿUzt ʾargaʿ in-nahār da.* – I wanted to return today.

III. Tadrībāt:

Targama

We didn't go to the club, because we had too much work. This will not be possible at all. Can you tell me when is your birthday? Please, take this plate away! Leave us your address, so that we can visit you. You must tell them your order, so that they would bring you the meal as you want it. Don't worry (f.), the weather will be fine. I will not be away (missing) for long. He opened the sarcophagus for him, so that he could look at the mummy. She was afraid for them, because they could get lost. Who wants to taste Oriental sweets? Why did you have to sell the theatre tickets? Will you (m.) let me drive the company car?

Kammil!

a) ḥa-yimūt b) ʾashūfak c) nibāt d) tiʾūlū e) ḥa-nisīb f) yifūtū g) gābū h) tiʾūm

1. Lāzim ... fi ʾl-funduʾ. 2. Mumkin ... ʾemta? 3. ... luku ʾl-ḥagāt di fēn?
4. Hiya ʿawza ... badri. 5. Mnēn ... ʾl-kitāb da? 6. Mumkin ... ʿalēku ʾn-nahār da?
7. Kunna khayfīn ʾinno ... 8. Lāzim ... lna ʿala ʾl-mauḍūʿ da.

IV. Mufradāt

ʿagūz (ʿawagīz)	old, old man
ʾakl (ʾakalāt)	food, meal
ʾalō!	hello! (on the phone)
ʿaraḍ (i)	to exhibit, offer, make an offer
ʾasar (ʾāsār)	monument
asarī	archaeologist, historical
ʿaṣr (ʿuṣūr)	time, era
ʿāsh (ī)	to live
ʿāz (ū)	to wish, to want
ʿaẓīm (ʿuẓama)	great, excellent, marvellous
bāʿ (ī)	to sell
badri	early, soon
bardī, -yāt	papyrus
bās (ū)	to kiss
bāt (ā)	to sleep, spend the night
bukra	tomorrow
dāʾ (ū)	to taste
dās (ū)	to step, step on
daula (duwal)	to stand
daulī	international
fāt (ū)	to pass
	to stop by, come by *(ʿala)* (for) someone
fataḥ (a)	to open
fīdyo	video
firʿaunī	pharaonic
furṣa (furaṣ)	occasion, chance
gāb (ī)	to bring, obtain
ghāb (ī)	to be missing
gouwa	inside
ḥaḍāra	culture, civilisation
ḥāḍir	current, present
ḥalawīyāt	sweets
ḥaras	security guards
khāf (ā)	to be afraid / *min* of something / *ʿala* for
khashabī	wooden
kamera	camera
maʿād (mawāʿīd)	term, meeting
maʿhad (maʿāhid)	institute
maḥmūl	cellular phone
maʿrūḍāt	objects on exhibition
māt (ū)	to die
mauḍūʿ (mawaḍīʿ)	theme, problem, affair
mūmiyā, - āt	mummy

nādī (ʾandiya)	club
nām (ā)	to sleep
nāwūs (nawawīs)	sarcophagus
ʾāl (u)	to say (something without preposition), reveal something *(ʿala)*
ʾām (u)	stand, stand up, start
ʾās (ī)	measure (concerning a means of transporation)
rāḥ (ū)	to go
risāla (rasāyil)	letter, master's or doctor's thesis
rūḥ (ʾarwāḥ)	spirit, soul
sāʾ (ū)	to drive
sāb (ī)	to leave, let, let go
safar	journey, departure
siyāḥa	tourism
ṣubḥ	morning
shāf (u)	to see
shāl (ī)	to carry, carry away, remove
shurṭa	police
shwayya	a little
tābūt (tawabīt)	coffin, sarcophagus
tāh (ū)	to get lost
ṭālib (ṭalaba / ṭullāb)	student
timsāl (tamasīl)	statue
tuḥfa (tuḥaf)	monument, antiquity
ʿumr (ʾaʿmār)	age, lifetime
yā	or
zāy? (ʾezzāy?)	how? like, as
zār (ū)	to visit
zamān	time, period
zmīl (zamāyil)	colleague

V. Taʿbīrāt:

bukra yā baʿdo	Tomorrow or the day after tomorrow.
fi ʾl-maʿād	in time
il-lelā di	tonight
min zamān	long time ago
Zayyak? (ʾEzzayyak?)	How are you? (m. sg.)
Zayyik? (ʾEzzayyik?)	How are you? (f. sg.)
Zayyuku? (ʾEzzayuku?)	How are you? (pl.)
Zay ḥaḍretak? (-tik)	How are you? (polite m. and f.)
Zaymā ʾenta ʿāwiz.	As you like.

Fi ʾl-ʾahwa

- Nifsī ʾashrab kubbāyit shāy. ʾĒ(h) raʾyak, ḥa-nikhushsh il-ʾahwa di?
- Yarēt, ʾana ʿaṭshān barḍo, wi riglayya – mish ḥāsis bihā khāliṣ.
- Ṭabʿan, laffēna ʾl-madīna ʾt-tārīkhīya min Bāb in-Naṣr li ghāyit Bāb Zuwēla. Baʿdēn ruḥna gāmiʿ Ibn Ṭulūn wi kān lāzim nimidd gāmid ʿashān nilḥaʾ niṭlaʾ il-madna btaʿto.
- Sāmiʿ, iz-zabāyin bi-yisʾalū: "Fēn il-yansūn?" "Il-ʾirfa btaʿtī fēn?" "ʾAhwa ziyāda, lau samaḥt!"
- Buṣṣ il-makān da, ʾana shayfo ẓarīf ʾawi. W ʾil-garson bi-yigīb il-mayya ʿala ṭūl.
- Mumkin ʾaṣubb(u) lku shwayya?
- Min faḍlak, wāḥid shāy, bas ma tiḥutt(i) līsh sukkar!
- Ḥāḍir, wi ḥaḍretak?
- Karkadē(h) sāʾiʿ.
- Tiḥibbū tishrabū shīsha?
- Gamīl, ḥa-nishrab shīsha, ʾana baḥibbahā ʾawi.
- Itfaḍḍal, yā bāsha. Gibt(e) lku ʾl-miʿassil bi ʾt-tuffāḥ. Ish-shīsha, ḥaḥuṭṭahā lku hena, ʿashān lāzim ʾarudd ʿa ʾt-telefōn bi-surʿa.
- ʾAna ḥallēt mushkiltī maʿa ʾt-tadkhīn.
- ʾEzzāy? Ma bi-tiḥibbish is-sagāyir?
- Mish bi ʾẓ-ẓabṭ, bas is-shīsha di ḥāga tanya.
- Baʿd ʾizn ḥaḍretak, mumkin tilimm ig-gurnān ʿashān ʾashīl il-kubbāyāt?
- Mā lak, sarḥān fī ʾē(h)?
- ʾAbadan. Mish ʿārif, ḥaṭṭēt il-maḥfaẓa btaʿtī fēn?
- Buṣṣ fī gēb ij-jakēt bitāʿak!
- Baṣṣēt fīh, bas mish maugūda hnāk.
- Ṭayyib, shuftahā ʾākhir marra ʾemta?
- Lammā kunna fī Khān il-Khalīlī wi kunt baʿidd il-flūs, ʿashān ʾagīb li-ʾukhtī gallabīya.

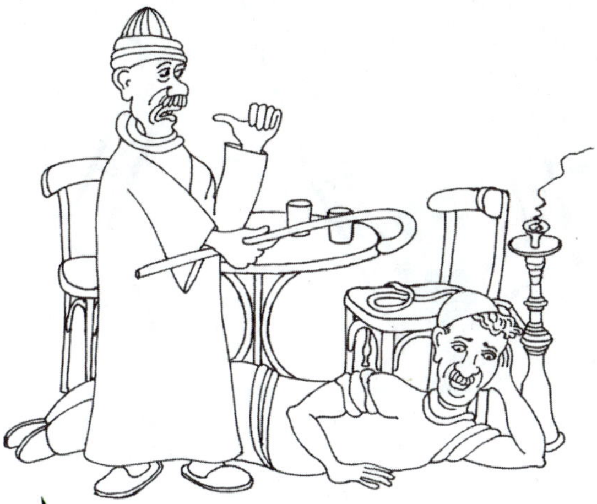

ʾEnta baʿdimā shribt mashrūb il-yansūn, nsīt ʾinn in-nōm bi-y(i)kūn ʿala ḥāga ismahā srīr.

After you had drunk the aniseed infusion, you have forgotten that we use bed for sleeping.

- Gāyiz ḥaṭṭēthā fī grāb il-basbōr bitāʿak.
- Il-ḥamdu li ʾllāh, il-mushkila maḥlūla wi ʿala fikra, il-ḥisāb ʿalayya ʾn-nahār da.

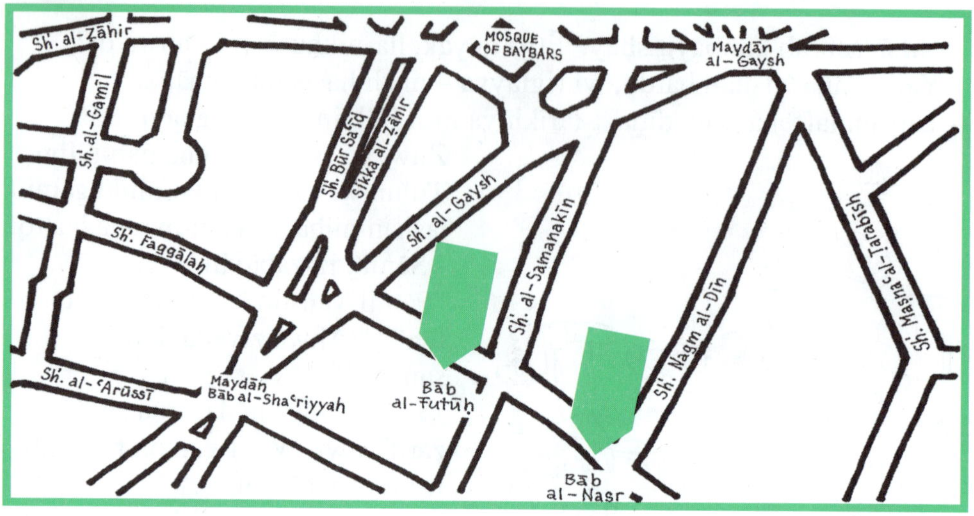

Báb il-Futūḥ
Báb in-Naṣr

I. ʾAsʾila:

1. Zuwwār il-Qāhira ʿawzīn yikhushshū ʾl-ʾahwa lē(h)?
2. Iz-zuwwār dōl laffū Halyūbulis?
3. Mīn kān ʿawiz jiṣubb(e) lhum mayya?
4. Mīn kān lāzim yirudd ʿa ʾt-telefōn?
5. Zāyir il-ʾahwa ḥall mushkilto maʿa ʾt-tadkhīn ʾezzāy?
6. Ig-garson kān ʿāwiz yilimm ig-gurnān lē(h)?
7. Ir-rāgel baṣṣ fī gēb ij-jakēt bitāʿo lē(h)?
8. Kān bi-jiʿidd il-flūs btaʿto ʾākhir marra ʾemta?

II. Qawāʿid:

1. Verbs with identical second and third consonants

These verbs have not in the perfect or imperfect form any vowel between the second and third consonant. They are conjugated according to the following paradigm:

ḤABB (to love, like)

perfect:

	singular:	negative:	plural:	negative:
3rd pers. m.	***ḤaBB***	***maḤaBB-ish***	***ḤaBB-ū***	***maḤaBB-ūsh***
3rd pers. f.	***ḤaBB-it***	***ma ḤaBB-itsh(i)***		
2nd pers. m.	***ḤaBB-ēt***	***ma ḤaBB-ētsh(i)***	***ḤaBB-ētū***	***maḤaBB-ētūsh***
2nd pers. f.	***ḤaBB-ēti***	***ma ḤaBB-ētīsh***		
1st pers.	***ḤaBB-ēt***	***ma ḤaBB-ētsh(i)***	***ḤaBB-ēna***	

imperfect:

	singular:	negative:	plural:	negative:
3rd pers. m.	***yi-ḤiBB***	***ma yi-ḤiBB(i)sh***	***yi-ḤiBB-ū***	***ma yi-ḤiBB-ūsh***
3rd pers. f.	***ti-ḤiBB***	***ma ti-ḤiBB(i)sh***		
2nd pers. m.	***ti-ḤiBB***	***ma ti-ḤiBB(i)sh***	***ti-ḤiBB-ū***	***ma ti-ḤiBB-ūsh***
2nd pers. f.	***ti-ḤiBBī***	***ma ti-ḤiBBī(sh)***		
1st pers.	***a-ḤiBB***	***m a-ḤiBB(i)sh***	***ni-ḤiBB***	***ma ni-ḤiBB(i)sh***

Imperative: *ḥibb!* (m.), *ḥibbī!* (f.), *ḥibbū!* (pl.).
Negative imperative: *ma tḥibb(i)sh!* (m.), *ma tḥibbīsh!* (f.), *ma tḥibbūsh!* (pl.). – the ***-i-*** of the prefix ***ti-*** is left out.

Active participle: *ḤāBiB* (m.) – loving, liking; *ḤāBBa* (f.), *ḤaBBīn* (pl.).
Passive participle: *maḤBūB* (m.) – beloved, favourite; *maḤBūBa* (f.), *maḤBūBīn* (pl.).

Other verbs following this paradigm: *LaMM (yi-LiMM)* – to collect, put together, assemble, *ShaMM (yi-ShiMM)* – to smell, *ʾaṢṢ (yi-ʾuṢṢ)* – to cut (with scissors), *KhaShSh (yi-KhuShSh)* – to enter, *ḤaṬṬ (yi-ḤuṬṬ)* – to put, to place something somewhere, *KhaFF (yi-KhiFF)* – to be cured, to recover.

Limm il-ghasīl! – Collect the laundry! *ʾAṣṣit shaʿrahā.* – She cut her hair. *Khushshū gouwa!* – Enter! *Ḥaṭṭēt il-muftāḥ fēn?* – Where did you put the key? *Lissa makhaffētsh(i) khāliṣ.* – I have not fully recovered yet.

– The verb ***ḤaBB***, "to like (to do something)", is followed, just like modal verbs, by the imperfect form: *Thiḥibbū tishrabū ʾē(h)?* – What would you like to drink? *Ma baḥibbish ʾarūḥ il-maḥall da.* – I don't like to go to this shop.

Bāb Zuwēla

Bāb il-Futūḥ

2. The particle *bitāʿ* :

The possessive particle ***bitāʿ*** is used to express:

a) the genitival phrase (appositional adjunct)

b) the possessive pronoun

a) The particle is placed between definite or indefinite nouns of the genitival phrase; its gender and number depends on the gender and number of the first component:

– if the first component is masculine, the particle assumes the form ***b(i)tāʿ***: *il-maktab bitāʿ is-safīr* / *maktab bitāʿ safīr* – the office of the ambassador, *il-maḥall b(i)tāʿ ʾl-ʿuṭūr* / *maḥall b(i)tāʿ ʿutūr* – the perfume shop.

– if the first component is feminine, the particle assumes the form ***btāʿ(i)t***: *il-ʿarabēya btaʿt il-mudīr* / *ʿarabēya btaʿit mudīr* – the car of the director, *it-tarabēza btaʿt il-ʾahwa* / *tarabēza btaʿit ʾahwa* – the café table.

– if the first component is plural, the particle assumes the form ***b(i)tūʿ***: *il-ʿummāl bitūʿ ish-shirka* / *ʿummāl bitūʿ shirka* – the workers of the company, *il-muwaẓẓafīn b(i)tūʿ il-wizāra* / *muwaẓẓafīn b(i)tūʿ wizāra* – the clerks of the ministry.

b) The particle takes the pronominal suffix and follows the noun:

(il-) mudarris b(i)tāʿī (my teacher) *(il-) mudarris b(i)tāʿna* (our teacher)

(il-) mudarris b(i)tāʿak (your [m.] teacher)

(il-) mudarris b(i)tāʿik (your [f.] teacher) *(il-) mudarris b(i)tāʿuku* (your teacher)

(il-) mudarris b(i)tāʿo (his teacher)

(il-) mudarris b(i)tāʿhā (her teacher) *(il-) mudarris b(i)tāʿuhum* (their teacher)

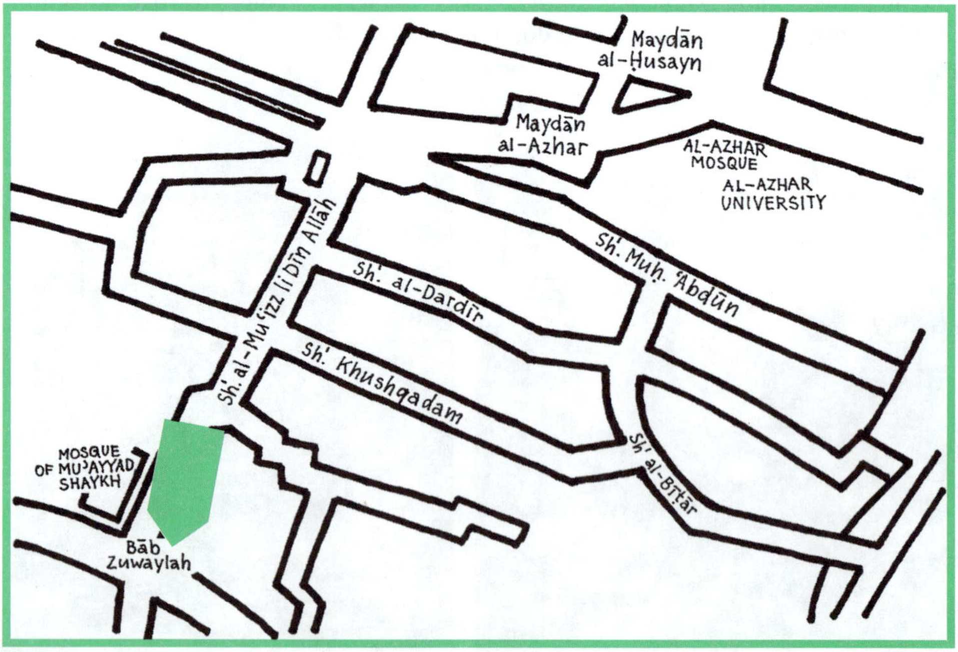

Bāb Zuwēla

Ibn Ṭulūn

(ish-) shanṭa btaʿtī (my bag)
(ish-) shanṭa btaʿtak (your [m.] bag)
(ish-) shanṭa btaʿtik (your [f.] bag)
(ish-) shanṭa btaʿ(i)to (his bag)
(ish-) shanṭa btaʿithā (her bag)

(ish-) shanṭa btaʿitna (our bag)
(ish-) shanṭa btaʿitku (your [pl.] bag)
(ish-) shanṭa btaʿithum (their bag)

(iṭ-) ṭalaba b(i)tūʿī (my students)
(iṭ-) ṭalaba b(i)tūʿak (your [m.] students)
(iṭ-) ṭalaba b(i)tūʿik (your [f.] students)
(iṭ-) ṭalaba b(i)tūʿo (his students)
(iṭ-) ṭalaba b(i)tūʿhā (her students)

(iṭ-) ṭalaba b(i)tūʿna (our students)
(iṭ-) ṭalaba b(i)tūʿuku (your [pl.] students)
(iṭ-) ṭalaba b(i)tūʿuhum (their students)

Plural nouns not denoting human beings are treated as singular feminine nouns: *il-kutub btaʿit il-madrasa* / *kutub btaʿit madrasa* school books, *iṣ-ṣuwar btaʿit ʾaṣḥābna* / *ṣuwar btaʿit ʾaṣḥābna* – photographs of our friends.

III. Tadrībāt:

Targama

Will you allow me to enter? I felt strong pain. They passed through the fruit and vegetable market. You must hurry up in order to catch the subway. Would you like me to give you sugar in your tea? Please, pour me some water. Why are you not answering our questions? Did you smell the scent? The cigarettes are not mine. The pocket of your jacket is torn. These are the photographs of our clients. She told me that she wants to recover fast. They don't like to go to the university buffet. She likes to wear her mother's dress. We like to taste various drinks. I (m.) like to visit Cairo cafés. We will have to solve the problem of the departure of the tourists. Who wants to go up to the minaret of the Ibn Tulun mosque? Look (f.) at the map!

Bāb-in Naṣr

Kammil!

forms of the particle ***bitāʿ***:

a) it-tawabīt ... il-Mathaf il-maṣrī b) ʿarabīyāt ... ish-shurṭa c) iz-zamāyil ... na d) iṭ-ṭalaba ... gamʿitna e) il-mawaʿīd ... hum f) iḍ-ḍuyūf ... o g) il-maʿāgim ... maktabitna h) is-sukkān ... il-madīna i) il-ʾalḥifa ... il-fonduʾ j) ir-rukkāb ... il-ʾotobīs in-nahrī

IV. Mufradāt

ʿadd (i)	to count
ʾākhir marra	the last time
ʾalam (ʾālām)	pain
ʾawwil marra	the first time
baṣṣ (u)	to look at, to look into *(fī)*
bāsha (bashawāt)	Mr., sir (also as a jocular address between friends)
gāyiz	maybe, perhaps
gallābīya (galālīb)	long, loose shirt-like dress
gamʿa (gāmiʿāt)	university
gāmid	strong, sturdy, tough, hard; strongly
gēb (guyūb)	pocket
ghasīl	laundry
grāb, -āt	cover, case
ḥabb (i)	to like, to love, to wish, to like to do something
ḥall (i)	to solve
ḥass (i)	to feel something *(bi)*
ḥaṭṭ (u)	to place, put something somewhere *(fī)*
khaff (i)	to recover, be cured
Khān il-Khalīlī	name of a Cairo Oriental market
khashsh (u)	to enter, come in
ʾirfa	cinnamon
ʿiṭr (ʿuṭūr)	perfume, scent
kafeteriya	buffet, canteen
karkadē(h)	drink made from hibiscus flowers
kubbāya	glass
laff (i)	to walk around, to pack
lamm (i)	to collect, assemble, put together
lammā	when
libis (i)	to put on
liḥiʾ (a)	to catch, to be in time
madd (i)	to extend, to hurry
madna (midan)	minaret
maḥfaẓa	purse
masʾala (masāʾil)	question, problem, affair
mashrūb, -āt	drink
mawgūd	present, occurring
miʿassil	tobacco for the waterpipe (usually scented)
mukhtalif	different, various
mushkila (mashākil)	problem
ʾahwa (ʾahāwī)	café

ʾaṣṣ (u)	to cut (with scissors)
radd (u)	to return, to answer to *(ʾala)*
raʾy (ʾārāʾ)	opinion
rīḥa (rawāyiḥ)	scent, smell
ṣabb (u)	to pour
safīr (sufara)	ambassador
sayyid (sāda)	master, mister, Sir
samaḥ (a)	to allow someone (*li*) to do something (*bi*)
sarḥān	thinking, thoughtful, contemplating something *(fī)*
sīgāra (sagāyir)	cigarette
suʾāl (ʾasʾila)	question
sukkar	sugar
ṣūra (ṣuwar)	picture, photograph
surʿa	speed
shaʿar	hair
shamm (i)	to smell
shīsha	waterpipe
tadkhīn	smoking
telefōn, - āt	phone
ṭiliʿ (a)	to go up, climb, ascend
wizāra	ministry
yansūn	aniseed
zāyir (zuwwār)	visitor
ẓarīf (ẓurāf)	kind, nice, pleasant
zbūn (zabāyin)	customer, client
ziyāda	rise, bonus, addition
jakēt (jawākit)	jacket

V. Taʿbīrāt:

ʾAbadan!	No, not at all. No problem.
ʿala fikra	by the way
ʾAna shayfo kwayyis.	I consider him good. I think he is good.
bi-surʿa	quickly
bi ʾẓ-ẓabṭ	exactly, verbatim
ʾE(h) raʾyak fī ...?	What do you think about…?
Il-ḥisāb ʿalayya.	I pay the bill.
Yarēt!	That would be great! Good idea!
Lau samaḥt/-i, -ū	If you were so kind!
Mā lak (li, lo, lhā, lku, lhum?)	What's wrong with you (him, her, you, them)?
Min ghēr laff wi dawarān.	Honestly. No beating about the bush.

Nifsī fī... (nifsak, nifsik, nifso, nifsahā nifsina, nifsuku, nifsuhum) — I would like to have…

ʾahwa ziyāda — very sweet coffee

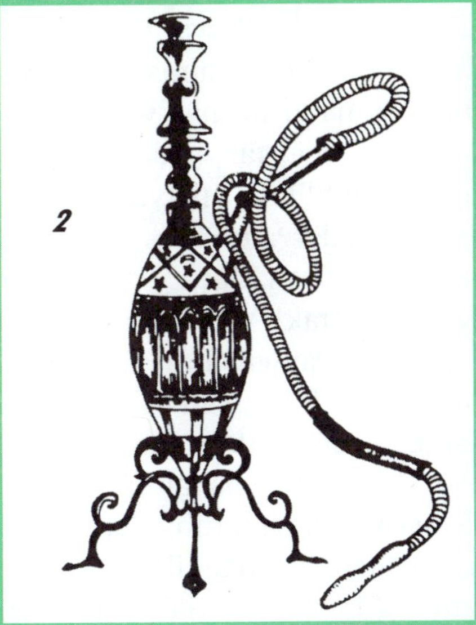

The life of an Arabic café would be impossible without the waterpipe. The presence of the waterpipe creates a cozy atmosphere for the café guests. There are different types of the waterpipe:

No. 1 – shīsha: a (ḥagar), b (ṭāsa), c (layy), d (bannūra), e (mabsam)

No. 2 – būrī

No. 3 – gōza: a (būsa/ghāba), b (ʾalb), c (buksha)

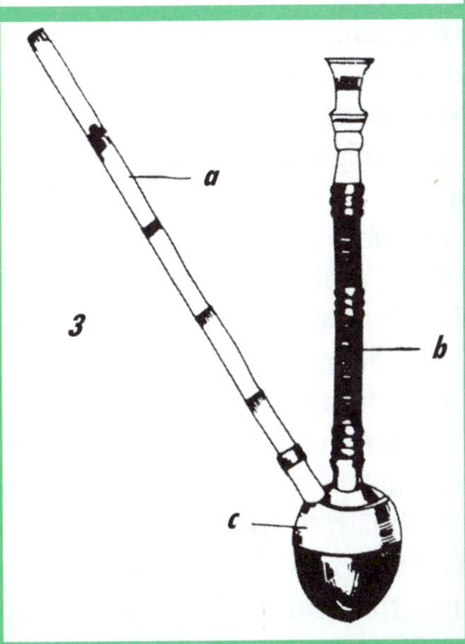

8

Id - Dars it-tāmin / Lesson 8

Maḥaṭṭit il-ʾuṭurāt

- Baʿd ʾizn ḥaḍretak, ʾana laʾēt ʿa ʾl-lōḥa ʾr-raʾīsīya mawāʿīd il-ʾuṭurāt li ʾl-ʾUʾṣur bas ma laʾ ētsh(i) ʾl-mawāʿīd li ʾAswān. ʾAṣlan, fī maktab il-istiʿlāmāt ʾiddū lī waraʾa ṣughayyara bi ʾl-maʿlūmāt di, w ʾana taʾrīban ramēthā fi ʾz-z(i)bāla maʿa ʾaurāʾī ʾl-ʾadīma. ʾUl lī, fī ḥad bi-yirmi ʾaurāʾo, min ghēr ma yishūfhā kwayyis?
- Maʿlesh, yā ʿustāz, ḥaḍretak mish lāzim tiḥki lī ḥikāyit ʾaurāʾak, ʾaʾdar ʾaddī lak il-maʿlūmāt il-maṭlūba.
- Kattar khērak! Yaʿnī, ʾemta ḥa-yiʾūm bukra ʾauwil ʾaṭr li ʾAswān?
- ʾAuwil ʾaṭr li ʾAswān bi-yiʾūm iṣ-ṣubḥ, is-sāʿa sitta ʾu nuṣṣ.
- Wi ʾākhir ʾaṭr in-nahār da?
- Da ḥa-yiʾūm baʿd rubʿ sāʿa, ʾin shā ʾallāh. ʿAshān tilḥaʾo, lāzim tigri, ʾaṣlo ḥa-yiʾūm min raṣīf talāta, naḥya tanya khāliṣ.
- *ʿala ʾr-raṣīf il-kumsarī saʾalna:*
- N(i)sītū ḥāga?
- ʾAh, ṣaḥḥ, nsīna nigīb yā gurnān yā magalla, ḥa-niʾra ʾē(h) fi ʾs-safar?
- Ma t(i)khafūsh, mish ḥa-tibʾū zahʾānīn, ʿashān il-ʾaṭr ḥa-yimshi fī ʾamākin gamīla ʾawi.
- ʾAkīd, ʾaṣḥābna ʾl-maṣrīyīn ʾālū lna, ʾinn riḥlit ʾAswān ḥa-tibʾa khaṭīra.
- Yā khabar, nsīna nigīb ʾizāzt il-mayya, yā ʾayyi ḥāga tanya mumkin nishrabhā fi ʾs-sikka.
- Yalla, igri wi hāt lina mayya maʿdanīya wi ma tinsāsh il-ʾAhrām barḍo! ʾAna grīt fiʿlan, ʿashān ma yifūtnāsh il-ʾaṭr b(i)taʿna. Lammā r(i)giʿt ir-raṣīf, kunt ʿāwiz ʾasʾal il-kumsarī ʿala ʿarabīyit in-nōm. Bas li ʾl-asaf, laʾēto mishi.

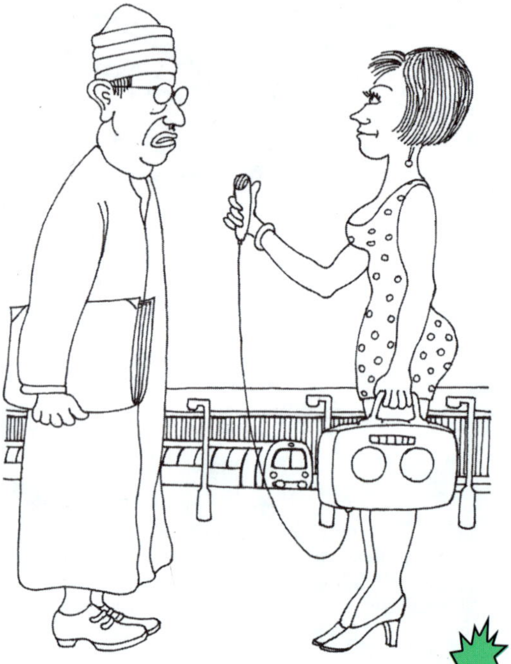

Yā ḥaḍret il-maʾzūn! Bi-tiḥibb tirkab ʾaṭr ʾē(ḥ) li-ʾAswān? ʾAṭr "il-ʿArūsa" ṭabʿan.

Reverend Sir, when going to Aswan, which train do you prefer ? "The Bride", of course.

البنك الأهلي المصري
البنك يضمن لك الراحة من خلال الصرف من أقرب ماكينة للمنزل في أي وقت
٣٠ صفحة
٥٠ قرشا
www.ahram.org.eg
E-mail:ahram@ahram.org.eg
الأهرام
رئيس مجلس الإدارة ورئيس التحرير
إبراهيم نافع
البنك الأهلي المصري
بطاقة الصرف والإيداع الآلي
A.T.M'S
(CASH 24)
لأكثر من ١٢٠ آلة
الطبعة الثانية
Al-Ahram 2 Dec. 2000

Title page of the most famous Egyptian newspaper al-Ahram

I. ʾAsʾila:

1. Mawāʿīd il-ʾuṭurāt li ʾl-ʾUʾṣur laʾēthā fēn?
2. ʾIddū lī ʾē(h) fī maktab il-istiʿlāmāt?
3. Ḥikāyit ʾaurāʾī ḥakēthā li mīn?
4. ʾEmta bi-yiʾūm ʾawwil ʾaṭr li ʾAswān?
5. Kumsarī saʾalna ʿala ʾē(h)?
6. Mīn ʾāl lina ʾinnā mish ḥa-nibʾa zahʾānīn fi ʾl-ʾaṭr?
7. ʾEzzāy ma gibnāsh il-mayya ʾl-maʿdanīya?
8. ʾAna grīt lē(h)?

Train ticket for the second-class train from Cairo to Alexandria. Second-class travelling through Egypt is very comfortable, but the purchasing of a ticket may be problematic. Each class (1st, 2nd, and 3rd) has its own counter, where tickets are sold according to the times in the schedules. The schedules hang over the corresponding counters. Tickets for longer distances are always sold with Apex. The figure shows a train ticket for a French train from Cairo to Alexandria (incl. Apex). When buying the ticket, one has to note the train number (0909), carriage (6) and seat (15), time of departure (10. 5. 1995, 9 o'clock), and ticket price (17 Egyptian pounds).

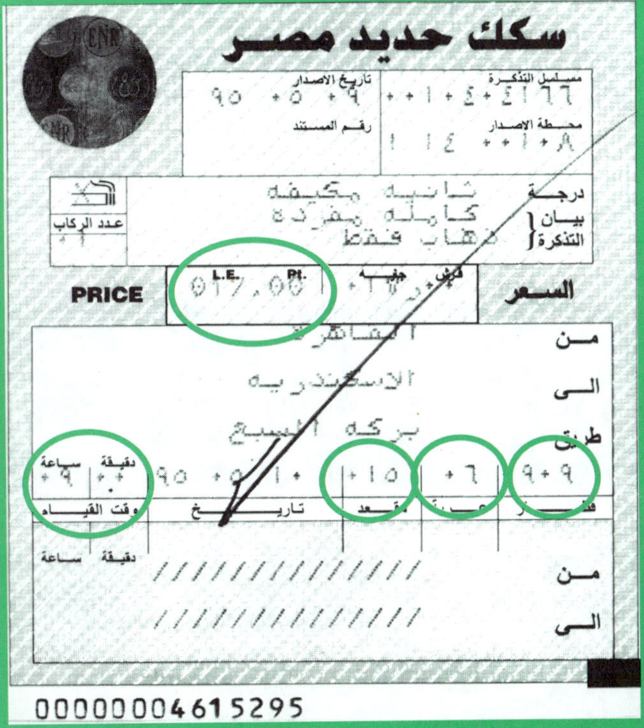
سكك حديد مصر
مسلسل التذكرة
تاريخ الاصدار
محطة الاصدار
رقم المستند
درجة
بيان التذكرة
ثانية مكيفة
كاملة مفردة
ذهاب فقط
عدد الركاب
PRICE
L.E. Pt.
017.00
جنيه قرش
السعر
من
القاهرة
الى
الاسكندرية
طريق
بركة السبع
ساعة دقيقة
وقت القيام
تاريخ
مقعد
١٥
٠٦
٠٩٠٩
من
الى
0000000461 5295

II. Qawāʿid:

1. Verbs with the third consonant *w* or *y*

These verbs end in the third person singular masculine perfect in the vowel ***–a*** or ***–i***, which was originally the third consonant **w** or **y**. They behave according to the following paradigms:

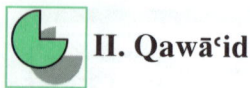

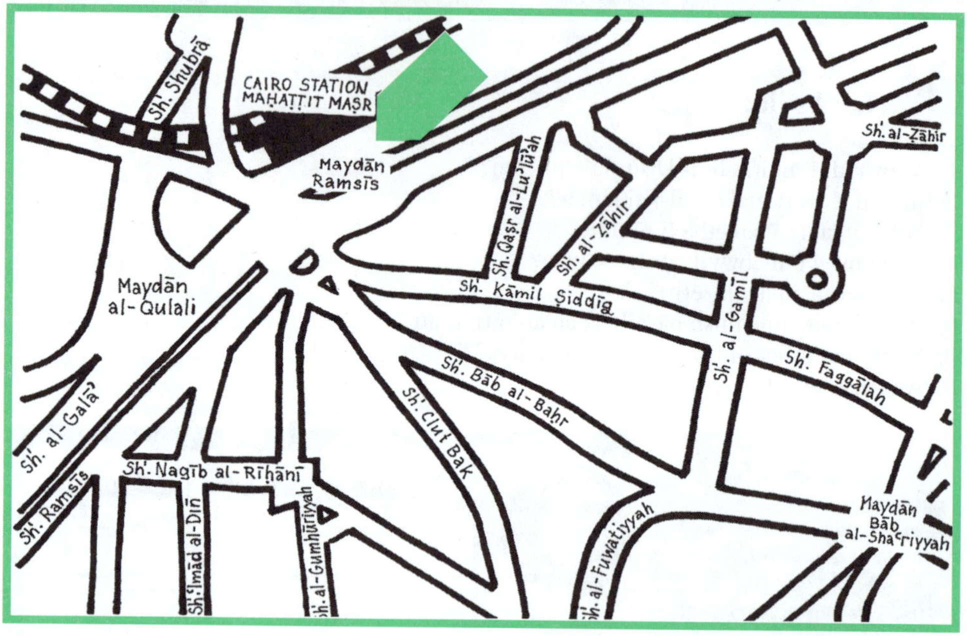

Cairo train station on the Ramsīs square

MIShI (to go)
perfect:

	singular:	negative:	plural:	negative:
3rd pers. m.	***MiShi***	***ma M(i)Sh-īsh***	***MiShY-ū***	***ma MiShY-ūsh***
3rd pers. f.	***MiShY-it***	***ma MiShY-itsh(i)***		
2nd pers. m.	***M(i)Sh-īt***	***ma MSh-ītsh(i)***	***M(i)Sh-ītū***	***ma M(i)Sh-ītūsh***
2nd pers. f.	***M(i)Sh-īti***	***ma MSh-ītīsh***		
1st pers.	***M(i)Sh-īt***	***ma MSh-ītsh(i)***	***M(i)Sh-īna***	***ma MiSh-īnāsh***

imperfect:

	singular:	negative:	plural:	negative:
3rd pers. m.	***yi-MSh-i***	***ma yi- MSh-īsh***	***yi-MSh-ū***	***ma yi-MSh-ūsh***
3rd pers. f.	***ti-MSh-i***	***ma ti- MSh-īsh***		
2nd pers. m.	***ti-MSh-i***	***ma ti- MSh-īsh***	***ti-MSh-ū***	***ma ti-MSh-ūsh***
2nd pers. f.	***ti-MSh-ī***	***ma ti- MSh-īsh***		
1st pers.	***a-MSh-i***	***ma- MSh-īsh***	***ni-MSh-i***	***ma ni-MSh-īsh***

Imperative: *imshi!* (m.), *imshī!* (f.), *imshū!* (pl.).
Negative imperative: *ma timshīsh!* (m.), *ma timshīsh!* (f.), *ma timshūsh!* (pl.).

Active participle: *MāShī* (m.) – going; *MaShYa* (f.), *MaShYīn* (pl.).
Passive participle: this group of verbs does not form the passive participle.

The verb *GiRi (yi-GRi)* – to pass, to run – follows this paradigm; however, there is also the verb *GaRa (yi-GRa)* – to happen, to occur, this verb appears only in the 3rd person masculine singular perfect and imperfect forms: *Gara lku ʾēh in-nahār da* – What happened to you today? *Ma gara lnāsh ḥāga.* – Nothing happened to us. *Mish ḥa-yigra lo ḥāga?* – Will he be all right? (lit. Will nothing happen to him?)

RAMA (to throw, throw away)
perfect:

	singular:	negative:	plural:	negative:
3rd pers. m.	***RaMa***	***ma RaM-āsh***	***RaM-ū***	***ma RaM-ūsh***
3rd pers. f.	***RaM-it***	***ma RaM-itsh(i)***		
2nd pers. m.	***RaM-ēt***	***ma RaM-ētsh(i)***	***RaM-ētū***	***ma RaM-ētūsh***
2nd pers. f.	***RaM-ēti***	***ma RaM-ētīsh***		
1st pers.	***RaM-ēt***	***ma RaM-ētsh(i)***	***RaM-ēna***	***ma RaM-ēnāsh***

imperfect:

	singular:	negative:	plural:	negative:
3rd pers. m.	***yi-RM-i***	***ma yi- RM-īsh***	***yi-RM-ū***	***ma yi-RM-ūsh***
3rd pers. f.	***ti-RM-i***	***ma ti- RM-īsh***		
2nd pers. m.	***ti-RM-i***	***ma ti- RM-īsh***	***ti-RM-ū***	***ma ti-RM-ūsh***
2nd pers. f.	***ti-RM-ī***	***ma ti-RM-īsh***		
1st pers.	***a-RM-i***	***ma- RM-īsh***	***ni-RM-i***	***ma ni-RM-īsh***

Imperative: *irmi!* (m.), *irmī!* (f.), *irmū!* (pl.).
Negative imperative: *ma tirmīsh!* (m.), *ma tirmīsh!* (f.), *ma tirmūsh!* (pl.).

Active participle: *RāMī* (m.) – throwing; *RaMYa* (f.), *RaMYīn* (pl.).
Passive participle: *maRMī* (m.) – thrown away; *maRMīYa* (f.), *maRMīYīn* (pl.).
Other verbs belonging to this group: *MaḌa (yiMḌi)* – to sign, *ḤaKa (yiḤKi)* – to tell, retell.

NISI (to forget)
perfect:

	singular:	negative:	plural:	negative:
3rd pers. m.	***NiSi***	***ma N(i)S-īsh***	***NiSY-ū***	***ma NiSY-ūsh***
3rd pers. f.	***NiSY-it***	***ma N(i)SY-itsh(i)***		
2nd pers. m.	***N(i)S-īt***	***ma N(i)S-ītsh(i)***	***N(i)S-ītū***	***ma N(i)S-ītūsh***
2nd pers. f.	***N(i)S-īti***	***ma N(i)S-ītīsh***		
1st pers.	***N(i)S-īt***	***ma N(i)S-ītsh(i)***	***N(i)S-īna***	***ma N(i)S-īnāsh***

imperfect:

	singular:	negative:	plural:	negative:
3rd pers. m.	***yi-NS-a***	***ma yi-NS-āsh***	***yi-NS-ū***	***ma yi-NS-ūsh***
3rd pers. f.	***ti-NS-a***	***ma ti-NS-āsh***		
2nd pers. m.	***ti-NS-a***	***ma ti-NS-āsh***	***ti-NS-ū***	***ma ti-NS-ūsh***
2nd pers. f.	***ti-NS-ī***	***ma ti-NS-īsh***		
1st pers.	***a-NS-a***	***m a- NS-āsh***	***ni-NS-a***	***ma ni-NS-āsh***

Imperative: *insa!* (m.), *insī!* (f.), *insū!* (pl.).
Negative imperative: *ma tinsāsh!* (m.), *ma tinsīsh!* (f.), *ma tinsūsh!* (pl.).

Active participle: *NāSī* (m.) – forgetting; *NaSYa* (f.), *NaSYīn* (pl.).
Passive participle: *maNSī* (m.) – forgotten; *maNSīYa* (f.), *maNSīYīn* (pl.).

BA'A (to become someone)
perfect:

	singular:	negative:	plural:	negative:
3rd pers. m.	***Ba'a***	***ma Ba'-āsh***	***Ba'-ū***	***ma Ba'-ūsh***
3rd pers. f.	***Ba'-it***	***ma Ba'-itsh(i)***		
2nd pers. m.	***Ba'-ēt***	***ma Ba'-ētsh(i)***	***Ba'-ētū***	***ma Ba'-ētūsh***
2nd pers. f.	***Ba'-ēti***	***ma Ba'-ētīsh***		
1st pers.	***Ba'-ēt***	***ma Ba'-ētsh(i)***	***Ba'-ēna***	***ma Ba'-ēnāsh***

imperfect:

	singular:	negative:	plural:	negative:
3rd pers. m.	***yi-B'-a***	***ma yi-B'-āsh***	***yi-B'-ū***	***ma yi-B'-ūsh***
3rd pers. f.	***ti-B'-a***	***ma ti- B'-āsh***		
2nd pers. m.	***ti-B'-a***	***ma ti- B'-āsh***	***ti-B'-ū***	***ma ti-B'-ūsh***
2nd pers. f.	***ti-B'-ī***	***ma ti-B'-īsh***		
1st pers.	***a-B'-a***	***ma- B'-āsh***	***ni-B'-a***	***ma ni-B'-āsh***

Imperative: *ib'a!* (m.), *ib'ī!* (f.), *ib'ū!* (pl.).
Negative imperative: *ma tib'āsh!* (m.), *ma tib'īsh!* (f.), *ma tib'ūsh!* (pl.).

Active participle: *Bā'ī* (m.) – becoming; *Ba'Ya* (f.), *Ba'Yīn* (pl.).
Passive participle: this group of verbs does not form the passive participle.

Other verbs following this paradigm: *MaLa (yiMLa)* – to fill, *'aRa (yi'Ra)* – to read, and also *La'a* – to find. The verb *La'a* follows the paradigm of *Ba'a* in the perfect. It has no imperfect in its 1st verbal stem. It uses the imperfect forms of the 3rd verbal stem instead (cf. Lesson 10):

	singular:	negative:	plural:	negative:
3rd pers. m.	***yi-Lā'-ī***	***ma yi-Lā'-īsh***	***yi-Lā'-ū***	***ma yi-Lā'-ūsh***
3rd pers. f.	***ti-Lā'-ī***	***ma ti-Lā'-īsh***		
2nd pers. m.	***ti-Lā'-ī***	***ma ti-Lā'-īsh***	***ti-Lā'-ū***	***ma ti-Lā'-ūsh***
2nd pers. f.	***ti-Lā'-ī***	***ma ti-Lā'-īsh***		
1st pers.	***a-Lā'-ī***	***ma- Lā'-īsh***	***ni-Lā'-ī***	***ma ni-Lā'-īsh***

2. The verb *iDDa* (to give)

perfect:

	singular:	negative:	plural:	negative:
3rd pers. m.	***iDDa***	***ma iDD-āsh***	***iDD-ū***	***ma iDD-ūsh***
3rd pers. f.	***iDD-it***	***ma iDD-itsh(i)***		
2nd pers. m.	***iDD-ēt***	***ma iDD-ētsh(i)***	***iDD-ētū***	***ma iDD-ētūsh***
2nd pers. f.	***iDD-ēti***	***ma iDD-ētīsh***		
1st pers.	***iDD-ēt***	***ma iDD-ētsh(i)***	***iDD-ēna***	***ma iDD-ēnāsh***

imperfect:

	singular:	negative:	plural:	negative:
3rd pers. m.	***yi-DD-ī***	***ma yi-DD-īsh***	***yi-DD-ū***	***ma yi-DD-ūsh***
3rd pers. f.	***ti-DD-ī***	***ma ti-DD-īsh***		
2nd pers. m.	***ti-DD-ī***	***ma ti-DD-īsh***	***ti-DD-ū***	***ma ti-DD-ūsh***
2nd pers. f.	***ti-DD-ī***	***ma ti-DD-īsh***		
1st pers.	***a-DD-ī***	***ma-DD-īsh***	***ni-DD-ī***	***ma ni-DD-īsh***

Imperative: *iddi!* (m.), *iddī!* (f.), *iddū!* (pl.).
Negative imperative: *ma tiddīsh!* (m.), *ma tiddīsh!* (f.), *ma tiddūsh!* (pl.).

Active participle: *miDDī* (m.) – giving; *miDDīYa* (f.), *miDDīYīn* (pl.).
Passive participle: this verb does not form the passive participle.

Iddēt lo ʿunwānī. – I gave him my address. *Bi-yiddū lhum furaṣ ʿaẓīma.* – They give them excellent opportunities.

If the verb ***idda*** is followed by a preposition with the 1st person singular or plural pronominal suffix, the preposition is left out and the pronoun is suffixed directly to the verb; 1st person singular uses the form ***-nī***: *Iddānī naṣīḥa kwayyisa.* – He gave me good counsel. *Bi-yiddūnā ʾl-magallāt di.* – They are giving us these magazines.
– However, forms with preposition are also possible: *Iddit lī h(a)dīya gamīla.* – She gave me a beautiful present.
– If the second object is expressed by a pronominal suffix, the preposition ***li*** is necessary: *Iddūhā lī* – They gave her to me.

III. Tadrībāt:

Targama

Do not (f.) forget to write us a letter! We hope that you will be ("become") satisfied here ("by us"). I began (came) to like these films. We will be happy (become happy) about your visit. Why do you have to go? Where can I throw it away? I can't forget him at all. Don't give it (f.) to him! I want to give it (m.) to you. You will find him in the café. I haven't found them yet. They didn't find us at home. Can you (f.) read them this message? Please fill (m.) these glasses. Nothing happened to them. You don't know this fairy tale, so I'll tell it to you. Where will I find you? You are (have become) bored, haven't you? She told us about the forgotten books. Please, give it (m.) to us! Run! I mustn't forget him. We can't go now. I have read (active participle *ʾara*) all these things very well. Can you (m.) please read the schedule for me, because I can't see it. Don't be (become) sad, it will go somehow.

Kammil!

a) tilāʾī b) irmī c) mishi d) baʾa e) tibʾū f) timshū g) tiddī h) ninsa i) nāsī j) ʾaʾra

1. ʾAkhūya ... mudarris. 2. Mish mumkin ... kum. 3. Lāzim ... mafatīḥak! 4. ʿAwzīn ... badri lē(h)? 5. Maʾdarsh(i) ... il-kilma di. 6. ... iz-zibāla hena! 7. Mumkin ... lī ʾl-ḥitta di? 8. ʾEnta ... dayman. 9. Il-ʾotobīs ... min shwayya. 10. Ḥa ... ʿaṭshānīn khāliṣ.

IV. Mufradāt

il-ʾAhrām	name of the most famous Egyptian newspaper "the Pyramids"
ʾakīd	certain, certainly
ʿarabīy(i)t in-nōm	sleeping car
ʾaṣl (+ pronominal suffix) (ʾaṣlo, ʾaṣlī, ʾaṣluku)	since, for, because
ʾaṣlan	because, for, originally
ʾaurāʾ	papers, documents, ID cards
baʾa (a)	to become
dayman	always
fiʿlan	really, indeed
gadwal (gadāwil)	list, schedule
gara (a)	to happen
giri (i)	to run, flow, pass
hadīya (hadāyā)	gift
ḥaddūta (ḥawadīt)	tale, fairy tale
ḥaka (i)	tell, retell
haram (ʾahrām / ʾahrāmāt)	pyramid
hāt!/hātī!/hātū!	give! pass!
ḥazīn	sad
ḥikāya	tale, story
ḥitta (ḥitat)	piece (of food, cloth)
khaṭīr	great, wonderful, excellent; dangerous
ʾidda (yiddi)	to give
istiʿlāmāt	information, questions
yā ... yā ...	either… or…
kilma (kalimāt)	word
laʾa (yilāʾī)	to find
lōḥa	desk, blackboard, canvas (painting)
maḍa (i)	to sign

magalla	magazine
makān (ʾamākin)	place
mala (a)	to fill
maʿlūmāt	information
maṭlūb	requested, wanted
min ghēr ma	without doing
mishi (i)	to walk, to go, go away, to stride
naḥya (nawāḥī)	side, look
naṣīḥa (naṣāyiḥ)	counsel
nisi (a)	to forget
nōm	sleep
ʾara (a)	to read
ʾaṭr (ʾuṭurāt)	train
ʾidir (a)	to be able, can, may
rama (i)	to throw, throw away
riḥla (raḥalāt)	journey, trip, flight
rubʿ (ʾarbāʿ)	quarter
taʾrīban	approximately, maybe, perhaps
il-ʾUʾṣur	Luxor
ʾustāz (ʾasatza)	Mr. (intellectual); professor
waraʾa	small piece of paper
zahʾān	bored, annoyed, frustrated
z(i)bāla	garbage
zihiʾ (a)	to be bored, annoyed, to have enough of something

note:

ʾahrāmāt (ʾahrāmāt il-Gīza)	pyramids (of Giza)
il-ʾAhrām	name of the Egyptian newspaper
(shāriʿ) il-Haram	Pyramid street

V. Taʿbīrāt:

Baʿd ʾiznak?	Excuse me please!
ʾE(h) da baʾa?	What's this? What's the meaning of this?
ʾE(h) ḥikaytak? (ʾē(h) ḥikaytik, ḥikayto, ḥikāyithā, ḥikāyitku, ḥikāyithum?)	What's wrong with you?
Gara ʾē(h)?	What happened?
Yā khabar!	Oh-oh! Oops! That's bad!
Yalla!	Come on!
Yalla baʾa!	Come on now! Let's go! Let's get going!
Yaʿnī ...	That means …
Yaʿnī ʾē(h) baʾa?	What's the meaning of this (then)?
Kattar khērak!	Thank you. You are very kind. (lit.: May God extend your fortune!)
Li ʾl-ʾasaf.	Unfortunately.
Māshī?	O.K.? Do you agree? Fine with you?
Māshī ʾl-ḥāl?	You're fine? All's well?
Māshī walla mish māshī?	Is it possible or not?
Mish keda?	Is it so? Indeed?

Fi ʾl-ḥafla

Kān lāzim ʾagahhiz nafsī, li ʾinnī kunt maʿzūm li ʾl-ḥafla ʾd-diblūmāsīya fi ʾs-sifāra ʾl-brīṭānīya. Ṭallaʿt badlitī min dolāb wi dawwart ʿala krafatta. Laʾēt waḥda, lākin lōnhā ḥayyarnī shwayya. Lammā ḥaḍḍart il-ʾamīṣ, fakkart fī bibyōna. Garrabtahā. ʿAgabitnī wi ʿashān keda ʾult li nafsī ʾinnī ḥalbishā. Lammaʿt gazmitī wi kharagt mi ʾl-bēt. ʾAʿḍāʾ is-sifāra raḥḥabū bīya fī madkhal ig-gnēna ʾl-m(i)nawwara. Ḥaram is-safīr ʾaddimit lī ṣaḥafīya amrīkīya kānit ʿawza tiʿmil ḥiwār maʿa ʾl-kātib il-maṣrī Nagīb Maḥfūẓ. Farraḥitnī ʾawi bi ʾl-khabar da w ʾana ʿaraḍt ʿalēhā, ʾinnī ḥadabbar lahā maʿād maʿāh. Il-qunṣul ʾaddim lī mudīr il-marāsim bi Wizart il-khārigīya ʾl-maṣrīya. Khilāl il-ḥafla kallimt il-mandūbīn bitūʿ ish-sharikāt il-inglīzīya. Farragūnī ʿala ṣuwar muntagāthum wi fahhimūnī ʿinn il-muntagāt di bi-tiʿmil sumʿa ṭayyiba li-baladna.

Il-ḥafla gouwa mabna ʾs-sifāra, bas illi huwa bi-yirūḥ lāzim yinzil il-bissīn il-ʾawwil.

The reception is in the embassy building, but the guests must first enter the pool.

Ṭūl il-waʾt kunt badawwar ʿala ʾl-mulḥaq is-saqāfī. Lammā laʾēto, ʿarrafnī ʿala ʾl-masʾūl ʿan il-ʿalāqāt il-khārigīya bi Wizart it-taʿlīm il-ʿālī ʾl-maṣrīya. ʾAddimt(e) lo nafsī wi warrēt lo ʾt-targama btaʿtī li ʾsh-shiʿr il-inglīzī...

- Mumkin ʾaʿarrafak ʿala ʾd-doktōr Muṣṭafa Ḥāzim min Wizart it-taʿlīm il-ʿālī?
- Da ḥa-yibʾa sharaf kbīr līya.
- Bravo ʿalēk! It-targama btaʿ(i)tak khallitnī ʾaḥibb ish-shiʿr il-inglīzī. Mish ʿāwiz tiwaddīhā ʾayyi magalla ʿashān tunshurhā?
- Bi-ṣarāḥa, lissa mafakkartish fi ʾl-mauḍūʿ da.
- Tismaḥū lī ʾaʾaddim luku zmīlī, bi-yidarris il-ʾadab il-ʾinglīzī fī Kullīyit il-ʾādāb Gamʿit il-Qāhira?
- Furṣa saʿīda!
- Lāzim ʾarauwaḥ di ʾl-waʾti, bas(i) yarēt t(i)sharrafūna fī bētna ʾurayyib.
- ʾIn shāʾ allāh. Sallim lina ʿala madām wi ʾawlādak!
- Allāh yisallimak!

I. ʾAsʾila:

1. ʾEzzāy gahhizt nafsī li ʾl-ḥafla?
2. Mīn raḥḥab bīya fī gnēnt is-sifāra?
3. ʾAnho khabar farraḥnī ʾawi?
4. Il-mandūbīn bitūʿ is-sharikāt ʾl-inglīzīya farragūnī ʿala ṣuwar muntagāthum lē(h)?
5. Kunt badawwar ʿala mīn ṭūl il-waʾt?
6. Mīn ʿarrafnī ʿala ʾl-masʾūl ʿan il-ʿalāqāt il-khārigīya?
7. ʾAna warrēt ʾē(h) li ʾd-doktōr min Wizart it-taʿlīm il-ʿālī?
8. ʾEmta waddēt it-targama btaʿtī magalla ʿashān tunshurhā?

Cairo University

II. Qawāʿid:

1. Extended verbal stems

Verbs introduced in Lessons 1–8 belong to the first basic verbal stem. Arabic verbs are divided into ten verbal stems: the first is the basic stem, and nine others represent the extended stems, formed by changes within the stems or by affixes. The conjugation of the extended stems uses the same prefixes and suffixes as the first (basic) stem.

The 2nd verbal stem

The meaning of the verbs of the 2nd verbal stem: They express an activity causing an activity or character expressed a) by the basic stem, b) by a noun, c) by an adjective:

a) *FiHiM* (to understand) – *FaHHiM* (to explain); *DaKhaL* (to enter) – *DaKhKhaL* (to put inside); *DaRaS* (to study) – *DaRRiS* (to teach); *ZiHi'* (to be bored) – *ZaHHa'* (to bore someone).
b) *ṢūRa* (to understand) – *ṢaWWaR* (to explain); *WaẒīFa* (function, job) – *WaẒẒaF* (to employ someone).
c) *KBīR* (big, great) – *KaBBaR* (to enlarge, magnify); *ṢGhaYYaR* (small) – *ṢaGhGhaR* (to make smaller); *GāHiZ* (to be ready, prepared) – *GaHHiZ* (to make ready, prepare).

perfect:

FaHHiM (to explain)
- the second consonant is geminated
- the first vowel is ***a***
- the second vowel is either ***i*** or ***a*** (above all next to glottal and emphatic phonemes and consonants ***r***, ***l***)

	singular:	negative:	plural:	negative:
3rd pers. m.	***FaHHiM***	***ma FaHHiM-sh(i)***	***FaHHiM-ū***	***ma FaHHiM-ūsh***
3rd pers. f.	***FaHHiM-it***	***ma FaHHiM-itsh(i)***		
2nd pers. m.	***FaHHiM-t***	***ma FaHHiM-tish***	***FaHHiM-tū***	***ma FaHHiM-tūsh***
2nd pers. f.	***FaHHiM-ti***	***ma FaHHiM-tīsh***		
1st pers.	***FaHHiM-t***	***ma FaHHiM-tish***	***FaHHiM-na***	***ma FaHHiM-nāsh***

imperfect singular:

		negative:
3rd pers. m.	***yi-FaHHiM***	***ma yi-FaHHiM-sh(i)***
3rd pers. f.	***ti-FaHHiM***	***ma ti-FaHHiM-sh(i)***
2nd pers. m.	***ti-FaHHiM***	***ma ti-FaHHiM-sh(i)***
2nd pers. f.	***ti-FaHHiM-ī***	***ma ti-FaHHiM-īsh***
1st pers.	***a-FaHHiM***	***m a-FaHHiM-sh(i)***

imperfect plural:

		negative:
3rd pers.	***yi-FaHHim-ū***	***ma yi-FaHHim-ūsh***
2nd pers.	***ti-FaHHim-ū***	***ma ti-FaHHim-ūsh***
1st pers.	***ni-FaHHim***	***ma ni-FaHHim-sh(i)***

Imperative: To form the imperative, the prefix ***ti-*** is detached from the 2nd person imperfect forms: *fahhim!* (m.), *fahhimī!* (f.), *fahhimū!* (pl.).
Negative imperative: *ma tifahhimsh(i)!* (m.), *ma tifahhimīsh!* (f.), *ma tifahhimūsḥ* (pl.).

Active and passive participles:
The participles are formed by means of the prefix ***mi-*** / ***mu*** (in the case of forms denoting a professional activity), the first consonant is followed by ***a***, the second by ***i*** (active participle only) or ***a*** (both active and passive participles). *muDaRRiS* (m.) – teacher, *muDaRRiSa* (f.), *muDaRRiSīn* (pl.); *muDaRRiB* – trainer; *muFaTTiSh* –

inspector, controller; *muṢaWWiR* – photographer; *muWaẒẒaF* – clerk; *miLaMMaʿ* – polished, burnished; *miRaWWaḤ* – going home; *miḤaYYaR* – embarrassing; *miʾaDDiM* – presenting.
- The difference between the active and the passive participle can be observed in the case of the pair: *muṢaWWiR* – photographer x *miṢaWWaR* – photographed.

Verbal noun:
- The derivation of verbal nouns from the first, basic verbal stem, follows a large number of various patterns and the nouns have to be learned separately as individual vocabulary units: *DaRS* – lesson, *ZiYāRa* – visit, *NōM* – sleep.
- Verbs of the second stem derive verbal nouns according to two patterns:
Pattern 1 (for most verbs of the 2nd stem): *ta-DRīS* – teaching, education; *ta-DRīB* – training; *ta-FTīSh* – control, inspection; *ta-ṢWīR* – photographing; *ta-LMīʿ* – polishing; *ta-ʿLīM* – learning, education.
Pattern 2 (mainly for verbs with the third consonant ***w*** or ***y*** or verbs with four stem consonants): *ta-GRiB-a* – attempt; *ta-SLiY-a* – fun, entertainment; *ta-RBiY-a* – education; *ta-RGaM-a* – translation; *DaRDaSha* – talking, chatting.

The 2nd stem of verbs with the third consonant ***w*** or ***y***:
ṢaWWaR (yiṢaWWaR) – to photograph; *RaWWaḤ (yiRaWWaḤ)* – to go home; *RaYYaḤ (yiRaYYaḤ)* – to oblige sb.; *NaYYiM (yiNaYYim)* – to put to sleep.

The 2nd stem of verbs with the first consonant ***w*** or ***y***:
Paradigm ***WaDDa*** (to bring to)

perfect:

	singular:	negative:	plural:	negative:
3rd pers. m.	***WaDDa***	***ma WaDD-āsh(i)***	***WaDD-ū***	***ma WaDD-ūsh***
3rd pers. f.	***WaDD-it***	***ma WaDD-itsh(i)***		
2nd pers. m.	***WaDD-ēt***	***ma WaDD-ētsh(i)***	***WaDD-ētū***	***ma WaDD-ētūsh***
2nd pers. f.	***WaDD-ēti***	***ma WaDD-ētīsh***		
1st pers.	***WaDD-ēt***	***ma WaDD-ētsh(i)***	***WaDD-ēna***	***ma WaDD-ēnāsh***

imperfect:

	singular:	negative:	plural:	negative:
3rd pers. m.	***yi-WaDD-i***	***ma yi-WaDD-īsh***	***yi-WaDD-ū***	***ma yi-WaDD-ūsh***
3rd pers. f.	***ti-WaDD-i***	***ma ti-WaDD-īsh***		
2nd pers. m.	***ti-WaDD-i***	***ma ti-WaDD-īsh***	***ti-WaDD-ū***	***ma ti-WaDD-ūsh***
2nd pers. f.	***ti-WaDD-ī***	***ma ti-WaDD-īsh***		
1st pers.	***a-WaDD-i***	***m a-WaDD-īsh***	***ni-WaDD-i***	***ma ni-WaDD-īsh***

Imperative: *waddi!* (m.), *waddī!* (f.), *waddū!* (pl.).
Negative imperative: *ma tiwaddish!* (m.), *ma tiwaddīsh!* (f.), *ma tiwaddūsh!* (pl.).
Active participle: *miWaDDi* (m.) – throwing; *miWaDDīYa* (f.), *miWaDDiYīn* (pl.).
Passive participle: verbs of this group do not form the passive participle.

Other verbs following this paradigm: *KhaLLa (yiKhaLLi), WaRRa (yiWaRRi), RaBBa (yiRaBBi)* – to sign, *SaLLa (yiSaLLi)*.

Verbs with four stem consonants are conjugated like verbs of the 2nd stem:

Paradigm ***TaRGiM*** (to translate)

perfect:

	singular:	negative:	plural:	negative:
3rd pers. m.	***TaRGiM***	***ma TaRGiM-sh(i)***	***TaRGiM-ū***	***ma TaRGiM-ūsh***
3rd pers. f.	***TaRGiM-it***	***ma TaRGiM-itsh(i)***		
2nd pers. m.	***TaRGiM-t***	***ma TaRGiM-tish***	***TaRGiM-tū***	***maTaRGiM-tūsh***
2nd pers. f.	***TaRGiM-ti***	***ma TaRGiM-tīsh***		
1st pers.	***TaRGiM-t***	***ma TaRGiM-tish***	***TaRGiM-na***	***ma TaRGiM-nāsh***

imperfect singular:

		negative:
3rd pers. m.	***yi-TaRGiM***	***ma yi-TaRGiM-sh(i)***
3rd pers. f.	***ti-TaRGiM***	***ma ti-TaRGiM-sh(i)***
2nd pers. m.	***ti-TaRGiM***	***ma ti-TaRGiM-sh(i)***
2nd pers. f.	***ti-TaRGiM-ī***	***ma ti-TaRGiM-īsh***
1st pers.	***a-TaRGiM***	***m a-TaRGiM-sh(i)***

imperfect plural:

		negative:
3rd pers.	***yi-TaRGiM-ū***	***ma yi-TaRGiM-ūsh***
2nd pers.	***ti-TaRGiM-ū***	***ma ti-TaRGiM-ūsh***
1st pers.	***ni-TaRGiM***	***ma ni-TaRGiM-sh(i)***

Imperative: *targim!* (m.), *targimī!* (f.), *targimū!* (pl.).
Negative imperative: *ma titargimshi!* (m.), *ma titargimīsh!* (f.), *ma titargimūsh!* (pl.).

Active participle: *muTaRGiM* (m.) – translator, interpreter; *muTaRGiMa* (f.), *muTaRGiMīn* (pl.).
Passive participle: *muTaRGaM* (m.) – translated; *muTaRGaMa* (f.), *muTaRGaMīn* (pl.).

Other verbs with four stem consonants: *DaRDiSh (yiDaRDiSh)* – to talk, chat; *FaRFiSh (yiFaRFiSh)* – to distract sb., to create a happy mood; *ḤaṢWiK (yiḤaṢWiK)* – to be overly careful, pedantic.

2. Conjunctions *ʾinn* (that), *liʾinn* (because of), *lākin* (but)

- These conjunctions are followed by nouns or pronominal suffixes functioning as subjects; the conjunctions assume the following forms with pronominal suffixes: *ʾinnī, (liʾinnī, lākinnī), ʾinnak, (liʾinnak, lākinnak), ʾinnik, (liʾinnik, lākinnik), ʾinno, (liʾinno, lākinno), ʾinnahā, (liʾinnahā, lākinnahā), ʾinnā, (liʾinnā, lākinnā), ʾinnuku, (liʾinnuku, lākinnuku), ʾinnuhum, (liʾinnuhum, lākinnuhum).*

ʾĀl lī ʾinn il-karnē(h) btāʿī gāhiz fī maktab il-mudīr. – He told me that my ID card was ready in the director's office. *ʾĀl lī ʾinno gāhiz fī maktab il-mudīr.* – He told me that it (my ID card) was ready in the director's office.
Ma ruḥnāsh il-fundu' liʾinn ʾasḥābna kānū taʿbānīn mi ʾs-safar. – We didn't go to the hotel, because our friends were tired from the journey. *Ma ruḥnahūsh liʾinnuhum kānū taʿbānīn mi ʾs-safar.* – We didn't go there (to it), because they (our friends) were tired from the journey.
Huwa ʿārif il-ʾadab il-ʿarabī kwayyis, lākin il-kitāb da ma ʾarahūsh. – He knows Arabic literature well, but he hasn't read this book.
Kānit ʿawza tizūr il-Matḥaf il-maṣrī, lākinnahā ma kānitsh(i) faḍya. – She wanted to visit the Egyptian Museum, but she didn't have time.

– After the conjunction ***lākin***, the pronominal suffix may be omitted:
Kānit ʿawza tizūr il-Matḥaf il-maṣrī, lākin ma kānitsh(i) faḍya.
She wanted to visit the Egyptian Museum, but (she) didn't have time.

III. Tadrībāt:

Targama

Greet from me all your Egyptian friends! When will you visit us? We heard that you have lifted the lid of the sarcophagus. He invited me to the party, because he wanted me to meet his colleagues from London. May I introduce myself to you? She translated for us the lyrics (words) of this song. This music makes me sleep. I wanted to distract you a little. Why don't you want to oblige us? This book is the reason that I fell in love with Egyptian antiquities. They will let you go there without us. Why do you want to grow a beard? He is still entertaining them with his words. Could you photograph us in front of this pyramid? Where should I bring these things? Leave them here! Don't let them sign into the hotel! We searched for your address, but we didn't find it. Don't search for it (f.)! Could you (polite) show me this street on the map? Did you show them your pictures from Egypt? We will show them to them. Do (pl.) not show them to them! Do (f.) not show them to him! Why do you have to go home early? What are you thinking about? May I try on the shirt? Do not arrange the meeting for tomorrow! We have to talk to you about this affair.

Kammil!

a) niʿaṭṭal b) tikhallaṣū c) tifahhimī d) ʾanazzil e) yidauwar f) kammil
g) tiʾaddimī h) niraggaʿ i) ma tirawwaḥsh j) rayyaḥ

1. Mumkin ... ish-shanṭa di? 2. ... il-gumla, min faḍlak! 3. ... di ʾl-waʾti!
4. Inshāʾallāh ḥa ... lku flūsku ʾurayyib! 5. Mumkin ... lna nafsik?
6. Mish ʿawzīn ... ku! 7. ʿAyzik ... nī ʾē(h) il-ḥikāya. 8. Mīn bi- ... ʾala mafatīḥo.
9. ...o wi iʾbal minno ʾl-hadīya di! 10. Kān lāzim ... shughluku ʾemta?

IV. Mufradāt

ʾadab (ʾādāb)	literature
ʿalāqa	relationship, intercourse
ʿallim II	to educate someone
ʾamrīkī (ʾamrīkān)	American
ʿarraf II	to introduce someone (without preposition) to someone/something *(ʿala/bi)*
ʿashān keda	therefore
ʿaṭṭal II	to interrupt someone, to distract someone from something *(ʿan)*
badla (bidal)	suit
bibyōna	bowtie
brīṭānī	British
dabbar II	to arrange
dakhkhal II	to put inside *(fī)*
daʾn (duʾūn)	beard
darrab II	to train, practice
dardish (yidardish)	to talk, chat with *(maʿa)*
darris II	to teach someone *(li)* something (without preposition)
dawwar II	to search for something *(ʿala)*
diblūmāsī	diplomatic, diplomat
doktōr (dakatra)	doctor
fahhim II	to explain something (without preposition) to someone (without preposition)
fakkar II	to think of *(fī)*
farfish (yifarfish)	to distract someone, to coax/induce someone into good mood
farrag II	to show something *(ʿala)* to someone (without preposition)
farraḥ II	to make someone (without preposition) happy
fattish II	to control, to check
gāhiz	ready, prepared
gahhiz II	to prepare, to make ready
garrab II	to try something, to attempt something
gazma (gizam)	shoes
ghinwa (ʾaghānī)	song
gumla (gumal)	sentence
ḥaḍḍar II	to prepare, to make, to create
ḥayyar II	to embarrass
ḥaram	husband, wife
ḥaṣwik (yiḥaṣwik)	to be overly careful, pedantic
ḥiwār	dialogue
khalla II	to let someone (do), to make someone (do)

khallaṣ II	to finish, end something
khārigī	foreign, external
khilāl	in the course of, while
ʾinglīzī (ʾinglīz)	English
kabbar II	to increase, enlarge
kallim II	to talk to (without preposition), to speak with (without preposition)
kammil II	to finish something
krafatta	tie
kullīya	faculty
kullīyit il-ʾādāb	faculty of arts
lākin	but
lammaʿ II	to polish
liʾinn	because, because of
madām	Mrs. (in the city, office and intellectual environment)
madkhal	entrance
mandūb	delegate, representative
marāsim	ceremony, protocol (diplomatic)
masʾūl	executive, responsible representative
m(i)nawwar	lighting
mudarrib	trainer
mufattish	inspector
muḥaḍra	lecture
mulḥaq	attaché
muntag, -āt	product
muṣawwir	photographer
nafs (nufūs)	soul
nayyim II	to coax/induce/help someone to sleep
nashar (u)	to publish (a book), to hang (laundry), to distribute
nazzil II	to put down, to bring down
ʾaddim II	to introduce someone/something to someone, to explain something to someone (*li*)
ʾibil (a)	to accept something
qunṣul (qanaṣla)	consul
rabba II	to educate, to keep, to grow a beard
raggaʿ II	to return something to someone *(li)*
raḥḥab II	to welcome someone, something *(bi)*
rayyaḥ II	to oblige to someone (without preposition)
rawwaḥ II	to go home
ṣaghghar II	to change
ṣaḥafī	journalist
salla II	to entertain someone
sallim II	to give over, to greet someone *(ʿala)* from someone *(li)*

saqāfī	cultural
ṣawwar II	to photograph, to film
sumʿa	name, reputation
sharaf	honour, dignity
sharraf II	to honour someone (without preposition) with something *(bi)*, to honour someone (without preposition) with a visit *(bi)*

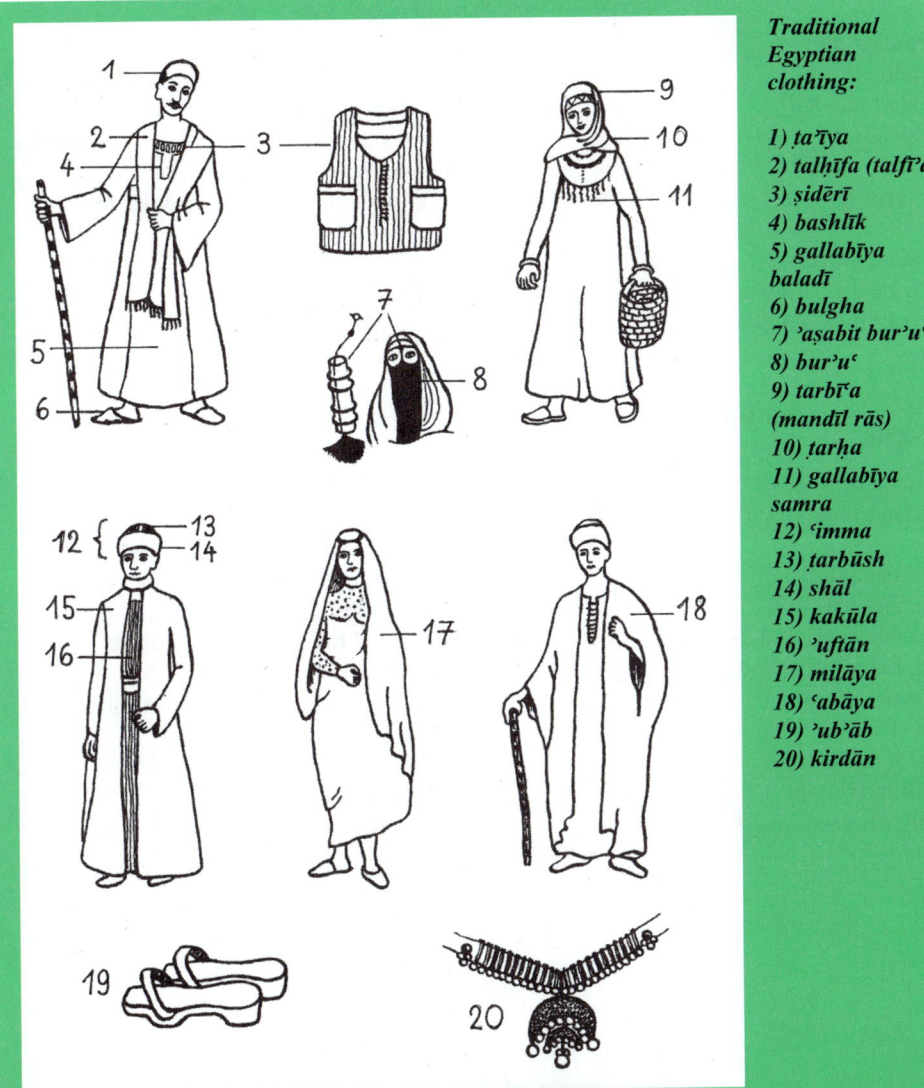

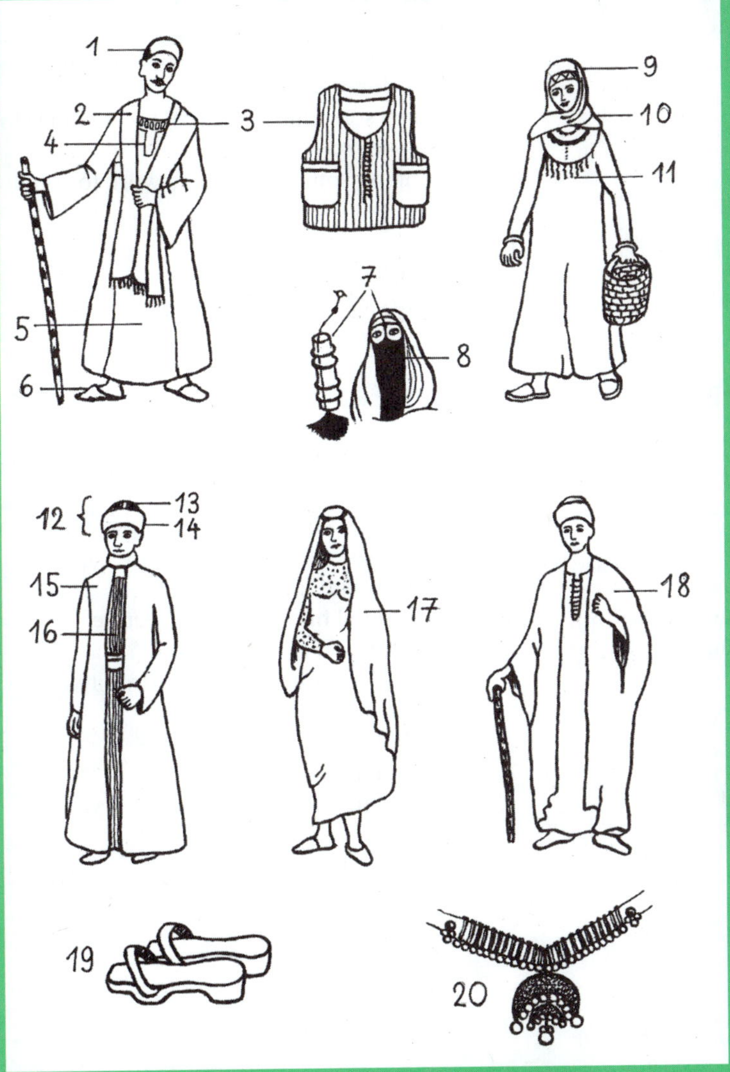

Traditional Egyptian clothing:

1) ṭaʾīya
2) talḥīfa (talfīʾa)
3) ṣidērī
4) bashlīk
5) gallabīya baladī
6) bulgha
7) ʾaṣabit burʾuʿ
8) burʾuʿ
9) tarbīʿa (mandīl rās)
10) ṭarḥa
11) gallabīya samra
12) ʿimma
13) ṭarbūsh
14) shāl
15) kakūla
16) ʾuftān
17) milāya
18) ʿabāya
19) ʾubʾāb
20) kirdān

shiʿr	poetry
shughl (ʾashghāl)	work
tagriba (tagārib)	attempt
taʿlīm	education
ṭallaʿ II	to take out, to take up, to lift; to make photos
targama (tarāgim)	translation
targim	to translate
ṭūl (il-waʾt)	in the course of (the whole time), for (the whole time)
ʿuḍw (ʾaʿḍāʾ)	member
wadda II	to take somebody somewhere, to bring to
walad (ʾawlād)	boy, (plural: children)
warra II	to show something (without preposition) to someone *(li)*
waẓẓaf II	to employ someone, to give work to some one
waẓīfa (waẓāyif)	job, office
wizart il-khārigīya	ministry of foreign affairs
wizart it-taʿlīm il-ʿālī	ministry of higher education

V. Taʿbīrāt:

Bravo ʿalēk!	Great! Excellent! You are great, excellent!
Furṣa saʿīda!	I'm pleased to meet you. (lit. "Happy occassion.")
- ʾAna ʾasʿad!	The pleasure is mine. (lit.: "I am happier.")
Gahhiz nafsak li ... !	Get ready for ... ! Prepare for … !
Gahhiz nafso li ʾl-muḥaḍra.	He prepared himself for the lecture.
Ḥa-tisharrafna ʾemta?	When are you going to visit us?
Ḥazūrku ʾurayyib, ʾin shāʾallāh.	answer (lit.: "I hope that I will visit you soon.")
ʾĀl li nafso ...	He told himself ...
Sallim lī ʿalēh!	Give him my best regards!
- ʾAllāh yisallimak!	answer (lit.: "May Allah preserve you.")

Id - Dars il-ʾāshir / Lesson 10

Fi ʾl-bosṭa

-Ḥaḍretak bi-tidawwar ʿala ḥāga?
-ʾA(h), baʿd ʾizn ḥaḍretik, mumkin t(i)sāʿidīnī? Lāzim ʾabʿat ṭard li ʾl-khārig.
- Sawānī, ḥanāwil lak istimāra. ʿĀwiz tibʿato ʿādī walla m(i)staʿgil walla musaggal?
- Mish ʿārif, ʾaṣlī barāsil ʾaṣḥābī fī ʾŪrubbā wi ʿāwiz ʾabʿat luhum shwayyit hadāyā bi-munasbit Rās is-sana.
- Li ʾŪrubbā, yibʾa bi ʾl-barīd il-gawwī, liʾinno sarīʿ wi maḍmūn barḍo.
- Ṭayyib, bas ʾalāʾī hena kartōna wi dubāra ʾaliff bihā ʾṭ-ṭard?
- La il-ḥagāt di ḥa-t(i)lāʾīhā fī mīdān il-ʿAtaba.
- Keda kwayyis? ʿUnwān il-mursal ʾilēh ḥaktibo ʿalā wishsh iṭ-ṭard. Wi ʿunwān il-mursil ḥaktibo ʿala ḍahro?
- La, iktibo fi ʾl-ḥitta di ʿala wishsh iṭ-ṭard barḍo.
- ʿAndī fikra khaṭarit bi-bālī di ʾl-waʾti, mumkin ʾabʿat luhum faks ʿashān ʾaṭammin ʿala ʾakhbārhum, ʾaṣluhum baʾa lhum ktīr ma raddūsh ʿala gawabātī.
- Il-faks fī mabna tānī, ʿandī gawabāt wi ṭurūd bas.
- ʿAshān mansāsh, ṭawābiʿ bosṭa ʿand ḥaḍretik? ʿĀwiz ḥedāshar ṭābiʿ bi-mīya khamsa ʾu ʿishrīn ʾirsh.

Mamnūʿ... maʾdarsh(i), ʾana ʿandī taʿlīmāt māshī ʿalēhā!

That's forbidden... I can't, I have instructions that I have to follow.

Fi ʾl-mīdān ʾābilt gārī mi ʾl-madīna ʾl-gamʿīya. Kān rāyiḥ il-bosṭa, ʿashān yibʿat shrīṭ tasgīl li ʾakhūh. Ḥaka lī, ʾinn ʾakhūh sāfir Bārīs, liʾinn il-mushrif bitāʿo fī Gamʿit Sorbōn ʿāwiz yishūf ʿamal ʾē(h) fī risalto li ʾd-doktōrāh.
-Ḥāga ʿaẓīma ʾinn il-ʾustāz il-faransī bi-yitābiʿ shughl ʾakhūk. W ʾenta bi-tizākir kwayyis il-ʾayyām di?
- ʾAna mish mabsūṭ min nafsī...
- Mish ʿāwiz ʾanāʾishak fi ʾl-mauḍūʿ da, ʾenta ṭālib mumtāz!
-Ma tigāmilnīsh! ʾĒ(h) raʾyak, yinfaʿ tisāʿidnī fī ḥāga?
- Ṭabʿan, ʾawi, ʾawi!
- ʾAllāh y(i)khallīk! Tiʾdar tirāgiʿ maʿāya ʾl-baḥs b(i)tāʿī? Lāzim ʾasallimo fī baḥr ʿusbūʿ.
-Min ʿēnayya. ʿAla fikra, il-muwaẓẓafīn fī maktab il-bosṭa ʾr-raʾīsī bi-yiʿām(i)lū ʾl-gumhūr muʿamla ḥelwa khāliṣ!

I. ʾAsʾila:

1. Mīn bi-yirāsil ʾaṣḥābo fī ʾŪrubbā?
2. Muwaẓẓaft il-bosṭa nāw(i)lit lo ʾl-istimāra lē(h)?
3. Fēn mumkin yilāʾī kartōna wi dubāra ʿashān yiliff bihā ʾṭ-ṭard?
4. ʿUnwān il-mursal ʾilēh lāzim yiktibo fēn?
5. Mursil iṭ-ṭard ʾābil mīn fi ʾl-mīdān?
6. ʾAkhū gāro sāfir Bārīs lē(h)?
7. Iṭ-ṭālib wāfiʾ ʿala ʾē(h)?
8. Il-muwaẓẓafīn fī maktab il-bosṭa ʾr-raʾisī bi-yiʿām(i)lū ʾl-gumhūr ʿezzāy?

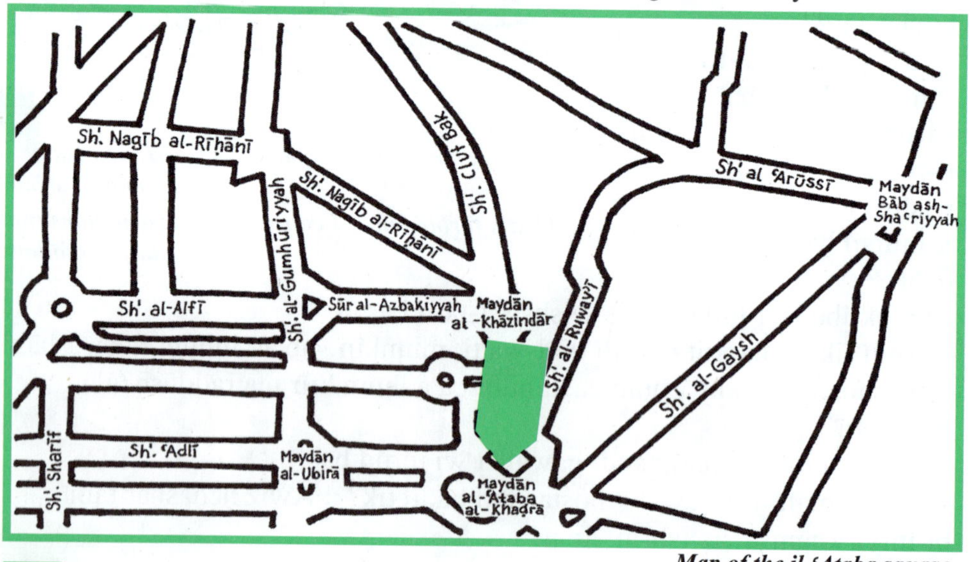

Map of the il-ʿAtaba square.

II. Qawāʿid:

1. The 3rd verbal stem

The meaning of the verbs of the 3rd verbal stem:

a) They express an activity of the subject in relationship to the object:
GāMiL (to flatter sb.); *RāSiL* (to exchange letters with sb.); *GāWiB* (to answer a question); *ʾāBiL* (to meet someone); *SāʿiD* (to help sb.); *NāʾiSh* (to argue with someone); *ʿāMiL* (to treat sb.).

b) They express an activity derived from a noun:
SaFaR (journey, travelling) – *SāFiR* (to travel); *TiGāRa* (trade, commerce) – *TāGiR* (to trade).

perfect:

RāSiL (to exchange letters)
- the first vowel is ***ā***
- the second vowel is ***i***

	singular:	negative:	plural:	negative:
3rd pers. m.	***RāSiL***	***ma RāSiL-sh(i)***	***RāSiL-ū***	***ma RāSiL-ūsh***
3rd pers. f.	***RāS(i)L-it***	***ma RāS(i)L-itsh(i)***		
2nd pers. m.	***RāSiL-t***	***ma RāSiL-tish***	***RāSiL-tū***	***ma RāSiL-tūsh***
2nd pers. f.	***RāSiL-ti***	***ma RāSiL-tīsh***		
1st pers.	***RāSiL-t***	***ma RāSiL-tish***	***RāSiL-na***	***ma RāSiL-nāsh***

Imperfect
- the perfect verbal stem takes imperfect prefixes and suffixes:

singular:

		negative:
3rd pers. m.	***yi-RāSiL***	***ma yi-RāSiL-sh(i)***
3rd pers. f.	***ti-RāSiL***	***ma ti-RāSiL-sh(i)***
2nd pers. m.	***ti-RāSiL***	***ma ti-RāSiL-sh(i)***
2nd pers. f.	***ti-RāS(i)L-ī***	***ma ti-RāS(i)L-īsh***
1st pers.	***a-RāSiL***	***ma-RāSiL-sh(i)***

plural:

		negative:
3rd pers.	***yi-RāS(i)L-ū***	***ma yi-RāS(i)L-ūsh***
2nd pers.	***ti-RāS(i)L-ū***	***ma ti-RāS(i)L-ūsh***
1st pers.	***ni-RāSiL***	***ma ni-RāSiL-sh(i)***

Imperative: To form the imperative, the prefix ***ti-*** is detached from the 2nd person imperfect forms: *rāsil!* (m.), *rās(i)lī!* (f.), *rās(i)lū!* (pl.).
Negative imperative: *ma t(i)rāsilsh(i)!* (m.), *ma t(i)rās(i)līsh!* (f.), *ma t(i)rās(i)lūsh!* (pl.).

Active and passive participles:

The participles are formed by means of the prefix ***mi- / mu-*** (in the case of forms denoting a professional activity), followed by the simple perfect stem of the verb; the second consonant is followed by ***i*** (active participle) or ***a*** (passive participle): *muRāSiL* (m.) – correspondent, *muRāSiLa* (f.), *muRāSiLīn* (pl.); *muSāʿiD* – assistant; *miSāFiR* – traveller, passenger; *miTāBiʿ* – watching, informed on; *miZāKiR* – studying, learning.

– Passive participle forms of the verbs of the 3rd verbal stem are very rare, indeed rather theoretical.

Samples of Egyptian postal stamps

Verbal noun:

- Verbal nouns are derived according to the following two patterns, depending on whether the principal meaning is verbal (the first pattern) or nominal (the second pattern).

Pattern 1: ***mu-RāSaLa*** – correspondence; *mu-SāʿaDa* – help; *mu-Nāʾasha* – discussion, defense; *mu-GāM(a)La* – flatter, compliment; *mu-ʾāBaLa* – meeting.

Pattern 2: ***DiFāʿ*** – defense; *ʿilāG* – treatment, therapy.

The third stem of verbs with the third consonant *w* or *y*:

These verbs are conjugated according to the paradigm ***SāWa*** (to equal, to have the value of):

perfect:

	singular:	negative:	plural:	negative:
3rd pers. m.	***SāWa***	***ma SaW-āsh(i)***	***SāW-ū***	***ma SāW-ūsh***
3rd pers. f.	***SāW-it***	***ma SāW-itsh(i)***		
2nd pers. m.	***SaW-ēt***	***ma SaW-ētsh(i)***	***SaW-ētū***	***ma SaW-ētūsh***
2nd pers. f.	***SaW-ēti***	***ma SaW-ētīsh***		
1st pers.	***SaW-ēt***	***ma SaW-ētsh(i)***	***SaW-ēna***	***ma SaW-ēnāsh***

Imperfect:
Cf. the imperfect forms of the verb ***yiLā'ī*** (to find) – Lesson 8.

Imperative: *sāwi!* (m.), *sāwī!* (f.), *sāwū!* (pl.).
Negative imperative: *ma t(i)sāwīsh!* (m.), *ma t(i)sāwīsh!* (f.), *ma t(i)sāwūsh!* (pl.).

Active participle: *miSāWī* (m.) – equaling; *miSāWīYa* (f.), *miSāW(ī)Yīn* (pl.).
Passive participle: verbs of this group do not form the passive participle.

Verbal noun: *mu-SāW-ā* (equality)

Other verbs following this paradigm: *WāZa (yiWāZī), Rā'a (yiRā'ī).*

2. The 4th verbal stem
The meaning of the verbs of the 4th verbal stem:
They express an activity that causes something to happen, they are created according to the paradigm: *sa'īd* (happy, content) – *'aS'aD* (to make happy);
- there are only few verbs of the 4th verbal stem in Egyptian colloquial Arabic: *'aKhRaG* (to direct); *'aShRaF* (to inspect something); *'a'LaN* (to declare, proclaim something).

Perfect:

'a-KhRaG (to direct)
- the first consonant is preceded by the prefix ***'a-***
- the vowel between the first and second consonant is omitted
- the vowel between the second and third consonants is ***a***

singular:

		negative:
3rd pers. m.	***'a-KhRaG***	***ma 'a-KhRaG-sh(i)***
3rd pers. f.	***'a-KhRaG-it***	***ma 'a-KhRaG-itsh(i)***
2nd pers. m.	***'a-KhRaG-t***	***ma 'a-KhRaG-tish***
2nd pers. f.	***'a-KhRaG-ti***	***ma 'a-KhRaG-tīsh***
1st pers.	***'a-KhRaG-t***	***ma 'a-KhRaG-tish***

plural:

		negative:
3rd pers.	***'a-KhRaG-ū***	***ma 'a-KhRaG-ūsh***
2nd pers.	***'a-KhRaG-tū***	***ma 'a-KhRaG-tūsh***
1st pers.	***'a-KhRaG-na***	***ma 'a-KhRaG-nāsh***

Imperfect
– the imperfect is formed by detaching the prefix ***'a-*** and attaching imperfect prefixes and suffixes; the second consonant is followed by the vowel ***i***
– imperfect forms of the verbs of the 4th verbal stem are identical to the imperfect forms of verbs of the 1st verbal stem with the imperfect vowel ***i***:

	singular:	negative:	plural:	negative:
3rd pers. m.	***yi-KhRiG***	***ma yi-KhRiG-sh(i)***	***yi-KhRiG-ū***	***ma yi-KhRiG-ūsh***
3rd pers. f.	***ti-KhRiG***	***ma ti-KhRiG-sh(i)***		
2nd pers. m.	***ti-KhRiG***	***ma ti-KhRiG-sh(i)***	***ti-KhRiG-ū***	***ma ti-KhRiG-ūsh***
2nd pers. f.	***ti-KhRiG-ī***	***ma ti-KhRiG-īsh***		
1st pers.	***a-KhRiG***	***ma-KhRiG-sh(i)***	***ni-KhRiG***	***ma ni-KhRiG-sh(i)***

Imperative: To form the imperative, the prefix ***ti-*** is detached from the 2nd person imperfect forms and replaced by the prefix ***ʾa***:
ʾakhrig! (m.), *ʾakhrigī!* (f.), *ʾakhrigū!* (pl.).
Negative imperative: *ma tikhrigsh(i)!* (m.), *ma tikhrigīsh!* (f.), *ma tikhrigūsh!* (pl.).

Active and passive participles:
The participles are formed by means of the prefix ***mu***; the second consonant is followed by ***i*** (active participle) or ***a*** (passive participle): *muRSiL* (m.) – sender, *muRSiLa* (f.), *muRSiLīn* (pl.); *muShRiF* – leader, overseer; *muRSaL* – addressee, sent; *muKhRaG* – recorded, directed; *muʿLaN* – announced, proclaimed.

Verbal noun:
– Verbal nouns are derived according to the following pattern: ***ʾi-RSāL*** – broadcast; *ʾi-KhRāG* – directorship, directing; *ʾi-ShRāF* – leadership, control; *ʾi-LāN* – announcement, proclamation.

The 4th stem of verbs with the second consonant *w* or *y*:

perfect: ***ʾa-Ḍ̣āF*** (to add, complete), *ʾa-ḌāF-it, ʾa-ḌaF-t, ʾa-ḌaF-ti, ʾa-ḌaF-t, ʾa-ḌāF-ū, ʾa-ḌaF-tū, ʾa-ḌaF-na / ma ʾa-ḌaF-shi, ma ʾa-ḌāF-itshi, ma ʾa-ḌaF-tish, ma ʾa-ḌaF-tīsh, ma ʾa-ḌaF-tish, ma ʾa-ḌāF-ūsh, ma ʾa-ḌaF-tūsh, ma ʾa-ḌaF-nāsh*
imperfect: (the forms of the imperfect are identical to the imperfect forms of verbs with the second consonant ***y***, cf. Lesson 6): *yi-ḌīF, ti-ḌīF, ti-ḌīF, ti-ḌīF-ī, ʾa-ḌīF, yi-ḌīF-ū, ti-ḌīF-ū, ni-ḌīF / ma-yi-ḌīF-sh(i), ma-ti-ḌīF-sh(i), ma-ti-ḌīF-sh(i), ma-ti-ḌīF-īsh, ma-ʾa-ḌīF-sh(i), ma-yi-ḌīF-ūsh, ma-ti-ḌīF-ūsh, ma-ni-ḌīF-sh(i).*
Imperative: *ʾaḍif! ʾaḍīfī! ʾaḍīfū!*
Negative imperative: *matiḍifshi!, ma tiḍīfīsh!, ma tiḍīfūsh!*
Active participle: *muḌīF*, ***passive participle***: *muḌāF*
Verbal noun: *ʾi-ḌāFa* (addition, appendix)

– other verbs following this paradigm: *ʾaFāD (yiFīD), ʾaShāR (yiShīR)*

The 4th stem of verbs with the third consonant *w* or *y*:

perfect: (these forms are identical with the perfect forms of verbs with the third consonant ***y***, cf. Lesson 8, *RaMa*) ***MaḌa*** (he signed)
imperfect: (these forms are identical with the imperfect forms of verbs with the third consonant ***y***, cf. Lesson 8, *yi-RM-i*) ***yi-MḌ-i*** (he signs)
Imperative: cf. the verb *RaMa (yi-RM-i)*

Negative imperative: cf. the verb *RaMa (yi-RM-i)*
Active participle: *māḌī, MaḌYa, MaḌYīn*
Passive participle: *maMḌī, maMḌīYa, maMḌīYīn*
Verbal noun: *ʾi-MḌā* (signature)

- other verbs following this paradigm: *ṬaFa (yiṬFi)*.

3. Basic numerals 11 and above

11 *ḥedāshar*	21 *wāḥid u ʿishrīn*	**31** *wāḥid ʾu talatīn*
12 *itnāshar*	22 *itnēn u ʿishrīn*	**40** *ʾarbaʿīn*
13 *talattāshar*	23 *talāta u ʿshrīn*	**50** *khamsīn*
14 *ʾarbaʿtāshar*	24 *ʾarbaʿa u ʿishrīn*	**60** *sittīn*
15 *khamastāshar*	25 *khamsa u ʿishrīn*	**70** *sabʿīn*
16 *sittāshar*	26 *sitta u ʿishrīn*	**80** *tamanīn*
17 *sabʿatāshar*	27 *sabʿa u ʿishrīn*	**90** *tisʿīn*
18 *tamantāshar*	28 *tamanya u ʿishrīn*	**100** *mīya*
19 *tisʿatāshar*	29 *tisʿa u ʿishrīn*	**101** *mīya ʾu wāḥid*
20 *ʿishrīn*	30 *talatīn*	**200** *mitēn*
263 *mitēn talāta ʾu sittīn*	**2000** *ʾalfēn*	**8000** *tamantālāf*
300 *tultumīya*	**3000** *talatālāf*	**9000** *tisʿitālāf*
311 *tultumīya ʾu ḥedāshar*	**4000** *ʾarbaʿtālāf*	**10 000** *ʿashrat ʾālāf*
400 *rubʿumīya*	**5000** *khamastālāf*	**100 000** *mīt ʾalf*
500 *khumsumīya*	**6000** *sittālāf*	**1 000 000** *mil(i)yōn*
600 *suttumīya*	**7000** *sabʿatālāf*	**5 000 000** *khamas malayīn*
700 *subʿumīya*		
800 *tumnumīya*		
900 *tusʿumīya*		
1000 *ʾalf*		

- basic numerals 11 and above take the counted object in the singular:
ḥedāshar ṭālib (11 students), *itnāshar ṣafḥa* (12 pages)
- the components of composite numerals combine in the following order:
unit – conjunction u / wi - ten:
khamsa u talatīn bardī (35 papyri), *tisʿa u sabʿīn ṣūra* (79 pictures, photographs)
- the components of higher composite numerals (over 100) combine in the following order:
millions – thousands – hundreds – tens /units – tens, the conjunction ***u / wi*** stands only between the last two components:
khamas malayīn tumnumīt ʾalf subʿumīya talāta ʾu ʿishrīn ginē (5 800 723 Egyptian pounds), *tamant ʾalāf khumsumīya ʾarbaʿa ʾu sittīn kīlo* (8 564 kilograms), *talat ʾālāf ʾu wāḥid ṭālib* (3001 students), *tusʿumīya tamanya ʾu talatīn ʿarabīya* (938 cars), *rubʿumīya wi sabʿīn kitāb* (470 books).

- if the counted objects follow the final digits 03 – 10, they take the plural form:
subʿumīya u sitt tamasīl (706 statues), *tumnumīya ʾu ʾarbaʿ nusakh* (804 copies), *mīya ʾu ʿasharit matāḥif* (110 museums), *mitēn ʾu tisʿ tazākir* (209 tickets).
- the numeral ***mīya*** and its composites change immediately in front of the counted object to ***mīt****: mīt yōm* (100 days), *khumsumīt sana* (500 years), *suttumīt ḥikāya* (600 stories)

III. Tadrībāt:

Targama

May I help you with something? Who did not agree with this program? Please, do not argue with me about this affair! Did you answer his letter? We have been exchanging letters with him for a number of years. They met us yesterday in front of the embassy. How will you treat him? I must follow these affairs. Can you (f.) pass me the map? We must learn the new vocabulary. Do not flatter (pl.) us! I thought he went (departed) to his family in Upper Egypt. Do you (pl.) know that they advertised their products in this Arabic newspaper? Can we meet you tomorrow? I am afraid that you (polite) will not approve of this project. They told us that they treat them very well. The minister of national defense conferred with his foreign guests. I know well that you do not like this flattery. She wrote to her that she takes care of her brother's children. He wanted to make this film this year. Would you like to add something? Where should I sign? Can we send this postcard by airmail? We will answer your question in the course of the week. Have you been here long? We have been in Egypt already a month. I want to make sure that you are all right. This engine will be no good for him. With whom did you revise the translation?

Kammil!
Yisāwī kām?

a) ***zāyid***
12 + 33 = …
96 + 115 = …
388 + 274 = ...
1599 + 745 = ...
256 + 837 = ...

b) ***nāʾiṣ***
197 -83 = …
2652 -931 = …
4237 - 2589 = ...
874 -326 = ...
1057 - 71 = ...

c) ***fī***
12 x 4 = …
15 x 7 = …
17 x 8 = …
19 x 5 = …
14 x 18 = …

d) ***ʿala***
216 : 9 = …
600 : 8 = …
234 : 6 = …
202 : 5 = …
441 : 7 = …

Li ʾl-ʾasaf mafish maʿāya flūs ziyāda ʾashtiri bihā ṣandūʾ ʾakbar shwayya.
Unfortunately I am not rich enough to buy a slightly bigger box.

IV. Mufradāt

ʾaḍāf IV	to add, complete
ʿādī	common, normal
ʾafād IV	to be useful, beneficient to sb. (without preposition)
ʾahl (ʾahālī)	family
ʿala	divided by (:)
ʾaʿlan IV	to declare, proclaim, advertise something *(ʿan)*
ʿālig III	to cure, treat sb.
ʿāmil III	to treat sb., to get along with sb. (without preposition)
ʾashār IV	to point to *(ʾila)*
ʾashraf IV	to oversee something *(ʿala)*, to direct, lead something *(ʿala)*
baḥs (ʾabḥās)	research, term paper, contribution (at a conference)
bāl	mind
barīd	post
Bārīs	Paris
barnāmig (barāmig)	programme
bosṭa	post office
dāfiʿ III	to defend something *(ʿan)*
ḍahr	back, reverse, reverse side
dubāra	rope, string
faks	fax
fī	times (x)
gāmil III	to flatter sb. (without preposition)
gār (gīrān)	neighbour
gawwī	by airmail, by air, by plain
gāwib III	to answer to *(ʿala)*
gihāz (ʾaghiza)	engine
gumhūr (gamahīr)	the public
il-khārig	abroad
ʾikhrāg	direction (film)
ʾimḍāʾ	signature
ʾiʿlān	declaration, proclamation, advertisement
ʾirsāl	broadcast
istimāra	questionnaire, document, form
ʾishāra	signal, traffic light
kart (kurūt)	post card
kartōna	paper, cardboard box
kurōna	crown (money)

mabna (mabānī)	building
maḍa (i)	to sign something *(ʿala)*
maḍmūn	guaranteed, safe, sure
mashrūʿ (mashārīʿ)	project, plan
mistaʿgil	express, fast
muʾabla	meeting, interview
muʿamla	behaviour, conduct, treating sb.
mugamla	flatter, compliment
munaʾsha	discussion, defense (of a master's, doctor's thesis)
murasla	correspondence
mursal ʾilēh	addressee
musaggal	written, noted, recommended
mursil	sender
mushrif	leader, inspector, overseer
nāʾiṣ	missing, incomplete, minus (-)
nāʾish III	to discuss, argue with someone (without preposition) about something *(fī)*
nāwil III	to pass something (without preposition) to sb. *(li)*
nifiʿ (a)	to be useful, beneficient; to suit sb. or something (without preposition)
nuskha (nusakh)	copy, printout, specimen
ʾābil III	to meet sb. (without preposition)
ʾirsh (ʾurūsh)	piastre
rāʿa III	to care for someone, something
rāgiʿ III	to make corrections, to revise, control something, to review (study materials)
rāsil III	to exchange letters with (without preposition)
Rās is-sana	New Year
risal(i)t id-doktorāh	doctor's thesis
sāfir III	to travel to a place (without preposition), to go to a person *(li)*
sāʿid III	to help someone (without preposition) with something *(fī)*
iṣ-Ṣaʿīd	Upper Egypt (southern Egypt)
sanya (sawānī)	second, moment
sarīʿ	fast
sāwa III	to equal something (without preposition)
shrīṭ (ʾashriṭa)	stripe, belt, girdle
shrīṭ it-tasgīl	cassette, tape
tābiʿ III	to watch something
ṭafa (i)	to quench
ṭammin II	to make sure about something *(ʿala)*

ṭard (ṭurūd)	packet
tasgīl	record
ʾŪrubbā	Europe
wāfiʾ III	to agree with *(ʿala)*
waṭanī	national
wāza III	to be parallel, equivalent something, to correspond to a sum (without preposition)
zāyid	plus (+)
zākir III	to study, learn something

V. Taʿbīrāt:

ʾAllāh y(i)khallīk!	Thank you very much! (lit.: May God preserve you!)
ʿĀwiz ʾaṭammin ʿalēku!	I want to make sure that you are all right.
Baʾa lī ktīr hena (baʾa lak, lik, lo, lhā, lna, lku, lhum).	I (you, he, she, we, you, they) have been here already a long time.
fī baḥr ...	in the course of … (time)
Khaṭar bi-bālī (bi-bālak, bālik, bālo, bālhā, bālna, bālku, bālhum).	I thought (had an idea).
yibʾa	so, thus
Keda kwayyis?	Is it all right this way?
Min ʿēnayya!	With pleasure!

Tahrir – main Cairo square

Id - Dars ḥedāshar /Lesson 11

Maʿhad il-lugha ʾl-ʿarabīya

- Mumkin ʾatkallim maʿa mudīr il-maʿhad?
- ʾAʾūl lo mīn?
- ʾAna ṭālib inglīzī wi ʿāwiz ʾatʿallim il-ʿarabī ʿanduku fi ʾl-maʿhad.
- Ḥaḍretak ʿāwiz titʿallim il-fuṣḥa walla ʾl-ʿāmmīya?
- ʾAna ʾtkharragt fī qism il-lugha ʾl-ʿarabīya, Maʿhad id-dirāsāt ish-sharʾīya, Gamʿit Oxford. Fi ʾl-gamʿa kunna bi-nitʿallim il-fuṣḥa wi ʾl-ʿāmmīya. Di ʾl-waʾti ʾana ʿāwiz mustawāya yitḥassin fi ʾl-ʾitnēn.
- ʾIn shāʾ allāh, itfaḍḍal ḥaḍretak maʿāya ʿashān titfarrag ʿala ʾuwaḍ wi qāʿāt maʿhadna wi titʿarraf ʿala manāhigna fī tadrīs il-ʿarabī li ʾl-ʾagānib.

ʾEnta wākhid maʿāk timsāl ʾaṣlī?
Di zikra basīṭa ʿashān mansāsh il-lugha ʾl-firʿaunīya.
You're taking an ancient Egyptian statue with you? That's a small souvenir, so that I wouldn't forget the language of the pharaohs.

- Ṭayyib, ʾezzāy il-wāḥid yiʾdar yibʾa mutamakkin mi ʾl-lugha wi huwa wusṭ nās ʾagānib bi-yitkallimū lughāt mukhtalifa wi hum mish nāṭiqīn ʾaṣlīyīn?
- Ma t(i)khafsh(i), ḥa-n(i)khallīk titṣarraf zay in-nāṭiq il-ʾaṣlī. Il-masʾala mish ṣaʿba ʾawi. Il-ʾawwil ḥa-titʿarrafū ʿala baʿḍuku, baʿdēn ḥa-titkallimū maʿa baʿaḍ, wi ḥa-titdarrabū ʿala ʾl-muḥadsa bi-mufradāthā, gumalhā wi taʿbīrāthā ʾl-muhimma.
- Wi mustawāya ḥa-yithaddid ʾemta wi zāy?
- In-nahār da baʿd iḍ-ḍuhr ḥa-niʿmil lak imtiḥān ʿashān niʿraf mustawāk.

... baʿd il-imtiḥān

- ʾAlf mabrūk, itʾakkidna min mustawāk, mumkin tudkhul il-mustawa ʾl-khāmis wi ḥa-titʿallim mi ʾl-kitāb it-tālit.
- Mutashakkir ʾawi, ḥaḍretak shāyif ʾinnī ʾaʾdar ʾatʾaddim fī baḥr ʾaddi ʾē(h)?

- Mithayya' lī, kurs mukassaf li-muddit shahr, shahr 'u nuṣṣ k(i)fāya 'ashān tit'addim bi-shakl kbīr. Ṭab'an, bi-sharṭ 'inn ḥaḍretak tib'a mutamassik bi-manāhigna 't-ta'līmīya.
- Ḥāḍir, bas 'atmanna 'at'assis kwayyis.
- Ṭammin ḥaḍretak, rabbina yiwaffa'ak. Di 'l-wa'ti mumkin titghadda fi 'l-maṭ'am bitā'na, mumkin titmashsha shwayya fī gnēnit ma'hadna. Bas matit'akhkharsh(i) 'ala ma'ād id-dars!
- La, 'in shā' allāh mish ḥat'akhkhar.
- 'Ala fikra, ma'hadna bi-yi'mil raḥalāt wi ḥaḍretak mumkin titfassaḥ ma'āna fī 'l-maṣyaf 'alā shāṭi' il-Baḥr il-'aḥmar.
- Shukran 'ala 'l-ma'lūmāt il-mufīda. 'Ana muta'assif giddan, 'innī 'aṭṭalt ḥaḍretak.
- 'Ezzāy ba'a, 'eḥna taḥt 'amrak!

I. 'As'ila

1. Mīn 'āwiz yitkallim ma'a mudīr il-ma'had?
2. Iṭ-ṭālib daras il-'arabī fēn?
3. 'Ē(h) hiya ṭarī'it tadrīs il-'arabī li 'l-'agānib?
4. 'Idart il-ma'had bi-tiḥaddid mustawa 'ṭ-ṭalaba 'ezzāy?
5. Iṭ-ṭālib il-inglīzī mumkin yudkhul 'anho mustawa?
6. 'Ezzāy yi'dar yit'addim fī baḥr shahr?
7. Mīn mumkin yitfassaḥ 'ala shāṭi' il-Baḥr il-'aḥmar?
8. Mīn muta'assif wi lē(h)?

II. Qawā'id:

1. The 5th verbal stem

The meaning of the verbs of the 5th verbal stem:

a) reflexive of verbs of the 2nd verbal stem:

FaRRaG – it-FaRRaG (to show – to look at); *DaRRaB – it-DaRRaB* (to train, exercise – to train oneself); *'aRRaF – it-'aRRaF* (to introduce – to meet); *ḤaSSiN – it-ḤaSSiN* (to make better – to get better); *'aLLiM – it-'aLLiM* (to teach – to learn, to study); *SaLLa – it-SaLLa* (to entertain – to have fun, entertain oneself)

b) passive of verbs of the 2nd verbal stem:

ShaRRaF- it-ShaRRaF (to honour – to be honoured); *ḤaDDiD – it-ḤaDDiD* (to set, determine – to be determined, set)

perfect:

it- FaRRaG (to look at)

- the prefix ***it-*** is attached to verbs of the 2nd verbal stem
- verbs of the 5th verbal stem are thus conjugated according to the same paradigm as verbs of the 2nd verbal stem

singular:

		negative:
3rd pers. m.	***it-FaRRaG***	***ma-t-FaRRaG-sh(i)***
3rd pers. f.	***it-FaRRaG-it***	***ma-t-FaRRaG-itsh(i)***
2nd pers. m.	***it-FaRRaG-t***	***ma-t-FaRRaG-tish***
2nd pers. f.	***it-FaRRaG-ti***	***ma-t-FaRRaG-tīsh***
1st pers.	***it-FaRRaG-t***	***ma-t-FaRRaG-tish***

plural:

		negative:
3rd pers.	***it-FaRRaG-ū***	***ma-t-FaRRaG-ūsh***
2nd pers.	***it-FaRRaG-tū***	***ma-t-FaRRaG-tūsh***
1st pers.	***it-FaRRaG-na***	***ma-t-FaRRaG-nāsh***

Imperfect
- the perfect verbal stem takes imperfect prefixes and suffixes:

singular:

		negative:
3rd pers. m.	***yi-t-FaRRaG***	***ma yi-t-FaRRaG-sh(i)***
3rd pers. f.	***ti-t-FaRRaG***	***ma ti-t-FaRRaG-sh(i)***
2nd pers. m.	***ti-t-FaRRaG***	***ma ti-t-FaRRaG-sh(i)***
2nd pers. f.	***ti-t-FaRRaG-ī***	***ma ti-t-FaRRaG-īsh***
1st pers.	***a-t-FaRRaG***	***m a-t-FaRRaG-sh(i)***

plural:

		negative:
3rd pers.	***yi-t-FaRRaG-ū***	***ma yi-t-FaRRaG-ūsh***
2nd pers.	***ti-t-FaRRaG-ū***	***ma ti-t-FaRRaG-ūsh***
1st pers.	***ni-t-FaRRaG***	***ma ni-t-FaRRaG-sh(i)***

Imperative: To form the imperative, the prefix ***ti-*** is detached from the 2nd person imperfect forms: *itfarrag!* (m.), *itfarragī!* (f.), *itfarragū!* (pl.).
Negative imperative: *ma titfarragsh(i)!* (m.), *ma titfarragīsh!* (f.), *ma titfarragūsh!* (pl.).

Active and passive participles:
The participles are formed by means of the prefix ***mi- / mu-*** (in the case of words taken over from standard Arabic context), followed by the perfect stem of the verb; the prefix ***mi- / mu-*** combines with the prefix ***it-*** into ***mit- / mut-***, as is the case of imperfect prefixes ***yit-***, ***tit-***, ***at-***, ***nit-***, and of the negative particle ***ma-*** > ***mat-***.

- After the second of the geminated consonants ***(-rr-, -dd-)***, the participles (active and passive) have the vowel ***i*** or, next to glottal or emphatic consonants and ***r*** and ***l*** : ***a*** (cf. Lesson 9).

- because of their meaning, verbs of the 5th verbal stem form only the **active participle** (i.e. trained, educated, graduated, delayed, etc.), irrespective of the vowel following the second consonant and the English translation:
mitDaRRaB – trained (m. sg.), *mitDaRRaBa* (f. sg.), *mitDaRRaBīn* (pl.); *mitʻaLLiM* – educated, *mitKhaRRaG* – graduated; *mitʼaKhKhaR* – delayed; *mitḤaDDiD* – set, determined

– words taken over from the standard Arabic context have the vowel ***-a-*** after the prefix ***mut-***: *mutaShaKKiR* – thanking, *mutaMaSSiK* – holding oneself, *mutaMaKKiN* – expert in, *mutaʼaSSiF* – regretting something .

Verbal noun:

– Verbal nouns are derived according to the following pattern: ***ta-ḤaSSuN*** – improvement; *ta-KhaRRuG* – graduation; *ta-ṢaRRuF* – behavior; *ta-MaSSuK* – holding, preserving

The 5th stem of verbs with the third consonant w or y :

these verbs follow the same paradigm as the verb ***BAʼA*** (cf. Lesson 8)
ITMAShShA (to go for a walk)

perfect singular:

		negative:
3rd pers. m.	***it-MaShSh-a***	***ma-t-MaShSh-āsh(i)***
3rd pers. f.	***it-MaShSh-it***	***ma-t-MaShSh-itsh(i)***
2nd pers. m.	***it-MaShSh-ēt***	***ma-t-MaShSh-ētsh(i)***
2nd pers. f.	***it-MaShSh-ēti***	***ma-t-MaShSh-ētīsh***
1st pers.	***it-MaShSh-ēt***	***ma-t-MaShSh-ētsh(i)***

plural:

		negative:
3rd pers.	***it-MaShSh-ū***	***ma-t-MaShSh-ūsh***
2nd pers.	***it-MaShSh-ētū***	***ma-t-MaShSh-ētūsh***
1st pers.	***it-MaShSh-ēna***	***ma-t-MaShSh-ēnāsh***

imperfect singular:

		negative:
3rd pers. m.	***yi-t-MaShSh-a***	***ma yi-t-MaShSh-āsh(i)***
3rd pers. f.	***ti-t-MaShSh-a***	***ma ti-t-MaShSh-āsh(i)***
2nd pers. m.	***ti-t-MaShSh-a***	***ma ti-t-MaShSh-āsh(i)***
2nd pers. f.	***ti-t-MaShSh-ī***	***ma ti-t-MaShSh-īsh***
1st pers.	***a-t-MaShSh-a***	***m a-t-MaShSh-āsh(i)***

plural:

		negative:
3rd pers.	***yi-t-MaShSh-ū***	***ma yi-t-MaShSh-ūsh***
2nd pers.	***ti-t-MaShSh-ū***	***ma ti-t-MaShSh-ūsh***
1st pers.	***ni-t-MaShSh-a***	***ma ni-t-MaShSh-āsh(i)***

Imperative: *itmashsha!* (m.), *itmashshī!* (f.), *itmashshū!* (pl.).
Negative imperative: *ma titmashshīsh!* (m.), *ma titmashshīsh!* (f.), *ma titmashshūsh!* (pl.).

Active participle: *mitMaShShi* (m.) – walking; *mitMaShShīYa* (f.), *mitMaShShīYīn* (pl.).
Passive participle: verbs of this group do not form the passive participle.

Verbal noun: (theoretically) ***ta-MaShSh-i*** (walking).

Other verbs following this paradigm: *it-GhaDDa (yi-t-GhaDDa), it-ʿaShSha (yi-t-ʿaShSha), it-SaLLa (yi-t-SaLLa), it-MaNNa (yi-t-MaNNa).*

2. Ordinal numerals:

	masculine	***feminine***
the first	*ʾawwil / ʾawwalānī*	*ʾūlā / ʾawwalānīya*
the second	*tānī*	*tanya*
the third	*tālit*	*talta*
the fourth	*rābiʿ*	*rabʿa*
the fifth	*khāmis*	*khamsa*
the sixth	*sādis*	*sadsa / satta*
the seventh	*sābiʿ*	*sabʿa*
the eighth	*tāmin*	*tamna*
the ninth	*tāsiʿ*	*tasʿa*
the tenth	*ʿāshir*	*ʿashra*

- from 11 upwards, the meaning of ordinal numerals is expressed by cardinal numerals placed behind the determined nouns: *il-yōm ḥedāshar* (the eleventh day) *is-sana taman ya ʾu talatīn* (the thirty-eighth year) , *iṣ-ṣandūʾ mīya wāḥid ʾu ʿishrīn* (the hundred and twenty-first box)

- ordinal numerals usually follow their noun as an attribute, and thus they agree with it in gender and number: *yōm sābiʿ / il-yōm is-sābiʿ* (the seventh day); *ʾōḍa rabʿa / il-ʾōḍa ʾr-rabʿa* (the fourth room); *shāriʿ ʾawwalānī / ish-shāriʿ il-ʾawwalānī* (the first street); *ṣūra ʾawwalanīya / iṣ-ṣūra ʾl-ʾawwalānīya* (the first photograph)

- ordinal numerals may also stand in front of the noun, in this case the numeral only takes the masculine form and the noun is indefinite: *ʾawwil riḥla* (the first way); *tānī sana* (the second year*), ʾawwil shahr* (the first month), *tānī matḥaf* (the second museum), *tālit dōr (*the third floor).

III. Tadrībāt:

Targama

Have you already had your lunch? I want to make sure that this information is correct (about the correctness of this information). We can't be late today. They dined in this restaurant with their English guests. We will practise the vocabulary of the ninth lesson. When did you graduate from the university? The students of the fourth grade advanced a lot in their study of the colloquial language. They told us that they would like to meet our Egyptian professor. The second date for the exam in standard Arabic has not been announced yet. Do not apologize, I know your situation. He has never been late. Do you (polite) think that we could have a look at the Abusir papyri tomorrow? With whom would you (polite) like to talk? He has been learning English since the third grade of the basic school. She was brought up in the family of her aunt. His level has improved a lot, hasn't it? I am afraid you have been delayed because of me. Would you like to have a little walk before dinner? We haven't thought about where we'd go for holidays yet. I wish you a good journey! I can assure to you (polite – f.) that our teachers use modern teaching methods. The Czech Institute of Egyptology was founded 40 years ago.

Kammil!

1. ʾAna ʾāsif ʾinnī ... (ʾakhkhart x itʾakhkhart) ʿala bidayit il-muḥaḍra.
2. Ḥa- ... (tikhallaṣū x titkhallaṣū) shughluku ʾemta?
3. ... (ʾaddimū x itʾaddimū) ṭalabhum li-mudīr il-maʿhad.
4. Hiya mabsūṭa ʾawi ʾinnā ... (ʾaddimna x itʾaddimna) fi ʾl-ʿarabī.
5. Nifsuhum ... (yiḥassinū x yitḥassinū) mustawāhum fi ʾl-inglīzī.
6. Katabū lna ʾinn ẓurūfhum ... (ḥassinit x itḥassinit).
7. ... (ḥaddidtū x itḥaddidtū) maʿād safarku li-Maṣr walla lissa?
8. Yitmanna ... (yiʿarraf x yitʿarraf) ʿala zamāyilku ʾl-maṣrīyīn ʾurayyib.
9. ... (kallimtū x itkallimtū) maʿa mīn fi ʾl-mauḍūʿ da?
10. Min faḍlik, ... (ʾakkidī x itʾakkidī) ʾinn il-ʿasha gāhiz.

IV. Mufradāt

ʾaḥmar	red
ʾakkid II	to assure someone *(li)*
ʿamm (ʾaʿmā,)	uncle (father's brother)
ʿāmmīya	colloquial Arabic
ʾanho / ʾanhi / ʾanhum?	which? (interrogative pronoun)
ʿasha	dinner
baʿḍ	some
baʿd iḍ-ḍuhr	afternoon
bidāya	beginning
daras (i)	to study, to be a student
dars (durūs)	lesson
dirāsa	study
dōr (ʾadwār)	storey; role, part
ḍuhr	noon
ghada	lunch
khāl (khīlān)	uncle (mother's brother)
ibtidāʾī	basic (school), initial
ʾidāra	directorate, administration
imtiḥān, -āt	test, exam in *(fī)*
ʾinsān (nās)	human (human beings); the noun *nās* is either feminine singular or plural
itʾaddim V	to make progress, to proceed in *(fī)*
itʾakhkhar V	to be late, to have a delay
itʾakkid V	to make sure about *(min)*
itʿallim V	to study, to learn
itʿarraf V	to meet, to be introduced to *(ʿala / bi)*
itʾassif V	to apologise to sb. *(li)* for something *(ʿan)*
itʾassis V	to be founded, to have good foundations
itʿashsha V	to dine
itʿaṭṭal V	to be distracted (from work)
itdarrab V	to practice, train something *(ʿala / fī)*
itfarrag V	to look at something *(ʿala)*
itfassaḥ V	to go out, to go for a walk, trip
itghadda V	to lunch
itḥaddid V	to be set, determined
ithayyaʾ V	to appear, seem to someone *(li)*
itḥassin V	to improve
itkharrag V	to graduate *(fī)*
itkallim V	to speak
itmakkin V	to be expert in, to be good at *(min)*
itmanna V	to wish, to hope
itmassik V	to follow something, to hold to (a method) *(bi)*

itmashsha V	to go for a walk
itrabba V	to be brought up
itsalla V	to have fun, be entertained
itṣarraf V	to behave, to manage something *(fī)*
itsharraf V	to be honoured by *(bi)*
fuṣḥa	standard Arabic
kurs, -āt	course (language)
lugha	language
manhag (manāhig)	method
maṣyaf (maṣāyif)	recreation site, seaside center
mudda	time, period
mufīd	useful, beneficient
mufrad, -āt	word, pl. vocabulary
muḥadsa	conversation
muhimm	important
mukassaf	intensive
mulaḥẓa	note, objection
mustawa, -yāt	level
mutashakkir	thanking
nāṭiq ʾaṣlī	native speaker
qāʿa	hall, audition hall
qism (ʾaqsām)	department
ṣaʿb	hard, difficult
ṣandūʾ (ṣanadīʾ)	box
ṣaḥḥa	health, correctness
shakl (ʾashkāl)	form, shape
sharṭ (shurūṭ)	condition
taʿbīr, -āt	expression
taʿlīmī	educating, educational
taqaddum	advance, rise
ṭarīʾa (ṭuruʾ)	way, method
ʾusra (ʾusar)	family
ẓarf (ẓurūf)	situation, conditions

V. Taʿbīrāt:

ʾAlf mabrūk!	Congratulations!
- ʾAllāh yibārik fīk!	(answer)
bi-shakl kbīr	very, profoundly
ʾEzzāy baʾa?	How can this be? How come?
fī baḥr ʾaddi ʾē(h)?	At what time?
yā tarā ...	Do you think?
maʿa baʿḍ (baʿḍina, baʿḍuku, baʿḍuhum)	one another, amongst

mithayyaʾ lī (lak, lik, lo, lhā, lna, lku, lhum)	it seems to me
Rabbina yiwaffaʾak!	Good luck! I cross my fingers for you!
ʿUmro ma kān (ma rāḥ)	He has never been (gone) to …

Mulaḥẓa:
If the noun ***ʿumr*** is used to express “never”, the negative particle ***sh*** of the negative form is omitted.

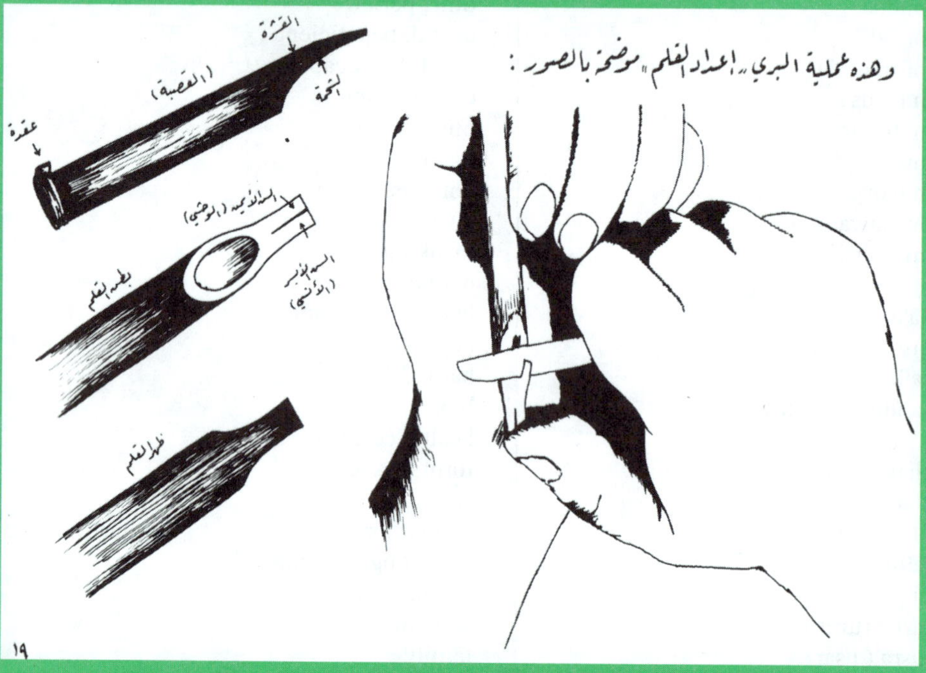

The making of an Arabic calligraphic pen

Iṣ-ṣafqa ʾt-tigārīya

Il-marra li gayya ibʿatū l(i)na ḥāga niftaḥ bihā ʾl-ʿilab.

So next time send us something with which we can open the boxes.

- Min faḍlak, il-bashmuhandis M(u)ḥammad maugūd?
- ʾĀ(h), ʾāʿid fi maktabo, itfaḍḍal, ḥaḍretak!
- ʾĒ(h) il-mufagʾa ʾg-gamīla di!
- ʾEzzayyak, yā bashmuhandis? ʾEzzay il-ʿēla?
- Il-ḥamdu liʾllāh, kullina kwayyisīn. Itfaḍḍal, tishrab ʾē(h)?
- Baʿd(i) shwayya. ʾAna lissa shārib fingān ʾahwa. ʾĒ(h) raʾyak fī ṣafqitna ʾg-gdīda? Mumkin nitnāʾish fīhā maʿa baʿḍ?
- Bi-ṣarāḥa, ʾana mabṣūṭ ʾawi ʾinn shirkitna bi-titʿāmil maʿa ʾsh-shirka btaʿitku. Baʾa lna ktīr bi-nitrāsil maʿa baʿḍ wi di ʾawwil marra bi-nitʾābil fīhā shakhṣīyan. Yalla bīna, ḥa-n(i)shūf iṣ-ṣafqa btaʿitna.
- Gamīl, ʾin shāʾ allāh ḥaḍretak mish ḥa-titḍāyīʾ min kalāmī, ʾaṣlan ʿāwiz ʾatnāʾish maʿāk fī kam mulaḥẓa.
- La, ʾabadan, da ḥaʾʾak, mish mumkin ʾatḍāyiʾ min ʾayyi mulaḥẓa mufīda tinfaʿ ʿamalna ʾl-mushtarak. Itfaḍḍal!
- ʾAna ṭabʿan mish ʿāwiz nitfāṣil fī ʾasʿār il-gulūd, maʿa ʾinnahā ghalya shwayya, bas ʿāwiz ʾatnāʾish maʿāk fī nauʿīyithā.
- ʾAhlan wa sahlan, yarēt tibʾū mutasāmiḥīn maʿāna, ʾeḥna shirka gdīda wi muntagātna ʾl-gildīya kullahā niz(i)lit is-sūʾ il-maḥallī min sanitēn.
- Zay mā ḥaḍretak ʿārif, ʾeḥna niʾdar nitfāhim maʿāku fī kull(i) ḥāga. Nifsina nitʿāwin maʿa shirkitku fī ṣināʿit ish-shunaṭ wi ʾl-gizam wi ʾl-ʾaḥzima ʾl-gildīya.
- Ṣaʿb nitnāzil ʿan ʾasʿār khāmitna, liʾinnahā gild ṭabīʿī mīya fi ʾl-mīya. ʿAla kull ḥāl ʾana muwāfiʾ ʿala takhfīḍ ʾasʿār il-muntagāt il-gahza.

- Ṭayyib wi ʾsh-shirka btaʿitku tiʾdar t(i)ṣaddar ʾaddi ʾē(h) min ʾintāghā kullo?
- ʾEḥna bi-nitʿāmil maʿa ʾs-sūʾ il-maḥallī wi ʾl-ʾkhārigī. Il-ʾawwalānī bi-yisāwī sittīn fi ʾl-mīya wi ʾt-tānī ʾarbaʿīn fi ʾl-mīya.
- Mithayyaʾ lī ḥatḥāyil ʿala ḥaḍretak, t(i)khallūna zbūnku ʾl-ʾagnabī ʾl-waḥīd.
- Mish lāzim titḥāyil ʿalayya, tigāritna maʿāku maṣlaḥitna zay mā hiya maṣlaḥitku. Iṣ-ṣafqa gahza. ʾAlf(i) mabrūk wi ʾashkurak giddan ʿala furṣit it-taʿāruf ig-gamīla!

I. ʾAsʾila:

1. Mīn ʿāwiz yitʾābil maʿa ʾl-bashmuhandis M(u)ḥammad?
2. Il-bashmuhandis M(u)ḥammad itḍāyiʾ min kalām zbūno?
3. Iz-zbūn ʿāwiz yitnāʾish maʿāh fī ʾē(h)?
4. Ish-shirka ʾl-ʾagnabīya ʿayza titʿāwin maʿa ʾsh-shirka ʾl-maṣrīya fī ʾanho magāl?
5. Ish-shirka ʾl-maṣrīya matiʾdarsh(i) titnāzil ʿan ʾasʿār khāmithā lē(h)?
6. Iz-zbūn ʿāwiz yitḥāyil ʿala ʾl-bashmuhandis M(u)ḥammad lē(h)?
7. Mīn mabsūṭ min taʿāmul ish-shirkitēn?
8. Iz-zbūn wi ʾl-bashmuhandis M(u)ḥammad yiʾdarū yitfāh(i)mū maʿa baʿḍ kwayyis?

II. Qawāʿid:

1. The 6th verbal stem

The meaning of the verbs of the 6th verbal stem:

a) reciprocity – verbs of the 6th verbal stem are derived from verbs of the 3rd verbal stem and take the preposition ***maʿa*** (with, together):
RāSiL – it-RāSiL (to exchange letters); *ʾāBiL – it-ʾāBiL* (to meet one another); *ʿāMiL – it-ʿāMiL* (to come to contact with, to cooperate with); *FāHiM – it-FāHiM* (to understand one another); *NāʾiSh – it-NāʾiSh* (to discuss with)

b) reflexive of the verbs of the 3rd verbal stem:
ḌāYiʾ – it-ḌāYiʾ (to annoy someone – to be annoyed, angry); *ʿāLiG – it-ʿāLiG* (to cure someone – to recover, cure oneself); *FāGiʾ – it-FāGiʾ* (to surprise someone – to be surprised, to surprise oneself); *SāWa – it-SāWa* (to equal something – to be equal, to equal one another)

c) gradual, incessant activity:
it-NāZiL (to give up something, to leave something); *it-ḤāYiL* (to insist on); *it-NāʾiSh* (to discuss something).

perfect:
it- RāSiL (to exchange letters with)
- the prefix ***it-*** is attached to verbs of the 3rd verbal stem
- the verbs of the 6th verbal stem thus follow the same paradigm as verbs of the 3rd verbal stem.

singular:

		negative:
3rd pers. m.	***it-RāSiL***	***ma-t-RāSiL-sh(i)***
3rd pers. f.	***it-RāS(i)L-it***	***ma-t-RāS(i)L-itsh(i)***
2nd pers. m.	***it-RāSiL-t***	***ma-t-RāSiL-tish***
2nd pers. f.	***it-RāSiL-ti***	***ma-t-RāSiL-tīsh***
1st pers.	***it-RāSiL-t***	***ma-t-RāSiL-tish***

plural:

		negative:
3rd pers.	***it-RāS(i)L-ū***	***ma-t-RāS(i)L-ūsh***
2nd pers.	***it-RāSiL-tū***	***ma-t-RāSiL-tūsh***
1st pers.	***it-RāSiL-na***	***ma-t-RāSiL-nāsh***

Imperfect
- the perfect verbal stem takes imperfect prefixes and suffixes:

singular:

		negative:
3rd pers. m.	***yi-t-RāSiL***	***ma yi-t-RāSiL-sh(i)***
3rd pers. f.	***ti-t-RāSiL***	***ma ti-t-RāSiL-sh(i)***
2nd pers. m.	***ti-t-RāSiL***	***ma ti-t-RāSiL-sh(i)***
2nd pers. f.	***ti-t-RāS(i)L-ī***	***ma ti-t-RāS(i)L-īsh***
1st pers.	***a-t-RāSiL***	***m a-t-RāSiL-sh(i)***

plural:

		negative:
3rd pers.	***yi-t-RāS(i)L-ū***	***ma yi-t-RāS(i)L-ūsh***
2nd pers.	***ti-t-RāS(i)L-ū***	***ma ti-t-RāS(i)L-ūsh***
1st pers.	***ni-t-RāSiL***	***ma ni-t-RāSiL-sh(i)***

Imperative: To form the imperative, the prefix ***t-*** is detached from the 2nd person imperfect forms: *itrāsil!* (m.), *itrās(i)lī!* (f.), *itrās(i)lū!* (pl.).
Negative imperative: *ma titrāsilshi!* (m.), *ma titrās(i)līsh!* (f.), *ma titrās(i)lūsh!* (pl.).

Active participle:
(Verbs of the 6th stem do not form the passive participle)
- the active participle is formed by means of the prefix ***mi- / mu-*** (in the case of words taken over from Standard Arabic context), followed by the perfect stem of the verb; the prefix ***mi- / mu-*** combines with the prefix ***it-*** into ***mit- / mut-***, as is the case of imperfect prefixes ***yit-***, ***tit-***, ***at-***, ***nit-***, and of the negative particle ***ma-*** > ***mat-***.

– **After the second consonant, the participle has the vowel *i***

mitRāSiL – exchanging letters (m. sg.), *mitRāS(i)La* (f. sg.), *mitRāS(i)Līn* (pl.); *mitFāHiM* – understanding one another; *mitNāZiL* – giving up something, leaving something; *mitʿāWiN* – cooperating with; *mitḤāYiL* – insisting; *mitDạYiʾ* – angry

– words taken over from the Standard Arabic context have the vowel ***-a-*** after the prefix ***mut-***: *mutaSāMiḤ* – tolerant.

Verbal noun:

– Verbal nouns are derived according to the following pattern: ***ta-SāMuḤ*** – tolerance; *ta-NāZuL* – compromise; *ta-FāHuM* – understanding; *ta-ʿāWuN* – cooperation

The 6th stem of verbs with the third consonant w or y:

– the perfect of these verbs follows the same paradigm as the verb ***SāWa*** (cf. Lesson 10), the imperfect follows the paradigm ***itSāWa*** (to equal together)

perfect singular:

		negative:
3rd pers. m.	***it-SāW-a***	***ma-t-SaW-āsh(i)***
3rd pers. f.	***it-SāW-it***	***ma-t-SaW-itsh(i)***
2nd pers. m.	***it-SaW-ēt***	***ma-t-SaW-ētsh(i)***
2nd pers. f.	***it-SaW-ēti***	***ma-t-SaW-ētīsh***
1st pers.	***it-SaW-ēt***	***ma-t-SaW-ētsh(i)***

plural:

		negative:
3rd pers.	***it-SaW-ū***	***ma-t-SaW-ūsh***
2nd pers.	***it-SaW-ētū***	***ma-t-SaW-ētūsh***
1st pers.	***it-SaW-ēna***	***ma-t-SaW-ēnāsh***

Imperfect singular:

		negative:
3rd pers. m.	***yi-t-SāW-a***	***ma yi-t-SāW-āsh(i)***
3rd pers. f.	***ti-t-SāW-a***	***ma ti-t-SāW-āsh(i)***
2nd pers. m.	***ti-t-SāW-a***	***ma ti-t-SāW-āsh(i)***
2nd pers. f.	***ti-t-SāW-ī***	***ma ti-t-SāW-īsh***
1st pers.	***a-t-SāW-a***	***m a-t-SāW-āsh(i)***

plural:

		negative:
3rd pers.	***yi-t-SāW-ū***	***ma yi-t-SāW-ūsh***
2nd pers.	***ti-t-SāW-ū***	***ma ti-t-SāW-ūsh***
1st pers.	***ni-t-SāW-a***	***ma ni-t-SāW-āsh(i)***

Imperative: *itsāwa!* (m.), *itsāwī!* (f.), *itsāwū!* (pl.).
Negative imperative: *ma titsāwāsh!* (m.), *ma titsāwīsh!* (f.), *ma titsāwūsh!* (pl.).

Factory halls in the city of 10th Ramadan (on the way from Cairo to Ismailiya)

Active participle: *mitSāWī* (m.) – equaling one other; *mitSāWīYa* (f.), *mitSāWīYīn* (pl.).
Passive participle: verbs of this group do not form the passive participle.

Verbal noun: ***ta-SāW-ī*** (equilibrium, agreement).

Other verbs following this paradigm: *it-ʿāLa*.

2. "kull"
The noun ***"kull"*** expresses ***"every", "entire, whole",*** and ***"all"***.

a) "**every**"
"kull" precedes the indefinite noun (and the vowel **"i"** is inserted between the two for easier pronunciation):
kull(i) kitāb – every book, *kull(i) bēt* – every house, *kull(i) sana* – every year, *kull(i) ḥāga* – everything, *kull(i) ʾakl* – every meal, *kull(i) shakhṣ* – every person, everyone, *kull(i) wāḥid* – every one = everyone.

b) "**entire**", "**whole**"
"kull" may precede the noun, which is determined
- by the article:
kull il-kitāb – the whole book, *kull il-bēt* – the whole house, *kull is-sana* – the whole year, *kull il-ʾakl* – the whole meal;
- or by the pronominal suffix:
(above all meaning "on all places", "over the entire surface"): *kull(i) wishshahā* – her entire face, *kull(i) ʾoḍtī* – my whole room).

Alternatively, "*kull*" follows the noun, which is determined by the article, pronominal suffix, or the second component of the genitival phrase; *"kull"* takes the pronominal suffix agreeing in number in gender with the preceding noun: *il-kitāb kullo / kitābī kullo / kitāb ʾustāzhum kullo* – the entire book / my entire book / the entire book of their professor; *il-bēt kullo / bēto kullo / bēt gārna kullo* – the whole house / his whole house / the whole book of our neighbour; *is-sana kullahā* – the whole year, *il-ʾakl kullo* – the whole meal.

c) "**all**"

"kull" either precedes or follows the plural noun, which is determined by the definite article, pronominal suffix, or the second component of the genitival phrase. When following the noun, *"kull"* takes the pronominal suffix agreeing with the noun it qualifies in number and gender.

- ***"kull"*** preceding the noun:

kull il-kutub – all books; *kull il-buyūt* – all houses; *kull is-sinīn* – all years; *kull il-ḥāgāt* – all things; *kull il-ʿummāl* – all workers; *kull iṣ-ṣuwar* – all pictures

kull(i) buyūto – all his houses; *kull(i) buyūto* – all his houses; *kull(i) kutubī* – all my books; *kull(i) buyūto* – all his houses; *kull(i) sinīnhā* – all her years; *kull(i) ʿummālna* – all our workers; *kull(i) ṣuwarku* – all your photographs

kull(i) kutub ʾabūya – all books of my father; *kull(i) buyūt il-madīna* – all houses of the city; *kull(i) sinīn ḥayātak* – all years of your life; *kull(i) ʿummāl il-biʿsa* – all workers of the expedition; *kull(i) ṣuwar il-mausūʿa* – all pictures of the encyclopedia

-***"kull"*** following the noun:

il-kutub kullahā / kutubī kullahā / kutub ʾabūya kullahā – all books / all my books / all the books of my father; *il-buyūt kullahā / buyūto kullahā / buyūt il-madīna kullahā* – all houses / all his house / all the houses of the city; *is-sinīn kullahā / sinīnhā kullahā / sinīn ḥayātak kullahā* – all years / all her years / all the years of your life; *il-ʿummāl kulluhum / ʿummālna kulluhum / ʿummāl biʿsitna kulluhum* – all workers / all our workers / all the workers of our expedition; *iṣ-ṣuwar kullahā / ṣuwarku kullahā / ṣuwar il-mausūʿa kullahā* – all pictures / all your pictures / all the books of the encyclopedia.

III. Tadrībāt:

Targama

All our students exchange letters with their friends in Egypt. May I discuss this problem with you? I think that she is not angry with them because of these comments. Were you not surprised by our visit? We wanted to surprise you. He will be recovering in this hospital for the whole month. Who treated you? They want to bargain the prices of all industrial products with you. She never changed her opinion. Everyone can confirm to you that the cooperation with foreign producers is very successful. Do you (polite) think that they will be able to meet the representative of the company tomorrow? Why do I have to insist that you explain to me what happened? All this vocabulary will help you (f.) communicate (understand one another) with the participants of the conference. He told me that he insisted that they be tolerant to these views. They wrote to us that they are satisfied with the cooperation of their faculty with our institute. This trade agreement is not identical with the preceding agreement. He thinks that this restaurant is able to compete with all other restaurants. I'll bet you (m.) that he'll soon bring us good news. He always competes with his classmates. They do not like their neighbours, because they are boastful.

Kammil!

1. Ish-shirka btaʿitku bi- ... (tiʿāmil x titʿāmil) maʿa ʾanhi sharikāt ʾagnabīya?
2. Mumkin ... (niʾābil x nitʾābil) maʿāku bukra yā baʿdo?
3. Tiḥibbī ... (ʾarāhin x ʾatrāhin) maʿāki?
4. Kānū bi- ... (yiḥāyilū x yitḥāyilū) ʿalēna ʿashān niṭlaʿ maʿāhum ir-riḥla li ʾl-gibāl.
5. Bi ... (tināfis x titnāfis) maʿa zamīlāthā fi ʾd-dirāsa.
6. Ḥa ... (niḥāsib x nitḥāsib) ʾemta?
7. ʾAna khāyif ʾinnuku ḥa ... (tiḍāy[i]ʾū x titḍāy[i]ʾū) min kalāmī.
8. Min faḍlak, ma (tifāṣilsh[i] x titfāṣilsh[i]) maʿāya fi ʾl-mauḍūʿ da!
9. Kunt bi- ... (tiʿālig x titʿālig) ʿand ʾanho ṭabīb?
10. ... (fāgiʾtū x itfāgiʾtū) bi ʾs-suʾāl da lē(h)?

Ḥa-niftaḥ il-mazād bi 200 000 dōlār. Da timsāl ʾaʿma! ʾUmmāl lau kān bi-yishūf?

The upset price is 200 000 dollars. And the statue is blind! Imagine it could see!

IV. Mufradāt

āmal (ʾaʿmāl)	work
ʿāmilīn	workers, employees
biʿsa	expedition, mission
ʿēla	family (closest family circle)
fāgiʾ III	to surprise someone
fāṣil III	to bargain with (without preposition)
fingān (fanagīn)	cup, mug
gabal (gibāl)	mountain
ghālī	expensive, dear, costly
gild (gulūd)	leather, skin
gildī	leather (adjective)
ḥayā	life
ḥaʾʾ (ḥuʾūʾ)	law
ḥāsib III	to settle (financially) with someone (without preposition)
ḥizām (ʾaḥzima)	waist, belt
khāma	material
ʾintāg	production
itʾābil VI	to meet someone *(maʿa)*
itʿāla VI	to boast *(ʿala)*
itʿālig VI	to be treated, cured
itʿāmil VI	to cooperate, to be in contact with *(maʿa)*
itʿāwin VI	to cooperate with *(maʿa)*
itḍāyiʾVI	to be angry with someone; because of *(min)*
itfāgiʾ VI	to be surprised by *(bi)*
itfāhim VI	to understand one another *(maʿa)*
itfāṣil VI	to bargain with someone *(maʿa)* about *(fī)*
itḥāyil VI	to insist on someone *(ʿala)*
itḥāsib VI	to settle (financially) with someone, to balance accounts with *(maʿa)*
itnāfis VI	to compete with *(maʿa)*
itnāʾish VI	to discuss with sb. *(maʿa)* about something *(fī)*
itnāzil VI	to give up something, to refrain from something *(ʿan)*
itrāhin VI	to bet with *(maʿa)* *(ʿala)*
itrāsil VI	to exchange letters with *(maʿa)*
itsābiʾ VI	to compete with *(maʿa)*
itsāwa VI	to equal one another *(maʿa)*
kam	how many, some, a few
kull	every, any, all, entire, whole
maʿa ʾinn	although, despite
magāl , -āt	area, sphere, field (abstract)
maḥallī	local

maṣlaḥa (maṣāliḥ)	use, benefit; administration
mausūʿa	encyclopaedia
mufagʾa	surprise
muntig, -īn	producer
mustashfa, -yāt	hospital
mushtarak	common
mushtarik, -īn	participant
muʾtamar, -āt	conference, congress
mutasāmiḥ	tolerant to *(maʿa)*
nāfis III	to be a competition for sb., to compete with sb. (without preposition)
nāgiḥ	successful
nauʿīya	kind, sort, type
rāhin III	to bet with (without preposition)
sābiʾ	preceding
sābiʾ III	to compete with (without preposition)
ṣaddar II	to export
ṣafqa (ṣafqāt)	agreement (trade)
ṣināʿa	production, industry
ṣināʿī	industrial
shakhṣ (ʾashkhāṣ)	person
shakhṣīyan	personally
taʿāmul	cooperation, contact
taʿāruf	meeting (one another), getting to know one another
taʿāwun	cooperation
ṭabīʿī	natural
tafāhum	(mutual) understanding
takhfīḍ	discount
tanāzul, -āt	compromise
tasāmuḥ	tolerance
tigārī	commercial
ʿummāl	workers (manual)
waḥīd	one, unique, the only

V. Taʿbīrāt:

ʾAhlan wa sahlan!	Welcome! Please, with pleasure!
ʿala kull(i) ḥāl	in every case
ʾawwil marra	for the first time
il-bashmuhandis	Mr. engineer
Da ḥaʾʾak!	It's your right!
Yalla bīna!	Let's go!
kull(i) ḥagtī / ḥagtī kullahā	all my things
Maṣlaḥt il-ʾāsār	Antiquities administration

ʿAnd iṭ-ṭabīb

- Itfaḍḍal il-ʾustāz, id-dōr ʿala ḥaḍretak! Ismak il-karīm yinkitib keda bi ʾl-ʾinglīzī?
- Maẓbūṭ. Maʿalesh, yā doktor, ʾana ʾāsif ʾinnī ḥatʿab ḥaḍretak maʿāya, lākin ʿandī shwayyit mashākil ṣiḥḥīya.
- Matitkisifsh(i) wi ʾul lī ʿala kull(i) ḥāga bi-ṣarāḥa.
- ʾAṣlan itʿazamt ʿala walīma ma haṣalitsh(i) wi hnāk itḥaṭṭit ʾuddāmī ʾaḥla ʾl-ʾashkāl wi ʾl-ʾalwān! ʾAḥsan ʾakl kalto fī ḥayātī. Shibiʿt ʾawi, bas ṣaḥbit il-bēt ʾālit ʾinn il-ʾakl mish ḥa-yitshāl li-ghāyit ma yikhlaṣ. Fagʾa ḥassēt ʾinn(i) nifsī itsaddit ... tiʿibt.

Itfaḍḍalī, iʾlaʿī yā madām, matitkis(i)fīsh, da ʾana ṭabīb il-ʿēla.

Please, madam, take off your clothes. Don't be shy, I am your family physician.

- Khēr, in shāʾ allāh, ḥakshif ʿalēk. Min faḍlak, iʾlaʿ ʾamīṣak, ʿashān ʾaṭṭammin ʿala baṭnak!
- Wi ʾḍ-ḍaghṭ lāzim yitʾās barḍo?
- ʾAḍman ... ir-roshetta bitaʿ(i)t ḥaḍretak!
- Id-dawa da yitgāb min ʾayyi ṣaydalīya?
- Ṭabʿan, ʿala fikra ʾaʾrab ṣaydalīya min hena ʾuṣād ʿayyadtī ganb(i) studiyo ʾt-taṣwīr.
- Ṭayyib, ḥaḍretak mish mumkin tifahhimnī, id-dawa da ḥakhdo ʾezzāy?
- Fī ʾaʿshāb ṭibbīya yitʿimil minhā mashrūb wi ʾl-mashrūb da yitshirib baʿd il-ʾakl. Il-ʾaʾrāṣ lāzim titbiliʿ ʾabl in-nōm wi ʾl-ḥabbāyāt di ʾafḍal dawa li ʾl-maghaṣ.
- ʾAna mish ʿāwiz ʾaʿaṭṭal ḥaḍretak, bas fī ḥāga kamān, riglī ʾl-yimīn warma khāliṣ, baʾa lhā keda ʾusbūʿ. ʾAṣlan ʾaktar riyāḍa baḥibbahā ʾl-kura wi di ʾn-natīga.

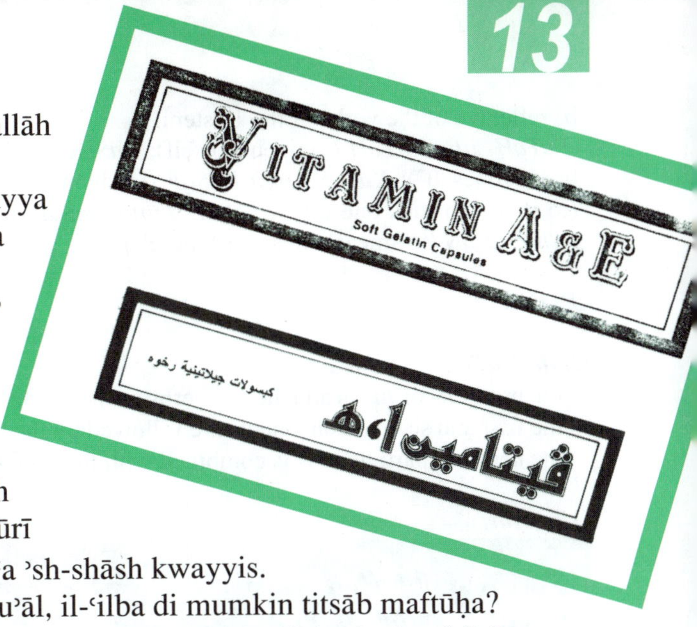

- ʾAlf salāma ʿalēk! In shāʾ allāh ḥāga basīṭa. Riglak lāzim titghisil kull(i) yōm bi ʾl-mayya wi ʾl-bābung wi baʿd(i) keda titdihin bi ʾl-marham da.
- Wi ʾsh-shāsh da yitribiṭ fōʾ il-mifṣal walla fōʾ mishṭ ir-rigl?
- Yarēt yitribiṭ fōʾ il-itnēn, lākin mish lāzim yitḥaṭṭ kullo, ʿashān da ʾaṭwal shāsh laʾēto fī dōlāb ʿayyadtī. Ḍarūrī yitlizīʾ bi-lāziʾ ṭibbī yimsik ʿa ʾsh-shāsh kwayyis.
- Maʿalesh ḥaḍretak, ʿandī suʾāl, il-ʿilba di mumkin titsāb maftūḥa?
- Khud bālak, da fītāmīn fawwār wi ʿashān keda ʿilbito lāzim titfitiḥ wi titʾifil ʿala ṭūl.
- ʾAna mutashakkir ʾawi, yā doktor, mamnūn lak khāliṣ.
- Il-ʿafw(u)! Matinsāsh ḥaḍretak, ir-roshetta matitrimīsh, ḥattā baʿdi mayitṣirif lak id-dawa fi ʾṣ-ṣaydalīya!

I. ʾAsʾila:

1. Il-marīḍ bi-yitkisif ʾuddām iṭ-ṭabīb lē(h)?
2. Mīn ʾāl ʾinn il-ʾakl mish ḥa-yitshāl li-ghāyit ma yikhlaṣ?
3. Id-dawa fi ʾr-roshetta bi-yitgāb ʾezzāy?
4. Id-dawa ʾsh-shurb bi-yitʿimil ʾezzāy wi yitshirib ʾemta?
5. ʾĒ(h) huwa ʾafḍal dawa li ʾl-maghaṣ?
6. ʾĒ(h) hiya ʾaktar riyāḍa bi-yiḥibbahā ʾl-marīḍ?
7. Riglo lāzim titghisil fi ʾl-mayya wi ʾl-yānsūn?
8. Ish-shāsh lāzim yitribiṭ foʾ ir-rukba?
9. Il-ʿilba mish mumkin titsāb maftūḥa lē(h)?
10. Ir-roshetta mafrūḍ ma titrimīsh lē(h)?

II. Qawāʿid:

1. The 7th verbal stem

The meaning of the verbs of the 7th verbal stem:

a) passive of the verbs of the 1st stem:

KaTaB – it/in-KaTaB (to be written); *ʿaZaM- it/in-ʿaZaM* (to be invited); *ʿaMaL – it/in-ʿaMaL* (to be done); *BaʿaT – it/in-BaʿaT* (to be sent); *ShāL – it/in-ShāL* (to be brought away); *ḤaṬṬ – it/in-ḤaṬṬ* (to be put/laid); *RaMa – it-RaMa* (to be thrown away)

b) reflexive of the verbs of the 1st stem:

FaTaḤ- it/in-FaTaḤ (to open oneself); *KaSaR – in/it-KaSaR* (to break something – to break [oneself]); *KaSaF– in/it-KaSaF* (to shame – to be ashamed); *LaZa'- in/it-LaZa'* (to stick – to stick oneself); *GhaSaL- in/it-GhaSaL* (to wash oneself); *DaHaN – in/it-DaHaN* (to smear – to smear oneself).

Perfect:

in/it- KaTaB (to be written)

- the prefix ***it-*** or ***in-*** is attached to verbs of the 1st verbal stem
- the first and second consonants are followed by the vowel ***a***
- the negative particle ***ma-*** is combined with the prefix ***it- / in-*** to ***mat- / man-***

singular:

		negative:
3rd pers. m.	***it-KaTaB***	***ma-t-KaTaB-sh(i)***
3rd pers. f.	***it-KaTaB-it***	***ma-t-KaTaB-itsh(i)***
2nd pers. m.	***it-KaTaB-t***	***ma-t-KaTaB-tish***
2nd pers. f.	***it-KaTaB-ti***	***ma-t-KaTaB-tīsh***
1st pers.	***it-KaTaB-t***	***ma-t-KaTaB-tish***

plural:

		negative:
3rd pers.	***it-KaTaB-ū***	***ma-t-KaTaB-ūsh***
2nd pers.	***it-KaTaB-tū***	***ma-t-KaTaB-tūsh***
1st pers.	***it-KaTaB-na***	***ma-t-KaTaB-nāsh***

Imperfect

- the perfect verbal stem takes imperfect prefixes and suffixes
- the first and second consonant is followed by the vowel ***i***
- imperfect prefixes combine with the prefix ***it- / in-*** to form ***yit-, tit-, at-, nit-***

singular:

		negative:
3rd pers. m.	***yi-t-KiTiB***	***ma yi-t-KiTiB-sh(i)***
3rd pers. f.	***ti-t-KiTiB***	***ma ti-t-KiTiB-sh(i)***
2nd pers. m.	***ti-t-KiTiB***	***ma ti-t-KiTiB-sh(i)***
2nd pers. f.	***ti-t-KiTiB-ī***	***ma ti-tKiTiB-īsh***
1st pers.	***a-t-KiTiB***	***m a-t-KiTiB-sh(i)***

plural:

		negative:
3rd pers.	***yi-t-KiTiB-ū***	***ma yi-t-KiTiB-ūsh***
2nd pers.	***ti-t-KiTiB-ū***	***ma ti-t-KiTiB-ūsh***
1st pers.	***ni-t-KiTiB***	***ma ni-t-KiTiB-sh(i)***

Imperative:
- there is no imperative of these verbs; theoretically it would take the following forms: *itkitib!* (m.), *itkit(i)bī!* (f.), *itkit(i)bū!* (pl.).

Active and passive participles:
- Verbs of the 7th stem do not form participles

Verbal noun:
- Verbal nouns are derived according to the following pattern: ***in-KiSāR*** – breaking oneself; *in-FiTāḤ* – opening oneself

The 7th stem of verbs with the second consonant w or y:
- these verbs follow the paradigm of the verb ***it-ShāL (yi-t-ShāL)***:
perfect: *it-ShāL, it-ShāL-it, it-ShaL-t, it-ShaL-ti, it-ShaL-t, it-ShāL-ū, it-ShaL-tū, it-ShaL-na*
imperfect: *yi-t-ShāL, ti-t-ShāL, ti-t-ShāL, ti-t-ShāL-ī, a-t-ShāL, yi-t-ShāL-ū, ti-t-ShāL-ū, ni-t-ShāL*
Passive participle: *mitShāL* (m.) – brought away, disposed of; *mitShāLa* (f.), *mitShāLīn* (pl.).
Verbal noun: no verbal nouns are derived from these verbs

7th stem of verbs with identical second and third consonants:
- *it-ḤaṬṬ, it-ḤaṬṬ-it, it-ḤaṬṬ-ēt, it-ḤaṬṬ-ēti, it-ḤaṬṬ-ēt, it-ḤaṬṬ-ū, it-ḤaṬṬ-ētū, it-ḤaṬṬ-ēna*
- *yi-t-ḤaṬṬ, ti-t-ḤaṬṬ, ti-t-ḤaṬṬ, ti-t-ḤaṬṬ-ī, a-t-ḤaṬṬ, yi-t-ḤaṬṬ-ū, ti-t-ḤaṬṬ-ū, ni-t-ḤaṬṬ*

The 7th stem of verbs with the third consonant w or y:
- these verbs follow the paradigm of the verb ***it-RaMa (yi-t-RiMi)***:
perfect: *it-RaMa, it-RaM-it, it-RaM-ēti, it-RaM-ēt, it-RaM-ū, it-RaM-ētū, it-RaM-ēna*
imperfect: *yi-t-RiM-i, ti-t-RiM-i, ti-t-RiM-i, ti-t-RiM-ī, a-t-RiM-i, yi-t-RiM-ū, ti-t-RiM-ū, ni-t-RiM-i*
Passive participle: these verbs do not form the passive participle
Verbal noun: no verbal nouns are derived from these verbs

2. Comparative and Superlative of Adjectives
- for both the comparative and the superlative, the so-called ***elative*** form of the adjective is used. The elative does not change with number and gender. The elative is formed according to the following principle: the prefix "a" precedes, between the first and the second consonant there is no vowel, between the second and the third there is "a". Adjectives with **w** or **y** as their third consonant – **w** or **y** merges with the preceding "a" = ***ā***:
KBīR – ʾaKBaR; GaMīL – ʾaGMaL; KTīR – ʾaKTaR; ṬWīL – ʾaṬWaL, ḤaSaN –ʾ aḤSaN, ṢGhaYYaR – ʾaṢGhaR, SaHL – ʾaSHaL, BaSīṬ – ʾaBSaṬ, RKhīṢ – ʾaRKhaṢ, KaRīM – ʾaKRaM, LaṬīF – ʾaLṬaF, ḤaDīS – ʾaḤDaS, WāḌiḤ – ʾaWḌaḤ, WiḤiSh – ʾaWḤaSh, Ṣaʿ aB – ʾaṢʿaB, GhāLī – ʾaGhLā, ʿāLī – ʾaʿLā, ʾuLaYYiL – ʾaʾaLL

The comparative

- the elative follows the noun: *bēt ʾaGMaL* (a nicer house); *matḥaf ʾakbar* (a bigger museum); *ʾōda ʾaṣghar* (a smaller room); *riḥla ʾaṭwal* (a longer road); *ṭalaba ʾaḥsan* (better students)

- the preposition ***min*** "than" is used to introduce the compared object: *il-bēt da ʾaGMaL min bēto* (this house is nicer than his house); *ʾenta ʾaṭwal minnī* (you are taller than I am); *tazkartik ʾarkhaṣ min it-tazkara btaʿithā* (your ticket is cheaper than her ticket); *ṭalabit kullīyitku ʾaṣghar min iṭ-ṭalaba b(i)tūʿna* (the students of your faculty are younger than our students)

- the comparative of the participles of extended verbal stems is formed by the participle followed by the elative, eg. *ʾaktar, ʾaḥsan, ʾaʾall: huwa mutasāmiḥ ʾaktar minhum* (he is more tolerant than they are); *hiya mitrabbīya ʾaḥsan min ʾikhwāthā* (she is more – better – brought up than her brothers and sisters); *humma mitdarrabīn ʾaʾall min zamāyilhum* (they are less well-trained than their colleagues).

- The comparative is also formed by means of the preposition ***ʿan*** (meaning "than"), followed by the compared object or the pronominal suffix, the basic form of the adjective is used instead of the elative:
ʾenta kbīr ʿan ʾakhūk (you are older than your brother); *huwa mutasāmiḥ ʿan zamaylo* (he is more tolerant than his colleagues); *hiya mitrabbīya ʿanhum* (she is better brought up than they); the preposition ***ʿan*** expresses an increase in quality or quantity.

The superlative

- the elative precedes the noun, which is

a) not determined and in the singular: *ʾagmal bēt* (the nicest house); *ʾakbar matḥaf* (the biggest museum); *ʾaṣghar ʾōda* (the smallest room); *ʾaṭwal riḥla* (the longest road)

b) determined and in the plural: *ʾakbar il-matāḥif* / *ʾakbarhā** (the biggest museum – the biggest of the museums – the biggest of them); *ʾagmal mudun Maṣr* / *ʾagmal il-mudun il-maṣrīya* / *agmal mudunhā* / *ʾagmalhā* (the most beautiful Egyptian town – the most beautiful of the Egyptian towns / its most beautiful town / the most beautiful of them)
- the superlative of the participles of extended verbal stems is formed by the elative preceding the numeral *wāḥid* / *waḥda,* followed by the participle: *huwa ʾaktar wāḥid mutasāmiḥ fīhum* (he is the most tolerant of them); *hiya ʾaḥsan waḥda mitrabbīya fī ʾikhwāthā* (she is the best brought up of her brothers and sisters); if the compared object is in the plural form, the verbal noun following the preposition ***fī*** is used instead of the participle: *humma ʾaʾalluhum fi ʾt-tadrīb* (they are the least trained of them).

3. The verb "*KhaD*" (to take)
perfect:

	singular:	negative:	plural:	negative:
3rd pers. m.	***KhaD***	***ma KhaD-sh(i)***	***KhaD-ū***	***ma KhaD-ūsh***
3rd pers. f.	***KhaD-it***	***ma KhaD-itsh(i)***		
2nd pers. m.	***KhaD-t***	***ma KhaD-tish***	***KhaD-tū***	***ma KhaD-tūsh***
2nd pers. f.	***KhaD-ti***	***ma KhaD-tīsh***		
1st pers.	***KhaD-t***	***ma KhaD-tish***	***KhaD-na***	***ma KhaD-nāsh***

* *-hā = matāḥif*

Imperfect:

	singular:	negative:	plural:	negative:
3rd pers. m.	***yā-KhuD***	***ma yā-KhuD-sh(i)***	***ya-KhD-ū***	***ma ya-KhD-ūsh***
3rd pers. f.	***tā-KhuD***	***ma tā-KhuD-sh(i)***		
2nd pers. m.	***tā-KhuD***	***ma tā-KhuD-sh(i)***	***ta-KhD-ū***	***ma ta-KhD-ūsh***
2nd pers. f.	***ta- KhD-ī***	***ma ta-KhD-īsh***		
1st pers.	***ā-KhuD***	***mā-KhuD-sh(i)***	***nā-KhuD***	***ma nā-KhuD-sh(i)***

Imperative: *khud!* (m.), *khudī!* (f.), *khudū!* (pl.).
Negative imperative: *ma tākhudsh(i)!* (m.), *ma takhdīsh!* (f.), *ma takhdūsh!* (pl.).
Active participle: *WāKhiD* (2nd person m. singular) – taking, *WaKhDa* (2nd person f. singular), *WaKhDīN* (2nd person pl.)
Passive participle: these verbs do not form the passive participle.

- The verb ***KaL*** "to eat" follows the same pattern.

III. Tadrībāt:

Targama

Your name was written in the Latin script? This drink must be drunk with sugar. Can something break here? The dough is made of flour, water and yeast. Was the fruit washed properly? This is the best way. This cheese is more tasty, because it wasn't stored out of the fridge for a long time. I think that it is necessary to paint this wall quickly. He told her, that old medicines should not be thrown away. Liquorice tablets must be swallowed on an empty stomach. Camomile balm must be stored in a cool place. The sand must be taken away in a truck. Can rewards be paid to them? When the patient's temperature becomes very high, ice should be placed on his head. It isn't necessary to fear this illness. To discover the real cause, an expert should see you. Can you tell us, how you spent your time? (with what did you busy yourself?) All these letters must be sent in the shortest possible time. These things must be acquired as soon as possible (at the nearest occasion).

Kammil!

a) tithạṭṭ, b) itkasaf c) yitsadd d) mayitkiwīsh e) yitkhitim f) mabiyitʾirīsh g) yitʿimil h) yitsimiʿ i) titbāʿ i) titgāb

1 ... yiʾūl lina ʿala ʾl mushkila di. 2. Il-maʿāgim di mumkin ... min wusṭ il-balad. 3. Ig-gawāb lāzim ... khitm il-gumhurīya. 4. ʾAḥla fakha ... fi ʾas-sūʾ ʾurayyib mi ʾl-kullīya. 5. Il-ʾaghiza di lāzim ... makān bārid. 6. ʾUlt(e) lhum ʾinn il-khurm da mafrūḍ ... 7. Wāḍiḥ ʾinn in-naṣṣ da ... bi-suhūla. 8. Matinsīsh, il-banṭalōn da ... 9. Fī ṣōt gamīl ... hena kull(i) yōm. 10. Ḥaḍretak khāyif ʾinn ish-shugl da mish ḥa- ... , ṣaḥḥ?

IV. Mufradāt

ʾafḍal	better, the best (elative)
ʿagīna (ʿagāyin)	dough
ʾahamm	more important, the most important (elative)
ʾaḥsan	better, the best (elative)
ʾakhiṣṣāʾī	specialist, expert physician
ʿayyāda	surgery
ʿarabīyt in-naʾl	truck, lorry
ʿarʾisūs	liquorice
ʾāsif	sorry
bābung	camomille
baʿdi ma	after
banṭalōn, -āt	trousers
bārid	cool, cold
basīṭ (busaṭa)	simple, common
bīr (ʾābār)	well, shaft
ḍaghṭ (ḍughūṭ)	pressure
dahan (i)	to smear
ḍaman (a)	to guarantee
dawa (ʾadwiya)	medicine
dawa shurb	syrup
diʾīʾ	flour
dinya/dunya	the world
fagʾa	suddenly
fawwār	effervescent
fītāmīn, -āt	vitamin
ḥabbāya	pill
ḥaʾīʾī	real
ḥarāra	temperature
ḥattā	even
ḥawāfiz	reward (financial), bonus
ḥēṭa (ḥīṭān)	wall
khad (jākhud)	to take
Khafraʿ	Khephren
khamīra	yeast
khatam (i)	to seal, to stamp
khitm (ʾakhtām)	stamp, seal
Khūfū	Khufu (Greek Kheops)
khurm (khurūm)	hole
ʾikhwāt	siblings
ʿilba (ʿilab)	box, chest
ʾismant	cement
itʾafal VII	to close oneself
itʿamal VII	to be made

it'ara' VII	to be read
itʿaraf VII	to be known (get known)
it'ās VII	to be measured
itʿazam VII	to be invited
itbaʿat VII	to be sent
itbalaʿ VII	to be swallowed
itbana VII	to be built
itdahan VII	to be smeared
itfataḥ VII	to open oneself
itgāb VII	to be acquired
itghasal VII	to wash oneself, to be washed
itḥasha VII	to be filled
itḥaṭṭ VII	to be put, placed
itkhatam VII	to be stamped, sealed
itkasaf VII	to be ashamed
itkasar VII	to break (oneself)
itkatab VII	to be written
itkawa VII	to be ironed
itlaza' VII	to stick to something
itrabaṭ VII	to be bandaged
itrakan VII	to be put aside
itrama VII	to be thrown away
itsāb VII	to be left, to be left behind
itsadd VII	to be stuffed, jammed, blocked
itsamaʿ VII	to be heard
itṣaraf VII	to be paid
itshaghal VII	to be employed, busy
itshāl VII	to be brought away, taken away, removed
itsharab VII	to be drunk (of a drink)
yimīn	right
kal (yākul)	to eat
kamān	also, further, too
karīm (kirām/kurama)	generous, honoured, respected
kashaf (i)	to look at, to diagnose someone *(ʿala)*
kura (kuwar)	ball, football
lātīnī	Latin
lazaʿ (a)	to stick, to stick to, to stick on
lāzi', -āt	bandage
mafrūḍ	it is necessary
maghaṣ	stomach, belly pain
maghrib	sunset
il-Maghrib	Morocco
mamnūn	grateful
manẓar (manāẓir)	view, scenery
maraḍ ('amrāḍ)	illness, sickness

marham (marāhim)	ointment
marīḍ (marḍa)	patient, sick one
Menkaraʿ	Menkaura (Greek Mycerinus)
mifṣal (mafāṣil)	joint
mishṭ (ʾamshāṭ)	comb
mishṭ(i) rigl	tarsus, toe
mōsim (mawāsim)	season
naṣṣ (nuṣūṣ)	text
natīga (natāyig)	result
nḍīf (nuḍāf)	pure
ʾalaʿ (a)	to undress, to take off
ʾulayyil, -īn	small

For the Medical Profession Only

EEEEEEEEEEEEEEEEEEEEEEEE EIPICO E

CONTA - FLU

Tablets

Anticatarrhal

Composition:

Each tablet contains:

Phenylpropanolamine hydrochloride	24 mg
Chlorpheniramine maleate	3 mg
Propyphenazone	200 mg

Action:

Conta - flu is a judicious combination of components which ensure a prompt relief from common cold. Phenylpropanolamine hydrochloride is a sympathomimetic amine which has an ephedrine like decongestant action with a negligible stimulating effect on the central nervous system. Chlorpheniramine maleate is a highly potent antihistaminic agent with a rapid onset of action. It is well tolerated and generally causes less sedation than other antihistaminics. Propyphenazone is a safe highly effective analgesic and antipyretic.

Indications:

Conta-flu is effective in the symptomatic relief of upper respiratory congestion, common cold, allergic rhinitis, acute rhinitis, rhinosinusitis, and Eustachian tube congestion.
If used early, it may abort such affections.

Precautions:

Although the dose of phenylpropanolamine is small, **Conta - flu** should be used with care in patients with hypertension, coronary insufficiency, hyperthyroidism and diabetes mellitus.
Avoid use of **Conta-flu** in conjunction with antihypertensives, antidepressants with monoaminooxidase inhibitor action or other medications containing sympathomimetic drugs.

Dosage:

1 tablet 3 times daily or as directed by the physician.

Packing:

2 Blisters of 10 tablets each. Keep out of reach of children.

E.I.P.I. CO.
EGYPTIAN INTERNATIONAL PHARMACEUTICAL INDUSTRIES CO.
TENTH OF RAMADAN CITY A. R. E.

للمهن الطبية فقط

EEEEEEEEEEEEEEEEEEEEEEEE ايبيكو E

كونتا ـ فلو

أقراص

لعلاج الزكام ونزلات البرد

بيان التركيب :

كل قرص يحتوى على :

ايدروكلوريد فينيل بروبانولامين	٢٤ مجم
ماليات الكلورفينيرامين	٣ مجم
بروبيفينازون	٢٠٠ مجم

الأثر الطبى :

كونتا ـ فلو مستحضر متميز مكوناته تضمن الشفاء العاجل لنزلات البرد . فمادة ايدروكلوريد فينيل بروبانولامين مركب امينى مقلد للعصب السمبثاوى ذو تأثير يماثل الأفيدرين كمزيل للاحتقان أما تأثيره على الجهاز العصبى المركزى فيمكن اهماله .
أما ماليات الكلورفينيرامين فهو مادة مضادة للهستامين قوية المفعول ويبدأ أثرها سريعاً كما أنه حسن التحمل وأقل مضادات الهستامين فى الأثر المسكن .
ومادة بروبيفينازون مضادة للألم وخافضة للحرارة وهى ذات تأثير قوى وآمن .

دواعى الاستعمال :

كونتا ـ فلو مستحضر فعال في علاج احتقان الجزء العلوى من الجهاز التنفسى وحالات الإصابة بالبرد ، التهاب الأنف بسبب الحساسية ، التهاب الأنف الحاد ، التهاب الأنف والجيوب الأنفية ، احتقان قناة استاكيوس وإذا استخدم مبكراً فقد ينهى مثل هذه الحالات .

الاحتياطات :

برغم صغر جرعة مادة أيدروكلوريد فينيل بروبانولامين لابد ان يستخدم **كونتا ـ فلو** بحرص فى المرضى ذوى ضغط الدم العالى والذين يعانون من القصور التاجى او فرط افراز الغدة الدرقية وارتفاع نسبة السكر فى الدم . ولا يستعمل **كونتا ـ فلو** فى ان واحد مع مضادات ضغط الدم العالى او مضادات الاكتئاب ذات الأثر المثبط لانزيم أحادىأمينوأوكسيديز أو الأدوية التى تحتوى على عقاقير مقلدة للعصب السمبثاوى .

الجرعة :

قرص واحد ثلاث مرات يومياً . أو حسب ارشادات الطبيب .

العبوة :

٢ شريط بكل ١٠ أقراص . يحفظ بعيداً عن متناول الأطفال .

ايبيكو
الشركة المصرية الدولية للصناعات الدوائية
مدينة العاشر من رمضان ـ ج . م . ع

Example of an information leaflet of Conta Flu, a commonly accessible remedy against flu and cold

ʾurṣ (ʾaʾrāṣ)	pill
raml (rimāl)	sand
riyāḍa	sport
roshetta	recipe
rukba (rukab)	knee
sabab (ʾasbāb)	reason, cause
sahl	easy, simple
ṣaydalīya	pharmacy
ṣiḥḥī	medical
studiyo ʾt-taṣwīr	photographic studio
sūr (ʾaswār)	wall, fence
shāsh	bandage
shibiʿ (a)	to be full, to eat to the full
shimāl	left
taʿab (a)	to make someone tired, to bother someone
takhaṣṣuṣ, -āt	field, specialisation
talg	snow, ice
ṭibbī	medical
tiʿib (a)	to get tired, to be tired
ṭūb	bricks
ʿushb (ʾaʿshāb)	plant
ʿushb ṭibbí	herb
wāḍiḥ	lear, evident
walīma (walāyim)	feast
wārim	swollen
wiḥish	bad, ugly

V. Taʿbīrāt:

ʾAḍman.	This will be more certain.
Il-ʿafw(u).	Please. Nothing happened. Not at all.
ʾaḥla ʾl-ʾashkāl wi ʾl-ʾalwān	The best kinds, to one's heart content.
ʾAlf salāma ʿalēk! (ʿalēki, ʿalēku...)	Get better soon! Good health!
- ʾAllāh yisallimak (yisallimik, yisallimku)	answer to the preceding sentence
ʾAna ʾāsif.	I am sorry.
ʿa ʾr-rīʾ	on an empty stomach
bi-suhūla	simply, easily
Id-dinya talg.	It's very cold.
Id-dōr ʿalayya (ʿalēk, ʿalēki, ʿalēh)	It's my time.
Khēr?!	We will see. Let's hope it will be all right.
Khud bālak (khudī bālik / khudū bālku!)	Take care!

Id - Dars ʾarbaʿtāshar /Lesson 14

Maktab is-siyāḥa

Mish faḥma ʾē(h) bas illi bi-yiʿgibak fi ʿṣ-ṣēf?!!
I don't understand … what makes you like the summer?!!

- Ṣabāḥ il-khēr!
- Ṣabāḥ in-nūr!
- Lau samaḥti, ḥaḍretik, ʾana gay, ʿashān istalamt minku gawāb bi-yiʿūl ʾinn barnāmig riḥlitī gāhiz.
- Lāzim ʾaʿtarif, ʾinnī n(i)sīt khāliṣ ḥaḍretak ikhtart ʾanhi riḥla.
- Maʾʾūl! Mish ʾana (i)ttaṣalt bi-ḥaḍretik wi (i)ktashafnā maʿa baʿḍ riḥla gamīla giddan mi ʾl-Qāhira li ʾl-wāḥāt.
- ʾĀ(h) ṣaḥīḥ, ʾaʿtazir li-ḥaḍretak, di ʾl-waʾt(i) iftakart. Yā salām ʿala ʾbtikārak il-hāyil! Yaʿnī bi ʾl-ʾaṭr li-ghāyit ʾAsyūṭ wi min hnāk bi ʾl-ʿarabīya. Ittafaʾna ʿala kull(i) ḥāga?
- ʾAna ma ʿandīsh ʾayyi iʿtirāḍ, il-barnāmig ʿāgibnī ʾawi w ʾana ḥāsis ʾinnī ḥanbisiṭ minno khāliṣ!
- Mumkin ʾawʿid ḥaḍretak ʾinnak ḥa-tiwṣal bi-ʿarabīyāt maktabna ʾagmal il-ʾamākin is-siyāḥīya fī Maṣr.
- Ṭayyib, ʿandī ṭalab tānī. Nifsī ʾaḥtafil bi-lēlit Rās is-sana fī Sīnā. ʾAna muntaẓir ziyārit ʾaraybī, ʿāwiz ʾafassaḥhum shwayya wi ʾafarraghum ʿala ʾl-manāẓir iṭ-ṭabīʿīya wi ʾl-ʿāsār it-tārīkhīya.
- Gamīl, mumkin nirattib luku riḥla ẓarīfa mi ʿl-Iskindirīya li-ghāyit ʾAswān wi min hnāk li-Sīnā ʿan ṭarīʿ il-ʾUʾṣur wi ʾl-Ghardaʾa.
- ʾAftikir ʾinnī ḥāgī tānī ʿashān ʾakallim ḥaḍretik fī riḥla zayyi di.
- La, mish ḍarūrī ḥaḍretak tīgī shakhṣīyan. K(i)fāya nittifiʾ bi ʾt-telefōn.

ʿAla kull(i) ḥāl, di furṣa ʿaẓīma wi ḍuyūfak yiʾdarū yiktish(i)fū ʾamāk in gdīda ʿumruhum ma shāfūhā.
- Da ʾakīd!
- ʿAwza ʾasʾal ḥaḍretak ʿala ḥāga bas mish ʿarfa ʾabtidi ʾezzāy. ʾAna khayfa, suʾālī ḥa-yisabbib lak ʾiḥrāg.
- Itfaḍḍalī ḥaḍretik! Mafīsh dāʿī li ʾl-khōf.
- ʾAna shayfa ʾaddi ʾē(h) ḥaḍretak murtabiṭ bi-Maṣr. ʿAndī iqtirāḥ ... mish ʿāwiz tishtaghal murshid siyāḥī fi ʾsh-shirka btaʿitna? Ḥaḍretak irtabakt lē(h)?
- Shaklī murtabik? ʾAṣlī ʾaftikir ʾinn shughl il-murshid mish sahl wi muḥtāg maʿrift il-lughāt wi ʾt-tārīkh wi ʾl-ʾāsār.
- Il-masʾala mish ṣaʿba awi. Lagnit Wizart is-saqāfa ḥa-tikhtabirak fi ʾl-lugha wi tārīkh Maṣr bi-ʾāsārhā wi ḥaḍārithā ʾl-firʿaunīya wi ʾl-ʾibṭīya wi ʾl-ʾislāmīya.
- Ṭayyib, mumkin ʾamtiḥin ʾemta ʾin shāʾallāh?
- Ḥaḍretak ḥa-tiʾaddim ṭalab wi ʾsh-shirka btaʿitna ḥa-tibʿat lak daʿwa li-ḥuḍūr il-imtiḥān.
- Wi lammā ʾangaḥ?
- Ḥa-tishtarik fi ʾd-daura ʾt-tadrībīya li ʾl-murshidīn.
- Wi baʿdi keda ḥa-yīgī lī shughl fi ʾsh-shirka btaʿitku bi-shakl muntaẓim?
- Bi ʾizn(i) ʾllāh, rabbina yiwaffaʾak!

I. ʾAsʾila:

1. Mīn istalam gawāb min maktab is-siyāḥa?
2. Il-muwaẓẓafa bi-tiʿtazir li ʾz-zbūn lē(h)?
3. Iz-zbūn lāzim yīgī tānī ʿashān yittifiʾ maʿa muwaẓẓaft il-maktab ʿala barnāmig ir-riḥla?
4. Iḍ-ḍuyūf il-ʾagānib ʿawzīn yiḥtaf(i)lū bi-lēlit Rās is-sana fēn?
5. Riḥlithum ḥa-tibtidi fēn?
6. Muwaẓẓaft il-maktab bi-tiqtariḥ ʾē(h) ʿala ʾz-zbūn?
7. Shughl zayy(i) da muḥtāg ʾē(h)?
8. Mīn bi-yimtiḥin murshidīn gudād?
9. Murshid gdīd lāzim jiʿmil ʾē(h) baʿd nagāḥo fi ʾl-imtiḥān?
10. Muwaẓẓaft il-maktab iktashafit ʾezzāy ʾinn iz-zbūn murtabiṭ bi-Maṣr?

II. Qawāʿid:

1. Verbs with the first consonant w

– follow the paradigm of the verb ***W a Z a N*** (to weigh)

perfect:

– cf. regular verbs

imperfect:

	singular:	negative:	plural:	negative:
3rd pers. m.	***yi-WZiN***	***ma yi-WZiN-sh(i)***	***yi-WZiN-ū***	***ma yi-WZiN-ūsh***
3rd pers. f.	***ti-WZiN***	***ma ti-WZiN-sh(i)***		
2nd pers. m.	***ti-WZiN***	***ma ti-WZiN-sh(i)***	***ti-WZiN-ū***	***ma ti-WZiN-ūsh***
2nd pers. f.	***ti-WZiN-ī***	***ma ti-WZiN-īsh***		
1st pers.	***a-WZiN***	***ma-WZiN-sh(i)***	***ni-WZiN***	***ma ni-WZiN-sh(i)***

Imperative: *iwzin!* (m.), *iwzinī!* (f.), *iwzinū!* (pl.).
Negative imperative: *ma tiwzinsh(i)!* (m.), *ma tiwzinīsh!* (f.), *ma tiwzinūsh!* (pl.).

Active participle:
WāZiN (m.) – weighing, *WaZNa* (f.), *WaZNīn* (pl.).
Passive participle:
maWZūN (m.) – weighed, balanced, *maWZūNa* (f.), *maWZūNīn* (pl.).
- Other verbs following this paradigm: *WiRiS (yiWRiS), WiSiʿ (yiWSaʿ), WiṢiL (yiWṢaL), WiLiD (yiWLiD), WaʿaD (yiWʿiD),WaGaʿ (yiWGaʿ), WiRiM (yiWRaM)*

- Imperfect prefixes ***yi-, ti-, ni-*** of verbs that have hamza ("***q***") as the second consonant combine with ***w*** to ***yū-, tū-, nū-***: *WiʾiF (yū-ʾaF, tū-ʾaF, nū-ʾaF), Wiʾiʿ (yū-ʾaʿ, tū-ʾaʿ, nū-ʾaʿ)*; in the first person singular, ***w*** is left out: *ʾaʾaF, ʾaʾaʿ*
Note the different consonants **ʿ** x **ʾ**.

2. The 8th verbal stem

The meaning of the verbs of the 8th verbal stem:
a) reflexive of the verbs of the 1st stem:
ʿiRiF – i-ʿ-ta-RaF (to confess); *ʿaZaR* (to excuse someone, to forgive someone) –

i-ʿ-ta-ZaR (to excuse oneself); *ShaGhaL* (to employ someone, to make someone busy) – *i-Sh-ta-GhaL* (to be employed, to work); *HaMM* (to interest someone) – *i-H-ta-MM* (to be interested in); *WiṢiL* (to come) – *i-t-ta-ṢaL* (to join someone); *KaL* – *i-t-tā-KiL* (to be eaten); *ShaKa* (to file a complaint about) – *i-Sh-ta-Ka* (to complain)

b) an activity performed by the agent in his own interest (for his own benefit):
i-Kh-ta-BaR (to screen someone); *i-M-ta-ḤaN* (to examine someone); *i-N-ta-ẒaR* (to wait for)

c) derived from a noun or an adjective:
i-F-ta-KaR (to think); *i-B-ta-KaR* (to invent); *i-Ḥ-ta-RaF* (to be a professional)

d) similar meaning to verbs of the 1st stem:
FaRaḌ (to expect) – *i-F-ta-RaḌ* (to expect); *KaShaF* (to discover) – *i-K-ta-ShaF* (to discover).

Perfect:

i - N - ta - Ẓ a R (to wait)
- the perfect is formed by the prefix ***i-*** and the morpheme ***-ta-*** following the first consonant
- the second consonant is always followed by the vowel ***a***
- the negative particle ***ma-*** is combined with the first consonant, eg. ***man-***; the prefix ***i-*** is left out.

singular:

		negative:
3rd pers. m.	***i-N-ta-ẒaR***	***ma-N-ta-ẒaR-sh(i)***
3rd pers. f.	***i-N-ta-ẒaR-it***	***ma-N-ta-ẒaR-itsh(i)***
2nd pers. m.	***i-N-ta-ẒaR-t***	***ma-N-ta-ẒaR-tish***
2nd pers. f.	***i-N-ta-ẒaR-ti***	***ma-N-ta-ẒaR-tīsh***
1st pers.	***i-N-ta-ẒaR-t***	***ma-N-ta-ẒaR-tish***

plural:

		negative:
3rd pers.	***i-N-ta-ẒaR-ū***	***ma-N-ta-ẒaR-ūsh***
2nd pers.	***i-N-ta-ẒaR-tū***	***ma-N-ta-ẒaR-tūsh***
1st pers.	***i-N-ta-ẒaR-na***	***ma-N-ta-ẒaR-nāsh***

Imperfect
- the perfect verbal stem takes imperfect prefixes and suffixes
– the consonant ***-t-*** is followed by the vowel ***i*** when the first consonant of the perfect stem is ***b***, ***f***, ***k***, ***m***, or ***s***; in other cases the consonant ***-t-*** is followed by the vowel ***-a-***
– the actual use of ***-ti-*** *or* ***-ta-*** depends on the speakers' level of knowledge of the Standard Arabic
– the second consonant is always followed by the vowel ***i***.
– imperfect suffixes combine with the first consonant and with the prefix ***i-***; eg. ***yin-***, ***tin-***, ***an-***, ***nin-***.

singular:

		negative:
3rd pers. m.	***yi-N-ta-ẒiR***	***ma yi-N-ta-ẒiR-sh(i)***
3rd pers. f.	***ti-N-ta-ẒiR***	***ma ti-N-ta-ẒiR-sh(i)***
2nd pers. m.	***ti-N-ta-ẒiR***	***ma ti-N-ta-ẒiR-sh(i)***
2nd pers. f.	***ti-N-ta-ẒiR-ī***	***ma ti-N-ta-ẒiR-īsh***
1st pers.	***a-N-ta-ẒiR***	***ma-N-ta-ẒiR-sh(i)***

plural:

		negative:
3rd pers.	***yi-N-ta-ẒiR-ū***	***ma yi-N-ta-ẒiR-ūsh***
2nd pers.	***ti-N-ta-ẒiR-ū***	***ma ti-N-ta-ẒiR-ūsh***
1st pers.	***ni-N-ta-ẒiR***	***ma ni-N-ta-ẒiR-sh(i)***

Imperative:
intaẓir! (m.), *intaẓirī!* (f.), *intaẓirū!* (pl.)
Negative imperative:
ma tintaẓirsh(i)! (m.), *ma tintaẓirīsh!* (f.), *ma tintaẓirūsh!* (pl.)

Active participle:
muNTaẒiR (m.) – waiting, *muNTaẒiRa* (f.), *muNTaẒiRīn!* (pl.)
Passive participle:
muNTaẒaR (m.) – awaited, expected, *muNTaẒaRa* (f.), *muNTaẒaRīn!* (pl.).
These verbs do not form the active participle.
Verbal noun:
– Verbal nouns are derived according to the following pattern: ***i-N-ti-ẒāR*** (waiting), *i-M-ti-ḤāN* (exam), *i-B-ti-KāR* (invention), *i-Ḥ-ti-FāL* (celebration), *i-ʿ-ti-RāḌ* (objection), *i-F-ti-ṚāḌ* (expectation), *i-ʿ-ti-ZāR* (excuse).

The 8th stem of verbs with the first (theoretical) consonant "hamza":
- ***"hamza"*** assimilates with the morpheme ***-ta-***: a geminated ***t*** (***-tt-***) is followed by ***ā***, the second consonant is followed by the vowel ***i***: *i-ʾ-ta-KaL* **>** ***i-ttā-KiL***
Perfect: cf. the paradigms of regular 8th stem verbs
Imperfect: *yi-ttā-KiL, ti-ttā-KiL, ti-ttā-KiL, ti-ttā-K(i)L-ī, a-ttā-KiL, yi-ttā-K(i)L-ū, ti-ttā-K(i)L-ū, ni-ttā-K(i)L*
Passive participle: *mittāK(i)L* (m.) – eaten, *mittāK(i)La* (f.), *mittāK(i)Līn* (pl.)

Verbal noun: verbal nouns are not derived from these verbs.
Other verbs following this paradigm: *i-ttā-KhiD (yi-ttā-KhiD).*

The 8th stem of verbs with the first consonant w:
- ***w*** assimilates with the morpheme ***–ta-***: *i-W-ta-ṢaL* **>** ***i-tta-ṢaL*** (to connect, to join)
Perfect: cf. the paradigm of the regular verbs of the 8th stem
Imperfect: *yi-tti-ṢiL, ti-tti-ṢiL, ti-tti-ṢiL, ti-tti-ṢiL-ī, a-tti-ṢiL, yi-tti-ṢiL-ū, ti-tti-ṢiL-ū, ni-tti-ṢiL*
Active participle: *mittiṢiL* (m.) – phoning; *mittiṢ(i)La* (f.), *mittiṢiLīn* (pl.).

Verbal noun: *i-t-ti-ṢāL* (connection); *i-t-ti-Fāʾ* (agreement).

The 8th stem of verbs with the second consonant w or y:

- these verbs follow the paradigm of ***i-Ḥ-t-āG (yi-Ḥ-t-āG)*** (to need)

Perfect: in the first and second person singular and plural, ***-ā-*** is reduced to ***-a-***:
i-Ḥ-t-āG, i-Ḥ-t-āG-it, i-Ḥ-t-aG-t, i-Ḥ-t-aG-ti, i-Ḥ-t-aG-t, i-Ḥ-t-āG-ū, i-Ḥ-t-aG-tū, i-Ḥ-t-aG-na
Imperfect: *yi-Ḥ-t-āG, ti-Ḥ-t-āG, ti-Ḥ-t-āG, ti-Ḥ-t-āG-ī, a-Ḥ-t-āG, yi-Ḥ-t-āG-ū, ti-Ḥ-t-āG-ū, ni-Ḥ-t-āG*
Active participle: *muḤtāG* (m.) – needing; *muḤtāGa* (f.), *muḤtāGīn* (pl.).

Verbal noun: *i-Ḥ-ti-YāG* (need); *i-Kh-ti-YāR* (choice).

The 8th stem of verbs with identical second and third consonants:

- these verbs follow the pattern of the verb ***i-H-t-aMM (yi-H-t-aMM)*** (to be interested)

Perfect:
i-H-t-aMM, i-H-t-aMM-it, i-H-t-aMM-ēt, i-H-t-aMM-ēti, i-H-t-aMM-ēt, i-H-t-aMM-ū, i-H-t-aMM-ētū, i-H-t-aMM-ēna
Imperfect:
yi-H-t-aMM, ti-H-t-aMM, ti-H-t-aMM, ti-H-t-aMM-ī, a-H-t-aMM, yi-H-t-aMM-ū, ti-H-t-aMM-ū, ni-H-t-aMM
Active participle: *muHTaMM* (m.) – interested in; *muHTaMMa* (f.), *muHTaMMīn* (pl.).

Verbal noun: *i-H-ti-MāM* (interest)
Other verbs belonging to this group include for example: *i-Ḥ-ta-GG (yi-Ḥ-ta-GG)* (to protest).

The 8th stem of verbs with the third consonant w or y:

- these verbs follow the paradigm of the verb ***i-B-ta-Da (yi-B-ti-Di)*** (to begin)

Perfect: *i-B-ta-Da, i-B-ta-D-it, i-B-ta-D-ēt, i-B-ta-D-ēti, i-B-ta-D-ēt, i-B-ta-D-ū, i-B-ta-D-ētū, i-B-ta-D-ēna*
Imperfect: *yi-B-ti-D-i, ti-B-ti-D-i, ti-B-ti-D-i, ti-B-ti-D-ī, a-B-ti-D-i, yi-B-ti-D-ū, ti-B-ti-D-ū, ni-B-ti-D-i*
Passive participle: appears above all in Standard Arabic context, the third consonant is *hamza*: *muBTaDiʾ* (m.) – beginner; *muBTaDiʾa* (f.), *muBTaDiʾīn* (pl.).

Verbal noun: (the third consonant is *hamza*): *i-B-ti-D-āʾ* (beginning)
To this group belong, among others, the following verbs: *i-Sh-ta-Ra (yi-Sh-ti-Ri)* (to buy); *i-Sh-ta-Ka (yi-Sh-ti-Ki)* (to complain).

3. Conjugation of the verb "*Ge*" (to come)

Perfect:

	singular:	negative:	plural:	negative:
3rd pers. m.	***Ge***	***ma Gā-sh(i)***	***Gu-m***	***ma Gū-sh***
3rd pers. f.	***Ga-t***	***ma Ga-tsh(i)***		
2nd pers. m.	***Gē-t***	***ma Gē-tsh(i)***	***Gē-tū***	***ma Gē-tūsh***
2nd pers. f.	***Gē-ti***	***ma Gē-tīsh***		
1st pers.	***Gē-t***	***ma Gē-tsh(i)***	***Gē-na***	***ma Gē-nāsh***

Imperfect:

	singular:	negative:	plural:	negative:
3rd pers. m.	***yī-Gī***	***ma yī-Gī-sh***	***yī-Gū***	***ma yī-Gū-sh***
3rd pers. f.	***tī-Gī***	***ma tī-Gī-sh***		
2nd pers. m.	***tī-Gī***	***ma tī-Gī-sh***	***tī-Gū***	***ma tī-Gū-sh***
2nd pers. f.	***tī-Gī***	***ma tī-Gī-sh***		
1st pers.	***ā-Gī***	***mā-Gī-sh***	***nī-Gī***	***ma nī-Gī-sh***

Imperative: *taʿāla!* (m.), *taʿālī!* (f.), *taʿālū!* (pl.).
Negative imperative: *ma tgīsh!* (m.), *ma tīgīsh!* (f.), *ma tīgūsh!* (pl.).
Active participle: *GaY* (2nd person m. singular) – coming, *GaYYa* (2nd person f. singular), *GaYYīN* (2nd person pl.)
Passive participle: these verbs do not form the passive participle.

III. Tadrībāt

Targama

I think that he'll come this afternoon. They haven't come yet. They called (us), that they are waiting for us at the airport. She has always complained about her financial situation. I must apologize (to you) that I did not come in time. Do you (don't you) need anything from the magazine? When are you going to celebrate his birthday? Who will inherit this house? What postcards did you (polite f.) choose? Can we negotiate the price of wood with you? Members of the expedition discovered new reliefs. He is very attached to his family. The exams will begin the day after tomorrow. They have chosen this course, because it is designed for beginners. They wanted to buy a bigger car. She must go to (enter) the hospital, since she will give birth in a few days. Where are you going to work tomorrow? He protested against this method. I think that you will have objections to the program of the journey. They admitted to us that they did not work according to their expectations these days. We still haven't begun to work (the work) in this pyramid. His objection wasn't justified (right). Where will we receive keys to the rooms? We would like to propose to you a visit to the monastery of St. Catherine in the Sinai. Do (m.) not apologize to me for anything! How do you want to discover another grave? Who will examine you (f.) in Arabic? What have you agreed on? I cannot promise you that I will come, but I will try. Take care (m.), this way you are going to fall. Which line shall we stand in? The committee would like to examine their knowledge of Egyptian history. You will need an umbrella on the beach. They were embarrassed when they heard our question. This meal is eaten with rice and "tahina" salad. This medicine must be taken on an empty stomach. All foreign guests will take part in today's party in the hotel garden. Does your (m.) arm hurt? They were very interested in historical monuments.

Kammil!

a) nishtaghal b) ikhtarti
c) ittafaʾtū d) nittiṣil e) ʾastilif
f) yikhtār g) tiʿtariḍ h) ʾastilim
i) tīgū j) tiḥtāgū

1 ʾEmta mumkin ... bīku?
2. Huwa ʿāwiz ... iṣ-ṣūra- di.
3. Mish ḥa- ... musāʿiditna?
4. Lāzim ... lēl nahār.
5. ... maʿa mīn ʿala barnāmig ir-riḥla? 6. Ḥa- ... shanṭitī fēn?
7. Mayinfaʿsh(i) ... lna ʾl-ʾusbūʿ da? 8. Hiya mish ḥa- ... ʿala ḥāga. 9. ... il-ʾakl walla lissa? 10. ʾAʾdar ... minku khamsīn ginē?

IV. Mufradāt

ʾaḥrag IV	to embarass, shame
ʿan ṭarīʾ	via, by way of
ʿazar (u)	to excuse someone, to forgive someone
baʿd(i) bukra	the day after tomorrow
blāje, -āt	beach
daʿwa	invitation
dēr (ʾadyira)	monastery
faraḍ (i)	to expect

fassaḥ II	to organize a trip, walk for someone (without preposition)
ge (yīgī)	to come to a place (without preposition), to a person *(li)*
il-Gharda'a	Hurghada
ḥaḍar (a)	to take (passive) part in
hāyil	great, wonderful, excellent
hamm (i)	to interest someone
ḥāwil III	to try, to attempt
ḥuḍūr	participation
khashab	wood
khōf	fear
ibtada VIII	to begin
ibtakar VIII	to invent
ibtikār, -āt	invention
iftakar VIII	to think, to opine
iftaraḍ VIII	to expect
iḥtafal VIII	to celebrate something *(bi)*
iḥtāg VIII	to need something *(li)* or (without preposition)
iḥtagg VIII	to protest against *(ʿala)*
ihtamm VIII	to be interested in *(bi)*
iḥtaraf VIII	to be a professional
iḥtigāg, -āt	protest
ikhtabar VIII	to screen someone, to examine something
ikhtār VIII	to choose
iktashaf VIII	to discover
imtaḥan VIII	to examine someone in *(fī)*
inbasaṭ VII	to be satisfied with *(min)*
intaẓam VIII	to regularly take part in *(fī)*
intaẓar VIII	to wait someone, something (without preposition)
iqtaraḥ VIII	to suggest something to someone *(ʿala)*
irtabak VIII	to be embarassed, to get embarassed
irtabaṭ VIII	to be connected with *(bi)*
'islāmī	Islamic, Muslim
istalaf VIII	to borrow
istalam VIII	to receive, to take over
ishtaghal VIII	to work, to be employed
ishtahar VIII	to become famous through *(bi)*
ishtaka VIII	to complain about *(min)*
ishtara VIII	to buy
ishtarak VIII	to take (active) part in *(fī)*
iʿtaraḍ VIII	to have objections to *(ʿala)*
iʿtaraf VIII	to confess something *(bi)*

iʿtazar VIII	to apologize to someone *(li)* for something *(ʿan)*
iʿtirāḍ, -āt	objection
itṣawwar V	to imagine, to be photographed
ittafaʾ VIII	to agree with someone *(maʿa)* about something *(ʿala)*
ittākhid VIII	to be taken, accepted
ittākil VIII	to be eaten
ittaṣal VIII	to be in contact with *(li)*, to turn to *(bi)*, to join someone *(bi)*
lagna (ligān)	committee
lēlit Rās is-sana	New Year's Eve
māddī	material
makhzan (makhāzin)	magazine
maqbara (maqābir)	grave, tomb
maʿʾūl	possible, rational, reasonable
maʿrifa (maʿārif)	knowledge
mubtadiʾ	beginner
nagaḥ (a)	to succeed, to be successful at *(fī)*
nagāḥ	success
naqsh bāriz (nuqūsh barza)	relief
ʾarīb (ʾarāyib)	relative
ʾibṭī (ʾaʾbāt)	Coptic
rattib II	to organize
sabbib II	to cause
salīm (sulām)	correct, faultless
Sant Katrīn	St. Catherine
saqāfa	culture
siyāḥī	touristic
Sīnā	Sinai
shaghal (i)	to employ, to make busy
shahar (i)	to make someone or something famous
shaka (i)	to complain, file a complaint against *(min)*
shamsīya (shamāsī)	parasol, umbrella
ṭābūr (ṭawabīr)	queue, line
tadrībī	training, practice
ṭarīʾ (turuʾ)	road, journey
tārīkh	history
waʿad (i)	to promise something *(bi)* to someone (without preposition)
wagaʿ (a)	to give pain, ache someone
wāḥa	oasis
wilid (i)	to give birth
wiʾiʿ (a)	to fall
wiʾif (a)	to stand, to stand up

wirim (a)	to swell
wiris (i)	to inherit
wisiʿ (a)	to be broad, to broaden
wiṣil (a)	to arrive at

V. Taʿbīrāt:

Bi ʾizn(i) ʾllāh.	If God gives. With Allah's consent.
bi-ʾanhi ṭarīʾa?	What way? How?
bi-shakl muntaẓim	regularly
yā salām ʿalā ...	that's great, wonderful
lēl nahār	day and night
mafīsh dāʿī li ...	there's no reason to ...
Ṣabāḥ il-khēr!	Good morning! (lit. a morning of goodness)
Ṣabāḥ in-nūr!	- answer (lit. a morning of light)
shaklak (-ī, -ik, -o, -ahā, -ina, -uku, -uhum) mabsūt	you (I, he, you, we, you, they) look satisfied
shughl zayy(i) da / furṣa zayy(i) di	such work / such occasion (the noun is always undetermined!)

Oasis in the Western desert

Stud(i)yo 't-taṣwīr

- Masā' il-khēr!
- Masā' in-nūr! Sawānī ḥaḍretak, 'ana gay lak ḥālan! 'U'mur!
- ʿAndī ṭalab makhṣūṣ, nifsī 'ashtirik fi 'l-musab'a btaʿit Wizart it-tarbiya wi 't-taʿlīm li-musāʿidit madāris iṣ-ṣumm wi 'l-bukm, ism il-musab'a "Gamāl iṭ-ṭabīʿa". Il-mushārikīn fīhā lāzim yiṣawwarū 'agmal il-manāẓir il-maugūda fi 'ṭ-ṭabīʿa ḥawālēna wi baʿdēn lāzim yiktibū taʿlī' ẓarīf ʿalēhā. W 'ana baṣawwar, la'ēt ḥāgāt gamīla ʿumrī ma shuftahā khallitnī 'aḥiss 'innī kunt 'aʿma wi fattaḥt.
- 'In shā'allāh ḥa-tifūz! Yaʿnī ḥa-niḥammaḍ il-film wi niṭallaʿ minno ṣuwar barḍo?
- Bi 'izn(i)'llāh. Bas 'argūk ḥaḍretak, khud bālak mi 'l-film da 'awi, ʿashān mish ḥa'dar 'aʿawwaḍo.
- Iṭṭammin siyadtak khālis! Mumkin tīgī bukra ʿa 'l-maghrib.

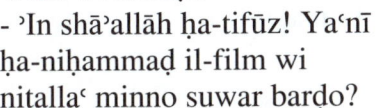

Mish ba'ūl lak, il-ḥumār da zayyak bi-yiḥibb iṭ-ṭabīʿa.
Don't I tell you, that donkey likes nature as much as you.

... tānī yōm...

- 'Alf mabrūk, itfaḍḍal ḥaḍretak, iṣ-ṣuwar! Zay mā 'enta shāyif, muʿẓamhā ḥelwa 'awi, bi-ṣarāḥa ma ḥaṣalitsh(i). Bas li 'l-'asaf, fī barḍo kam ṣūra ma ṭiliʿitsh(i) kwayyis. Buṣṣ ḥaḍretak, masalan it-tuffāḥāya di iḥmarrit fī 'ṣ-ṣūra khālis, bi 'l-ʿaks il-kummitrāya di iṣfarrit bi-shakl gharīb. Wi hena – 'aywa iṣ-ṣūra di, il-khalfīya btaʿithā ighma''it wi ʿashān keda il-bar'ū'āya mish waḍḥa, izra''it li-daragit 'innahā mish bayna.
- 'Ana kunt khāyif giddan mi 'l-ḥikāya di. Kunt ba'ūl li nafsī, il-fakha mumkin tiḥmarr, tiṣfarr, tikhḍarr, tizra'' wi 'l-manāẓir yā tighma'' yā tib'a fatḥa khāliṣ. Bas il-ḥamdu li 'llāh, mafīsh ṣuwar ibyaḍḍit yā 'swaddit kullahā.
- La, ṭabʿan, buṣṣ ḥaḍretak, masalan il-mōz da, maʿa ʿinno mitṣawwar fī ʿizz in-nahār, il-'aṣfar bitāʿo gamīl, bas lōn il-ghēṭ, fī ra'yī, ikhḍarr ziyāda shwayya.

- Bi-sabab it-taṣwīr bitāʿ ī?
- La, bi-sabab it-taḥmīḍ.
- Di ʾl-waʾt(i) mumkin tikabbarū baʿḍ iṣ-ṣuwar ʿashān tibʾa gahza li ʾl-musabʾa?
- Min ʿēnayya ʾl-itnēn! Barḍo ḥa-n(i)ḥāwil nifaṭṭaḥ iṣ-ṣuwar btaʿit il-khalfīya ʾl-ghamʾa.
- Kattar khērak! ʿAla fikra, ʿashān mansāsh, ʾana muḥtāg kamān ṣurtēn li-gawāz safarī, yinfaʿ niṣaghghar iṣ-ṣūra di?
- ʾAḥsan niʿmil ṣūra gdīda. Fi ʾṣ-ṣūra di ḥaḍretak mismirr wʾ ana khāyif ʾinn(i) wishshak ḥa-yiṭlaʿ miḥmirr sinna, lammā niṣaghghar iṣ-ṣūra ʾl-ʾadīma.

I. ʾAsʾila:

1. Il-musabʾa btaʿit Wizart it-tarbiya wi ʾt-taʿlīm ḥa-t(i)sāʿid mīn?
2. ʾEzzāy ḥass il-mushārik fi ʾl-musabʾa ʾinno kān ʾaʿma wi fattaḥ?
3. Iṣ-ṣuwar kullahā ṭiliʿit kwayyis?
4. Il-barʾūʾāya mish waḍḥa lē(h)?
5. Il-mushārik kān khāyif ʾinn(i) ʾalwān il-fakha mish ḥa-tiṭlaʿ ḥelwa?
6. Fī manāẓir ighmaʾʾit khāliṣ?
7. Il-mōz kān mitṣawwar ʾemta?
8. Il-ghēṭ fi ʾṣ-ṣūra ikhḍarr ziyāda shwayya lē(h)?
9. ʿĀmil stud(i)yo ʾt-taṣwīr khāyif lē(h), ʾinn wishsh iz-zbūn ḥa-yiṭlaʿ miḥmirr?
10. Iṣ-ṣūra mumkin tibyaḍḍ khāliṣ ʾemta?

II. Qawāʿid:

1. Adjectives expressing colours, qualities, and corporal impairments
- these adjectives are formed the following way:

	singular		plural
masculine	***a S M a R***	(tanned, dusky)	***S u M R***
feminine	***S a M R a***		***S u M R***

Colours:
aḤMaR (ḤaMRa, ḤuMR) – red; *aṢFaR (ṢaFRa, ṢuFR)* – yellow; *aKhḌaR (KhaḌRa, KhuḌR)* – red; *aZRaʾ (ZaRʾa, ZuRʾ)* – blue
Note the irregularities in the following forms:
aByaḌ (BēḌa, BīḌ) – white; *iSWiD (SōDa, SūD)* – black

Qualities and corporal impairments:
aKhRaS (KhaRSa, KhuRS) – dumb; *aBKaM (BaKMa, BuKM)* – dumb; *aṬRaSh (ṬaRSha, ṬuRSh)* – deaf; *aṢaMM (ṢaMMa, ṢuMM)* – deaf; *aḤDaB (ḤaDBa, ḤuDB)* – hunchbacked; *aʿRaG (ʿaRGa, ʿuRG)* – limping
Note the irregularities in the following forms:
aʿWaR (ʿōRa, ʿūR) - one-eyed; *aḤWaL (ḤōLa, ḤūL)* – squinting; *aʿMa (ʿaMYa, ʿuMY)* – blind.

2. The 9th verbal stem

***The meaning of the verbs of the 9th verbal stem*:**

a) to express colours and changes of colours:
i-SMaRR (to become tawny, to get tanned); *i-ḤMaRR* (to turn red) - *i-ṢFaRR* (to turn yellow); *i-KhḌaRR* (to turn green) - *i-ZRa"* (to turn blue); *i-BYaḌḌ* (to turn white); *i-SWaDD* (to turn black)
b) to express qualities and corporal impairments:
i-ḤWaLL (to squint); *i-ḤDaBB* (to be hunchbacked).

Perfect:

i - S M a R R (to get tanned)
- the perfect is formed by – the prefix ***i-***
  – gemination of the third consonant
- the second consonant is always followed by the vowel ***a***
- the negative particle ***ma-*** is combined with the first consonant, eg. ***mas-***; the prefix ***i-*** is left out.

singular:

		negative:
3rd pers. m.	***i-SMaRR***	***ma-SMaRR-ish***
3rd pers. f.	***i-SMaRR-it***	***ma-SMaRR-itsh(i)***
2nd pers. m.	***i-SMaRR-ēt***	***ma-SMaRR-ētsh(i)***
2nd pers. f.	***i-SMaRR-ēti***	***ma-SMaRR-ētīsh***
1st pers.	***i-SMaRR-ēt***	***ma-SMaRR-ētsh(i)***

plural:

		negative:
3rd pers.	***i-SMaRR-ū***	***ma-SMaRR-ūsh***
2nd pers.	***i-SMaRR-ētū***	***ma-SMaRR-ētūsh***
1st pers.	***i-SMaRR-ēna***	***ma-SMaRR-ēnāsh***

Imperfect
- the perfect verbal stem takes imperfect prefixes and suffixes
- the second consonant is always followed by the vowel ***a***.
- imperfect suffixes combine with the first consonant and with the prefix ***i-***;
eg. ***yis-, tis-, as-, nis-.***

singular:

		negative:
3rd pers. m.	***yi-SMaRR***	***ma yi-SMaRR-ish***
3rd pers. f.	***ti-SMaRR***	***ma ti-SMaRR-ish***
2nd pers. m.	***ti-SMaRR***	***ma ti-SMaRR-ish***
2nd pers. f.	***ti-SMaRR-ī***	***ma ti-SMaRR-īsh***
1st pers.	***a-SMaRR***	***ma-SMaRR-ish***

plural:

		negative:
3rd pers.	***yi-SMaRR-ū***	***ma yi-SMaRR-ūsh***
2nd pers.	***ti-SMaRR-ū***	***ma ti-SMaRR-ūsh***
1st pers.	***ni-SMaRR***	***ma ni-SMaRR-ish***

Imperative:
ismarr! (m.), *ismarrī!* (f.), *ismarrū!* (pl.)
Negative imperative:
ma tismarrish! (m.), *ma tismarrīsh!* (f.), *ma tismarrūsh!* (pl.)

Active participle:
miSMiRR (m.) – tanned, *miSMiRRa* (f.), *miSMiRRīn* (pl.)
Note the irregular forms: *miBYaḌḌ (miBYaḌḌa, miBYaḌḌīn).*

Verbal noun:
- Verbal nouns are derived according to the following pattern: ***i-SMiRāR*** (turning tanned), *i-ḤMiRāR* (turning red), *i-ṢFiRāR* (turning yellow), *i-KhḌiRāR* (turning green).

3. Collective nouns
- denote the species of plants, fruits, animals and materials
- take the masculine singular form
- in order to express the amount "one", "a piece", they take the suffix ***–a***, or its emphatic form ***-āya***: *tuffāḥ* (apples) – *tuffāḥa* / *tuffāḥāya* (an apple); *burtuʾān* (oranges) – *burtuʾāna* / *burtuʾānāya* (an orange); *kurumb* (cabbage) – *kurumba* / *kurumbāya* (a head of cabbage); *khōkh* (peaches) – *khōkha* / *khōkhāya* (a peach); *khiyār* (cucumbers) - *khiyāra* / *khiyārāya* (a cucumber); *ṭamāṭim* (tomatoes) – *ṭamāṭima* / *ṭamāṭimāya* (a tomato); *shagar* (trees) – *shagara* / *shagarāya* (a tree); *ward* (roses) – *warda* / *wardāya* (a rose); *samak* (fish) – *samaka* / *samakāya* (a fish); *ḥadīd* (iron) – *ḥadīda* / *ḥadīdāya* (a piece of iron); *ḥagar* (stone) – *ḥagara* / *ḥagarāya* (a stone); *khashab* (wood) – *khashaba* / *khashabāya* (a piece of wood).

- collective nouns with adjectives: *baṭṭīkh kbīr* (big melons); *baṭṭīkha** / *baṭṭīkhāya kbīra* (a big melon); *ḥagar ʾabyad* (white stones); *ḥagara* / *ḥagarāya bēḍa* (a white stone); *samak gamīl* (beautiful fish); *samak(i)tēn gumāl* (two beautiful fish); *ward ʾaḥmar* (red roses); *wardītēn ḥumr* (two red roses); *khashab ṭwīl* (long wood) *khashaba* / *khashabāya ṭwīla* (a long piece of wood).

* A "piece" is treated like a singular feminine noun (cf. Lesson 1).

- the collective noun *mōz* "bananas" uses the noun *ṣubāʿ* "finger" to express "one banana": *ṣubāʿ mōz* (one banana), *mōza* denotes also "sirloin".

III. Tadrībāt:

Targama

I'll come immediately. We will compensate all losses for you. Look (polite), your hand has turned completely red (completely turned red). Can you (f.) pass me one big orange? Where did you get so tanned? They want to get tanned, and therefore they sit long hours in the sun. Let (m.) the apples turn red a bit. Do you (polite) only want to develop the film? Please, do (f.) not forget to take the fruit out of the bag! Can you make pictures out of this negative? Do not enlarge these two photographs! She talked with us about the problems of the whites in South Africa. They were interested in American Indian culture. I am afraid your leg will turn blue. The wall turned nicely white. For a fruit salad you need two bananas, a big pomegranate, two mangoes and one small orange. When spring comes, all the trees will turn green. Do not put a whole onion into the soup! Take all these bricks away! Should I increase the amount of garlic? Who played the part of the one-eyed corsair? Did you hear of his new film "the Hunchback of Notre Dame"? His right leg limps, because he had broken it (it was broken). Do you prefer black or green tea? Bandage (m.) your finger with this piece of cloth. Do not (f.) speak so loudly to them, they're not deaf! This kind of mango must be dark green. Are you (polite) looking for the blue glass? Do not write (pl.) with a red pen! The doctor examined him and then he told him that he had hepatitis. The sky turned utterly dark before the storm. Do you (f.) want the yolk, the eggwhite or the whole egg?

Kammil!

a) ʾaʿma b) bukm c) ʾiswid d) khaḍra e) ṣufr f) miḥmirr g) ʿarga
h) sōda i) ʾuṣayyara j) sumr

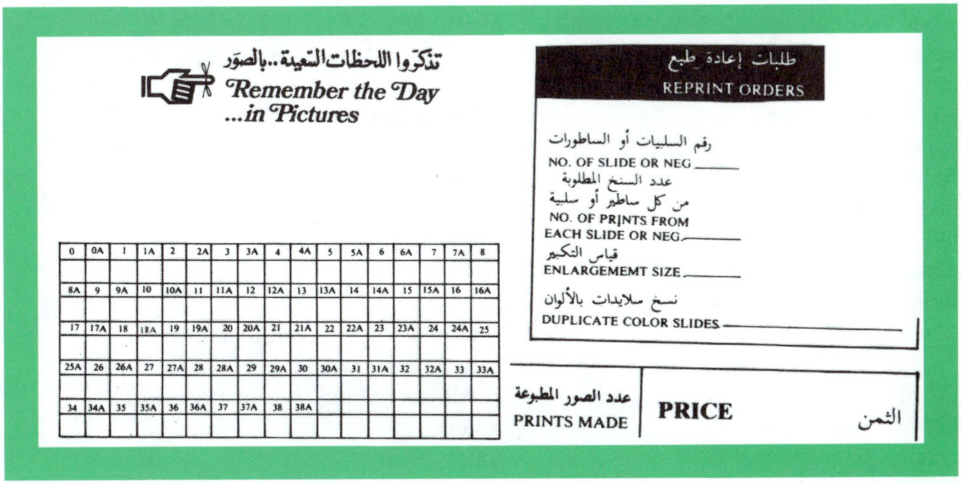
تذكّروا اللحظات السّعيدة.. بالصّور
Remember the Day ...in Pictures

0	0A	1	1A	2	2A	3	3A	4	4A	5	5A	6	6A	7	7A	8
8A	9	9A	10	10A	11	11A	12	12A	13	13A	14	14A	15	15A	16	16A
17	17A	18	18A	19	19A	20	20A	21	21A	22	22A	23	23A	24	24A	25
25A	26	26A	27	27A	28	28A	29	29A	30	30A	31	31A	32	32A	33	33A
34	34A	35	35A	36	36A	37	37A	38	38A							

طلبات إعادة طبع
REPRINT ORDERS
رقم السلبيات أو الساطورات
NO. OF SLIDE OR NEG ______
عدد النسخ المطلوبة
من كل ساطير أو سلبية
NO. OF PRINTS FROM EACH SLIDE OR NEG. ______
قياس التكبير
ENLARGEMEMT SIZE ______
نسخ سلايدات بالألوان
DUPLICATE COLOR SLIDES ______

عدد الصور المطبوعة
PRINTS MADE
PRICE الثمن

1. Is-suyyāḥ rigiʿū mi ʾl-maṣyaf ... khālis. 2. Dayman bi-yiʾūlʾinn il-ḥubb ... . 3. Ḥa-tilbisī fustān ... ? 4. ʿĀwiz tishtiri badla bēda walla ... ? 5. Ikhtar tuffāḥ ... shwayya! 6. Yalla bīna, il-ishāra ... ! 7. Bi-tidarris li ʾl-banāt il- ... . 8. Il-ghanama ma bi-timshīsh kwayyis ʿashanhā ... . 9. Khud il-ḥadīdāya ʾl-... di! 10. Iddīnī warditēn ... barḍo!

IV. Mufradāt

ʾabyaḍ	white
ʾabkam	dumb
ʿafrīta	negative
ʾaḥdab	hunchbacked
ʾaḥwal	squinting
ʾakhḍar	green
ʾakhras	dumb
ʿallaʾ II	to hang to comment *(ʿala)*
ʾaʿma	blind
ʾamar (u)	to command someone (without preposition) to do something *(bi)*
ʾaʿrag	limping, lame
ʾaṣamm	deaf
ʾaṣfar	yellow
il-ʾaṣfar	yellow colour
ʿāṣifa (ʿawāṣif)	storm
ʾaṭrash	deaf
ʿawwaḍ II	to compensate something *(ʿan)* to someone (without preposition)
ʾaʿwar	one-eyed
ʾazraʾ	blue
bayāḍ	1. white colour 2. eggwhite
bāyin	evident, visible
bāyin ʾinn	it seems that
barʾūʾ	plums
baṣal	onion
bēḍ	eggs
bīḍ	whites (Caucasians)
daraga	grade
fātiḥ	light
fattaḥ II	1. to make light, to enlighten 2. to be enlightened
fāz (u)	to win something *(bi)* (in a contest)
gamāl	beauty
ganūb	south

gawāz (gawāzāt) safar	passport
gharīb	weird, special
ghāmiʾ	dark
ghanam	sheep
ghēṭ (ghīṭān)	field, arable land
ḥagar	stone
ḥadīd	iron
ḥālan	immediately
ḥammaḍ II	to develop a film
hindī (hunūd)	Indian
hindī ʾaḥmar	American Indian
khalfīya	background
khōkh	peaches
kh(u)sāra (khasāyir)	damage, loss
ibyaḍḍ IX	to become white
ʾIfrīqiyā	Africa
ighmaʾʾ IX	to turn dark
iḥdabb IX	to be hunchbacked
iḥmarr IX	to turn red
iḥwall IX	to be squinting, to squint
ikhḍarr IX	to turn green
iṣfarr IX	to turn yellow
ismarr IX	to get tanned, to become tanned
iswadd IX	to turn black
ʾiswid	black
izraʾʾ IX	to turn blue
kattar II	to increase the amount, to make more numerous
kummitra	pears
kurumb	cabbage
makhṣūṣ	special
manga	mango
masalan	for example
massil II	to play (theatre)
mōza	sirloin
musabʾa	contest
mushārik	participant
muʿẓam	majority
nahār	daytime, day (from sunrise to sunset)
nōʿ (ʾanwāʿ)	kind, type
ʾalam (ʾiʾlām)	pen, pencil
ʾumāsh	cloth, textile
qurṣān (qaraṣna)	corsair, pirate
rabaṭ (u)	to bind, to tie
rabīʿ	spring

rummān	pomegranate
ṣafār	yolk
ṣafra	hepatitis
salaṭit fawākih	fruit salad
sinna	a little, a bit
ṣubāʿ (ṣawābiʿ)	finger
sūd	blacks, African Americans
shagar	trees
ṭabīʿa	nature
taḥmīḍ	film development
taʿlīʾ, -āt	commentary
taṣwīr	photography, filming
tōm	garlic
ward	roses

V. Taʿbīrāt:

ʾAḥsan niʿmil ...	We'd better do ...
ʾArgūk /-ki / -ku	Would you please be so kind …
bi ʾl-ʿaks	to the contrary
bi-sabab ...	because of ..., for the reason of ...
bi-ṣōt ʿālī	loudly
bi-shakl gamīl	nicely, beautifully
bi-shakl gharīb	oddly, weirdly
fī ʿizz in-nahār	right at noon
fī raʾyī (-ak, -ik, -o, -ahā, -ina, -uku, -uhum)	in my (his, her, your, our, your, their) opinion
siyadtak/-ik	very polite address (dear / honoured ...)

Id - Dars sittāshar /Lesson 16

Mukalma telefonīya

fi ʾd-dukkān

- Itfaddal yā ʾustāz, istarayyaḥ! Id-dinya ḥarr, ʾaftaḥ lak hāga sāʾ(i)ʿa?
- ʾĀ(h), yarēt, bas ma tikunsh(i) mitalliga ʾawi, ʿashān zōrī bi-yiwgaʿnī shwayya. Baʿd ʾiznak, yā bē(h), mumkin ʾastakhdim it-telefōn? ʾAṣlī ʿāyiz ʾaṭṭammin ʿala ʾusritī fi ʾs-Swīd.
- Maʿalesh, ʾanā ʾāsif, it-telefōn da bi-yishtaghal gouwa ʾl-Qāhira bas, wi ʿashān keda ma tiʾdarsh(i) tistaʿmilo li ʾl-mukalma ʾd-daulīya.
- Il-mushkila ʾinnī mistaʿgil shwayya. Ittafaʾt maʿa māma ʾu bāba ʿala maʿād wi hum(ma) mistannīn mukalmitī fi baḥr nuṣṣ(i) sāʿa.
- Yibʾa mafrūḍ ma titʾakhkharsh(i) ʿalēhum. ʾAʾūl lak ʿala ḥall. Shāyif il-mabna ʾl-ʾaṣfar fī ʾākhir ish-shāriʿ da?

ʾArgūki yā māma, taʿālī khudīnī li ʾinno māniʿnī ʾatkallim fi ʾt-telefōn!

Mom, please, come and take me home. He has forbidden me to talk on the phone!

- ʾAywa, shayfo. Ganbo yafṭa kbīra maktūb ʿalēha "ʾAḥsan istismārāt ʿumruku fī ʾaḥdas bunūk ʿaṣrina".
- ʾAho da mabna ʾs-sentrāl wi henāk mumkin tiʿmil trank, bas il-masāfa tākhud ḥawālī rub sāʿa mashy. Buṣṣ, maʿāya kart telefōn, mumkin tistafīd minno fī mukalma ʾuṣayyara. Il-kushk ʾuṣād il-furn il-ʾafrangī ʿala ṭūl.
- ʾAna mish ʿāwiz ʾastahlik il-kart bitāʿak.
- Lā, walā yihimmak! ʾAhamm ḥāga tiṭammin ʾahlak.
- Kattar khērak! Ṭayyib ʾastaʾzin ʿashān ʾarūḥ is-sentrāl.
- Itfaḍḍal, maʿa ʾalf salāma!

fi ʾs-sentrāl

- Lau samaḥti ḥaḍretik, mumkin ʾastashīrik fī ḥāga?
- Laḥẓa, ʾaywa ʾana samʿāk.
- ʾAna ʿāwiz ʾaʿmil mukalma daulīya, ʾaṭlub trank walla ʾashtiri kart telefōn?
- Di ʾl-waʾt(i) mafīsh zaḥma, ḥaḍretak mumkin tistaʿidd fī kushk nimra talāta w ʾana ḥaṭlubhā lak ḥālan.
- Ṭayyib, ʿandī suʾāl mustafizz shwayya, il-mukalma bi ʾl-kart mish ʾarkhaṣ?
- Suʾālak mish mustafizz ʾabadan wi yarēt ḥaḍretak ma tistaghrabsh(i) min ʾigabtī barḍo. Il-itnēn bi-siʿr wāḥid. ʾAna ʾstantigt min kalāmak ʾinn ḥaḍretak ʿāwiz tiṭṭammin ʿala ʾahlak barra wi ma tiḍmansh(i) ṭūl il-mukalma. Mukalmitak mi ʾs-sentrāl bi-tiddī lak furṣa timiddahā zay mā ʾenta ʿāwiz liʾinn il-muwaẓẓafa btaʿitna bi-tisʾalak fī nihāyit kull(i) mudda. Il-kart mumkin yikhlaṣ wi ḥaḍretak ʿāwiz tikammil mukalmitak.
- Bi-ṣarāḥa, ʾana wākhid ʿala ʾt-telefōn bi ʾl-kart. Yibʾa ʾashtiri kartēn ʿala ṭūl ʿashān yikaffūnī wi ʾaʾdar ʾakallim bīhum mukalma ṭwīla. Mumkin ʾastaʿīr min ḥaḍretik dalīl it-telefōnāt ʿashān ʾatʾakkid min kōd madīnit ʾahlī fī ʾs-Swīd?
- Istanna ḥaḍretak sawānī, id-dalīl di ʾl-waʾt(i) maʿa zbūn tānī.

Lā, khalāṣ, iz-zbūn gay wi gaybo maʿāh. Itfaḍḍal!
- ʾAna mitshakkir ʾawi ʿala ṣabr ḥaḍretik maʿāya!

I. ʾAsʾila:

1. Mīn ʿāwiz yistakhdim it-telefōn?
2. Lē(h) mish mumkin yistaʿmilo li ʾl-mukalma ʾd-daulīya?
3. Iṭ-ṭālib mistaʿgil lē(h)?
4. Iṭ-ṭālib ʿāwiz yistaḍīf ʾusrito fī Maṣr?
5. Iṭ-ṭālib ʿāwiz yistashīr muwaẓẓaft is-sentrāl fī ʾē(h)?
6. Iz-zbūn mumkin yistaʿidd fī kushk is-sentrāl ʿala ṭūl?
7. Iṭ-ṭālib istafazz il-muwaẓẓafa bi suʾālo?
8. Il-muwaẓẓafa ʾstantigit ʾē(h) min kalāmo?
9. Iṭ-ṭālib ʿāwiz yistaʿīr minhā dalīl it-telefōnāt lē(h)?
10. Il-mukalma ʾd-daulīya ʾṭ-ṭwīla bi-tistahlik kam waḥda?

II. Qawāʿid:

1. The 10th verbal stem

The meaning of the verbs of the 10th verbal stem:

a) verbs expressing attempt derived from verbs of the 1st stem:

KhaDaM (to serve) – *ista-KhDiM* (to use, to employ); *ʿaMaL* – *ista-ʿMiL* (to use, to employ); *KhaRaG* – *ista-KhRaG* (to mine, to quarry); *ḤaMaL* (to carry) – *ista-ḤMiL* (to endure)

b) reflexive of verbs of the 4th verbal stem:
ʾaNTaG (to produce) – *ista-NTiG* (to inferr, derive, deduce something); *ʾaSLaM* (to become Muslim, to give oneself to the will of God) – *ista-SLiM* (to give up, to capitulate); *ʾaShāR* – *ista-ShāR* (to take counsel with, to consult with)

c) verbs meaning "to consider (for)":
ista-GhRaB (to wonder, "to consider odd"); *ista-KTaR* (to consider something as being too great amount); *ista-RKhaS* (to consider cheap); *ista-KhSaR* (to consider something as being a loss, or damage)

d) verbs derived from nouns:
ʿaGaLa (hurry) – *ista-ʿGiL* (to hurry); *ʾiZN* (permission) – *ista-ʾZiN* (to ask for permission); *HaWa* (air) – *ista-HWa* (to catch a cold).

Perfect:
ista - H L i K (to use, to consume)
- the perfect is formed by the prefix ***ista-***
- the second consonant is followed by the vowel ***i-***;

if the second or third consonant is ***r***, an emphatic or glottal consonant, the second consonant is followed by the vowel ***-a-*** (with the exception of the verb ***ista-SMiR*** – to invest)
- the negative particle ***ma-*** is combined with the first consonant, eg. ***masta-***; the vowel ***i-*** is left out.

singular:

		negative:
3rd pers. m.	***ista-HLiK***	***masta-HLiK-sh(i)***
3rd pers. f.	***ista-HLiK-it***	***masta-HLiK-itsh(i)***
2nd pers. m.	***ista-HLiK-t***	***masta-HLiK-tish***
2nd pers. f.	***ista-HLiK-ti***	***masta-HLiK-tīsh***
1st pers.	***ista-HLiK-t***	***masta-HLiK-tish***

plural:

		negative:
3rd pers.	***ista-HLiK-ū***	***masta-HLiK-ūsh***
2nd pers.	***ista-HLiK-tū***	***masta-HLiK-tūsh***
1st pers.	***ista-HLiK-na***	***masta-HLiK-nāsh***

Imperfect
- the perfect verbal stem takes imperfect prefixes and suffixes
- the second consonant is followed by the vowel ***i-***; if the second or third consonant is ***r***, an emphatic or glottal consonant, the second consonant is followed by the vowel ***-a-***
- there are several exceptions to the above rule – mostly words taken over from the standard context: *yista-KhRiG* (he mines, quarries); *yista-MiRR* (he goes on, persists); *yista-SMiR* (he invests)
- imperfect prefixes combine with the prefix ***ista-***; eg. ***yista-, tista-, asta-, nista-***

singular:

		negative:
3rd pers. m.	***yista-HLiK***	***ma yista-HLiK-sh(i)***
3rd pers. f.	***tista-HLiK***	***ma tista-HLiK-sh(i)***
2nd pers. m.	***tista-HLiK***	***ma tista-HLiK-sh(i)***
2nd pers. f.	***tista-HLiK-ī***	***ma tista-HLiK-īsh***
1st pers.	***asta-HLiK***	***masta-HLiK-sh(i)***

plural:

		negative:
3rd pers.	***yista-HLiK-ū***	***ma yista-HLiK-ūsh***
2nd pers.	***tista-HLiK-ū***	***ma tista-HLiK-ūsh***
1st pers.	***nista-HLiK***	***ma nista-HLiK-sh(i)***

Imperative:
istahlik! (m.), *istahlikī!* (f.), *istahlikū!* (pl.)
Negative imperative:
ma tistahliksh(i)! (m.), *ma tistahlikīsh!* (f.), *ma tistahlikūsh!* (pl.)

Active participle:
mustaHLiK (m.) – consumer, *mustaHLiKa* (f.), *mustaHLiKīn* (pl.)
Active non-agentive participle, denoting the bearer of the most common human actions, takes the prefix ***mista-***:
mistaʿGiL – rushing, *mistaḤMiL* (enduring), *mistaGhRaB* (wondering), *mistaNNī* (waiting)
Passive participle:
muSTaHLaK (m.) – used up, consumed; *muSTaHLaKa* (f.), *muSTaHLaKīn* (pl.)

Verbal noun:
- Verbal nouns are derived according to the following pattern: ***isti-HLāK*** (usage, consumption), *isti-KhDāM* (use), *isti-ʿMāL* (use), *isti-KhRāG* (mining), *isti-SMāR* (investment).

The 10th stem of verbs with the second consonant w or y:

- these verbs follow the paradigm of ***ista-ShāR (yista-ShīR)*** (to take counsel)

perfect: in the first and second person singular and plural, ***-ā*** is reduced to ***-a***:
ista-ShāR, ista-ShāR-it, ista-ShaR-t, ista-ShaR-ti, ista-ShaR-t, ista-ShāR-ū, ista-ShaR-tū, ista-ShaR-na

imperfect: *yista-ShīR, tista-ShīR, tista-ShīR, tista-ShīR-ī, asta-ShīR, yista-ShīR-ū, tista-ShīR-ū, nista-ShīR*
Imperative:
istashir! (m.), *istashīrī!* (f.), *istashīrū!* (pl.)
Negative imperative:
ma tistashirsh(i)! (m.), *ma tistashīrīsh!* (f.), *ma tistashīrūsh!* (pl.)

Active participle:
mustaShīR (m.) – requesting consultation, *mustaShīRa* (f.), *mustaShīRīn* (pl.)
Passive participle:
mustaShāR (m.) – used up, consumed; *mustaShāRa* (f.), *mustaShāRīn!* (pl.)
Verbal noun:
isti-ShāR-a (consultation), *isti-FāD-a* (use, benefit), *isti-ḌāF-a* (hospitality)

The verb *ista-RaYYaḤ (yista-RaYYaḤ)* (to rest) is conjugated according to the paradigm of *istaHLiK,* active participle: *mistaRaYYaḤ, mistaRaYYaḤa, mistaRaYYaḤīn.*

The 10th stem of verbs with identical second and third consonants:

- these verbs follow the pattern of the verb ***ista-FaZZ (yista-FiZZ)*** (to provoke)

Perfect:
ista-FaZZ, ista-FaZZ-it, ista-FaZZ-ēt, ista-FaZZ-ēti, ista-FaZZ-ēt, ista-FaZZ-ū, ista-FaZZ-ētū, ista-FaZZ-ēna
Imperfect:
yista-FiZZ, tista-FiZZ, tista-FiZZ, tista-FiZZ-ī, asta-FiZZ, yista-FiZZ-ū, tista-FiZZ-ū, nista-FiZZ
Active participle:
mustaFiZZ (m.) – teasing; *mustaFiZZa* (f.), *mustaFiZZīn* (pl.).
Passive participle:
mustaFaZZ (m.) – incited; *mustaFaZZa* (f.), *mustaFaZZīn* (pl.).
Verbal noun:
isti-FZāZ (provocation), *isti-MRāR* (continuation), *isti-ʿDāD* (readiness)

The 10th stem of verbs with the third consonant w or y:

- these verbs follow the paradigm of the verb ***ista-RKh-a (yista-RKh-i)*** (to relax)

perfect: *ista-RKh-a, ista-RKh-it, ista-RKh-ēt, ista-RKh-ēti, ista-RKh-ēt, ista-RKh-ū, ista-RKh-ētū, ista-RKh-ēna*
imperfect: *yista-RKh-i, tista-RKh-i, tista-RKh-i, tista-RKh-ī, asta-RKh-i, yista-RKh-ū, tista-RKh-ū, nista-RKh-i*
Imperative:
istarkhi! (m.), *istarkhī!* (f.), *istarkhū!* (pl.)
Negativ imperative:
ma tistarkhīsh! (m.), *ma tistarkhīsh!* (f.), *ma tistarkhūsh!* (pl.)
Active participle:
mistaRKhi (m.) – relaxed; *mistaRKhīYa* (f.), *mistaRKhīYīn* (pl.).
Verbal noun: (the third consonant is *hamza*):
isti-RKhāʾ (relaxation)

Other verbs following this paradigm: *ista-HWa* (to catch cold) *(yista-HWa, tista-HWa, tista-HWa, tista-HWī, asta-HW-a, yista-HW-ū, tista-HW-ū, nista-HW-a*); *ista-NN-a (yista-NNa)* (to wait)
Imperative: *istanna!* (m.), *istannī!* (f.), *istannū!* (pl.)
Negative imperative:
ma tistannāsh! (m.), *ma tistannīsh!* (f.), *ma tistannūsh!* (pl.)

III. Tadrībāt:

Targama

This foreign company invested its financial means in our project. Get ready for the journey! Do not use this lift! Do not scrimp (consider for cheapness, m.) and buy a good thing! May I use your (polite) phone? Do not hurry (f.), you have enough time. Wait (m.) for me a moment! Can you wait for us in the restaurant? We will wait for you at the terrace of the hotel. Why didn't you (f.) wait for them? Let's hope that they will use their experience with modern electronic equipment. Who used up all the warm water? We would like to discuss this thing (this theme) with you (polite). Why are you (f.) provoking him? I was wondering a lot why they didn't call you. Can we borrow these books from you? The Gulf states extract oil. I want you (m.) to rest! Did you (pl.) rest a little? She is afraid that we will not endure the great heat in the summer months. Relax and do not think about anything! Do not (m.) give up! Excuse us (apologize for ourselves), but we must say goodbye, in order to catch the last train. They hosted them in their house the entire month. Will you go on with us? Close (pl.) the window, so that you don't catch cold! All the tourists were ready in front of the bus. The trade councillor introduced us to a delegation of foreign investors. Why didn't you borrow from them a detailed map of the Sinai? We didn't want to impede them, since they were in a great hurry.

Kammil!

a) yistanna b) tistaghrab c) tistaʿīr d) nistarayyaḥ e) tistaʿiddū f) yistaʾzinū g) istafadna h) yistammir i) tistakhrig j) tistaʿmilū

1 ʿAwzīn ... ʿashān yikhushshū yināmū badri. 2. ʾAddi ʾē(h) ... min naṣāyiḥku ʾl-hayla. 3. Il-barnāmig ḥa- ... li-ghāyit ʾemta? 4. Ḥa ... ʾanhi ṣūra? 5. Ma ...-sh(i) min suʾālī! 6. Nifsina ... shwayya. 7. Rāḥit il-maktaba ʿashān ... il-magalla di. 8. Mīn ḥa- ... ku fi ʾl-maṭār? 9. ʾAnhi daula bi-... il-faḥm? 10. Ḥa-n(i)sību di ʾl-waʾt(i) ʿashān ...li ʾl-imtiḥān.

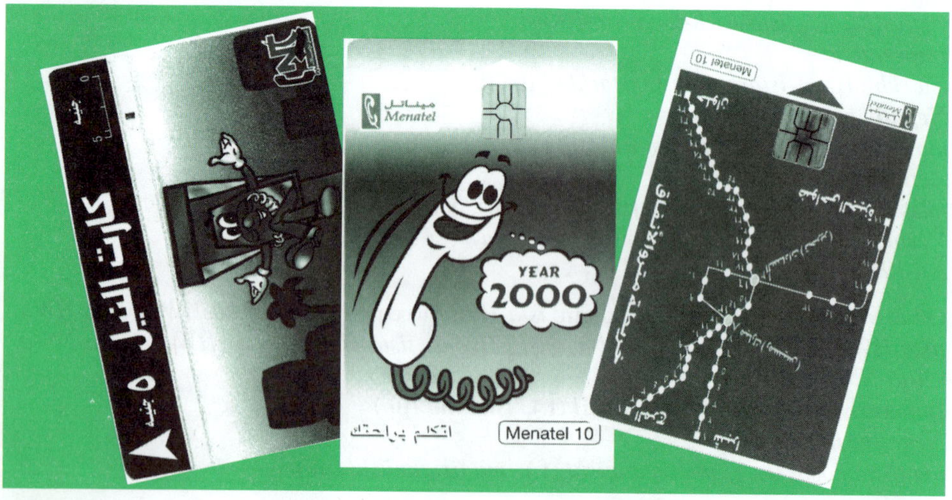

IV. Mufradāt

ʾafrangī	foreign (particularly when referring to breads and pastries)
ʿagala	rush, hurry
ʾantag IV	to make, produce
ʾaslam IV	to become a Muslim, to give oneself into God's will
bāba	daddy
bank (bunūk)	bank
betrōl	oil
dalīl	guide, list
dalīl it-telefōnāt	phone book
daula (duwal)	state, country
dukkān (dakakīn)	shop
furn (ʾafrān)	oven, bakery
ḥall (ḥulūl)	solution
ḥamal (i)	to carry
ḥamal (a)	become pregnant – the imperfect vowel is **a!**
ḥarr	heat
hawa	air
khadam (i)	to serve someone or something (without preposition)
khalīg (il-Khalīg)	gulf (the Gulf)
khibra	experience
ʾilīktrūnī	electronic
istaʿadd X	to get ready for *(fī)*
istaʿār X	to borrow from *(min)*
istaḍāf X	to host, to have guests
istafād X	to make use of, to benefit from *(min)*
istafazz X	to provoke
istaghrab X	to wonder at *(min)*
istaʿgil X	to hurry
istahlik X	to use up, to consume
istaḥmil X	to bear, to endure
istahwa X	to catch cold
istakhdim X	to use
istakhrag X	to mine, quarry
istakhsar X	to consider something as a loss, or as damage
istaktar X	to consider something as a great amount
istamarr X	to continue (uninterruptedly)
istaʿmil X	to use something
istanna X	to wait, wait for someone, something (without preposition)

A leaflet of the Egyptian mobile network MobiNil. When answering the phone, the Arabs say "'Alō!" Thereafter they ask "Mīn ma'āya?" (Who's speaking?) The leaflet tells us the price of a minute of phonecall: 75 'irsh, i.e. 75 piastres.

istantig X	to deduce something, to infer something from *(min)*
istarayyaḥ X	to rest, to have a rest
istarkha X	to relax
istarkhaṣ X	to consider something very cheap
istaslim X	to give up, capitulate
istasmir X	to invest
istashār X	to take counsel with someone (without preposition) about
ista'zin X	to ask for permission
istismār, -āt	investment
'izn	permission
yafṭa (yufaṭ)	notice, signpost
kaffa II	to keep up with (without preposition)

kōd, -āt	code, country code
māl (ʾamwāl)	finances, financial means
māma	mum
mashy	walk
mitallig	frozen, chilled
mufaṣṣal	detailed
mukalma	phonecall, talk
mustafizz	provoking, inciting
mustasmir	investor
mustashār	councillor, consultant, chancellor
nihāya	end
nimra (nimar)	number
ṣēf	summer
sentrāl, -āt	telephone exchange
shdīd	strong, relentless, strict
shurfa (shuraf)	terrace
is-Swīd	Sweden
swīdī	Swedish
telefōnī	phone
trank	intercity or international phone call
ṭūl (ʾaṭwāl)	length
wafd (wufūd)	delegation
waḥda	unit, unity
zaḥma	(traffic) jam, crowd
zōr	throat, neck

V. Taʿbīrāt:

ʾākhir ish-shāriʿ da	At the end of this street.
ʿAmal mukalma.	He was on the phone.
ʾAsta ʾazin	Excuse me. May I go?
Itfaḍḍal!	– answer
Id-dinya ḥarr.	It's hot.
Maʿa (alf) salāma!	Goodbye!
Walā yihimmak!	Don't mention it!

17

Id - Dars sab'atāshar /Lesson 17

ʾIsm il-būlīs

- Itfaḍḍalī ḥaḍretik, istarayyaḥī il-ʾawwil wi ʾūlī lī mushkiltik ʾē(h).
- ʾAna gayya li-ḥaḍretak ʿashān ʾaurāʾī kullahā ḍāʿit minnī.
- Wi da ḥaṣal ʾezzāy ?
- ʾAna kunt rakba ʾl-ʿarabīya btaʿit gōzī fī ṭarīʾ il-ʾIsmaʿīlīya wi hnāk ḥaṣalit lī ḥadsa. Kān ʾuddāmī ʿarabīya karro malyāna ʾaṣab sukkar, makhadtish bālī minhā, ḥāwilt ʾahaddiʾ is-surʿa, bas dakhalt fī ʾawwil shagara ganb iṭ-ṭarīʾ.
- Il-ḥamdu li ʾllāh ʾinn(i) ḥaḍretik bi-khēr! Wi ʾl-kalām da ḥaṣal ʾemta?
- Il-ḥadsa ḥaṣalit iṣ-ṣubḥ, yōm il-gumʿa, 23 (talāta ʾu ʿishrīn) māris, bēn is-sāʿa 10, 30 (ʿashara u nuṣṣ) wi 11 (ḥedāshar).
- Mumkin tiḥkī lī ʾl-mauḍūʿ bi ʾt-tafṣīl ?
- Id-dinya kānit faḍya, mafīsh ghēr ʾotobīs siyāḥī kān miʿaddi wi ʾs-sawwāʾ b(i)tāʿo, ʾawwilmā shāfnī nazla mi ʾl-ʿarabīya, kān ʿāwiz yuṭlub lī ʾl-ʾisʿāf, bas laʾānī salīma wi ʾāl ʾinno ḥa-yittiṣil bi ʾl-murūr. Gōzī kān ʾayyāmīhā fī Būr Saʿīd wi lammā kallimto ʿa ʾl-maḥmūl, ʾāl lī ʾinno ḥa-yīgī ʾawwilmā yikhallaṣ shughlo. Ge fī ḥudūd is-saʿa ʾtnēn wi f(i)ḍilna fi ʾl-ʾIsmāʿīlīya li-ghāyit yōm is-sabt. ʿAmalna ʾl-maḥḍar wi waddēna ʾl-ʿarabīya titṣallaḥ.
- Ṭayyib, di ʾawwil marra ḥaḍretik bi-tisūʾī ʾl-ʿarabīya fī Maṣr?
- La, gōzī mandūb shirka ʾalmanīya wi ʿashān keda bi-yisūʾ il-ʿarabīya kull(i) yōm. ʾAna bākhudhā minno marritēn talāta kull(i) shahr.

Wi ʾṭṭammina ʿala ʾt-tabūt sitta wi talatīn wi ʾt-tābūt sabʿa ʾu talatīn wi laʾēna ʾl-mūmiyāt fī makānhā. Sitta wi talatīn yiḍumm mūmiyā ʾl-wazīr Semkh-ka-raʿ mi ʾl-uṣra ʾr-rabʿa bi ʾl-Menūf, sabʿa ʾu talatīn yiḍumm mūmiyā ʾl-ḥarāmī ʿAbdo Ḥanafī mi ʾl-uṣra tamantāshar bi-Būlāʾ id-Dakrūr.

We checked coffins number 36 and 37. We found the mummies at their places. Number 36 contains the mummy of vizier Semkhkara from the 4th dynasty in Memphis, number 37 contains the mummy of the thief Abd Hanafi of the 18th dynasty in Bulaq id-Dakrur.

- Bas hiya di ʾawwil marra kunti bi-tisūʾī ḥaḍretik fī ṭarīʾ il-Ismāʿīlīya, mish keda?
- Da ṣaḥīḥ, lākin ʾabli keda ruḥt il-Ismāʿīlīya maʿa gōzī ḥawālī khamas marrāt.
- Ḥaḍretik maʿāki ṭabʿan rukhṣa daulīya?
- ʾĀ(h) ṭabʿan, ʿamaltahā ʾabli māgī Maṣr ʿashān ʾaʾdar ʾasūʾ hena.
- Ḥaḍretik gēti Maṣr ʾemta?
- 26. (sitta ʾu ʿishrīn) september 1998 (ʾalf tusʿumīya tamanya ʾu tisʿīn), bas gōzī sabaʾnī bi-shahr ʾu nuṣṣ taʾrīban.
- Gamīl, yibʾa maʿāki di ʾl-waʾt(i) maḥḍar il-būlīs bitāʿ il-ḥadsa min ʾism il-Ismāʿīlīya?
- Maẓbūṭ. Il-maḥḍar maugūd, lākin il-mushkila fī ʾaurāʾī, ir-rukhṣa id-daulīya wi gawāz is-safar wi kart it-taʾmīn is-siḥḥī wi ʾaurāʾ tanya. Kull(i) da ḍāʿ fī makān il-ḥadsa.
- Il-ʾaurāʾ ir-rasmīya masʾala muhimma ʾawi, ʾeḥna lāzim niʿmil li-ḥaḍretik maḥḍar gdīd tiʾdarī titḥarrakī bīh li-ghāyit ma titḥall il-mushkila. ʿAla ṭūl ḥattiṣil bi-zamāyilna fi ʾl-Ismāʿīlīya ʿashān yisʾalū ʿala ʾaurāʾik.
- Maʿrafsh(i) ʾashkur ḥaḍretak ʾezzāy!
- Il-ʿafw(u), ʿala ʾē(h)? Da wāgib, yā madām! ʾŪlī lī ḥaḍretik tārīkh wi makān mīlādik!
- 14. (ʾarbaʿtāshar) yūniyō 1965(ʾalf tusʿumīya khamsa u sittīn) fī Myūnikh.
- Waẓīftik?
- Fī ʾAlmāniyā mudarrisa, hena fī Maṣr rabbit manzil.
- Ṭayyib wi nimrit telefōnik?
- Il-bēt fi ʾl-Qāhira - 02/3315250, maktab gōzī 891613 wi ʾl-maḥmūl b(i)tāʿo 0124592077.
- Shukran, ḥa-nittiṣil bi-ḥaḍretik ʾawwilmā yiruddū ʿalēna min ʾl-Ismāʿīlīya.

I. ʾAsʾila:

1. Mīn kān bi-yisūʾ il-ʿarabīya fī ṭarīʾ il-Ismāʿīlīya?
2. Il-ʿarabīya dakhalit ish-shagara ganb iṭ-ṭarīʾ lē(h)?
3. Sawwāʾ il-ʾotobīs is-siyāḥī kān ʿāwiz yiʿmil ʾē(h) ʾawwilmā shāf il-ḥadsa?
4. Gōz is-sitt il-ʾalmanīya ʾāl ʾinno ḥa-yīgī ʾemta, lammā kallimito ʿa ʾl-maḥmūl?
5. Is-sitt il-ʾalmanīya ma kānitsh(i) bi-tisūʾ il-ʿarabīya fī Maṣr ʾabl(i) keda?
6. Mrāt mandūb ish-shirka ʾl-ʾalmanīya ʿamalit ir-rukhṣa ʾd-daulīya ʾemta?
7 Is-sitt il-ʾalmanīya rāḥit ʾism il-būlīs lē(h)?
8. Iẓ-ẓābit ʾāl lahā ʾē(h)?
9. Is-sitt il-almanīya muḥtāga maḥḍar gdīd lē(h)?
10. ʾIsm il-būlīs ḥa-yittiṣil bi-mrāt mandūb ish-shirka ʾl-ʾalmanīya ʾemta?

II. Qawāʿid:

1. Expressions of time

Is-sāʿa kam? – What's the time?

- in order to express whole hours, Arabic uses the noun ***sāʿa*** (hour) and cardinal numerals in the feminine form: *is-sāʿa waḥda* (it's one o'clock), *is-sāʿa ʾtnēn* (it's two o'clock), *is-sāʿa talāta* (it's three o'clock), *is-sāʿa ʾarbaʿa* (it's four o'clock), *is-sāʿa khamsa* (it's five o'clock), *is-sāʿa sitta* (it's six o'clock), *is-sāʿa sabʿa* (it's seven o'clock), *is-sāʿa ḥedāshar* (it's eleven o'clock), *is-sāʿa ʾtnāshar* (it's twelve o'clock)
- phrases like **"it's half past one"** are expressed by means of the noun ***sāʿa*** (hour), the cardinal numeral, the conjunction ***wi / ʾu*** (and), and the noun *nuṣṣ* (half): *is-sāʿa waḥda ʾu nuṣṣ* (it's half past one), *is-sāʿa ʾtnēn ʾu nuṣṣ* (it's half past two), *is-sāʿa talāta ʾu nuṣṣ* (it's half past three)
- phrases like **"its quarter past one"** are expressed by means of the noun ***sāʿa*** (hour), the cardinal numeral, the conjunction ***wi/ʾu*** (and), and the noun ***rubʿ*** (quarter): *is-sāʿa waḥda ʾu rubʿ* (it's quarter past one), *is-sāʿa ʾtnēn ʾu rubʿ* (it's quarter past two), *is-sāʿa talāta ʾu rubʿ* (it's quarter past three), *is-sāʿ ʾarbaʿa ʾu rubʿ* (it's quarter past four)
- phrases like **"its quarter to two"** are expressed by means of the noun ***sāʿa*** (hour), the cardinal numeral, the conjunction ***ʾillā*** (but, without), and the noun ***rubʿ*** (quarter): *is-sāʿa ʾtnēn ʾillā rubʿ* (it's quarter to two), *is-sāʿa talāta ʾillā rubʿ* (it's quarter to three), *is-sāʿa ʾarbaʿa ʾillā rubʿ* (it's quarter to four)
- phrases like **"it's twenty past one"** are expressed by means of the noun ***sāʿa*** (hour), the cardinal numeral, the conjunction ***wi/ʾu***, and the noun ***tilt*** (a third, i.e. 20 minutes): *is-sāʿa waḥda ʾu tilt* (it's twenty past one), *is-sāʿa ʾtnēn ʾu tilt* (it's twenty past two), *s-sāʿa talāta ʾu tilt* (it's twenty past three)
- phrases like **"it's twenty to two"** are expressed by means of the noun ***sāʿa*** (hour), the cardinal numeral, the conjunction ***ʾillā*** (but, without), and the noun ***tilt*:** *is-sāʿa ʾtnēn ʾillā tilt* (it's twenty to two), *is-sāʿa talāta ʾillā tilt* (it's twenty to three)
- in order to express 1 – 10 minutes to or past the whole hour, the numeral stands after the cardinal numeral and the conjunction ***wi/u*** ("past") or ***ʾillā*** ("to"): *is-sāʿa tamanya ʾu khamsa* (it's five minutes past eight), *is-sāʿa tisʿa ʾu sabʿa (sabʿa daʾāʾy)* (it's seven minutes past nine), *is-sāʿa ʿashara ʾu talāta* (it's three minutes past ten), *is-sāʿa tamanya ʾillā khamsa (khamas daʾāʾy)* (it's five minutes to eight), *is-sāʿa tisʿa ʾillā sabʿa (sabʿa daʾāʾy)* (it's seven minutes to nine), *is-sāʿa ʿashara ʾillā talāta (talāt daʾāʾy)* (it's three minutes to ten)
- in order to express 1 – 5 minutes to or past half an hour, the numeral stands after the cardinal numeral, the noun ***nuṣṣ*** and the conjunction ***wi/u*** ("past") or ***ʾillā*** ("to"): *is-sāʿa tamanya ʾu nuṣṣ ʾu khamsa (khamas daʾāʾy)* (it's eight thirty-five), *is-sāʿa tamanya ʾu nuṣṣ ʾillā khamsa (khamas daʾāʾy)* (it's eight twenty-five), *is-sāʿa ʿashara ʾu nuṣṣ ʾu ʾarbaʿa (ʾarbaʿa daʾāʾy)* (it's ten thirty-four), *is-sāʿa talāta ʾu nuṣṣ ʾillā diʾīʾtēn* (it's three twenty-eight)
- another way to express time is to express the whole hour by the cardinal number and the minutes past after the conjunction ***wi/u*:** *is-sāʿa waḥda ʾu sabʿatāshar (diʾīʾa)* (it's 1 o'clock 17 minutes), *is-sāʿa ʾtnēn ʾu talāta ʾu ʿishrīn (diʾīʾa)* (it's two twenty-three),

is-sāʿa sitta ʾu tamanya ʾu talatīn (diʾȳʾa) (it's six thirty-eight), *is-sāʿa sabʿa ʾu arbaʿa ʾu ʾarbaʿīn (diʾȳʾa)* (it's seven forty-four), *is-sāʿa ḥedāshar ʾu tisʿa ʾu ʾarbaʿīn (diʾȳʾa)* (it's eleven forty-nine).

2. The date, the calendar and days of the week

In-nahār da kam*?* – What's the date today?

In-nahār da wāḥid ʾaghusṭus (talāta fabrāyir / sabʿa yūniyū / itnāshar nofember / khamsa ʾu ʿishrīn māyū) sanit ʾalfēn ʾu wāḥid. Today is the 1st of August (3rd of February / 7th of June / 11th of November / 25th of May) 2001.

- the date (day, month and year) is expressed by cardinal numerals in the feminine form (with the exception of the numeral "one"), names of months and the noun *sana* (year), which forms a genitival phrase with the following number.

Shuhūr is-sana ʾl-higrīya (ish-shuhūr il-ʾamarīya)

1. *muḥarram*	7. *ragab*
2. *ṣafar*	8. *shaʿbān*
3. *rabīʿ il-ʾawwal*	9. *ramaḍān*
4. *rabīʿ it-tānī*	10. *shawwāl*
5. *gamād ʾawwal*	11. *zū ʾl-qaʿda*
6. *gamād tānī*	12. *zū ʾl-ḥigga*

- the Muslim era begins with the *higra* (the moving of the Prophet Muḥammad from Mekka to Medina on the 16th of July 622), the year 2001 of the Christian calendar corresponds to year 1425 of the Muslim calendar
- the Muslim month has 29 or 30 days (according to the appearance of the new moon in the sky)
- the Muslim months begin annually 11 days earlier than the year before

Shuhūr is-sana ʾl-mīlādīya (ish-shuhūr ish-shamsīya):
(the Gregorian calendar)

1. *yanāyir*	7. *yūliyū*
2. *fabrāyir*	8. *ʾaghusṭus*
3. *māris*	9. *september*
4. *ʾabrīl*	10. *ʾoktōber*
5. *māyū*	11. *nofember*
6. *yūniyū*	12. *dīsember*

Shuhūr is-sana ʾl-ʾibṭīya (ish-shuhūr ish-shamsīya):
(the Coptic calendar)

1. *tūt*	7. *baramhāt*
2. *bābah*	8. *barmūda*
3. *ḥātūr*	9. *bashans*
4. *khiyāk*	10. *baʾūna*
5. *tūba*	11. *ʾabīb*
6. *ʾamshīr*	12. *misrā*

- Coptic months occupy an important place in folk tradition – they are rooted in the daily ritual of the inhabitants of the countryside, who use them to place the meteorological situation, natural conditions or the state of agricultural works in time, e.g.: *khiyāk ṣabāḥak masāk, tiʾūm min nōm tiḥaḍḍar ʿashāk.* - The *"khiyak"* morning is like the evening, you get up and prepare dinner. *Baramhāt ruḥ il-ghēṭ wi hāt!* – *"Baramhat"* has come, go to the field and bring (the yield of the first harvest)!
- each Coptic month has 30 days, the month of *tūt* begins around the 10th of September (the date fluctuates); the month of *misrā* is followed by a period called *nasīʾ* (its length varies between 4 and 6 days), which evens the difference between the Gregorian and the Coptic calendar.

ʾAyyām il-ʾusbūʿ:
(yōm) ʾl-itnēn (Monday), *(yōm) ʾit-talāt* (Tuesday), *(yōm) il-ʾarbaʿ* (Wednesday), *(yōm) il-khamīs* (Thursday), *(yōm) il-gumʿa* (Friday), *(yōm) is-sabt* (Saturday), *(yōm) il-ḥad* (Sunday).

3. Multiplicative numerals
- multiplicative numerals are formed by cardinal numerals in the masculine form and the noun ***marra***: ***Kam marra?*** – How many times? Please note exceptions by "once" and "twice" – cf. Lesson 4.
marra (waḥda) (once), *marritēn* (twice), *talāt marrāt* (three times), *ʾarbaʿ marrāt* (four times), *khamas marrāt* (five times), *sitt(i) marrāt* (six times), *sabʿ marrāt* (seven times), *taman marrāt* (eight times), *tisʿ marrāt* (nine times), *ʿashar marrāt* (ten times), *ḥedāshar marra* (eleven times), *itnāshar marra* (twelve times), *ʿishrīn marra* (twenty times), *talāta ʾu talatīn marra* (thirty-three times), *mīt marra* (a hundred times), *khumsumīt marra* (five hundred times), *ʾalf marra* (a thousand times)

4. Numeral adverbs
- numeral adverbs are formed by ordinal numerals in masculine form followed by the noun *marra*: *ʾawwil marra* (the first time), *tānī marra* (the second time), *tālit marra* (the third time), *rābiʿ marra* (the fourth time), *khāmis marra* (the fifth time),

sādis marra (the sixth time), *sābiʿ marra* (the seventh time), *tāmin marra* (the eighth time), *tāsiʿ marra* (the ninth time), *ʿāshir marra* (the tenth time).

5. Temporal clauses
- temporal clauses are introduced by the following temporal conjunctions:
lammā (when), ***ʾablimā*** (before), ***baʿdimā*** (after, when), ***kullimā*** (every time when, whenever), ***ʾawwilmā*** (as soon as), ***li-ghāyit mā*** (until)
- the ***mā*** of the temporal conjunctions is often reduced, with the following verb form of the first person singular imperfect it combines to ***-ma-/-mā-***:

lammā:
Shufna ʾl-film da, lammā kunna fī Bārīs. – We saw this film when we were in Paris.
Lammā kallimtenī, kunt fī ʾl-metro. – When you called me, I was in the subway.
Lammā tīgū Maṣr, ʿaddū ʿalēna! – Come by when you come to Cairo!

ʾablimā:
ʾAblimā taklī, ighsilī ʾīdēki kwayyis! – Wash (f.) your hands properly before you eat!
Lāzim nirawwaḥ, ʾablimā ʾd-dinya tiḍallim – We must come home before it gets dark.
ʾAblimā tibtidū tiftaḥū ʾt-tābūt, itʾakkidū ʾinn il-ḥabl ḥa-yistahmil il-ghaṭa! – Before you start opening the coffin, make sure the rope will hold the lid!

baʿdimā:
Baʿdimā tiʾfilū ʾṣ-ṣandūʾ, waddūh il-makhzan! – After you lock the box, take it to the magazine!
Ḥabbēt il-kātib da, baʿdimā ʾarēt riwayto ʾl-ʾakhīra. – I began to like this author after I had read his last novel.
Baʿdimā nitfarrag ʿa ʾl-maʿraḍ, mumkin nishrab ḥāga fi ʾl-ʾahwa di. – After we see the exhibition we may have something to drink in this café.

kullimā:
Kulli maḥāwil ʾattaṣil bīku, ʾalāʾī telefōnku mashghūl. – Every time I try to call you, your phone is busy (I find your phone busy).
Kullimā nukhrug, ninsa nitfi ʾn-nūr shababīk il-ʾōḍa. – Every time we go away we forget to turn off the light.
Kullimā yishrab ḥāga sāʾ(i)ʿa, yikuḥḥ. – Whenever he drinks something cold, he coughs.

ʾawwilmā
ʾAwwilmā tirgaʿū mi ʾr-riḥla, ittaṣilū bīna! – As soon as you return from the trip, call us!
ʾAwwilmā s(i)miʿna ʾl-khabar, f(i)riḥna ʾawi. – As soon as we heard the news, we were very happy.
ʾAwwilmā tīgī, ḥa-nibtidi nishtaghal. – We will start to work as soon as you come.

li-ghāyit mā:
Lāzim tifḍal fi ʾs-srīr li-ghāyit mā tikhiff. – You must stay in bed until you recover.
Sībī ʾl-ghasīl fi ʾl-balakōna li-ghāyit mā yinshaf khāliṣ! – Leave (f.) the laundry on the balcony until it's completely dry!
Istannū li-ghāyit māgī! – Wait (pl.) until I come!

III. Tadrībāt:

Targama

How many times did you visit this museum? We visited it about eight times. Every time I hear this music, I remember our beautiful holiday. Every time we speak about the journey in front of her, she starts crying. This is the third time this problem happened (happens) to us. Before we set out the protocol, we must ask you several questions. Before you start the car, check (measure) the oil! After they had taken the statue out of the tomb, they took it for restoration (brought it away in order to be restored). Would you like to go for a little walk after you drink the tea? I was very happy when he told me that he had succeeded in the exam. When we were in Egypt for the first time, we did not understand many words. When you finish your work, you must rest. When and where were you born? I was born (I am born) on the 7th of July 1972 in Prague, but my sister was born on the 1st of September 1976 in Cairo. These products come from the factories in the cities of the 10th Ramadan and 6th October. My passport was issued by the Passport department on the 15th of December 1998. When he's got time, he goes on Friday and Saturday to Alexandria. After they had reserved the flight tickets, they went to the embassy for their visas. As soon as you (f.) recover, we will go to the sea. Wait (pl.) here until the bus comes. I will wait (for you) (polite) in the library until you return. As soon as I learn anything I'll tell you. Every time we want to go out, it is raining. He must stay in the hospital until his health improves. Before you (f.) open the bottle, shake it well. Before you go to the passport department, make copies (photographs) of your ID cards!

Kammil!

Is-sāʿa kam?

a)	6:09	f)	2:43 ......
b)	11:40	g)	4:29 ......
c)	7:56	h)	12:35 ......
d)	10:50	i)	5:18 ......
e)	3:21	j)	9:32 ......

IV. Mufradāt

ʿadda II	to go around, to stop by
ʾayyāmīhā	then, on that day
ʿayyaṭ II	to cry
ʾawrāʾ (rasmīya)	ID papers, documents
ʾawwilmā	as soon as, when
baʿdimā	after, afterwards
būlīs	police
Būr Saʿīd	Port Said
ḍāʿ (ī)	to get lost
ḍallim II	to dusk, to get dark
dawwar II	to start (a car) (without preposition)
fiḍil (a)	to stay, to remain
firiḥ (a)	to be happy
ghēr	outside, but for, besides, except for
gōz (ʾagwāz)	husband, pair
ḥabl (ḥibāl)	rope
ḥadd (ḥudūd)	frontier, limit
haddaʾ II	to calm down, to reduce (speed)
ḥadsa	accident
ḥāla	state, condition, case
ʾisʿāf	first help, ambulance
itḥall V	to be solved
itḥarrak V	to move
itrammim V	to be restored, reconstructed
itṣallaḥ V	to be repaired
kaḥḥ (u)	to cough
kalām	affair, event
karro	trolley, carriage
kaza	some, several
kullimā	every time, whenever
li-ghāyit mā	until
maʿraḍ (maʿāriḍ)	exhibition, book-fair
mandūb	representative

maṣnaʿ (maṣāniʿ)	factory
maṭṭar II	to rain
mawlūd (mawālīd)	born
mrāt (mrāto, mrāt mandūb shirka)	(before a pronoun, pronominal suffix or the first component of a genitival phrase) woman, wife (his wife, wife of company representative)
murūr	traffic
nishif (a)	to become dry
ʾablimā	before
ʾamar (ʾaʾmār)	moon
ʾaṣab sukkar	sugar cane
ʾism (ʾaqsām)	(police) station
ʾism ig-gawazāt	passport department
rabbit manzil	housewife
ragg (u)	to shake, shake something (without preposition)
rasmī	official
riwāya	novel
rukhṣa (rukhaṣ)	driver's license
sabaʾ (a)	to go / come before, to make something be fore someone else (without preposition)
ṣadar (a)	to be issued by/at *(min)*
sana higrīya	Muslim year
sana mīlādīya	Christian year
taʾmīn, -āt	insurance
tazkarit ṭayarān (tazākir)	flight ticket
tilt	a third
wāgib, -āt	duty, task

V. Taʿbīrāt:

bi-tafṣīl	in detail
fī ḥudūd	about, approximately
Id-dinya ḍallimit	It got dark.
Id-dinya faḍya.	There was nobody there.
Id-dinya maṭṭarit.	It was raining.
Il-ḥamdu li ʾllāh ʾinnak bi-khēr!	Thank God you (m.) are all right!
In-nahār da kām?	What's the date today?
Is-sāʿa kām?	What's the time?
Dakhal fī ...	He hit ...
Kam marra?	How many times?
kaza ḥāga	several things, a number of things
kaza ḥad / wāḥid	several people, a number of people
Ma khadsh(i) bālo min ...	He did not notice ...
marritēn talāta!	two or three times

Ish-sha''a

- Is-salāmu ʿalēku! ʾAna gay ʿashān il-ʾiʿlān ʾilli nizil fi ʾl-ʾAhrām ʾembāreḥ. ʾAna mutargim biʿsit il-Maʿhad it-tshīkī li ʾl-ʾāsār il-maṣrīya ʾl-ʾadīma wi maʿhadna muḥtāg ḍarūrī sha''a wāsiʿa li-ʾaʿḍāʾ il-biʿsa ʾl-gudād.
- ʾAhlan wa sahlan, bas ʾana mish ṣāḥib ish-sha''a.
- Mish ḥaḍretak il-ʾustāz Raʾūf ʾilli kallimto ʾembāreḥ bi ʾl-lēl?
- La, da ʾakhūya li kallim ḥaḍretak fī mauḍūʿ taʾgīr ish-sha''a. Sawānī, ʾandahū lak.
- Yā marḥab! ʾEzzāy ḥaḍretak? Kwayyis ʾinnak gēt in-nahār da ʿala ṭūl, ʾaṣlan fī kaza wāḥid ittaṣal bīna ʿashān mauḍūʿ ish-sha''a, ʾālū l(i)na ʾinn ish-sha''a bi-nafs il-muwāṣafāt fī nafs il-manṭiʾa bi-titʾaggar ʾaghla bi-ktīr mi ʾs-siʿr ʾilli ṭalabnāh fi ʾg-gurnān.

Sittī, sittī ... laʾēt ʾīd il-maknasa maksūra ?! Maʿalesh ... ʾaṣl sīdak ge ʾembāreḥ mitʾakhkhar shwayya!!

Granny, granny ... I found a broken broomstick?! Don't worry ... your grandpa came a bit late yesterday!

- Bas ʾana shāyif ʾinn il-mablagh ʾilli ḥaḍretak ʿaraḍto ʿalayya fi ʾt-telefōn, maʿʾūl giddan. Bi-ṣarāḥa, sumʿit il-maʿhad it-tshīkī ʾṭ-ṭayyiba wi ʾsh-shughl ʾilli bi-yiʿmilo, da li yikhallī lku ʾl-ʾaulawīya.
- ʾAllāh y(i)khallīk! Ḥaḍretak s(i)miʿt ʿan ʾl-iktishāfāt it-tshīkīya fī ʾAbū Ṣīr?
-Ṭabʿan, ʾeḥna fi ʿēlitna bi-n(i)ḥibb it-tārīkh. ʿAla fikra, ʾakhūya ʾlli ḥaḍretak sallimt ʿalēh min shwayya, khirrīg Kullīyit il-ʾāsār. ʾAna nafsī mitābiʿ kull il-ḥāgāt ig-gdīda li bi-yiktishifhā ʾl-ʾasarīyīn fī Maṣr.
- Ṭayyib, itfaḍḍal ḥaḍretak maʿāya, ḥafarragak ʿala ʾsh-sha''a!
- Ish-sha''a mafrūsha bi-shakl gamīl. Di sofra maftūḥa ʿala ṣāla, mish keda?

- ʾĀ(h), wi ʾl-ʾōḍa ʾlli ʾehna dākh(i)līnhā di ʾl-waʾt(i) kānit makhzan, shilna rufūf il-khashab illi kānit fīhā wi khalēnāhā ʾoḍt in-nōm.
- Ṭayyib, ʾeḥna ʿawzīn ish-shaʾʾa di li ʾn-nās ʾilli bi-yīgū ʾaktar min marra khilāl il-mōsim, bas kull(i) marra ma bi-yuʾʿdūsh ghēr mudda basīṭa.
- Iṣ-ṣāla li ḥaḍretak shuftahā, mumkin niʾfilhā wi nigīb lahā nafs is-sarāyir ʾilli ḥaṭṭēnāhā fi ʾoḍt in-nōm.
- Gamīl ʾu di ʾl-waʾt(i) baʿd ʾiznak, mumkin nibuṣṣ baṣṣa ʿala ʾl-maṭbakh? Fi ʾl-ḥaʾīʾa, ʾana mish ʿārif, in-nās ʾilli ḥa-yiskunū hena ḥa-yuṭbukhū bi-nafsuhum walla ḥa-yigībū ʾakl gāhiz.
- Bi-rāḥithum, ʿala kull(i) ḥāl, ḥa-tilāʾī fi ʾl-maṭbakh kull(i) ḥāga. ʿAndak hena butagāz wi khallāṭ wi kubbāyāt wi fanagīl wi ʾaṭbāʾ wi ṣawānī wi ḥilal wi ṭāsāt tīfāl wi shuwak wi maʿāliʾ wi sakakīn wi kamān fuwaṭ maṭbakh!
- Ṭayyib, fī ḥad bi-yīgī yinaḍḍaf ish-shaʾʾa?
- Mrāt il-bawwāb hiya li mumkin tittif(i)ʾū maʿāhā ʿala masʾal(i)t it-tanḍīf. ʿUmūman, ʾadawāt it-tanḍīf, zay il-gardal wi ʾl-gārūf wi il-maʾashsha, fī ʾl-ʾōḍa ʾṣ-ṣ(u)ghayyara li ʾuddām ḥaḍretak ʿala ṭūl.
- Maʿlesh ya ʾl-ʾustāz Raʾūf, mumkin ʾasʾalak suʾāl shakhṣī shwayya?
- ʾAwi, ʾawi!
- ʾEntū bi-tiʾaggarū ʾsh-shaʾʾa ʾl-gamīla di lē(h)? Ḥaʾūl li ḥaḍretak ... ish-shaʾʾa di kānit btaʿit ʿammitna li ʿāshit fīhā ʾl-ʿumr kullo. Mātit is-sana di, ʾAllāh yirḥamhā. Is-sinīn li fātit kullahā li kānit fīhā li-waḥdahā, makānitsh(i) ʿayza tighayyar fīhā ʾayyi ḥāga wi fī nafs il-waʾt kānit rafḍa tīgī tuʾ ʿud maʿa ʾayyi wāḥid fīna. ʾAna nafsī kunt batḥāyil ʿalēhā ʾinn fī ḥāgāt lāzim titṣallaḥ ʿashān ish-shaʾʾa tifḍal fī ḥāla kwayyisa. Baʿd wafātha ʾibtadēna niṣallaḥ fīhā – il-ḥanafīya kānit bi-t(i)naʾʾaṭ, il-ballāʿa fi ʾl-ḥammām kānit masdūda wi ʾl-ḥōḍ kān maksūr. Il-ḥāgāt di khadit minnā maghūd wi flūs, fa-ʾulna niʾaggarhā li ʾn-nās ʾilli tiʾaddar ʾīmithā ʾu fī nafs il-waʾt tiḥāfiz ʿalēhā.

- Yaʿnī ma bi-tifakkarūsh tibīʿūhā?
- La, nawyīn nisībhā li-w(i)lādna.
- Ittafaʾna ʿala ʾl-ʾīgār?
- ʾĀ(h) khalāṣ, ʾalf mabrūk. Ma tinsāsh ḥaḍretak maḥbas il-ghāz fi ʾl-maṭbakh ʾu maḥbas il-mayya fi ʾl-ḥammām taḥt is-sakhkhān wi ʿaddād il-kahraba ganb(i) bāb ish-shaʾʾa!

I. ʾAsiʾla:

1. Mīn li kallimo mutargim biʿsit il-maʿhad it-tshīkī fī mauḍūʿ taʾgīr ish-shaʾʾa?
2. Ish-shaʾʾa bi nafs il-muwāṣafāt wi fi nafs il-manṭiʾa bi-titʾaggar bi ʾs-siʿr ʾilli ṭalabo ʾaṣḥābhā fi ʾg-gurnān?
3. ʾĒ(h) li bi-yikhallī ʾl-ʾaulawīya li ʾl-maʿhad it-tshīkī?
4. Rufūf il-khashab ʾilli kānit fi ʾl-makhzan itshālit lē(h)?
5. In-nās ʾilli ha-yīgū ʾaktar min marra khilāl il-mōsim, ḥa-yuʾʿudū kull(i) marra ʾaddi ʾē(h)?
6. In-nās ʾilli ḥa-yiskunū fi ʾsh-shaʾʾa, ḥa-yuṭbukhū bi-nafsuhum walla ḥa-yigībū ʾakl gāhiz?
7. Mīn li mumkin yittif(i)ʾū maʿāh ʿala tanḍīf ish-shaʾʾa?
8. Mīn li kān ʿāyish fi ʾsh-shaʾʾa ʾs-sinīn li fātit?
9. ʾĒ(h) hiya ʾl-ḥāgāt ʾilli kān mafrūḍ titṣallaḥ?
10. Il-ʾustāz Raʾūf wi ʾakhūh ʿayzīn yiʾaggarū ʾsh-shaʾʾa li mīn?

II. Qawāʿid:

1. The relative pronoun *ʾilli / li*

- the relative pronoun has two forms, *ʾilli* (long) and *li* (short– mostly after words ending in a vowel). It follows the defined noun and does not change with gender or number:
ish-shahr ʾilli / li gay (next month), *il-ʾusbūʿ ʾilli / li fāt* (last week), *is-sana li gayya* (next year), *is-sinīn ʾilli fātit* (last years), *ish-shuhūr ʾilli / li gayya* (next months), *il-yōmēn ʾilli fātū* (the last two/few days)

- the short form of the relative pronoun is often used in sentences with interrogative pronouns ***mīn*** and ***ʾē(h)***: *Mīn li gāb ig-gawāb da?* – Who (is it who) brought this letter? *Mīn li saʾalak ʿala ʾl-mauḍūʿ da?* – Who asked you about this affair? *Mīn li ʿāwiz yīgī maʿāna?* – Who wants to go with us? *ʾĒ(h) li ʾenta shāy(i)lo?* – What is it that you are carrying with you? What are you carrying with you? *ʾĒ(h) li ʾenti gāy(i)bāh?* – What have you brought? *ʾĒ(h) li ʾentū muḥtāgīno?* – What do you need? What is it that you need?

2. The relative clause

a) the relative clause with a relative pronoun; the antecedent of the relative pronoun is the subject of the main clause:

Il-muwaẓẓaf ʾilli dakhal gāb lina gawāb. – The official who came in gave us a letter. *Iṭ-ṭayyāra li nizlit gayya mi ʾr-Riyād.* – The plane that landed came from Riyad. *It-tamasīl ʾilli bi-titrammim hena, min il-ʿaṣr il-bīzānṭī.*
– The statues that are restored here come from the Byzantine period.
Il-rukkāb ʾilli kharugū mi ʾl-maṭār, mistannīn il-ʾotobīs.
– The passengers who walked out of the airport are waiting for the bus.

b) the relative clause with a relative pronoun; the antecedent of the relative pronoun is the object of the verb or of an active participle:
- the pronominal suffix of the 3rd person is attached to the verb or participle and agrees in gender and number with the noun that governs the relative clause:
Il-kitāb ʾilli gibto, maktūb bi ʾl-ʿarabī. – The book that I have brought is written in Arabic. *Il-ʾōḍa li ḥagaznāhā, gamīla giddan.* – The room that we reserved is very beautiful. *Il-ʾakl ʾilli ṭalabtūh, ʿalēh shaṭṭa.* – The meal that you have ordered is with chilli peppers. *Is-suyyāḥ ʾilli ʾābilnāhum, kānū min ʾAlmāniyā.* – The tourists we have met were from Germany. *Il-kitāb ʾilli ʾenta shayfo ʿa ʾr-raff, maktūb bi ʾl-ʿarabī.* – The book that you see on the bookshelf is written in Arabic. *Il-ʾōḍa li humma ḥāg(i)zīnhā, gamīla giddan.* – The room that they reserved is very beautiful. *Il-ʾaghānī li ʾentū sām(i)ʿīnhā, mi ʾn-Nūba.* – The songs that you hear are from Nubia.

If the noun is left out, a pronominal suffix of the 3rd person masculine singular is attached to the verb or participle, which is often preceded by a personal pronoun – the relative clause is governed only by the relative pronoun:
ʾIlli ʾenta gibto, kān gamīl. – (The thing) that you have brought was nice. *ʾIlli simiʿito, ʿagabhā ʾawi.* – She liked what she heard very much. *ʾIlli shāfūh fi ʾl-film, laʾūh mubālagh fīh.* – The thing that they saw in the film appeared exaggerated to them. *ʾIlli hiya fakrāh, huwa ʾinno kān fi ʾl-fatra ʾl-ʾakhīra taʿbān giddan.* – What she remembers is that he was very sick lately. *ʾIlli ʾeḥna ʿāwizīno, salamitku.* – What we want is that you become well. *ʾIlli hena, ʿār(i)fo kwayyis, bas ʾilli henāk, maʿarafūsh khāliṣ.* – That which is here I know very well, but that which is there I do not know at all.

c) the relative clause with a relative pronoun; the antecedent of the relative pronoun is the object of a preposition
- the pronominal suffix of the 3rd person is attached to the preposition and agrees in number and gender with the antecedent:
Il-ṭālib ʾilli ʾtkallimtū maʿāh, bi-yidris it-tārīkh. – The student with whom you have spoken studies history. *Iṣ-ṣūra li dawwarit ʿalēhā, kānit fī durg il-maktab.* – The picture she was looking for was in the drawer of the desk. *Ish-shunaṭ ʾilli shālū fīhā ʾl-kutub, itʾaṭṭaʾit khāliṣ.* – The bags in which they carried the books got completely torn. *In-nās ʾilli n(i)zilna ʿanduhum, ʾarāyib mrātī.* – The people with whom we have stayed are the relatives of my wife.

If the noun is left out, a pronominal suffix of the 3rd person masculine singular is attached to the preposition – the relative clause is governed only by the relative pronoun:
ʾIlli dawwarit ʿalēh, kān fī durg il-maktab. – (The thing) she was looking for was in the desk drawer. *ʾIlli kallimū ʿanno, muhimm giddan.* – (The thing) that they talked about is very important. *ʾIlli istaghrabna minno, ṭarīʾit istiʿmāl il-gihāz da.* – That which you were wondering about is the way to use this appliance.

d) the relative clause with the relative pronoun in the accusative case: "whose"
- the pronominal suffix of the 3rd person singular or plural is attached to the possessed noun, the suffix agrees in number and gender with the noun which governs the relative sentence:

Ittaṣalū bi ʾl-muhandis ʾilli ʾiddēt lhum ʾembāreḥ nimrit telefōno.
- They called the engineer, whose telephone number I had given to them yesterday.
Shuftū ʾsh-shaʾʾa li ʾaʿlanū ʿan siʿrahā fī ʾg-gurnān?
- Did you see the flat the price of which was advertised in the newspaper?
Hiya di ʾsh-shirka li rigiʿ mudīrhā min London ʾurayyib.
- This is the company whose manager has recently returned from London.
Dōl gīrānna ʾilli bi-nishūf wilādhum bi-yilʿabū fi ʾg-gnēna.
- These are our neighbours, whose children we see playing in the garden.

e) the relative clause with the relative pronoun functioning as the subject "he who", "that which":
- the relative pronoun *ʾilli* stands at the beginning of the sentence:
ʾIlli bi-yikallim fi ʾr-radiyo di ʾl-waʾt(i), ʾakīd maṣrī.
He who is now talking on the radio is certainly an Egyptian.
ʾIlli maugūd fi ʾs-sūʾ il-ʾayyām di, ghālī ʾawi.
- That which is found on the market these days is very expensive.
ʾIlli biʿīd ʿan il-ʿēn, biʿīd ʿan il-ʾalb.
- That which is far from the eye is far from the heart.
ʾIlli maʿāh daʿwa, yitfaḍḍal.
- He who has an invitation may enter.

3. "The same" and "alone"
- "The same" is expressed by means of a genitival phrase consisting of the noun ***nafs*** (soul) and the qualified noun:
nafs il-bēt (the same house), *nafs ish-shirka* (the same company), *nafs il-mashākil* (the same problems), *nafs iṣ-ṣuwar* (the same pictures), *nafs il-ʿummāl* (the same workers).
- "Alone, the only" is expressed by means of the phrase ***li-waḥd*** with the pronominal suffix (*li-waḥdī, li-waḥdak, li-waḥdik, li-waḥdo, li-waḥdahā, li-waḥdina, li-waḥduku, li-waḥduhum*):
Kunt henāk li-waḥdī. – I was there alone. *Ḥa-tirawwaḥī li-waḥdik?* – Will you go home alone? *Ma tinzilūsh il-baḥr li-waḥduku!* – Do not go into the sea alone!
- "***Alone***", "***on one's own***", "***personally***" is expressed by means of the phrase ***bi-nafs*** with the pronominal suffix
(*bi-nafsī, bi-nafsak, bi-nafsik, bi-nafso, bi-nafsahā, bi-nafsina, bi-nafsuku, bi-nafsuhum*):
Ish-shughl da lāzim ʾaʿmilo bi-nafsī. – I must do this work personally/on my own.
ʿĀwiz tishūf iṣ-ṣuwar di bi-nafsak? – Would you like to see these pictures personally?
Mumkin tisʾalūhum ʿala ʾl-mauḍūʿ da bi-nafsuku! – You can ask them about this affair personally!
- The emphatic "***alone***", "***oneself***" is expressed by means of the noun ***nafs*** with the pronominal suffix (*nafsī, nafsak, nafsik, nafso, nafsahā, nafsina, nafsuku, nafsuhum*):
ʾAna nafsī mish ʿārif. – I myself (even I) don't know.
Hiya nafsahā muhtamma bi ʾl-ḥāgāt di. – She herself is interested in these things.
Humma nafsuhum ṭalabū minna musāʿada. – They themselves asked us for help.

III. Tadrībāt:

Targama

Is this the picture of the hotel where you have lived? The problems that you were talking about were solved. Who is the man who greeted me so heartily? They offered us the same price that was advertised in the newspaper. Did you acquaint yourselves with the objects that were dicovered by the Czech Institute of Egyptology? Do you know the people who will live in this flat? Please place (f.) the cutlery that you have polished on the table. Where are the devices with which you survey the excavation sites? Last year they went on holiday with the same travel agency. With whom can we arrange the cleaning of the apartment? What are you looking for? (What is it that you are looking for?) Who talked with you about this affair? The workers who are unloading bricks here come from Abu Sir. The mosques that we photographed are from the Fatimid period. The books that they ordered from abroad came very quickly. The map that I asked about is sold out. (That what) we felt (was) that they indeed liked us. (What) I understood from his speech (is) that he will be very busy in the next days. What they remember is that it was warm and humid (high humidity). What the director of the company asked of you is punctuality. Please, may I borrow your (f.) pen; the one I had brought with me stopped writing. Are you (m. polite) allergic to the medicine that I had prescribed to you? We liked the films that we have seen in the last months very much. This is the building of the Faculty of Arts, where I graduated 14 years ago. These are the students whose Egyptian friends phoned us yesterday. Did you visit this museum, the objects of which can be seen in exhibitions in Egypt and abroad? I think that they studied the same subject. She does not want to stay here alone. They arranged the scholarships for the university themselves. We do not know ourselves who will be entrusted with this task.

Kammil!

a) bi-nafsuku b) li-waḥdo c) bi-nafsina d) li-waḥduhum e) nafso f) bi-nafsuhum g) bi-nafso h) nafsahā i) li-waḥdina j) nafs

1 ʾEntū gētū ʿala ... iṭ-ṭayyāra?
2. Huwa ... mish ʿārif, ḥa-yinzil fī ʾanho funduʾ.
3. Baʿd wafāt mrāto kān ʿāyish sinīn ṭwīla ... .
4. Gamīl ʾinnuku ʾidirtū titargimū ʾn-naṣṣ kullo ... .
5. Iḍ-ḍuyūf kulluhum mishyū w ʾeḥna f(i)ḍilna fi ʾl-maṭʿam ... .
6. Hiya ... saʾalitnī ʿala saḥḥitak.
7. Kān ʿāwiz yiṣallaḥ ... il-ḥanafīya li bi-tinaʾʾaṭ.
8. Fi ʾl-maṣyaf ḥa-nuṭbukh ... .
9. Yaʿnī humma ... khadū ʾt-taks wi gum li-ghāyit il-bēt?
10. Ma bi-tisībsh(i) wilādhā ... ʾabadan.

IV. Mufradāt

ʾabadan	not at all, never
ʾadā (ʾadawāt)	tool, device
ʿaddād, -āt	meter (electrometer, water meter, taxameter)
ʾaggar	to rent, to lease
ʾAlmāniyā	Germany
ʾaulawīya	priority, preference
ballāʿa	outlet (in the bathroom)
baṣṣa	look (at / into)
bawwāb, -īn	doorkeeper, housekeeper
bīzanṭī	Byzantine
butagāz, -āt	stove (gas)
durg (ʾadrāg)	drawer (of a desk), shelf
farash (i)	to equip, decorate an apartment; to set, lay the table
fāṭimī	Fatimid
fatra (fatarāt)	time, era
fūṭa (fuwaṭ)	towel
fūṭit maṭbakh	dishcloth
gardal (garādil)	bucket
garūf (gawarīf)	shovel
ghayyar II	to change
ghāz, -āt	gas
ḥāfiẓ III	to save, keep *(ʿala)*
ḥaf(a)rīyāt	excavations, archaeological excavations
ḥalla (ḥilal)	pot
ḥanafīya	water tap
ḥassāsīya	allergy, sensitivity
ḥōḍ (ʾaḥwāḍ)	sink
khallāt, -āt	mixer
khirrīg	graduate, alumnus
ʾīgār	rent
iltizām, -āt	keeping of something *(bi)*, duty, obligation
iltizām bi ʾl-mawāʿīd	punctuality (keeping the terms)
itʾaggar V	to be rented
itʾaṭṭaʿ V	to be torn, cut
kahraba	electricity
kallif II	to charge someone with *(bi)*, to cost someone (a sum)
kasar (a)	to break (into pieces)
kullīy(i)t il-ʾāsār	Faculty of Archaeology
liʿib (a)	to play
mablagh (mabāligh)	sum (financial)

maghūd	effort
maḥbas (maḥābis)	stopper (gas, water)
maʿlaʾa (maʿāliʾ)	spoon
manṭiʾa (manāṭiʾ)	area, region
maʾashsha	broom
maṭbakh (maṭābikh)	kitchen
mauqiʿ (mawāqiʿ)	site, position (geographical)
minḥa (minaḥ)	stipend, scholarship, financial contribution
mubālagh *fīh/fīhā*	exaggerated (m./f.)
muhimma (mahāmm)	task, duty
muwāṣafāt	parametres, characteristics
nadah (a)	to call to someone *(li)*
naḍḍaf II	to clean
naʾʾaṭ II	to drip
nāwī	intending
in-Nūba	Nubia
ʾoḍt in-nōm (ʾuwaḍ in-nōm)	bedroom
ʾaddar II	to value
ʾalb (ʾulūb)	heart
qīma (qiyam) = ʾīma (ʾiyam)	value
rafaḍ (u)	to refuse
raff (rufūf)	shelf
rāḥa	peace, rest
ruṭūba	humidity
sadd (i)	to stuff, to plug; to cover (a debt)
sakhkhān, -āt	water-heater
sakan (u)	to live
salāma	good health, recovery, safe return, peace
ṣallaḥ II	to repair
sallif II	to lend someone (*li*) something (without preposition)
sarāyir	beds
sikkīna (sakakīn)	knife
ṣīnīya (ṣawānī)	tray
sofra	table (dining), dining room
shakhṣī	personal
shaʾʾa (shuʾaʾ)	flat
shaṭṭa	chilli peppers
shōka (showak)	fork
taʾgīr	rent
ṭayyāra	aeroplane
ṭāsa	frying pan
tīfāl	teflon
wafā (wafayāt)	death
wāsiʿ	wide, broad, spacious, extensive

V. Taʿbīrāt:

ʾAllāh yirḥamo/hā!	God will pity him/her! - reaction to the announcement of someone's death or to the utterance of the name of a deceased.
ʾaktar min marra	many times, several times
ʾAna shāyif ʾinn ...	It seems to me that ...
bi-ḥafāwa (shdīda)	(very) warmly, warm-heartedly
bi-raḥtak/raḥtik, raḥtī/raḥto, rāḥithā, rāḥitna/rāḥitku/rāḥithum!	As you (I, he, she, we, you, they) like
bi ʾr-rāḥa	easily, comfortably
Da li yikhallī lku ʾl-ʾaulawīya.	That's what gives you the superior position.
fi ʾl-ḥaʾīʾa	In reality, indeed
Yā marḥab!	Welcome!
kull(i) marra	Every time, each time
Mish ḥaḍretak ... / mish ʾenta ... ?	You are not ... ?
ʿUmūman ...	Be it as it may ..., simply ...

Id - Dars tisʿatāshar /Lesson 19

Munasbāt igtimāʿīya

Faraḥ

- Mumkin tisharrafna yōm il-khamīs?
- Khēr!
- ʾAkhūya dukhlito yōm il-khamīs li gay, is-sāʿa tamanya bi ʾl-lēl.
- ʾAlf mabrūk!
- ʾAllāh yibārik fīk!
- Fī ḍuyūf, ʾiza gū lī mish ḥaʾdar ʾaḥḍar il-faraḥ, bas ʾiza ma gūsh, ḥaḥḍar ṭabʿan. ʿAla kull(i) ḥāl ḥāgī lku fi ʾṣ-ṣabāḥīya.
- Tisharraf fī ʾayyi waʾt!

Lā muʾakhza, yā ʿamm, yā maʾzūn – muddit ṣalāḥīyito intahit. ʿAyza wāḥid ghēro!

Don't be angry with me, Reverend Sir, but he has expired. I want a new husband!

- Bi ʾl-munasba, ʾiza gēt fi ʾṣ-ṣabāḥīya, ʾaʾūl ʾē(h) li ʾl-ʿirsān bi ʾẓ-ẓabṭ?
- ... *"Ṣabāḥīya mubār(a)ka"*, wi fi ʾl-ḥāla di ḥa-yiruddū:*"ʾAllāh yibārik fīk!"* Wi lau ʾult:*"Rabbina yitammim bi-khēr!"* ḥa-yiruddū:*"ʿOʾbāl ʿanduku!"*

Wilāda

- Mumkin ʾashīl maʿāk shwayya?
- *"ʿOʾbāl ʿanduku!"* Di hāgāt ʿashān subūʿ ibn ʾukhtī.
- *"ʾAlf mabrūk!"*, *"Rabbina yikhalli!"*
- *"ʾAllāh yikhallīk!"* Lau kunt ʿārif ʾinn is-subūʿ muḥtāg hāgāt ktīr keda, kunt gibt ḥad maʿāya.
- ʾAkīd da ʾawwil ṭifl?
- ʾAywa. Dōl lissa mitgawwizīn min sana ʾu nuṣṣ.
- ʾIza kunt muḥtāg ḥāga tānī, mumkin ʾarūḥ ʾana ʾashtirīhā lak.
- La, mutashakkir ʾawi, keda k(i)fāya!
- ʿUmūman, lau kunt ʿāwiz musāʿiditī fī ʾayyi ḥāga, ittaṣil bīya. Maʿāk nimrit telefōnī, mish keda?
- ʾĀ(h), ṭabʿan. ʾIza kunt fāḍī ʾn-nahār da shwayya, ʿaddi ʿalayya fi ʾl-bēt. Lau tiḥibb, mumkin nuʾʿud fī ʾayyi makān barra.

- Gamīl, lau la'ēt nafsī fāḍī, ḥattiṣil bīk 'ala ṭūl!

'Aza

- Mā lak? 'Enta shaklak za'lān 'awi!
- Ṣadīqī wāl(i)do māt in-nahār da.
- Il-ba'īya fī ḥayātak!
- Shukran!
- Lau raddēt keda, ḥa-yibān 'innak 'agnabī.
- 'Ummāl 'a'ūl 'ē(h)?
- Lau ḥad 'āl lak: *"Il-ba'īya fī ḥayātak"*, ti'ūl lo: *"Ḥayātak il-bā'(i)ya!"*
- Wi 'iza kunt 'āyiz 'astakhdim 'ibāra kamān?
- Mumkin ti'ūl lo:*"Shidd(i) ḥēlak!"*, wi fi 'l-ḥāla di ḥa-yi'ūl lak:*"Ish-shidda 'ala 'llāh!"*
- Mutashakkir 'awi!

-Il-'afw(u)! 'Ala 'ē(h)?

I. 'As'ila:

1. 'Iza 'ḍ-ḍuyūf gum, iṭ-ṭālib ḥa-yi'dar yiḥḍar il-faraḥ?
2. Il-wāḥid yi'ūl 'ē(h) li 'l-'arīṣ wi 'l-'arūsa, 'iza ge fi 'ṣ-ṣabāḥīya ?
3. Lau 'āl luhum "Rabbina yitammim bi-khēr!", ḥa-yiruddū 'ezzāy ?
4. Lau kān ir-rāgel 'ārif 'inn is-subū' muḥtāg ḥāgāt ktīr keda, kān ḥa-yi'mil 'ē(h)?
5. Iṭ-ṭālib mumkin yi'addi 'ala ṣaḥbo 'l-maṣrī 'emta?
6. Iṭ-ṭālib ḥa-yittiṣil bi-mīn, lau la'a nafso fāḍī?
7. 'Emta ḥa-yibān 'inn iṭ-ṭālib 'agnabī?
8. 'Iza kān 'āyiz yistakhdim 'ibāra kamān, ḥa-yi'ūl 'ē(h)?
9. Lau ruḥt tibārik li 'akhūk 'ashān ṭifl gdīd, kunt ḥa-ti'ūl lo 'ē(h)?
10. Lau ruḥna ni'azzi, ḥa-ni'ūl 'ē(h) li 'aṣḥāb il-'aza?

II. Qawā'id:

1. Conditional clauses

- conditional clauses use the following conjunctions: ***'iza*** (if, when), ***lau*** (if) and ***'in*** (if, when)
- generally the conjunctions ***'iza***, ***lau*** (if) and ***'in*** share the same meaning and are therefore interchangeable

- in certain temporal and semantic contexts, as well as in fixed phrases and proverbs, the use of a particular one of these conjunctions is obligatory:
- the conjunction ʾin is used less frequently than ʾiza and lau, it often appears in fixed phrases, proverbs and song texts
- unlike ʾiza and lau, the conjunction ʾin is always followed by a verbal form.

a) the past perfect

the conjunction ʾiza / lau / ʾin is followed by:
the perfect of the verb kān + the perfect of the semantic verb,
or the perfect of the verb kān + the noun functioning as the subject and + perfect of the semantic verb,

the matrix sentence is introduced by:
the perfect of the verb kān + the perfect of the semantic verb, or the perfect of the verb kān + ḥa + the imperfect of the semantic verb,
or the imperfect of the semantic verb,
or the imperative:

ʾIza / lau / ʾin kuntū ruḥtū ʾl-Matḥaf il-maṣrī, kuntū shuftū ʾl-ʾāsār di. – If you had gone to the Egyptian Museum, you would have seen these monuments. ʾIza / lau / ʾin kunt shuftak, kunt ʾult(e) lak. – If I had seen you, I would have told you. ʾIza / lau / ʾin kuntū ruḥtū ʾl-Matḥaf il-maṣrī, kānū ḥa-y(i)shūfū ʾl-ʾāsār di. – If you had gone to the Egyptian Museum, you would have seen these monuments. ʾIza/lau/ʾin kān ʾaṣḥābhum rāḥū ʾl-Matḥaf il-maṣrī, kānū ḥa-yishūfū ʾl-ʾāsār di. – If their friends had gone to the Egyptian museum, they would have seen these monuments. ʾIza /lau / ʾin kunna laʾēna nimrit telefōnku, kunna ʾttaṣalna bīku. – If we had found your telephone number, we would have called you. ʾIza / lau / ʾin kunna laʾēna nimrit telefōnku, kunna ḥa-nittiṣil bīku. – If we had found your telephone number, we would have called you. ʾIza / lau / ʾin kānit zmīlitna laʾit nimrit telefōnna, kānit ittaṣalit bīna. – If our colleague had found our telephone number, she would have called us.

Negative forms:

ʾIza / lau / ʾin ma kuntūsh ruḥtū ʾl-Matḥaf il-maṣrī, ma kuntūsh shuftū ʾl-ʾāsār di. – If you had not gone to the Egyptian Museum, you would not have seen these monuments. ʾIza / lau/ ʾin ma kuntish shuftak, ma kuntish ʾult(e) lak. - If I had not seen you, I would not have told you.

ʾIza / lau / ʾin ma kuntūsh ruḥtū ʾl-Matḥaf il-maṣrī, ma kuntūsh ḥa-t(i)shūfū ʾl-ʾāsār di. – If you had not gone to the Egyptian Museum, you would not have seen these monuments.

ʾIza / lau / ʾin ma kānsh(i) ʾaṣḥābhum rāḥū ʾl-Matḥaf il-maṣrī, ma kānūsh ḥa-yishūfū ʾl-ʾāsār di.

– If their friends had not gone to the Egyptian museum, they would not have seen these monuments.

ʾIza / lau / ʾin ma kunnāsh laʾēna nimrit telefōnku, ma kunnāsh ʾittaṣalna bīku. - If we had not found your telephone number, we could not have had called you.

ʾIza / lau / ʾin ma kunnāsh laʾēna nimrit telefōnku, ma kunnāsh ḥa-nittiṣil bīku. – If we had not found your telephone number, we could not have called you.

ʾIza / lau / ʾin ma kānitsh(i) zmīlitna laʾit nimrit telefōnna, ma kānitsh(i) ittaṣalit bīna. – If our colleague had not found our telephone number, she could not have called us.
ATTENTION:
ʾIza / lau / ʾin ma kuntūsh ruḥtū ʾl-Mathaf il-maṣrī, ḥāw(i)lū t(i)zūrūh fī ʾaʾrab furṣa. – If you have not been to the Egyptian Museum, try to visit it as soon as possible.
ʾIza / lau / ʾin makuntūsh ruḥtū ʾl-Matḥaf il-maṣrī, yibʾa ma tiʿrafūsh kunūz il-ḥaḍāra ʾl-firʿawnīya. – If you have not been to the Egyptian Museum, you do not know the treasures of the pharaonic civilisation.

b) the present tense

the conjunction ***ʾiza / lau / ʾin*** is followed by:
the perfect of the verb *kān* + *bi* + the imperfect of the semantic verb,
or the perfect of the verb *kān* + the active participle

the matrix sentence is introduced by:
ḥa + the active participle of the semantic verb,
ḥa + the imperfect of the semantic verb,
or the impersonal form ***mumkin/lāzim***,
or the particle ***fī***,
or the preposition expressing the verb "to have",
or the imperative:

ʾIza / lau / ʾin kunt bi-t(i)sāfir ktīr, ḥa-t(i)kūn ʿārif il-ḥāgāt di.
– If you travel often, you will know these things.
ʾIza / lau / ʾin kānit id-dinya bi-timaṭṭar, ḥa-nuʾʿud fi ʾl-bēt.
– If it is raining, we will stay at home.
ʾIza / lau / ʾin kunt bi-titfarrag ʿa ʾt-telefiz(i)yōn, lāzim tilbis in-naḍḍāra.
– If you are watching the TV, you must wear glasses.
ʾIza / lau / ʾin kuntū shāyfīn ḥall tānī, ʾūlū lna ʿalēh!
– If you see (know) another solution, tell us!
ʾIza / lau / ʾin kānū taʿbānīn, mumkin yistarayyaḥū hena.
– If they are tired, they can rest here.
ʾIza / lau / ʾin kunti bi-tiʾrī, wallaʿī ʾl-ʾabazhōra!
– If you are reading, turn on the lamp.

Negative forms:
ʾIza / lau / ʾin ma kuntish bi-t(i)sāfir ktīr, mish ḥa-t(i)kūn ʿārif il-ḥāgāt di.
– If you do not travel often, you will not know these things.
ʾIza / lau / ʾin ma kānitsh(i) id-dinya bi-timaṭṭar, ḥa-nukhrug.
– If it is not raining, we will go out.
ʾIza / lau / ʾin ma kuntish bi-titfarrag ʿa ʾt-telefiz(i)yōn, mish lāzim tilbis in-naḍḍāra.
– If you are not watching the TV, you needn't wear glasses.
ʾIza / lau / ʾin ma kuntūsh shāy(i)fīn ḥall(i) tānī, iʾbalū ʾl-ḥall bitāʿna!
– If you do not see (know) another solution, accept ours!
ʾIza / lau / ʾin ma kānūsh taʿbānīn, mumkin yirgaʿū mashy(i).
– If they are not tired, they can return on foot.
ʾIza / lau / ʾin kuntīsh bi-tiʾrī, itfī ʾl-ʾabazhōra!
– If you are not reading, turn off the lamp!

c) the future tense

the conjunction ***ʾiza / lau / ʾin*** is followed by:
the perfect of the semantic verb,
or the perfect of the verb *kān* + *ḥa* + the imperfect of the semantic verb,
or the perfect of the verb *kān* + the active participle,
or the perfect of the verb *kān* + the active participle + the imperfect of the semantic verb, or the noun functioning as the subject

the matrix sentence is introduced by:
the imperfect of the semantic verb,
or *ḥa* + the imperfect of the semantic verb,
or the perfect of the verb *kān* + *ḥa* + the imperfect of the semantic verb,
or the impersonal form ***mumkin/lāzim***,
or the particle ***fī***,
or the preposition expressing the verb "to have",
or the imperative:

ʾIza / lau / ʾin ruḥtū ʾl-Matḥaf il-maṣrī, ḥa-t(i)shūfū hnāk il-ʾāsār di.
– If you go to the Egyptian museum, you will see these monuments there.
ʾIza / lau / ʾin shuftak, kunt ḥaʾūl lak.
– If I saw you, I would have told you.
ʾIza / lau / ʾin ḥabbēt, mumkin nishrab shāy.
– If you want, we could drink tea.
ʾIza / lau / ʾin ʿirift ʾayyi ḥāga, kallimnī!
– If you learn anything, give me a call!
ʾIza / lau / ʾin ruḥtū ʾl-Matḥaf il-maṣrī, lāzim tizūrū qism il-mūmīyāt.
– If you go to the Egyptian Museum, you have to see the department of the mummies.
ʾIza / lau / ʾin ruḥtū ʾl-Matḥaf il-maṣrī, itfarragū ʿala magmūʿit il-bardīyāt.
– If you go to the Egyptian Museum, have a look at the collection of papyri.
ʾIza / lau / ʾin ḥa-t(i)ruḥtū ʾl-Matḥaf il-maṣrī, khudū maʿāku ʾd-dalīl da!
– If you go to the Egyptian Museum, take this guide with you!
ʾIza / lau / ʾin kānū nāz(i)līn fi ʾl-funduʾ da, kānū ḥa-y(i)shūfū ʾl-ʾahrāmāt min shibbāk ʾōḍithum.
– If they stay in this hotel, they would see the pyramids from the window of their room.
ʾIza / lau / ʾin kuntū ʿayzīn t(i)rūḥū ʾl-Matḥaf il-maṣrī, mumkin tirkabū ʾl-metro li-ghāyit it-Taḥrīr.
– If you want to go to the Egyptian Museum, you can take the subway to Tahrir.
ʾIza / lau / ʾin il-ʿummāl khallaṣū shughluhum badri, ibdaʾū bi-ḥāga gdīda.
– If the workmen finish their work earlier, start with something new!
ʾIza / lau / ʾin zmīlak rāḥ il-Matḥaf il-maṣrī, mumkin yitfarrag hnāk ʿala magmūʿit il-bardīyāt.
– If your colleague goes to the Egyptian Museum, he can have a look at the collection of papyri.

Negative forms:
ʾIza / lau / ʾin ma ruḥtūsh ʾl-Matḥaf il-maṣrī, mish ḥa-t(i)shūfū hnāk il-ʾāsār di.
– If you do not go to the Egyptian museum, you will not see these monuments.

ʾIza / lau / ʾin ma shuftaksh(i), kunt ḥasīb lak khabar.
– If I do not see you, I will leave you a message.
ʾIza / lau / ʾin ma ḥabbētūsh titfarragū ʿa ʾt-telefiz(i)yōn, iftaḥū ʾr-rad(i)yo.
– If you do not want to watch TV, turn on the radio.
ʾIza / lau / ʾin ma laʾētsh(i) ʾl-kharīṭa fī ash-shanta, dawwar ʿalēhā fi ʾl-maktaba.
– If you do not find the map in the bag, look for it in the library!
ʾIza / lau / ʾin ma ruḥtūsh ʾl-Matḥaf il-maṣrī ʾn-nahār da, iʿmilū riḥla li ʾl-Fayyūm.
– If you do not go to the Egyptian Museum today, make a trip to the Fayyum.
ʾIza / lau / ʾin ma kānūsh ḥāg(i)zīn ʾōḍa fi ʾl-fundu, kān mumkin yibātū ʿandina.*
– If they have not reserved a room in the hotel, they could stay with us.
ʾIza / lau / ʾin makuntūsh ʿayzīn t(i)rūḥū ʾl-Matḥaf il-maṣrī ʾn-nahār da, mumkin t(i)rūḥūh bukra.
– If you do not want to go to the Egyptian Museum today, you can go there tomorrow.
ʾIza / lau / ʾin il-ʿummāl ma khallaṣūsh shughluhum, mish ḥa-niʾdar niʾfil il-maqbara.
– If the workmen haven't finished their work earlier, we will not be able to close the tomb.
ʾIza / lau / ʾin zmīlak ma rāḥsh(i) ʾl-Matḥaf il-maṣrī, lāzim yizūr Matḥaf il-ʾUʾṣur.
– If your colleague does not go to the Egyptian Museum, he must visit the Luxor Museum.

- **phrases with an obligatory use of a certain conjunction:**
lau
+ **the perfect of the semantic verb:**
Lau tiḥibbū, mumkin nuʾʿud hena.
– If you like, we can sit here.
Lau ma bi-t(i)ḥibbish il-ʾakl da, nuṭlub ḥāga tanya.
– If you do not like this meal, we will order something else.
Lau tiʿraf, yā ḥabībī, baḥibbak ʾaddi ʾē(h)!
– If you knew, my love, how much I love you! (song text)
+ **the active participle:**
Lau ʿayza ʾṣ-ṣūra di, ḥagībhā lik.
– If you want this picture, I will bring it to you.
Lau mish ʿāyiz kart il-ʾahrāmāt, khud kart in-Nīl.
– If you do not want the postcard with the pyramids, take the postcard with the Nile.
+ **the particle fī:**
Lau fī laban, ḥuṭṭ(e) lī shwayya!
– If there is milk, pour me some!
Lau mafīsh laban, ḥuṭṭ(e) lī sukkar bas!
– If there's no milk, give me only sugar!

ʾin:
+ **the perfect of the semantic verb**
ʾIn shāʾallāh! - If God gives!
ʾIn dibil il-ward, rīḥto fīh!
– If a rose fades, it still will smell (its odour is within it). (Arab proverb)
ʾIn khuft, ma tiʾulshi, ʾin ʾult, matkhafshi!
– If you are afraid, do not speak, if you have spoken, have no fear! (Arab proverb)

+ the perfect of the verb *kān*, followed by:
a preposition with the pronominal suffix,
or a noun functioning as the subject,
or the active participle:
ʾIn kān ʿalayya ... – If it depended on me ...
ʾIn kān gārak fī khēr, ifraḥ lo! – If your neighbour lives in richness, rejoice about him!
ʾIn kunt nāsī, ʾafakkarak ... ! – If you have forgotten, I will remind you ... ! (song text)

2. Indirect questions
- indirect questions are introduced by conjunctions ***ʾiza*** or ***ʾin***, meaning "whether," followed by the perfect of the verb ***kān:***
- the forms of the verb ***kān*** are followed by the perfect or imperfect of the semantic verb, the particle ***fī***, preposition, impersonal form ***mumkin*** / ***lāzim***, or the active participle,
- at the end of the sentence is the expression ***walla laʾ*** "or not"

Mish ʿārif ʾiza / ʾin kunt shuft il-film da walla laʾ.
– I don't know whether I have seen the film (or not).
ʿĀwiz yiʿraf ʾiza / ʾin kuntū bi-takhdū ʾd-dawa da bi ʾntiẓām walla laʾ.
– He wants to know whether you have been taking the medicine regularly or not.
Ma katabū lhumsh ʾiza / in kānū ḥa-yinzilū fī nafs il-funduʾ walla laʾ.
– They did not ask them (write to them) whether they would stay in the same hotel.
Isʾalhā ʾiza / ʾin kān fī ṭabaʾ fāḍī hena walla laʾ.
– Ask her if there is an empty plate here or not.
Ma ʾāl līsh ʾiza / ʾin kān ʿando waʾt baʿd iḍ-ḍuhr walla laʾ.
– He did not tell me, whether he will have time in the afternoon or not.
Mish ʿār(i)fa ʾiza / ʾin kān mumkin timidd ʾiqāmithā fī Maṣr walla laʾ.
– She does not know whether she will be able to prolong her stay in Egypt.
Mish ʿāri(i)fīn ʾiza / ʾin kān lāzim niʾaddim ṭalab rasmī walla k(i)fāya nistaʾzin il-mudīr.
– We don't know whether it is necessary to file an official request, or whether it is enough to ask the manager's permission.
Saʾalnī ʾiza / ʾin kunt ʿāwiz iṣ-ṣuwar di walla laʾ.
– He asked me whether I would want these photographs.
Ma ʾālū lnāsh ʾiza / ʾin kānū ʿāw(i)zīn yikammilū dirāsithum fi ʾl-gamʿa walla laʾ.
– They did not tell us whether they intend to continue their university studies.
Isʾalūhūm ʾiza / ʾin kānū ʾāʿidīn shwayya walla laʾ.
– Ask them whether they would stay (sit) for a while or not.

III. Tadrībāt:

Targama
If you have any question, ask (turn to) your guide. If you find the picture, leave it on my desk. If you come back before lunch, we will manage to finish the translation. If the pain doesn't get better (milder), they will operate on him (they will perform an operation). If you want to visit the Karnak temple, you have to take a carriage or a taxi.

If they do not like this flat, we will find them another one. If the program of the journey changes, we will let you know. If this date would not suit you, tell me. If I stay longer, I will call you. If you are hungry, there is food (prepared) in the fridge. If there is lemon juice, I'll drink some, because I am very thirsty. If you (f.) are cold, take a sheet out of the case. If I miss the bus, I can go by train. If you like this place, you can stay here. If we knew when you would come, we would have waited for you at the airport. If they think the price too high, they can cancel the agreement. If she could also speak English, she could work in tourism. Tell me (f.), if you find the book! If you (m.) have time, pay me a visit. If it's dark in the tomb, turn on the reflector! If you (pl.) are hot, turn on the air conditioning! If we do not manage to dine in the hotel, we will go to a restaurant after the concert. If the museum is closed, make a boat trip on the Nile. If they do not have an official invitation, they will not be able to get the visa. If you go to congratulate the newlyweds, do not forget to bring them a box of chocolates. If you go out, leave the key of the room at the reception. If you do not go to the sea, we can ride horses at Saqqara. If this sum were not enough, I would have to go to the bank to fetch (so that I would fetch) more money. If you see them, greet them from us! If we do not see you before your journey, we will see you after you will have returned. If I can't reach you on the phone, I will send you an SMS to your cellphone. If I fall asleep, wake me up at 7 o'clock! She did not tell me if she graduated from the faculty this year or the last. I would like to know if the photographs turned out well. Ask them if they want to return to Cairo today or tomorrow. We have no idea whether they liked the programme.

Kammil!

a) ʾIn shāʾallāh! b) ʾAllāh yirḥamo! c) Ḥayātak il-bāʾ(i)ya. d) ʾAllāh yibārik fīk! e) W ʾenta bi ʾṣ-ṣaḥḥa wi ʾs-salāma! f) ʾAllāh yibārik fīk! g) Il-ʿafw(u)! h) ʿOʾbāl ʿanduku! i) Ish-shidda ʿala ʾllāh! j) ʾAllāh yikhallīk!

1. Rabbina yitammim bi-khēr! ....

2. Kull(i) sana w ʾenta ṭayyib! ....

3. ʾAlf mabrūk! ....

4. Shiddi ḥēlak! ....

5. Mutashakkir ʾawi! ....

6. Giddo māt. ....

7. Mumkin t(i)sharrafna bukra? ....

8. Rabbina yikhalli! ....

9. Il-baʾīya fī ḥayātak! ....

10. Ṣabāḥīya mubār(a)ka! ....

IV. Mufradāt

ʾabazhōra	desk lamp (*zh* pronounce like French *j* in *jour*)
ʿamalīya	operation (medical, military), action
ʿarīs	bridegroom
ʿarūsa	bride
ʿaṣīr (ʿaṣāyir)	juice
ʿaza	condolence
ʿazza II	to condole someone (without preposition)
badaʾ (a)	to begin with *(fī)*
bān (ā)	to look like, to be seen somewhere, on some one / something *(ʿala),* to come out that *(ʾinn)*, to appear that *(ʾinn)*
bāʾī	remaining
il-bāʾī	remaining money, change
baʾīya (bawāʾī)	rest, remain
bardān	feeling cold
bārik III	to congratulate someone *(li)*, to bless someone *(li)*, may God bless you *(fī)*
baṭanīya	sheet, cover
dibil (a)	to fade
dukhla	wedding night, wedding ritual celebrating the marriage
faraḥ (ʾafrāḥ)	wedding
gaʿān	being hungry
gidd (ʾagdād)	granddad, grandparent
ḥabīb (ḥabāyib)	beloved
ḥafla mūsīqīya	concert
ḥanṭūr (ḥanaṭīr)	carriage
ḥarrān	feeling warm, hot
ḥēl	force, energy
khēl (khuyūl)	horses
ʿibāra	expression, word
igtimāʿī	social
ʿilbit shokolāta	box of chocolates
ʾin	if
ʿirsān	newlyweds
itgawwiz V	to marry someone
itghayyar V	to change oneself
ʾiza	if
kashshāf, -āt	reflector
kinz (kunūz)	treasure
lagaʾ (a)	to turn to someone, something *(li)*

lamūn	lemon
lau	if, when
maʿbad (maʿābid)	temple
mabrūk	blessed
magmūʿa	group, collection
maktab il-istiʾbāl	reception
mubārak	blessed
naḍḍāra	glasses
nāsib III	to suit someone (without preposition)
ʾāfil	being closed (institution)
rabb	God, Lord, lord (landlord)
ṣabāḥīya	wedding ritual after the first waking (the first morning) as a married couple
ṣadīq (ʾaṣdiqāʾ)	friend (an expression of the standard language, which expresses respect, esteem and deep feeling for the person in question)
saḥab (a)	to withdraw
ṣaḥḥa II	to wake up someone
ṣāḥib il-ʿaza	the surviving person; the one who accepts condolence
Saʾʾāra	Saqqara
subūʿ	celebration of the birth of a child (a week of its life)
shāʾ (a)	to wish
shadd (i)	to tighten, strengthen
shaghghal II	to turn on, launch
shidda	strength, force; downbeat
shokolāta	chocolate
takyīf	airconditioning
tammim II	to organise, arrange, bring to a happy end
il-wāḥid	man, someone, one
wālid (plural: ʾābāʾ)	father, parent
wallaʿ II	to turn on the light, to ignite
wilāda	birth
zaʿlān	angry with someone, about something *(min)* sorry, sad about someone, something, worried about *(ʿashān)*
ziʿil (a)	to be angry with someone, about something *(min)* to be sorry, sad about someone, something, worried about *(ʿashān)*

V. Taʿbīrāt :

ʾAna bardān/a	I am cold.
ʾAna gaʿān/a	I am hungry.
ʾAna ḥarrān/a	I am warm / hot.
Bāyin ʾinno ʾagnabī.	It seems he is a foreigner.
Il-baʾīya fī ḥayātak!	Please accept my condolences! (lit. "The rest of your life!")
	Reply:
Ḥayātak il-bāʾ(i)ya!	(lit. : "Your remaining life!")
bi ʾl-munasba	by the way, (at the occassion)
bi ʾntiẓām	regularly
fi ʾl-ḥāla di	in this case

Note the difference between the following two expressions:

Ḥāga tānī?	Something else (more of anything, of any kind)?
ḥāga tanya	something else (of the same kind)

Khēr!?	Something happened? What's up?
ʾIdda l(i)na khabar.	Let us know.
Itfaḍḍal, il-bāʾī!	There you are, here's your change.
Kull(i) sana w ʾenta ṭayyib!	Best wishes! (for birthday, religious festivals, lit.: "every year and you are fine")
	answer:
Wʾ enta bi ʾṣ-ṣaḥḥa wi ʾs-salāma!	(lit.: "And may you be in health and prosperity!")
Maʿandīsh fikra!	I have no idea!
Rabbina yikhalli!	Best wishes! (a wish at the birth of a child, lit.: "May God preserve!")
	answer:
ʾAllāh yikhallīk!	(lit.: "May God preserve you!")
Rabbina yitammim bi-khēr!	Best wishes! (a wish for the newlyweds on the first day of their life as a married couple, lit.: "God will give (you) happiness and prosperity!")
	answer:
ʿOʾbāl ʿanduku!	(lit.: "May you celebrate (soon) too! May you be happy (soon)!")
Rāḥ fi ʾn-nōm.	He fell asleep.
Ṣabāḥīya mubār(a)ka!	Congratulations! (to the newlyweds on the first day of their life as a married couple)
ʾAllāh yibārik fīk!	answer to the preceding congratulation

Shidd(i) ḥēlak!	Please accept my (our) condolences! (lit.: “Be strong!”) answer:
Ish-shidda ʿala ʾllāh!	(lit. “Allah gives strength!”)
T(i)sharraf fī ʾayy(i) waʾt.	You are always welcome!
ʾUmmāl ... ?	How then ...? What ...?

20

Id-Dars il-ʿishrīn / Lesson 20

Ḥa-tiwḥashīna yā Maṣr

(A)

Andrew wi mamit Karīm:

- ʾAlō, mumkin ʾakallim Karīm?
- Mīn ʿāwizo?
- ʾAna Andrew.
- ʾAhlan yā Andrew, ʿāmil ʾēh?
- ʾAna kwayyis yā ṭant wi ʾezzay ḥaḍretik?
- Il-ḥamd liʾllāh. Khalāṣ misāfir yā Andrew?
- ʾĀ(h) baʿd yōmēn.
- ʾAkīd ʾenta farḥān ʿashān ḥa-tishūf mamtak wi babāk wi ʾikhwātak.
- ʾAna fiʿlan farḥān, bas ḥaʾīʾī ḥa-tiwḥashūnī!
- W ʾenta kamān ḥa-tiwḥashna, ḥa-tīgī tānī ʾurayyib mish keda?
- Ṭabʿan yā ṭant, ʾurayyib ʾawi.
- Ṭayib, sallim lina ʿala māma wi bāba wi ʾikhwātak. Wi fī ḥāga ṣughayyara baʿtāhā lhum, min faḍlak, waṣṣalhā wi ballaghhum salāmātna wi ʾashwāʾna. ʾAho Karīm ge, khud kallimo.

(B)

Andrew wi Karīm:

- ʾAhlan! ʾEzzayak yā bāsha, ṣabāḥ il-full!
- Ṣabāḥ in-nūr!
- Ha, ʿamalt ʾēh yā ʿamm, gahhizt kull(i) ḥāga? Kull(u) tamām yā bēh?
- Tamām it-tamām, ṣawwart il-makhṭūṭa min Dār il-kutub ʿashān il-baḥs bitāʿī wi ʾshtarēt il-muʿgam wi shwayit marāgiʿ. Fāḍil magallit ʾAlif.
- Ma tiḥmilsh(i) hamm, ʾana ruḥt ʾembāreḥ maktab(i)t il-Gamʿa ʾl-ʾamrīkīya wi gibt(e) lak nuskha maʿāya. ʾĒh li naʾiṣ mi ʾl-hadāyā?
- Lissa ʿāyiz ʾagīb shwayit ʿuṭūr wi T-shirtāt ʿalēhā rusūm firʿaunīya. Mish ʿārif ʾalāʾī fēn miʿassil tuffāḥ ʿashān wāḥid ṣāḥ(i)bī miwaṣṣīnī ʿalēh.
- Basīṭa, ʾeḥna keda keda ḥa-nirūḥ Khān il-Khalīlī wi ḥa-tilāʾī kull(u) da henāk.
- Lissa kunt ḥaʾūl lak niʿaddi ʿala ʾl-Ḥusēn wi nishrab tamr hindī. ʿĀwiz ʾashbaʿ shwaya mi ʾl-gauw ish-sharʾī fī ḥayy il-ʾAzhar, ʾaslo ḥa-yiwḥashnī. ʿAla fikra yā Karīm, mumkin tiddīnī nimrit telefōn

Ṭāriʿ, kān bi-yiʾūl lo ḥad ʿando warshit mashghūlāt fannīya.
- ʾAwi, ʾawi, iktib ʿandak: 0107543928.

(C)

Andrew wi Ṭāriʿ:

- ʾAlō, masāʾ il-khēr!
- Masāʾ in-nūr!
- Mumkin ʾakallim Ṭāriʿ min faḍlak?
- ʾAna Ṭāriʾ, min ʾilli bi-yitkallim?
- ʾAna Andrew, ṣāḥib Karīm.
- ʾAhlan yā Andrew, ma simiʿnāsh ṣōtak min yōm ma ʾtʾābilna fī khuṭūbit Mona wi Hishām.
- Kunt mashghūl giddan, ʿashān bagahhiz nafsī li ʾs-safar.
- Ṣaḥīḥ, misāfir? Khusāra! Kān nifsina tiʾaḍḍi maʿāna waʾt ʾaṭwal, bas ḥa-tīgī tānī mish keda?
- Ḍarūrī ḥāgī.
- Bi-yiʾūlū ʾilli yishrab min mayit in-Nīl lāzim yirgaʿ tānī.
- ʿAndak ḥaʾʾ. Maṣr waḥshānī min di ʾl-waʾti wi ʾin shāʾallāh ḥa-yikūn ʿandī furṣa ʾāgī fī ʾagāzit nuṣṣ is-sana.
- ʾAʿtabir da waʿd? Ḥa-nakhdak tizūr ir-rīf il-marra di wi tikūn ḍēfna fī ʿizbitna fi ʾl-Fayyūm. ʾAna ʿārif ʾinnak ruḥt ʾamākin ktīra, shuft shawāṭiʾ gamīla wi ghuṣt fi ʾl-Baḥr il-ʾaḥmar wi zurt il-ʾāsār il-ʾislāmīya wi ʾl-ʾibṭīya wi ʾl-firʿaunīya. ʿAndina fi ʾl-Fayyūm mazāriʿ ʿinab wi nakhīl wi mumkin tiṣṭād fī buḥeyrit Qārūn.
- ʾAllāh yikhallīk! Kunt bi-tiʾūl ʾinn ʿanduku warsha li ʾl-mashghūlāt il-fannīya? ʿĀwiz ʾashtiri shwayit hadāyā mumayaza, masalan kharṭūsh dahab li-ʾukhtī ʾṣ-ṣughayara wi ʿilba ṣadaf li-gidditī.
- ʾĀh, da ʾakhūya ʾl-k(i)bīr, ʿando warsha, taʿāla itfarrag wʾ ana mutaʾakkid ʾinnak ḥa-tilāʾī ṭalabak ʿandina. Wi ṭabʿan līk siʿr makhṣūṣ.
- Ṭayib, min faḍlak ʾiddīnī ʾl-ʿunwān wi ʾul lī mumkin ʾāgī ʾemta ʿashān ʾana misāfir baʿd yōmēn.
- Tīgī fī ʾayy waʾt. ʾAna ḥakūn henāk in-nahār da bi ʾl-lēl. Tiʾdar tiʿaddi ʿalaya is-sāʿa tisʿa masalan.
- Kwayyis ʾawi, ṭayib mumkin tigahhiz lī tashkīla ʾakhtār minhā.
- ʿAndina tamasīl marmar wi fukhār wi mashghūlāt faḍḍa wi dahab wi nuḥās wi ʾizāz kamān. Wi ʾl-ʿunwān 15 shāriʿ is-Sulṭān Ḥasan.
- Mutashakkir khāliṣ. Ḥakūn ʿandak is-sāʿa tisʿa bi ʾt-tamām.

(D)

Andrew wi Karīm:

- ʾAlō, ʾana Karīm yā Andrew.
- ʾAhlan yā Karīm.
- Bakallimak ʿashān ʾaṭṭammin ʿala ʾaḥwālak, ʾaffilt ish-shunaṭ? Fī ḥāga naʾṣāk?
- ʾIṭṭammin, khallaṣt kull(i) ḥāga.
- Ṭayartak ḥa-tiʾūm is-sāʿa kām bi ʾẓ-ẓabṭ?
- Is-sāʿa khamsa ʾu nuṣṣ mi ʾl-Maṭār ig-gdīd.
- Yaʿnī lāzim nikūn fi ʾl-maṭār is-sāʿa talāta ʾu nuṣṣ, bi ʾl-ktīr ʾarbaʿa. Khalāṣ ḥa-niʿaddi ʿalēk bi ʾl-ʿarabīya is-saʿa talāta, il-masāfa tākhud lahā nuṣṣ is-sāʿa, ʾenta ʿārif bi ʾl-lēl is-sikka faḍya. Bāba ḥa-yiwaṣṣalna ʿashān ʿāwiz yisallim ʿalēk bi-nafso. Wi māma kamān gaya maʿāna.
- Mish ʿārif ʾaʾūl lak ʾē(h).
- Ma tiʾulsh(i) ḥāga, da ʾeḥna ʾikhwāt, wi kullahā kam shahr wi tirgaʿ tānī.
- Bi ʾt-taʾkīd, Maṣr ḥa-tiwḥashnī …

Mufradāt wi taʿbīrāt:

ʾahlan	wellcome
ballagh II	to deliver, announce
basīṭa (= ḥāga basīṭa)	no problem, that is easy
bi ʾl-ktīr	at most, at the latest
bi ʾt-taʾkīd	sure, certainly
buḥeyra	lake
dahab	gold
Dār il-kutub	The National Library
faḍḍa	silver
fannīy	artistic, art, of art,
fukhār	ceramics
ghāṣ (u)	to dive
ḥāl (ʾaḥwāl)	situation, state, condition
ḥayy (ʾaḥyāʾ)	quarter
hamm (humūm)	worry, concern
ma tiḥmilsh(i) hamm	do not worry
ḥaʾʾ	law, truth
ʿandak ḥaʾʾ	you are right

il-Ḥusēn	the Mosque of Sayyidna Husēn in Cairo
iʿtabar VIII	regard somebody / something as, consider somebody / something as
ʿinab	grapes
iṣṭād VIII	hunt, fish
ʿizba (ʿizab)	farmstead, farm, holding
keda keda	in any case, at any rate
kharṭūsh (kharaṭīsh)	cartouche
khuṭūba	engagement
makhṭūṭa	manuscript
margiʿ (marāgiʿ)	source (in research, primary source)
mashghūlāt	handmade goods
marmar	marble
mazraʿa (mazāriʿ)	farm, plantation
mumayaz	remarkable, noteworthy, conspicuous
nakhīl	palms
nuḥās	copper
ʾizāz	glass
ʾaffil II	close, conclude
rasm (rusūm)	drawing
ṣadaf	mother-of-pearl
salām (salāmāt)	greeting
shōʾ (ʾashwāʾ)	yearning, longing, craving, memory
tamr hindī	tamarisk
ṭant	auntie (a familiar address of a female relative or a close acquaintance)
tamām	entirely, exactly, so
bi ʾt-tamām	precisely
kull(u) ʾt-tamām	allright, ok
tashkila	assortment, range (of goods)
T-shirt (T-shirtāt)	T-shirt
waʿd (wuʿūd)	promise
waḥash (a)	miss somebody / something
warsha (wirash)	workshop, shop, workroom
waṣṣa II	recommend somebody (no preposition like in English) somehing *(ʿala)* ask somebody for *(ʿala)* something
waṣṣal II	deliver, convey
yaʿnī	i.e., that means

21

Id-Dars wāḥid ʾu ʿishrīn / Lesson 21

Rubāʿīyāt Ṣalāḥ Jāhīn

Ṣalāḥ Jāhīn – the bard of Egyptian soul

Rubāʿīyāt are an ancient form of poetry and an Egyptian folk method of expression. The author brings to life the distinct traits of the Egyptian character with its wisdom, faith, sadness, optimism and irony, all of which combine to form a very special quality of soul.

Rubāʿīyāt – Four-verse

1.

Dakhal ir-rabīʿ yiḍḥak laʾānī ḥazīn
nadah ir-rabīʿ ʿala ʾismī lam ʾult mīn
ḥaṭṭ ir-rabīʿ ʾazhāro ganbī wi rāḥ
wi ʾēsh tiʿmil il-ʾazhār li ʾl-mayyitīn
ʿagabi!!

دخل الربيع يضحك لقانى حزين
نده الربيع على إسمى لم قلت مين
حط الربيع أزهاره جنبى وراح
وإيش تعمل الأزهار للمَيتين
عجبى !!

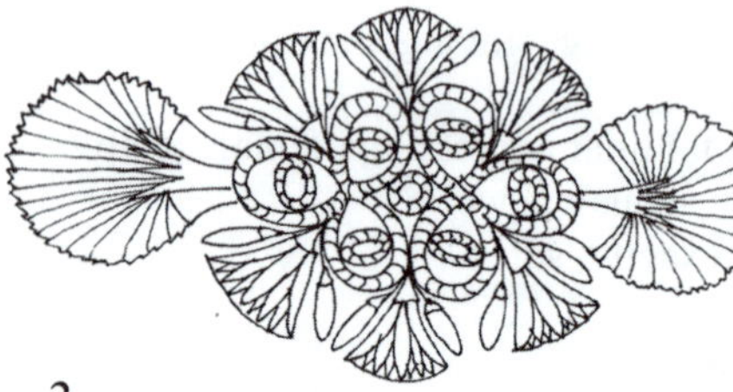

Spring came with smiles and found me full of woe
Spring called my name but I refused to hear
Spring lay its flowers and turned away to go
What can flowers do for a man in his bier?

2.

ʾAna shābb lākin ʿumrī walā ʾalf ʿām
waḥīd walākin bēn ḍulūʿī ziḥām
khāyif walākin khōfī minnī ʾana
ʾakhras walākin ʾalbī malyān kalām
ʿagabi!!

أنا شابّ لكن عمرى ولا ألف عام
وحيد ولكن بين ضلوعى زحام
خايف ولكن خوفى منى أنا
أخرس ولكن قلبى مليان كلام
عجبى !!

I am a thousand years, yet I am young
Alone, yet in my heart lives a throng
Afraid and knowing it's myself I fear
Silent but with much to say ...

3.

Ḥaddūta ʿan guʿrān wi ʿan khunfisa
itʾābilū ḥabbū baʿḍ sāʿit misa
walā ʾāl luhum ḥad ikhtishū ʿēb ḥarām
walā ḥad ʾāl di ʿalāqa mitdannisa
ʿagabi!!

حدوته عن جعران وعن خُنفسه
اتقابلوا حَبّوا بعض ساعة مِسَا
ولا قال لهم حد اختشوا عيب حرام
ولا حد قال دى علاقة متدنسه
عجبى !!

I have a story about a scarab and a beetle.
One evening they met and made love for an hour.
No one considered it a sin, nor gossiped their tale
Nor said their love was nasty, evil or even sour ... !

4.

– Id-dinya min ghēr ir-rabīʿ mayyita
waraʾit shagar ḍaʿfāna wi mifatfita
– Laʾ yā gadaʿ ghalṭān taʾammal
wi shuf zahr ish-shita
ṭāliʿ fī ʿizz ish-shita
ʿagabi!!

- الدنيا من غير الربيع ميّته
ورقة شجر ضعفانه ومفتفته
- لأ يا جدع غلطان تأمّل وشوف
زهر الشتا طالع فى عز الشتا
عجبى ! !

– The world without
spring is dismal and dead
A flimsy leaf, tattered to a shred ...
– Oh no! You ’re wrong, look around you and see
Even in the cold, the winter flower rears its head ...!

5.

ʾAʿraf ʿuyūn hiya ʾl-gamāl wi ʾl-ḥusn
wi ʾaʿraf ʿuyūn tākhud il-ʾulūb
bi ʾl-ḥuḍn
wi ʿuyūn mukhīfa wi ʾāsiya wi ʿuyūn
ktīr
wi baḥiss fīhum kulluhum bi ʾl-ḥuzn
ʿagabi!!

أعرف عيون هى الجمال والحسن
واعرف عيون تاخد القلوب بالحضن
وعيون مخيفة وقاسية وعيون كتير
وباحسّ فيهم كلهم بالحزن
عجبى !!

I know the eyes that give beauty to a face
And eyes whose looks are a warm embrace
And fearsome eyes, and eyes of solid steel
In all of them sadness do I feel ...

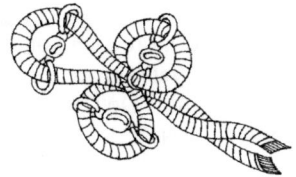

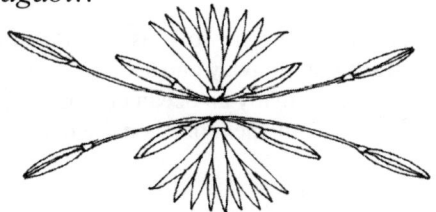

6.

ʾĒsh tuṭlubī yā nafsī fōʾ kull(i) da
ḥaẓẓik bi-yiḍḥak w ʾenti mitnakkida
raddit ʾālit li ʾn-nafs: ʾUl li ʾl-bashar
ma yibuṣṣū līsh bi-ʿuyūn ḥazīna keda
ʿagabi!!

إيش تطلبى يانفسى فوق كلّ ده
حظك بيضحك وانتى متنكدة
ردت قالت لى النفس : قول للبَشر
ما يبصوليش بعيون حزينة كده
عجبى !!

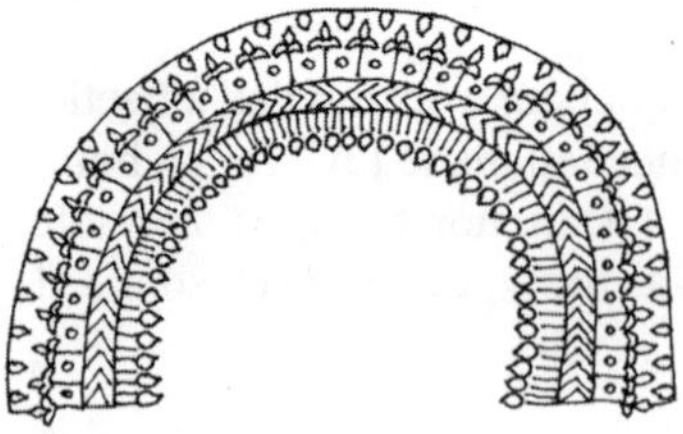

What could you want O self more than you own?
Fortune is smiling, yet you are forlorn ...
Myself with sadness said to me: “Do tell humanity
Not to look at me with eyes so full of misery!”

7.

Wara kull(i) shibbāk ʾalf ʿēn maftūḥīn
w ʾana w ʾenti mashyīn yā gharāmī ʾl-ḥazīn
lau iltaṣaqna nimūt bi-ḍarbit ḥagar
wi lau iftaraqna nimūt mitḥassarīn
ʿagabi!!

ورا كل شباك ألف عين مفتوحين
وانا وانتى ماشيين ياغرامى الحزين
لو التصقنا نموت بضربة حجر
ولو افترقنا نموت متحسّرين
عجبى !!

A thousand eyes behind a thousand windows pry
As you and I my forlorn love are walking by
If we stick close they can kill us with one stone
If we part, of loneliness we are bound to die ...

8.

Lē(h) yā ḥabibtī ma benna dayman safar
da ʾl-buʿd zanb kbīr lā yughtafar
lē(h) yā ḥabibtī ma benna dayman buḥūr
ʾaʿaddi baḥr ʾalāʾī ghēro itḥafar
ʿagabi!!

ليه ياحبيبتى ما بيننا دايماً سفر
ده البعد ذنب كبير لا يُغتفر
ليه ياحبيبتى ما بيننا دايماً بحور
أعدى بحر ألاقى غيره اتحفر
عجبى !!

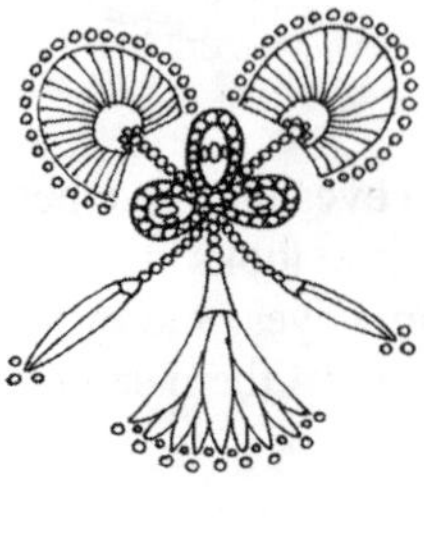

To always meet then part, my love, is a mortal sin
You ’re always out, or away and seldom ever in
Between us many an ocean do you keep
When I cross one, the next one is more deep ...

ʼAsʼila:

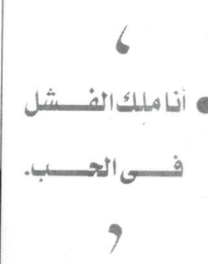

صلاح جاهين

• أنا ملك الفشل في الحب.

ʼAna malik il-fashal fi ʼl-ḥubb.
Ṣalāḥ Jāhīn
I am the king of unrequited love.

1. Shakl ish-shāʻir kān farḥān lammā dakhal ir-rabīʻ?
2. Ir-rabīʻ ḥaṭṭ ʼazhāro fēn?
3. Ish-shāʻir shābb walla ʻagūz?
4. Guʻrān wi khunfisa itʼāb(i)lū ʼemta?
5. Mīn ʼāl l(u)hum ikhtishū ʻēb?
6. Id-dinya kānit ḥa-t(i)mūt, ʼiza ma kānsh(i) fīhā ʼē(h)?
7. Waraʼit shagar tibʼa ḍaʻfāna wi mifatfita ʼemta?
8. Mīn li bi-yākhud il-ʼulūb bi ʼl-ḥuḍn?
9. Ish-shāʻir ḥāsis bi ʼē(h) fi ʼl-ʻuyūn il-mukhīfa wi ʼl-ʼās(i)ya ?
10. Ish-shāʻir bi-yiʼūl ʼē(h) li nafso?
11. In-nafs mish ʻāy(i)za ʼl-bashar yibuṣṣū lhā ʼezzāy?
12. Kam ʻēn maftūḥa wara kull(i) shibbāk?
13. Lau ish-shāʻir wi ḥabibto iltaṣaqū, kānū ḥa-yimūtū ʼezzāy?
14. Wi lau iftaraqū, kānū ḥa-yimūtū ʼezzāy?
15. ʼĒ(h) li dayman bēn ish-shāʻir wi ḥabibto?

Muʻgam ʻarabī ʻarabī:

Ṣalāḥ Jāhīn	***ʼism ish-shāʻir il-maṣrī***
ʻagabi!	ʼaddi ʼē(h) y(i)kūn da gharīb!
bashar	in-nās kulluhum
buʻd (ʼabʻād)	ʻaks ʼurb: biʻīd ʻaks ʼurayyib
ḍaʻfān	mafūsh ḥēl
ʻēb	ḥarām / ḥāga marfūḍa
ʼēsh	ʼē(h)
gadaʻ (gidʻān)	rāgel ḥaʼīʼī
ghalṭān	mish ṣaḥḥ
gharām	ḥubb kbīr: bi-yiḥibbū baʻḍ ʼawi
ḥarām	ʻēb
ḥuḍn (ʼaḥḍān)	ḥuḍn il-ʼumm ʼilli mās(i)ka fīh ṭiflahā
ḥusn	gamāl
ḥuzn (ʼaḥzān)	ʼinsān ḥazīn ḥāsis bi ʼl-ḥuzn
iftaraqna VIII	sibna baʻḍ
ikhtasha VIII	itkasaf VII
iltaṣaqna VIII	baʼēna ʼurayibīn giddan min baʻḍ
itḥafar VII	baʼa maḥfūr

lam ʾult	ma ʾultish
mayyit	ʾinsān ʾilli māt / warda ʾilli mātit
mifatfit	mitʾaṭṭaʿ ḥitat ṣ(u)ghayyara
misa	masāʾ
mitdannis	mish n(i)ḍīf
mitḥassar	ʾinsān ḥāsis bi ʾl-ʾasaf wi ʾl-ḥuzn
mitnakkid	zaʿlān
mukhīf	ḥāga bi-n(i)khāf minhā
ʾāsī	shdīd ʾawi
shābb	mish ṭifl wi lissa mish kbīr fi ʾs-sinn
shāʿir (shuʿarāʾ)	kātib bi-yiktib ish-shiʿr
shita	faṣl min fuṣūl is-sana, bi-yīgī baʿd il-kharīf wi ʾabl ir-rabīʿ
taʾammal! V	buṣṣ kwayyis!
zahr(a) (zuhūr / ʾazhār)	ward
ziḥām	zaḥma

Muʿgam ʿarabī ʾinglīzī:

dār (dūr)	house (above all specialised for a certain activity)
ḍarab (a)	to strike, to beat
ḍarba	a stroke
ḍiḥik (a)	to laugh
ḍilʿ (ḍulūʿ)	rib
guʿrān (gaʿārīn)	scarab beetle
ḥafar (u)	to excavate, to conduct (archaeological) excavations
khaṭṭ (khuṭūṭ)	line, writing, script
khunfisa (khanāfis)	beetle
lā yughtafar	unforgivable
manaʿ (a)	to forbid someone (without preposition) to do something *(min)*
ʾōberā	opera
rakkib II	to compose
rubāʿīyāt	four-verse poem
zanb (zunūb)	guilt

بسم الله الرّحمن الرحيم

الحمد لله رب العالمين الرّحمن الرّحيم ملك يوم الدّين إياك نعبد

وإياك نستعين اهدنا الصّراط المستقيم صراط الذين أنعمت

عليهم غير المغضوب عليهم ولا الضالين ..... آمين

صدق الله العظيم

Il-khaṭṭ il-ʿarabī

– the Arabic alphabet has 28 consonants, that differ in their graphic and phonetic form
– the Arab script encodes consonants and long vowels
– the Arab script is written from right to left
– short consonants are encoded only by diacritic signs in a vocalised text
– each consonant has four forms, the graphic form of each consonant depends on its position in the word.

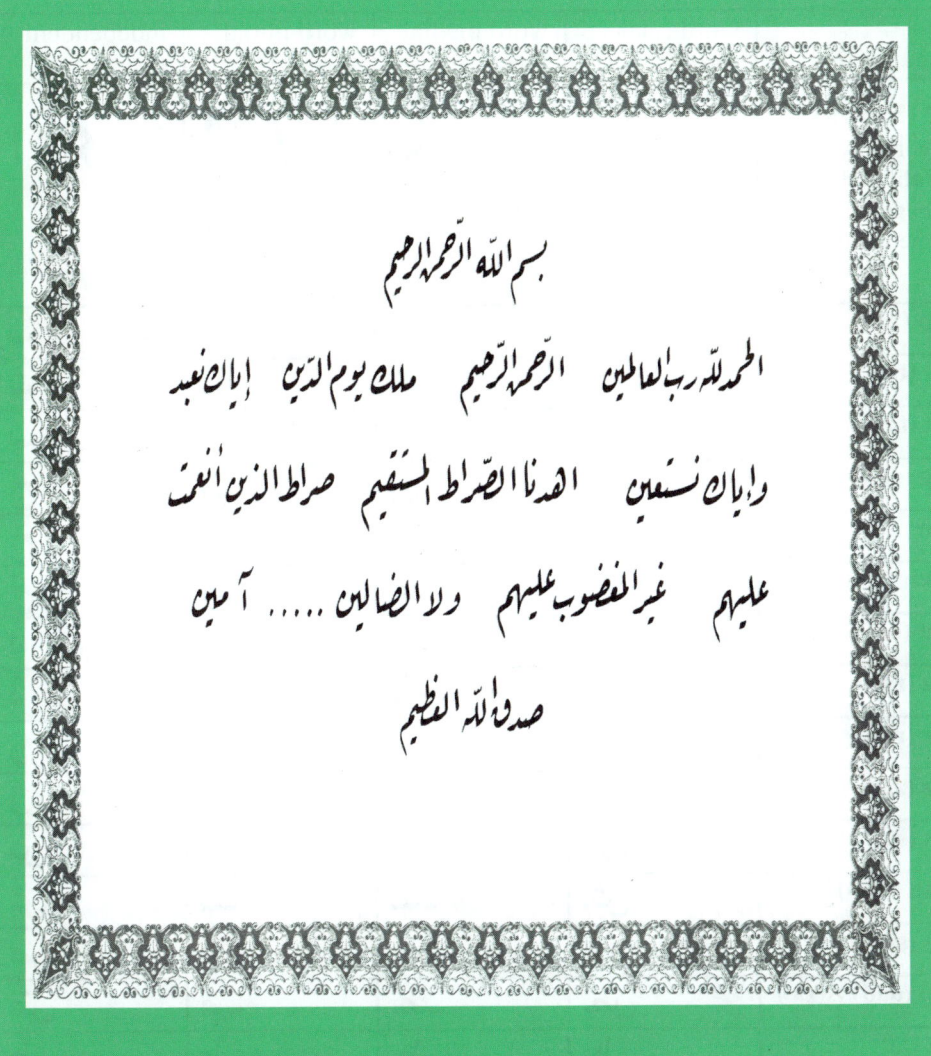

Consonants:

	word final form	word medial form	word initial form	independent form
ʾ (hamza), borne by **ʾalif** at the beginning of the word	ـأ/ء	ـأ	إ / أ	أ/ء
b (bāʾ)	ـب	ـبـ	بـ	ب
t (tāʾ)	ـت	ـتـ	تـ	ت
t (tāʾ)/s (sāʾ)	ـث	ـثـ	ثـ	ث
g (gīm)	ـج	ـجـ	جـ	ج
ḥ (ḥāʾ)	ـح	ـحـ	حـ	ح
kh (khāʾ)	ـخ	ـخـ	خـ	خ
d (dāl)	ـد	ـد	د	د
z (zāl)	ـذ	ـذ	ذ	ذ
r (rāʾ)	ـر	ـر	ر	ر
z (zāy)	ـز	ـز	ز	ز
s (sīn)	ـس	ـسـ	سـ	س
sh (shīn)	ـش	ـشـ	شـ	ش
ṣ (ṣād)	ـص	ـصـ	صـ	ص
ḍ (ḍād)/ẓ (ẓāʾ)	ـض	ـضـ	ضـ	ض
ṭ (ṭāʾ)	ـط	ـطـ	طـ	ط
ẓ (ẓāʾ)	ـظ	ـظـ	ظـ	ظ
ʿ (ʿēn)	ـع	ـعـ	عـ	ع
gh (ghēn)	ـغ	ـغـ	غـ	غ
f (fāʾ)	ـف	ـفـ	فـ	ف
q (qāf)	ـق	ـقـ	قـ	ق
k (kāf)	ـك	ـكـ	كـ	ك

l (lām)	ـل	ـلـ	لـ	ل
m (mīm)	ـم	ـمـ	مـ	م
n (nūn)	ـن	ـنـ	نـ	ن
h (hā')	ـه	ـهـ	هـ	ه
w (wau)	ـو	ـو	و	و
y (yā')	ـى	ـيـ	يـ	ى

– *qāf* ق is mostly pronounced as glottal stop – *hamza* ء : قلب ʾ *ʾalb / qalb*

– *ḍād* ض is often pronounced as *ẓā'* ظ : *maẓbūṭ* مضبوط

VOWELS
short:

a	*ma*	*(Maṣr)*	مصر
e	*te*	*(telefizyōn)*	تليفزيون
i	*hi*	*(il-Qāhira)*	القاهرة
o	*ʾo*	*(ʾoʿbālak)*	عقبالك
u	*ṣu*	*(ṣubḥ)*	صبح

– when the vowel ***a*** is part of a demonstrative pronoun, it is written as ***"hā'"*** ه :

da ده

– if the vowel ***i*** is part of a demonstrative pronoun, it is written as ***"yā'"*** ى :

di دى

– when the vowel ***o*** functions as a pronominal suffix, is written as ***"hā'"*** ه :

lo له

kitābo كتابه

shāy(i)fo شايفه

long:
– long vowels are written as follows:

ā	*"ʾalif"*	*mā*	ما
ē	*"yā'"*	*lē(h)*	ليه
ī	*"yā'"*	*fī*	فى
ō	*"wau"*	*nōm*	نوم
ū	*"wau"*	*fūl*	فول

Notes to the writing:

the consonants ***ʾalif, dāl, zāl, rāʾ, zāy*** and ***wau* :** أ , د , ذ , ر , ز , و

– are not connected with the consonants following them, and therefore their word intial and word medial forms do not have the connecting line, ـ by which all other consonants are connected with the ones following them

tāʾ marbūṭa ة **:**

the ending ***–a*** of feminine nouns (and of masculine nouns ending with ***– a***) is written in the Arabic script by the so-called *tāʾmarbūta :*

ṭāliba طالبة *ʿomda* عمدة

– the definite article ***il-*** **is written as :** ال

– if ***lām*** **is followed by** ***ʾalif*** , the resulting sequence is written as follows: لا

– when the preposition ***li*** ل **is followed by a noun with the definite article,** the *ʾalif* of the definite article is omitted: *il-kitāb – li ʾl-kitāb* للكتاب

reduplicated consonants are written as single consonants, in vocalised texts, they are marked by the so-called : ّ *kull* كلّ

– when a word begins with the long vowel ***ā***, the Arab script uses instead of an *ʾalif* with *hamza* and another (prolongational) *ʾalif* only a single *ʾalif* with the diacritic sign ***madda*** **~ :** آ *ʾālām* آلام

– ***protective ʾalif* :**

verbs in the 2nd and 3rd person plural perfect and imperfect and in the plural imperative have the so-called ***protective ʾalif*** at the end of the word.

(when the verb form is followed by a pronominal suffix or by a preposition with the pronominal suffix, *ʾalif* is omitted)

katabtū	كتبتوا	but!	*katabtūhā*	كتبتوها
katabū	كتبوا		*katabūh*	كتبوه
tiktibū	تكتبوا		*tiktibūhā*	تكتبوها
yiktibū	يكتبوا		*yiktibū lna*	يكتبولنا
iktibū!	اكتبوا!		*iktibūh!*	اكتبوه!

– The diacritic sign ً: ً is written by singular masculine nouns in front of the ***protective ʾalif*** of the ending – ***an***, i.e. by the forms of singular masculine nouns that would in the standard language be in the genitive case:

ʾahlan wa sahlan! **! أهلاً و سهلاً** , *shukran!* **!شكراً** *dayman!* **!دايماً**

Numerals:

1	**١**
2	**٢**
3	**٣**
4	**٤**
5	**٥**
6	**٦**
7	**٧**
8	**٨**
9	**٩**
0	**٠**

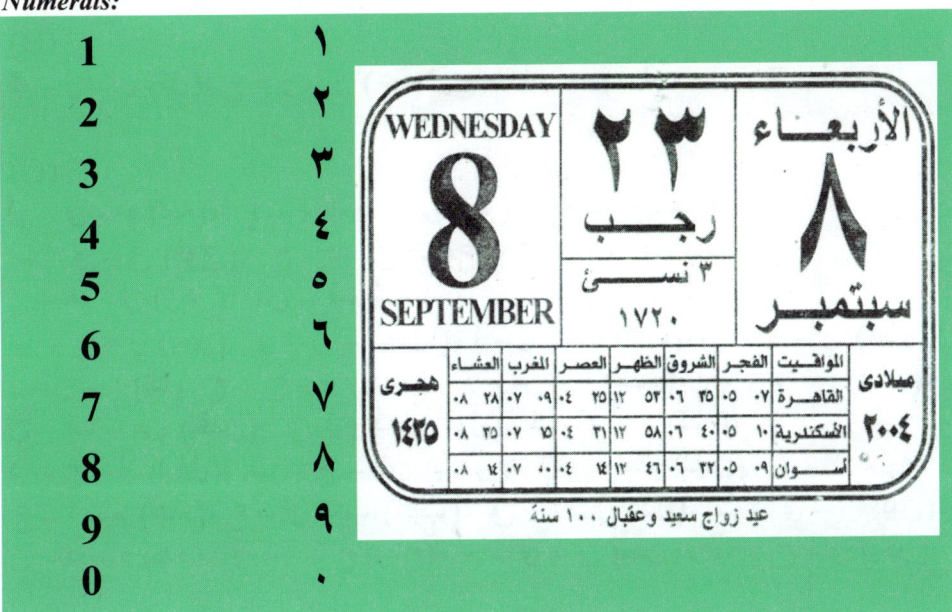

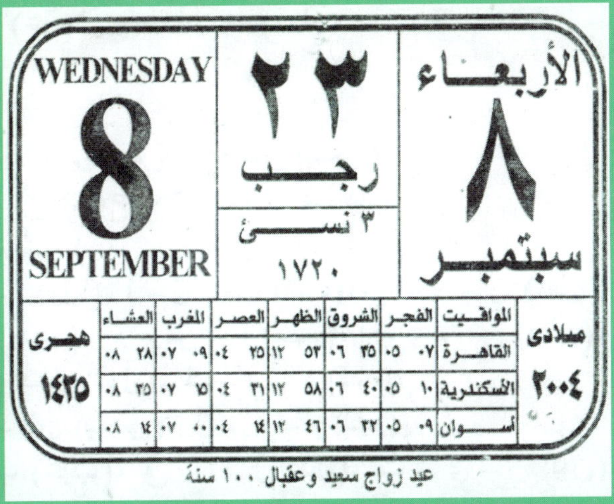

Numerals are combined from left to right:

29/4/1973	١٩٧٣/٤/٢٩
8/12/2004	٢٠٠٤/١٢/٨
705382	٧٠٥٣٨٢
00420218039657	٠٠٤٢٠٢١٨٠٣٩٦٥٧
0020125714803	٠٠٢٠١٢٥٧١٤٨٠٣

Tarkīb il-kalimāt

(A)

ف – ى (فى)، م – ن (من)، ى – ا (يا)، ل – أ (لأ)، م – ا (ما)، ل – ا (لا)،
د – ه (ده)، ل – و (لو)، هـ – ى (هى)، ل – ى (لى)، ع – ن (عن)،
ح – د (حد)، د – ى (دى)، ل – م (لم)

(B)

ك – ل – ل (كلّ)، ع – ز – ز (عزّ)، ح – ط – ط (حطّ)

(C)

ل – ى – ه (ليه)، غ – ى – ر (غير)، ش – ج – ر (شجر)،
ف – و – ق (فوق)، ج – د – ع (جدع)، ش – و – ف (شوف)،
ز – هـ – ر (زهر)، س – ف – ر (سفر)، ذ – ن – ب (ذنب)،
ب – ح – ر (بحر)، و – ر – ا (ورا)، أ – ل – ف (ألف)، ع – ى – ن (عين)،
أ – ن – ا (أنا)، ح – ج – ر (حجر)، م – س – ا (مسا)، إ – ى – ش (إيش)،
ن – ف – س (نفس)، ق – و – ل (قول)، ك – د – ه (كده)،
د – خ – ل (دخل)، ب – ع – ض (بعض)، ل – ه – م (لهم)،
ع – ا – م (عام)، ع – ى – ب (عيب)، ق – ا – ل (قال)، ب – ى – ن (بين)،
ن – د – ه (نده)، ر – ا – ح (راح)، م – ى – ن (مين)، ب – ح – ر (بحر)

(D)

ع – م – ر – ى (عمرى)، و – ح – ى – د (وحيد)، ز – ح – ا – م (زحام)،
ك – ل – ا – م (كلام)، أ – خ – ر – س (أخرس)، خ – و – ف – ى (خوفى)،
ق – ل – ب – ى (قلبى)، ع – ج – ب – ى (عجبى)، ط – ا – ل – ع (طالع)،
خ – ا – ى – ف (خايف)، ى – ض – ح – ك (يضحك)،
أ – ع – ر – ف (أعرف)، غ – ى – ر – ه (غيره)، ب – ح – و – ر (بحور)،
ا – س – م – ى (اسمى)، و – ر – ق – ة (ورقة)، ح – ز – ى – ن (حزين)،
ت – ع – م – ل (تعمل)، ج – ن – ب – ى (جنبى)، ك – ب – ى – ر (كبير)،
ن – م – و – ت (نموت)، ع – ى – و – ن (عيون)، ت – ا – خ – د (تاخد)،
ك – ت – ى – ر (كتير)، ف – ى – ه – م (فيهم)، ن – ف – س – ى (نفسى)
ح – ر – ا – م (حرام)، و – ل – ك – ن (ولكن)،
ر – د – د – ت (ردّت)، ح – ظ – ظ – ك (حظّك)

(E)

م – ل – ى – ا – ن (مليان)، ض – ل – و – ع – ى (ضلوعى)،
ل – ق – ا – ن – ى (لقانى)، غ – ل – ط – ا – ن (غلطان)،
د – ا – ى – م – ا (دايماً)، ى – غ – ت – ف – ر (يغتفر)،
أ – ل – ا – ق – ى (ألاقى)، ا – ت – ح – ف – ر (اتحفر)،
أ – ع – د – د – ى (أعدّى)، ت – أ – م – م – ل (تأمّل)،
م – ى – ى – ت – ة (ميّتة)، ش – ب – ب – ا – ك (شبّاك)،
غ – ر – ا – م – ى (غرامى)، ب – ض – ر – ب – ة (بضربة)،
ب – ى – ن – ن – ا (بيننا)، م – خ – ى – ف – ة (مخيفة)،
ق – ا – س- ى – ة (قاسية)، ب – أ – ح – س – س (بأحسّ)،
ك – ل – ل – ه – م (كلّهم)، ت – ط – ل – ب – ى (تطلبى)،
ب – ى – ض – ح – ك (بيضحط)، ح – ز – ى – ن – ة (حزينة)،
ج – ع – ر – ا – ن (جعران)، خ – ن – ف – س – ة (خنفسة)،
ح – ب – ب – و – ا (حبّوا)، ع – ل – ا – ق – ة (علاقة)

(F)

أ – ز – ه – ا – ر – ه (أزهاره)، ض – ع – ف – ا – ن – ة (ضعفانة)،
م – ف – ت – ف – ت – ة (مفتفتة)، ح – ب – ى – ب – ت – ى (حبيبتى)،
م – ا – ش – ى – ى – ن (ماشيين)، ح – د – د – و – ت – ة (حدّوتة)،
ا – خ – ت – ش – و – ا (اختشوا)

(G)

م – ف – ت – و – ح – ى – ن (مفتوحين)،
م – ت – ن – ك – ك – د – ة (متنكّدة)،
ا – ل – ت – ص – ق – ن – ا (التصقنا)،
ا – ف – ت – ر – ق – ن – ا (افترقنا)،
م – ت – د – ن – ن – س – ة (متدنّسة)

(H)

م – ت – ح – س – س – ر – ى – ن (متحسّرين)،
ى – ب – ص – ص – و – ل – ى – ش (يبصّوليش)،
ا – ت – ق – ا – ب – ل – و – ا (اتقابلوا)

(I)

ا-ل – ر – ب – ى – ع (الربيع)، ا – ل – أ – ز – ه – ا – ر (الأزهار)،
ل – ل – م – ى – ى – ت – ى – ن (للميتين)، ا – ل - ش – ت – ا (الشتا)،
ا – ل – د – ن – ى – ا (الدنيا)، ا – ل – ب – ع – د (البعد)،
ا – ل – ح – ز – ى – ن (الحزين)، ا – ل – ح – س – ن (الحسن)،
ا – ل – ج – م – ا – ل (الجمال)، ا – ل – ق – ل – و – ب (القلوب)،
ب – ا – ل – ح – ض – ن (بالحضن)، ب – ا – ل – ح – ز – ن (بالحزن)،
ل – ل – ب – ش – ر (للبشر)

Tadrībāt:

Rakkib il-kalimāt

(ر م ا ط)، (ك س ا ت)، (د ف ن ق)، (ى ص ف ر)، (ط م ع م)،
(ب و ة ر ش)، (ح ت ف م)، (ة ا ى ز ر)، (ه ة و ق)، (د ى م ن ة)،
(ك س ر ك)، (ى ش ة ش)، (ر ا ة س ف)، (ط ة ب س و)، (ض إ م ا ء)،
(ع م د ه)، (ش ت ى م س ف)، (ب ى ط ب)، (ا م ة ج ع)، (ة ص د ى ل ى)،
(و ى د ت و س)، (ف ن ت و ل ى)، (و د ة ل)، (ع م ج ا)، (ف ح ر)،
(ا ت ر ا ب ى ع)، (ك ن ب)، (ع ا ر ن ج)، (ت م ك ة ب)، (ك ب ش ب ا)،
(ح ط ة ط م)، (و ر م ت)، (ر ا ش ع)، (ى د ن م ا)، (ا ت ا س ل ا ت ع م)،
(م د خ ا ت س ا)

Iktib bi ʾl-khaṭṭ il-ʿarabī

a) il-Gumhūrīya ʾt-tshīkīya, Maṣr, ʾAswān, il-Gīza, maʿa ʾs-salāma!, il-ʾAhrām, doktōr, furṣa saʿīda!, Rās is-sana, ʾirsh, ʾŪrubbā, ṣafqa, ʾahlan wa sahlan!, il-bashmuhandis, barʾūʾ, gawāz safar, mustashār, il-gumʿa, kull(i) sana w ʾenta ṭayyib!, maktab il-istiʾbāl, mukalma, ish-shaʾʾa li ʾl-ʾīgār, gadwal il-muḥāḍrāt, in-nahār da, kumsarī, is-sana li gayya
b) Istalamt il-mablagh. Imḍi hena, min faḍlak! Ḥa-nistannāku ʾuddām il-funduʾ! Ma-tinsūsh il-mafatīḥ! Ma titʾakhkharīsh! Ikhtārū li ʾentū ʿāw(i)zīno! Sallim lī ʿala wilādak! Lau laʾētū nafsuku fāḍ(i)yīn, fūtū ʿalēna baʿd iḍ-ḍuhr! Ḥa-t(i)sharrafūna ʾemta ʾin shāʾallāh? Mish it-tadkhīn mamnūʿ hena? ʾAywa, kalāmak maẓbūṭ!

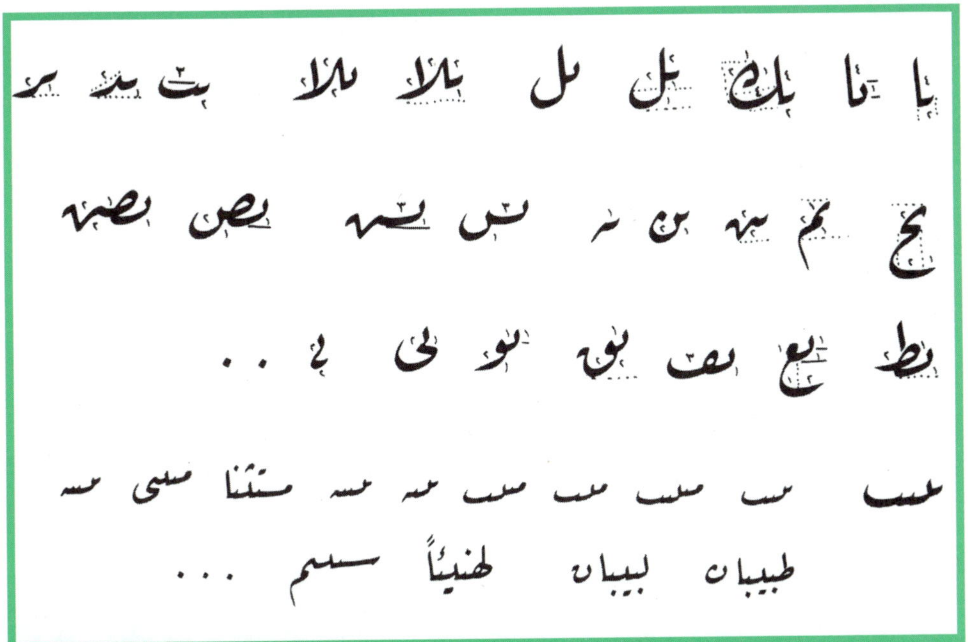

Samples of Arabic calligraphy

Iktib bi ʾl-khaṭṭ il-lātīnī

لندن، الحمد للّه!، السلام عليكم!، القاهرة، تليفزيون، ألف شكر!، قنصل،
استمارة، مرسل، سقّارة، بكره، كمّترى، رمّان، برتقان، فراولة،
بوليس، مدير، طيّارة، موظّف، أغسطس، يوليو، أكتوبر، مكتب السياحة،
سنترال، محطّة، وزارة الخارجية، أبو صير، استثمار، دار الأوبرا،
عيد الميلاد، جهاز التسجيل
لا يغتفر، لسّه مشفتهاش، القلم ده مبيكتبش كويّس، همّ بيراسلونا من
زمان، بتحبّوا قهوة ولا شاى؟، اتعرّفتوا عليهم إمتى؟، الحاجات اللى جبتوها
من السوق، حطّيتوها فين؟، إذا مجوش، لازم نروح لهم، لو فيه
أىّ مشكلة اتّصلوا بنا على الطول!،
نتمنّى لكو نجاح كبير فى مذاكرة العاميّة المصرية!!!

Ḥall it-tamrīnāt / The key

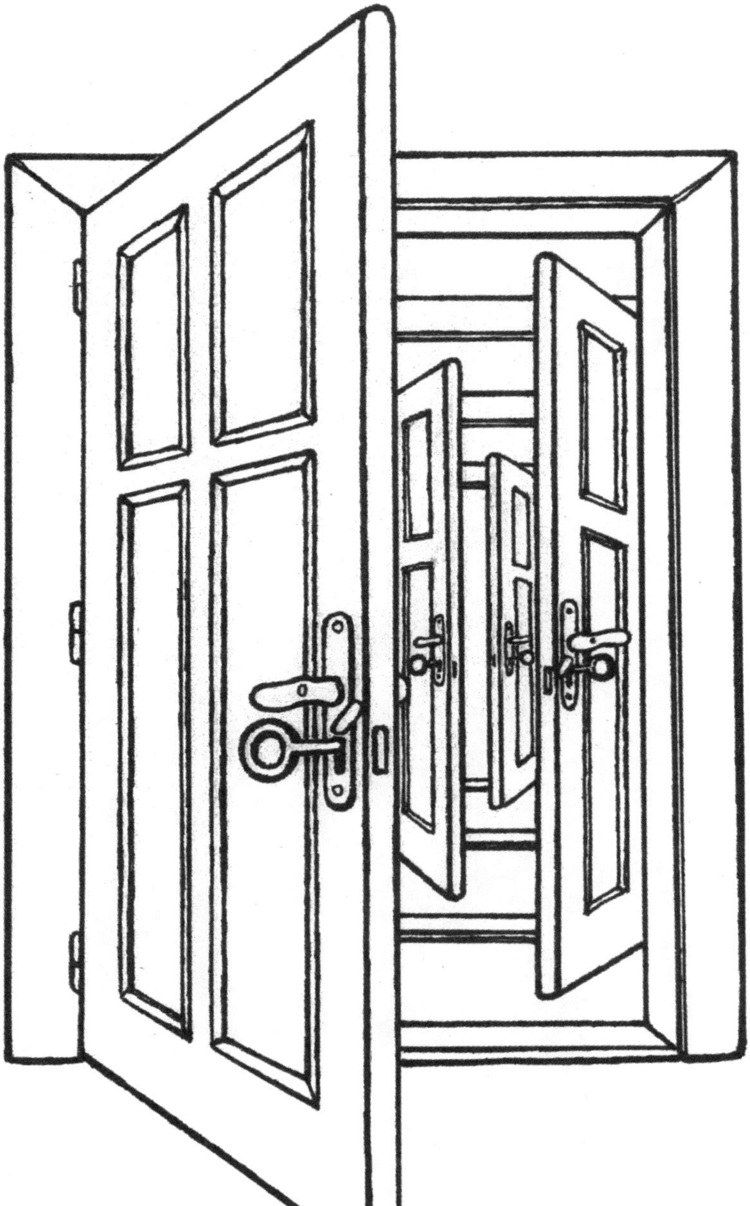

Lesson 1

ʾIgābāt:

1. Iṭ-ṭālib min London, min ʾIngilterra.
2. Il-gauw kwayyis hnāk.
3. Il-basbōr gdīd khāliṣ.
4. Iṭ-ṭālib ʾinglīzī .
5. Laʾ, ish-shanṭa tiʾīla shwayya.

Targama:

Iṭ-ṭālib maṣrī. Il-maṭār il-ʾadīm fēn? Il-ʾahwa ʾt-tiʾīla hena. Il-gauw fī ʾl-Qāhira ḥelu (gamīl). Il-basbōr il-brīṭānī fēn? Iṭ-ṭabīb ig-gdīd mnēn? Ish-shanṭa ʾl-kbīra fēn? Il-warda gamīla ʾawi.

Kammil: fī, min, fī, fī, fī

Lesson 2

ʾIgābāt:

1. ʾAywa, huwa fākir ʾism il-funduʾ.
2. Sauwāʾ it-taks rākin ganb(i) maḥaṭṭit il-ʾotobīs.
3. Iṭ-ṭālib sāmiʿ ṣōt gamīl.
4. La, huwa mish rāgiʿ il-maṭār.
5. La, huwa sākin wusṭ il-balad, ʿala ʾl-kornīsh.
6. ʾAywa, huwa ʿārif ʾUmm Kulsūm, il-muṭriba ʾl-maṣrīya ʾl-mashhūra.
7. Huwa wākhid il-ʾagāza min in-nahār da.
8. Is-sauwāʾ ʿāwiz fakka.

Targama:

ʾEnti mashya lē(h)? ʾAna mish ʾalmānī, ʾana tshīkī. ʾEnta rākin fēn? Hiya lissa mish nayma. ʾEḥna lissa waklīn. ʾEntū saknīn wusṭ il-balad? Ḥaḍretak ʿāwiz ḥāga min Maṣr? ʾEḥna mish shayfīn ḥāga. Bārīs ʿāṣimit Faransā. Murshid il-fōg il-ʾalmānī gāyib ʿunwān is-sifāra. Ḥaḍretik wakhda ʿala ʾl-akl il-ʿarabī? ʾAna mish ʿārif maḥaṭṭit Ḥelwān. Hum mish fahmīn ḥāga. ʾEnta rāyih fēn? ʾAna rāyiḥ li ʾṭ-ṭabīb. ʾEḥna ray(i)ḥīn il-maṭār.

Kammil: 1c, 2f, 3b, 4a, 5d, 6e

Lesson 3

ʾIgābāt:

1. La, mafīsh fī ʾl-funduʾ ʾōḍa faḍya bi ʾl-balakōna.
2. ʾAywa, it-tallāga kānit fī ʾl-ʾōḍa.
3. ʾAywa, kān mabsūṭ fīh ʾawi.
4. ʾIsmo maktūb ʿala biṭāʾit il-funduʾ.
5. ʾAywa, il-funduʾ ʿāg(i)bo giddan.
6. Muwaẓẓaf maktab il-istiʾbāl kān farḥān bīh.
7. Kānit ganb(i) bāb ʾodṭo.
8. ʾĀ(h), kānit bi ʾl-fiṭār.

Targama:
Kunti ʾembāreḥ ʿand ʾukhtik? Makansh(i) maʿāya ʾl-basbōr. Min faḍluku, maʿākūsh fakka? Lissa makunnāsh fī funduʾna. Lē(h) kuntū hnāk min ghērna? Malūsh ʾab walā ʾumm. Shanṭithā kānit tiʾīla ʾawi. Mīn kān hena ʾablina? Maʿāku miftāḥ ʿarabīyitku? Ṣūrithum kānit fī ʾg-gurnān. ʾIqāmitna fī ʾAswān kānit ʾusayyara. Samʿānī kwayyis? ʾEmta kuntū fī maḥaṭṭit Ramsīs? Kunna fīhā min sāʿa.

Kammil: 1c, 2a, 3f, 4b, 5e, 6d

Lesson 4

ʾIgābāt:

1. Iṭ-ṭālib il-ʾinglīzī nizil sūʾ is-Sayyida maʿa ʾaṣḥābo ʾl-maṣrīyīn.
2. Ṭalabhā minhum ʿashāno ma kansh(i) ʿārif sikkit is-sūʾ.
3. Rik(i)bū ʾl-metro wi ʾl-ʾotobīs.
4. Saʾalūʾ ʿalēhā wāḥid mi ʾl-bayyāʿīn.
5. Ir-rāgel ma wazan l(u)humsh(i) tuffāḥ.
6. Ig-gazzār ʿamal luhum siʿr kwayyis.
7. Shakarūhā ʿala ʾl-khuḍār iṭ-ṭāze ʾr-rkhīṣ.
8. Shir(i)būhā ʿashān kānū ʿaṭshānīn khāliṣ.

Targama:
ʿAmalit lī talāt ʾirghifa bi-gibna. Khamas rukkāb nizlū fī ʾl-Maḥaṭṭa ʾr-raʾīsīya. Il-ʾuwaḍ bi ʾl-balakōna kānit maḥgūza. Lissa ma katabt(e)lkūsh ʿunwānī fī ʾl-Qāhira. Ma ʿazamtūhūsh lē(h)? ʾEmta simiʿti ʾl-ʾaṣwāt? Lo ʾukhtēn ṣ(u)ghayyarīn. Ig-gawāmiʿ it-tārīkhīya ʾuddāmku ʿala ṭūl. Il-bībān ma kanitsh(i) maʾfūla. Lē(h) ma ʾaʿadtūsh ganb ish-shibbāk? Wazant(e) lī ʾt-tuffāḥ barḍo? Il-film lissa ma kh(i)lissh(i). Gawabāthā ʾl-ʾakhīra kānit ṭwīla giddan. Ma ḥaddish saʾalna ʿala ḥāga. Ma ṭalabūsh minna ḥāga.

Kammil:
gamīla, gudād, ḥelwīn, kwayyisa, ṭwīla, maṣrīyāt, ʾadīma, tiʾīla

Lesson 5

ʾIgābāt:

1. Il-ʾauwil kānū ʿawzīn yishrabū ḥāga sāʾiʿa.
2. ʾAywa, bi-yikhbizo.
3. ʾAywa, bi-yiʿmilhā.
4. Wāḥid mi ʾḍ-ḍuyūf kān ʿāwiz yighsil ʾīdēh.
5. Saʾalūh ʿala ʾl-iḥtifāl bi-munasbit ʿīd mīlād zmīlhum.
6. La, ma kansh(i) lāzim yiḥgizū ʾl -makān ʿala ṭūl.
7. Kān lāzim yibʿatūh li-ṣāḥib il-maṭʿam.
8. Ḥa-yidfaʿūh baʿd il-ḥafla.

Targama:
Mish ʿayzīn tuʾʿudū ganb ish-shibbāk? Mumkin tiʿmilī l(i)na samak mashwī? Lāzim nuṭlub ḥāga li ʾl-ʾakl. Is-suyyāḥ il-ʾinglīz dōl bi-yirgaʿū bi-ʾotobīs il-funduʾ. Il-ʾakhbār di

basmaʿhā ktīr ʾawi. Hiya mish ḥa-tirkab it-taks. Lāzim ʾaghsil ʾīdayya! Matinzilsh(i) fī ʾl-maḥaṭṭa di! Irkabī ḥāga tanya! Min faḍluku, idfaʿū ḥisābku ʾn-nahār da! Huwa ʿāwiz yiʿzimna li ʾl-iḥtifāl bi ʿīd mīlādo. Il-film da mish ḥa-yiʿgibhum. Mish ha-yifhamūnā. Lāzim nisʾalku ʿala ʿunwān il-maṭʿam da. Ig-garson ʿāyiz yiʿraf ʿadad iḍ-ḍuyūf. Il-mashākil di ma bi-tiḥṣalsh(i) fī shirkitna. Lē(h) mish ha-tishrabū ḥāga? Mish mumkin niḥgiz lo tazākir il-masraḥ. Ibʿatū l(i)na ṭalabku ʾl-ʾusbūʿ da!

Kammil!
a) dōl, b) da, c) di, d) di, e) di, f) da, g) dōl, h) di

Lesson 6

ʾIgābāt:

1. Zamaylī min Maʿhad il-ʾāsār il-maṣrīya ʾl-ʾadīma ʾālū lī ʾl-kalām da.
2. Kunt ʿāwiz ʾasībū lo ʿashān yirūh maʿāya.
3. Ṭalabt minno yifūt ʿalayya bukra ʾṣ-ṣubḥ.
4. Kunt shāyil fīhā kamerit fīdyo.
5. Ṭalabhā minnī ʿashān yigīb lina tazākir li ʾṭ-ṭalaba.
6. Rāgel ʿagūz kān bi-yibīʿhā ʾuddām il-matḥaf.
7. Sibtahā maʿa ḥaras il-matḥaf.
8. Tuhna gouwāh, ʿashān it-tamasīl kānit kbīra.

Targama:
Ma ruhnāsh in-nādī ʿashān kunna mashghūlīn khāliṣ. Da mish ḥa-yikūn mumkin ʾabadan. Mumkin tiʾūl lī ʿīd mīlādak ʾemta? Min faḍlak, shil iṭ-ṭabaʾ da! Sībū lna ʿunwānku ʿashān nizūrku. Lāzim tiʾūlū lhum ʿala ṭalabku ʿashān yigībū lku ʾl-ʾakl zaymā ʾentū ʿawzīn. Ma t(i)khafīsh, il-gauw ḥa-yikūn gamīl ʾin shāʾallāh! Mish ḥaghīb ktīr. Fataḥ lo ʾn-nāwūs ʿashān yishūf il-mūmiyā. Kānit khayfa ʿalēhum ʿashān ma yitūhūsh. Mīn ʿāwiz yidūʾ ḥalawīyāt sharʾīya? Kān lāzim tibīʿū tazākir il-masraḥ lē(h)? Ḥa-t(i)sībnī ʾasūʾ ʿarabīyt ish-shirka?

Kammil!
1c, 2b, 3e, 4h, 5g, 6f, 7a, 8d

Lesson 7

ʾIgābāt:

1. Zuwwār il-Qāhira ʿawzīn yikhushshūhā ʿashānhum ʿaṭshānīn wi taʿbānīn.
2. La, ma laffūhāsh, bas laffū ʾl-madīna ʾt-tārīkhīya min Bāb in-Naṣr li-ghāyit Bāb Zuwēla wi min hnāk rāḥū gāmiʿ Ibn Ṭulūn.
3. Ig-garson kān ʿāwiz yisubb(u) lhum mayya.
4. Ig-garson kān lāzim yirudd ʿalēh.
5. Ḥabb ish-shīsha wi ʿāwiz yishrabhā ʿala ṭūl.
6. Ig-garson kān ʿāwiz yilimmo ʿashān yishīl kubbāyāt.
7. Baṣṣ fīh ʿashān yishūf il-maḥfaẓa btaʿto.
8. Kān bi-yiʿiddahā lammā kān ʿāwiz yigīb gallabīya li-ʾukhto.

Targama:
Tismaḥū lī ʾakhushsh(i) gouwa? Ḥassēt bi-ʾalam gāmid. Laffū ʾs-sūʾ bitāʿ il-fakha wi ʾl-khuḍār. Lāzim timiddū ʿashān tilḥaʾū ʾl-metro. Mumkin / Tiḥibb ʾaḥuṭṭ(e) lak sukkar fi ʾsh-shāy? Min faḍlak ḥaḍretak, ṣubb(i) lī shwayyit mayya! Lē(h) ma bi-truddūsh ʿala ʾl-ʾasʾila btaʿitna? Shammētū ʾr-rīḥa di? Is-sagāyir di mish btaʿtī. Gēb ij-jakēt b(i)tāʿak maʾṭūʿ. Di ʾṣ-ṣuwar btaʿit zabāyinna. ʾĀlit lī ʾinnahā ʿawza tikhiff bi-surʿa. Ma bi-yihibbūsh yirūḥū kafeteriy(i)t il-gamʿa. Bi-tiḥibb tilbis fustān bitāʿ ʾummahā. Bi-n(i)ḥibb nidūʾ mashrūbāt mukhtalifa. Baḥibb ʾazūr ʾahāwī ʾl-Qāhira. Ḥa-yikūn lāzim niḥill masʾalit safar is-suyyāḥ. Mīn ʿāwiz yiṭlaʿ il-madna btaʿit gāmiʿ Ibn Ṭulūn? Buṣṣī fi ʾl-kharīṭa!

Kammil!
a) btaʿit, b) btaʿit, c) b(i)tūʿ, d) b(i)tūʿ, e) btaʿit, f) b(i)tūʿo
g) btaʿit, h) b(i)tūʿ, i) btaʿit, j) b(i)tūʿ

Lesson 8

ʾIgābāt:
1. Laʾēthā ʿa ʾl-lōḥa ʾr-raʾīsīya fi ʾl-maḥaṭṭa.
2. ʾIddū lī fīh waraʾa ṣ(u)ghayyara bi-mawāʿīd il-ʾuṭurāt.
3. Ḥakēthā li-muwaẓẓaf shibbāk it-tazākir.
4. Bi-yiʾūm iṣ-ṣubḥ, is-sāʿa sitta ʾu nuṣṣ.
5. Saʾalna ʿala ḥāga n(i)sīnāhā ʾabl(i) ʾs-safar.
6. ʾAṣḥābna ʾl-maṣrīyīn ʾālū lna il-ḥikāya di.
7. Bi-basāṭa, nsīna n(i)gībhā.
8. ʾAna grīt ʿashān ʾalḥaʾ il-ʾaṭr.

Targama:
Ma tinsīsh tiktibī lna gawāb. ʾIn shāʾallāh, ha-tibʾū mabsūṭīn ʿandina! Baʾēt ʾaḥibb il-ʾaflām di. Ḥa-nibʾa farhānīn bi-ziyāritku! Lāzim timshū lē(h)? Mumkin ʾarmi da fēn? Mish mumkin yinsūh ʾabadan. Ma tiddīhā lūsh! ʿĀwiz ʾaddīhū lak. Ḥa-tilāʾīh fi ʾl-ʾahwa. Lissa ma laʾēthumsh(i). Ma laʾūnāsh fi ʾl-bēt. Tiʾdarī tiʾrī lhum il-khabar da? Min faḍlak, ʾimla il-kubbāyāt di! Ma gara lhumsh(i) ḥāga. Ma tiʿrafsh(i) ʾl-ḥaddūta di, yibʾa ḥaḥkīhā lak. Ḥalāʾīku fēn? Baʾētū zahʾānīn, mish keda? Ḥakit lina ʿan il-kutub il-mansīya. Min faḍluku, ʾiddūhū lna! ʾIgri! Mafrūḍ mansahūsh. Di l-waʾt(i) mish mumkin nimshi. Il-ḥāgāt di, ʾana ʾārīhā kwayyis ʾawi. Min faḍlak, tiʾdar tiʾra lī gadwal il-mawāʿīd, ʾaṣlī ʾana mish shayfo. Ma tibʾīsh ḥazīna, il-ʾumūr ḥa-timshi, ʾin shāʾallāh.

Kammil!
1d, 2h, 3a, 4f, 5j, 6b, 7g, 8i, 9c, 10e

Lesson 9

ʾIgābāt:
1. Ṭallaʿt badlitī min dōlāb, ḥaḍḍart il-ʾamīṣ wi bibyōna wi lammaʿt gazmitī.
2. ʾAʿḍāʾ is-sifāra ʾl-brīṭānīya raḥḥabū bīya hnāk.

3. Farraḥnī ʾl-khabar, ʾinn(i) ṣaḥafīya ʾamrīkīya ʿawza tiʿmil ḥiwār maʿa ʾl-kātib il-maṣrī Nagīb Maḥfūẓ.
4. Farragūnī ʿalēhā liʾinnahā bi-tiʿmil sumʿa ṭayyiba li-baladhum.
5. Kunt badauwar ʿala ʾl-mulḥaq is-saqāfī.
6. Il-mulḥaq is-saqāfī ʿarrafnī ʿalēh.
7. Warrēt lo ʾt-targama btaʿtī li-ʾsh-shiʿr il-ʾinglīzī.
8. Lissa ma waddēthāsh ʾayy(i) magalla.

Targama:
Sallimū lī ʿala ʾaṣḥābku ʾl-maṣrīyīn! Ḥa-tisharrafūna ʾemta? S(i)miʿna ʾinnuku ṭallaʿtú ghaṭa ʾn-nāwūs. ʿAzamnī li ʾl-ḥafla, liʾinno kān ʿāwiz yiʿarrafnī ʿala zamaylo min London. Mumkin ʾaʾaddim luku nafsī? Targimit lina kalimāt il-ghinwa di. Il-mūsīqā di bi-tinayyimnī. Kunt ʿāwiz ʾafarfishak shwayya. Mish ʿawzīn t(i)rayyaḥūna lē(h)? Il-kitāb da khallānī ʾaḥibb il-ʾāsār il-maṣrīya ʾl-ʾadīma. Mish ḥa-yikhallūku trūḥū hnák min ghērna. ʿĀwiz tirabbi daʾnak lē(h)? Dayman bi-yisallīhum bi-kalāmo. Mumkin tiṣauwarūna ʾuddām il-haram da? Ḥawaddi ʾl-ḥāgāt di fēn? Khallīhā hena! Ma tikhallūhumsh(i) yinzilū fī ʾl-funduʾ! Dauwarna ʿala ʿunwānku, lākin ma laʾēnahūsh. Ma tidauwarīsh ʿalēh! Ḥaḍretak mumkin tiwarrīnī ʾsh-shāriʿ da ʿa ʾl-kharīṭa? Warrētū lhum iṣ-ṣuwar btaʿitku min Maṣr? Ḥa-niwarrīhā lhum. Ma tiwarrūhā lhumsh(i). Ma tiwarrīhā lūsh! Lāzim tirauwaḥū badri lē(h)? Bi-tifakkar fī ʾē(h)? Mumkin ʾagarrab il-ʾamīṣ da? Ma t(i)dabbarūsh il-maʿād da li-bukra! Lāzim nikallimku fī ʾl-mauḍūʿ da.

Kammil!
1d, 2f, 3i, 4h, 5g, 6a, 7c, 8e, 9j, 10b

Lesson 10

ʾIgābāt:
1. Iṭ-ṭālib il-ʾinglīzī bi-yirāsilhum.
2. Nāwilithā lo ʿashān yibʿat iṭ-ṭard li-ʾŪrubba.
3. Il-ḥāgāt di mumkin yilāʾīhā fī mīdān il-ʿAtaba.
4. Lāzim yiktibo ʿala wishsh iṭ-ṭard.
5. ʾĀbil henāk gāro mi ʾl-madīna ʾl-gamʿīya.
6. ʾAkhū gāro sāfir Bārīs ʿashān yiwarri li ʾl-mushrif b(i)tāʿo ʿamal ʾē(h) fī risalto li ʾd-doktōrāh.
7. Iṭ-ṭālib il-ʾinglīzī wāfiʾ ʿala musāʿidit gāro fī muragʿit il-baḥs b(i)tāʿo.
8. Bi-yiʿām(i)lūh muʿamla ḥelwa ʾawi.

Targama:
Mumkin ʾasāʿidku fī ḥāga? Mīn ma wāfiʾsh(i) ʿa ʾl-barnāmig da? Min faḍlak, ma t(i)nāʾishnīsh fi ʾl-mauḍūʿ da! Raddēti ʿala gawābo? Bi-n(i)rāsilhum sinīn ṭwīla. ʾĀb(i)lūna ʾembāreḥ ʾuddām is-sifāra. Ḥa-t(i)ʿāl(i)gūh ʾezzāy? Lāzim ʾatābiʿ il-ʾakhbār di. Mumkin tināwilīnī il-kharīṭa di? Lāzim nizākir kalimāt gdīda. Ma t(i)gāmilūnāsh! Khatar bi-bālī, ʾinno sāfir li-ʾahlo fi ʾṣ-Ṣaʿīd. ʾEntū ʿarfīn ʾinnuhum ʾaʿlanū ʿan muntagāt ish-shirka btaʿithum fi ʾg-gurnān il-ʿarabī da? Mumkin niʾābilku bukra? ʾAna khāʾyif ʾinn ḥaḍretak mish ḥa-tiwāfiʾ ʿala ʾl-mashrūʿ da. ʾĀlū lna ʾinnuhum bi-yiʿām(i)lūhum

mu'amla ḥelwa 'awi. Wazīr id-difā' il-waṭanī nā'ish ḍuyūfo 'l-'agānib. 'A'raf kwayyis 'innik ma bi-tiḥibbīsh il-mugamlāt di. Katabit lahā 'innahā bi-t(i)rā'ī 'aulād 'akhūhā. Kān 'āwiz yikhrig il-fīlm da lissa 's-sanā di. 'Awzīn tiḍīfū ḥāga? Ḥamḍi fēn? Mumkin nib'at il-kart da bi 'l-barīd ig-gauwī? Ḥa-n(i)gāwib 'ala su'ālku fī baḥr 'usbū'. Ba'a lku hena ktīr? Ba'a lna shahr fī Maṣr. 'Āwiz 'aṭṭammin 'alēku! Il-gihāz da mish ḥa-yinfa'o. Rāgi'tū 't-targama ma'a mīn?

Kammil!

a) khamsa 'u 'arba'īn, mitēn 'u ḥedāshar, suttumīya 'itnēn 'u sittīn, 'alfēn tultumīya 'arba'a wi 'arba'īn, 'alf talāta 'u tis'īn
b) mīya wi 'arba'tāshar, 'alf sub'umīya wāḥid 'u 'ishrīn, 'alf suttumīya tamanya 'u 'arba'īn, khumsumīya tamanya wi 'arba'īn, tus'umīya sitta wi tamanīn
c) tamanya 'u 'arba'īn, mīya wi khamsa, mīya sitta 'u talatīn, khamsa 'u tis'īn, mitēn itnēn wi khamsīn
d) 'arba' 'u 'ishrīn, khamsa 'u sab'īn, tis'a 'u talatīn, wāḥid 'u 'arba'īn, talāta 'u sittīn

Lesson 11

'Igābāt:

1. Iṭ-ṭālib il-'inglīzī 'āwiz yitkallim ma'āh.
2. Daras il-'arabī fī qism il-lugha 'l-'arabīya, Ma'had id-dirāsāt ish-shar'īya, Gam'it Oxford.
3. Iṭ-ṭalaba 'l-'agānib bi-yitdarrabū 'ala 'l-muḥadsa bi-mufradāthā wi gumalhā wi ta'bīrāthā 'l-muhimma.
4. Bi-ti'mil luhum imtiḥān 'ashān ti'raf mustawāhum.
5. Mumkin yudkhul il-mustawa 'l-khāmis.
6. Lāzim yib'a mutamassik bi-manāhig il-ma'had it-ta'līmīya.
7. Ṭalabit il-ma'had mumkin yitfassaḥū hnák.
8. Iṭ-ṭālib muta'assif li'inn(i) mudīr il-ma'had it'aṭṭal ma'āh.

Targama:

Itghaddētū walla lissa? 'Āwiz 'at'akkid min ṣiḥḥit il-ma'lūma di. In-nahār da mish mumkin nit'akhkhar. It'ashshū fi 'l-maṭ'am da ma'a ḍuyūfhum il-'inglīz. Ḥa-nitdarrab 'ala 'l-mufradāt mi 'd-dars it-tāsi'. Ḥaḍretak itkharragt fi 'l-gam'a 'emta? Ṭalabit is-sana 'r-rab'a 'amalū taqaddum hāyil fī diras(i)t il-'āmmīya. 'Ālū lna, 'innuhum yiḥibbū yit'arrafū 'ala 'ustāzna 'l-maṣrī. Tānī ma'ād li 'l-imtiḥān fi 'l-fuṣḥa lissa matḥaddidsh(i). Ma tit'assifsh(i), 'ana 'ārif ẓurūfak kwayyis! 'Umro ma 't'akhkhar. Yā tarā ḥaḍretak, mumkin nitfarrag bukra 'ala 'l-bardīyāt min 'Abū Ṣīr? Ḥaḍretak 'āwiz titkallim ma'a mīn? Bi-yit'allimū 'l-'inglīzī mi 's-sana 't-talta ibtidā'ī. Itrabbit fī 'usrit khālithā. Mustawāh itḥassin ktīr 'awi, mish keda? 'Ana khāyif 'innuku 't'aṭṭaltū ma'āya. Tiḥibbū titmashshū shwayya 'abl il-'asha? Lissa ma fakkarnāsh ḥa-nitfassaḥ fēn fi 'l-'agāza bta'itna. 'Atmanna lku riḥla sa'īda! Mumkin 'a'akkid li-ḥaḍretik 'inn il-mudarrisīn b(i)tū'na mutamassikīn bi 'l-manāhig it-ta'līmīya 'l-ḥadīsa. Il-ma'had it-tshīkī li 'l-'āsār il-maṣrīya 'l-'adīma it'assis min 'arba'īn sana.

Kammil!

1. itʾakhkhart	2. tikhallaṣū	3. ʾaddimū	4. itʾaddimna	5. yiḥassinū
6. itḥassinit	7. ḥaddidtū	8. yitʿarraf	9. itkallimtū	10. itʾakkidī

Lesson 12

ʾIgābāt:

1. Iz-zbūn il-ʾagnabī ʿāwiz yitʾābil maʿāh.
2. ʾAbadan, matḍāyiʾsh(i) min kalāmo khāliṣ.
3. ʿĀwiz yitnāʾish maʿāh fī kam mulaḥẓa, masalan fī nauʿīyt il-gulūd.
4. ʿAyza titʿāwin maʿāhā fī ṣināʿit ish-shunaṭ wi ʾl-gizam wi ʾl-ʾaḥzima ʾl-gildīya.
5. Matiʾdarsh(i) titnāzil ʿanhā, ʿashānhā gild tabīʿī mīya fi ʾl-mīya.
6. ʿĀwiz yitḥāyil ʿalēh ʿashān yikhallīh zbūno ʾl-ʾagnabī ʾl-waḥīd.
7. Il-bashmuhandis M(u)ḥammad mabsūṭ ʾawi min taʿāmul ish-shirkitēn.
8. ʾĀ(h), yiʾdarū yitfahmū maʿa baʿḍ kwayyis giddan.

Targama:

Ṭullābna kulluhum bi-yitrās(i)lū maʿa ʾaṣhābhum fī Maṣr. Mumkin ʾatnāʾish maʿāk fi ʾl-mushkila di? Mithayyaʾ lī ʾinnahā ma bi-titḍāyiʾsh(i) minhum ʿashān il-mulāḥaẓāt di. Matfāgiʾtūsh bi-ziyāritna? Kunna ʿayzīn nifāgiʾku. Ish-shahr kullo ḥa-yitʿālig fi ʾl-mustashfa da. Mīn kān bi-yiʿāl(i)gak? ʿAwzīn yitfāṣ(i)lū maʿāku fī ʾasʿār il-muntagāt iṣ-ṣināʿīya kullahā. ʿUmrahā matnāz(i)lit ʿan raʾyahā. Kull wāḥid yiʾdar yiʾakkid luku ʾinn taʿāwunna maʿa ʾl-muntigīn il-ʾagānib nāgiḥ giddan. Yā tarā ḥaḍretak, ḥa-yiʾdarū yitʾāb(i)lū bukra maʿa mandūb ish-shirka di? Lē(h) lāzim ʾatḥāyil ʿalēk ʿashān tifahhimnī ḥaṣal ʾē(h)? Il-kalimāt di kullahā ḥa-t(i)sāʿidik titfāh(i)mī maʿa ʾl-mushārikīn fi ʾl-muʾtamar. ʾĀl lī ʾinno kān bi-yitḥāyil ʿalēhum ʿashān yibʾū mutasām(i)ḥīn maʿa ʾl-ʾārāʾ di. Katabū lna ʾinnuhum mabsūṭīn min taʿāwun il-kullīya btaʿithum maʿa maʿhadna. Iṣ-ṣafqa di ma bi-titsāwāsh maʿa ʾṣ-ṣafqa ʾs-sabʾa. Huwa shāyif ʾinn il-maṭʿam da yiʾdar yināfis kull il-matāʿim it-tanya. ʾArāh(i)nak ʾinno ḥa-yigīb lina ʾurayyib ʾakhbār kwayyisa. Dayman bi-yitsābiʾ maʿa zamaylo. Ma bi-yiḥibbūsh gīrānhum ʿashānhum bi-yitʿālū ʿalēhum.

Kammil!

1. titʿāmil	2. nitʾābil	3. ʾatrāhin	4. yitḥāy(i)lū	5. titnāfis
6. nitḥāsib	7. titḍāy(i)ʾū	8. titfāṣilsh(i)	9. titʿālig	10. itfāgiʾtū

Lesson 13

ʾIgābāt:

1. Il-marīḍ bi-yitkisif ʿashān ʿando shwayyit mashākil ṣiḥḥīya wi mish ʿāwiz yitʿab iṭ-ṭabīb maʿāh.
2. Ṣaḥbit il-bēt ʾālit il-kalām da.
3. Id-dawa fi ʾr-roshetta yitgāb min ʾayyi ṣaydalīya.
4. Id-dawa ʾsh-shurb bi-yitʿimil min ʾaʿshāb ṭibbīya wi yitshirib baʿd il- ʾakl.
5. Il-ḥabbāyāt hiya ʾafḍal dawa li ʾl-maghaṣ.
6. ʾAktar riyāḍa bi-yiḥibbahā ʾl-marīḍ hiya ʾl-kura.
7. La, riglo lāzim titghisil fi ʾl-mayya bi ʾl-bābung.
8. La, ish-shāsh lāzim yitribiṭ fōʾ il-mifṣal wi mishṭ ir-rigl.

9. Il-ʿilba mish mumkin titsāb maftūḥa ʿashān fīhā fītāmīn fauwār.
10. Ir-roshetta mafrūḍ ma titrimīsh ʿashān iṭ-ṭabīb mumkin yishūfhā tānī.

Targama:
Ism ḥaḍretak inkatab bi ʾl-ʾinglīzī? Il-mashrūb da lāzim yitshirib bi ʾs-sukkar. Fī hena ḥāga mumkin titkisir? Il-ʿagīna bi-titʿimil min diʾīʾ wi mayya wi khamīra. Il-fakha di itghasalit kwayyis? Di ʾaḥsan ṭarīʾa. Il-gibna di ʾaḥla liʾinnahā matrakanitsh(i) ktīr barra ʾt-tallāga. Mithayyaʾ lī ʾinn il-ḥēṭa di lāzim titdihin bi-surʿa. ʾĀl lahā ʾinn il-ʾadwiya ʾl-ʾadīma matitrimīsh. Il-ʾaʾrāṣ bi ʾl-ʿarʾisūs lāzim titbiliʿ ʿa ʾr-rīʾ. Il-marham bi ʾl-bābung mafrūḍ yitḥaṭṭ fī makān bārid. Ir-raml lāzim yitshāl bi-ʿarabīy(i)t in-naʾl. Mumkin titṣirif l(u)hum ḥawāfiz? Lammā tibʾa ḥarar(i)t il-ʿayyān ʿalya ʾawi, yitḥaṭṭ it-talg ʿala dimāgho. Il-maraḍ da ma yitkhafsh(i) minno. ʿAshān titʿirif il-ʾasbāb il-ḥaʾīʾīya, lāzim yishūfak ʾakhiṣṣāʾī. Mumkin tiʾūlū lī inshaghaltū fī ʾē(h)? Ig-gawabāt di kullahā mafrūḍ titbiʿit fī ʾasraʿ waʾt. Il-ḥāgāt di lāzim titgāb fī ʾaʾrab furṣa.

Kammil!
1b, 2i, 3e, 4j, 5a, 6c, 7f, 8d, 9h, 10g

Lesson 14

ʾIgābāt:
1. Iz-zbūn istalam gawāb min maktab is-siyāḥa.
2. Bi-tiʿtazir lo ʿashānhā maftakaritsh(i) ibtikāro ʾl-hāyil ʿala ṭūl.
3. La, mish lāzim yīgī tānī, mumkin yittifiʾ maʿāhā ʿa ʾr-riḥla bi ʾt-telefōn.
4. Iḍ-ḍuyūf il-ʾagānib ʿawzīn yiḥtif(i)lū bi-lēlit Rās is-sana fī Sīnā.
5. Riḥlithum ḥa-tibtidi fi ʾl-ʾIskindirīya.
6. Bi-tiqtariḥ ʿalēh shughl il-murshid is-siyāḥī.
7. Shughl zayy(i) da muḥtāg maʿrift il-lughāt wi ʾt-tārīkh wi ʾl-ʾāsār.
8. Lagnit Wizart is-saqāfa bi-timtiḥinhum.
9. Lāzim yishtarik fi ʾd-daura ʾt-tadrībīya.
10. Iktashafit il-ḥaʾīʾa di min kalāmo ʿan Maṣr wi ḥaḍāritha.

Targama:
ʾAftikir ʾinno ḥa-yīgī ʾn-nahār da baʿd iḍ-ḍuhr. Lissa ma gūsh. Ittaṣalū bīna ʾinnuhum muntaẓirīnna fī ʾl-maṭār. Dayman kānit bi-tishtiki min ẓurūfhā ʾl-māddīya. Lāzim ʾaʿtazir luku ʾinnī ma gētsh(i) fi ʾl-maʿād. Mish muḥtāgīn ḥāga mi ʾl-makhzan? ʾEmta ḥa-tiḥtiflū bi-ʿīd mīlādo? Mīn ḥa-yiwris il-bēt da? Ḥaḍretik ikhtarti ʾanhi kurūt? Mumkin nittifiʾ maʿāku ʿala siʿr il-khashab? ʾAʿḍāʾ il-biʿsa iktashafū nuqūshāt barza gdīda. Huwa murtabiṭ ʾawi bi-ʾusrito. Il-imtiḥānāt ḥa-tibtidi baʿd(i) bukra. Ikhtārū ʾl-kurs da ʿashāno li ʾl-mubtadiʾīn. Kānū ʿawzīn yishtirū ʿarabīya ʾakbar. Lāzim tikhushsh il-mustashfa ʿashānhā ḥa-tiwlid baʿd kam yōm. Bukra ḥa-tishtaghalū fēn? Iḥtagg ʿala ʾṭ-ṭarīʾa di. ʾAna ḥāsis ʾinnuku ḥa-tiʿtariḍū ʿala barnāmig ir-riḥla. Iʿtarafū lna ʾinnuhum mashtaghalūsh il-ʾayyām dizay mā kānū mutaṣauwirīn. Lissa mabtadēnāsh shughl fi ʾl-haram da. Il-iʿtirāḍ bitāʿo ma kansh(i) salīm. Fēn ḥa-nistilim mafatīḥ il-ʾuwaḍ? ʿAwzīn niqtariḥ ʿalēku ziyārit dēr Sant Katrīn fī Sīnā. Ma tiʿtazir līsh ʿan ḥāga! Bi-ʾanhi ṭarīʾa ʿawzīn tiktish(i)fū maqbara tanya? Mīn ḥa-yimtiḥ(i)nik fi ʾl-ʿarabī?

Ittafa'tū ʿala 'ē(h)? Ma'darsh(i) 'awʿidku 'innī ḥāgī, bas ḥaḥāwil. Khud bālak, keda ḥa-tū'aʿ. Ḥa- nū'af fī 'anho ṭābūr? Il-lagna ʿawza tikhtabir maʿrifithum fī tārīkh Maṣr. ʿAla 'l-blāje ḥa-tiḥtāgū shamsīya. Lammā simiʿū su'ālna, irtabakū. Il-'akl da bi-yittākil maʿa ruzz wi salaṭit ṭ(i)ḥīna. Id-dawa da lāzim yittākhid ʿa 'r-rī'. Iḍ-ḍuyūf il-'agānib kulluhum ḥa-yiḥḍarū 'l-iḥtifāl bitāʿ in-nahār da fī gnēnt il-fundu'. 'Īdak bi-tiwgaʿak? Kānū muhtammīn giddan bi 'l-'āsār it-tārīkhīya.

Kammil!
1d, 2f, 3j, 4a, 5c, 6h, 7i, 8g, 9b, 10e

Lesson 15

'Igābāt:

1. Il-musab'a btaʿit Wizart it-tarbiya wi 't-taʿlīm ḥa-t(i)sāʿid madāris iṣ-ṣumm wi 'l-bukm.
2. Lammā kān bi-yiṣauwar, la'a ḥāgāt gamīla ʿumro ma shāfhā, khallito yiḥiss bi 'l-'iḥsās da.
3. La, bas muʿẓamhā ṭiliʿit kwayyis 'awi.
4. Il-bar'ū'āya mish waḍḥa, ʿashān il-khalfīya btaʿithā ighma''it.
5. 'Ā(h), kān khāyif giddan mi 'l-ḥikāya di.
6. Mafīsh manāẓir ighma''it khāliṣ.
7. Il-mōz kān mitṣauwar fī ʿizz in-nahār.
8. Il-ghēṭ ikhḍarr ziyāda shwayya bi-sabab it-taḥmīḍ.
9. Wishsho mumkin yiṭlaʿ miḥmirr sinna, li'inno mismirr fi 'ṣ-ṣūra 'l-'adīma.
10. Iṣ-ṣūra tibyaḍḍ khāliṣ, lammā niftaḥ il-film 'abl(i) taḥmīḍo.

Targama:
'Ana gay ḥālan. Ḥa-niʿauwaḍku ʿan kull il-khasāyir. Buṣṣ ḥaḍretak, 'īdak iḥmarrit khāliṣ. Mumkin t(i)nawilīnī burtu'ānāya kbīra? Ismarrētū keda fēn? ʿAwzīn yismarrū wi ʿashān keda 'āʿ(i)dīn sāʿāt ṭwīla fi 'sh-shams. Sib it-tuffāḥ yiḥmarr shwayya! Ḥaḍretak ʿāwiz tiḥammaḍ il-film bas? Min faḍlik, ma tinsīsh tiṭallaʿī 'l-fakha mi 'sh-shanṭa! Mumkin tiṭallaʿū 'ṣ-ṣuwar mi 'l-ʿafrīta di? Ma tikabbarūsh iṣ-ṣur(i)tēn dōl! Itkallimit maʿāna ʿan mashākil bēn bīḍ wi sūd fī ganūb 'Ifrīqiyā. Ihtammū bi-ḥaḍār(i)t il-Hunūd il-ḥumr. 'Ana khāyif 'inn rigl ḥaḍretak ḥa-tizra''. Il-ḥēṭa ibyaḍḍit bi-shakl gamīl. Li-salaṭit fawākih 'entū muḥtāgīn ṣubāʿēn mōz, rummānāya, mangaytēn wi burtu'ānāya ṣghayyara. Lammā yīgī 'r-rabīʿ, il-'ashgār kullahā bi-tikhḍarr. Ma t(i)ḥuṭṭīsh fi 'sh-shurba il-baṣalāya kullahā! Shil iṭ-ṭūb da kullo! 'Akattar tōm? Mīn massil dōr il-qurṣān il-'aʿwar? S(i)miʿtū ʿan filmo 'g-gdīd "'Aḥdab Notre-Dame"? Riglo 'l-yimīn ʿarga li'innahā kānit maksūra. Bi-tiḥibbū shāy 'iswid walla 'akhḍar? 'Urbuṭ ṣubāʿak bi 'l-'umāshāya di! Ma t(i)kallimhumsh(i) bi-ṣōt ʿālī, hum(ma) mish ṭursh! In-nōʿ da mi 'l-manga lāzim yib'a 'akhḍar ghāmi'. Ḥaḍretak bi-tidauwar ʿala 'l-kubbāya 'z-zar'a? Is-sama ighma''it khāliṣ 'abl(i) 'l-ʿāṣifa. ʿAyza 'ṣ-ṣafār walla 'l-bayāḍ walla 'l-bēḍa kullahā?

Kammil!
1j, 2a, 3c, 4h, 5f, 6d, 7b, 8g, 9i, 10e

Lesson 16

ʾIgābāt:

1. Iṭ-ṭālib is-swīdī ʿāwiz yistakhdimo.
2. Mish mumkin yistaʿmilo li ʾl-mukalma ʾd-daulīya ʿashāno bi-yishtaghal gouwa ʾl-Qāhira bas.
3. Huwa mistaʿgil ʿashān mamto wi babāh mistannīn mukalmito fī baḥr nuṣṣ(i) sāʿa.
4. La, huwa ʿāwiz yiṭṭammin ʿalēhā fi ʾt-telefōn.
5. Iṭ-ṭālib ʿāwiz yistashīrhā fī mauḍūʿ il-mukalma ʾd-daulīya.
6. ʾAywa, mumkin yistaʿidd fīh ʿala ṭūl.
7. ʾAbadan, hiya mish shayfāh mustafizz khāliṣ.
8. Istantigit minno ʾinno ʿāwiz yiṭṭammin ʿala ʾahlo barra wi ma yiḍmansh(i) ṭūl il-mukalma.
9. ʿĀwiz yistaʿīro minhā ʿashān yitʾakkid min kōd madīnit ʾahlo fī ʾs-Swīd.
10. Il-mukalma ʾd-daulīya ʾṭ-ṭwīla bi-tistahlik waḥdāt ktīr giddan.

Targama:

Ish-shirka ʾl-ʾagnabīya istasmirit ʾamwālhā fi ʾl-mashrūʿ b(i)tāʿna. Istaʿiddū li ʾs-safar! Ma tistakhdimūsh il-ʾasansēr da! Ma tistarkhaṣsh(i) wi hāt ḥāga kwayyisa! Mumkin ʾastakhdim it-telefōn b(i)tāʿ ḥaḍretak? Ma tistaʿgilīsh, ʿandik waʾt ktīr. Istannānī shwayya! Mumkin tistannūna fi ʾl-maṭʿam? Ḥa-nistannāku fī shurfit il-funduʾ. Mastannētīhumsh lē(h)? ʾIn shāʾallāh ḥa-yistafīdū min khibrithum maʿa ʾl-aghiza ʾl-ʾilīktrūnīya ʾl-ḥadīsa. Mīn istahlik il-mayya ʾs-sokhna kullahā? ʿAwzīn nistashīr ḥaḍretak fi ʾl-mauḍūʿ da. Bi-tistafizzīh lē(h)? ʾAna ʾstaghrabt ʾawi ʾinnuhum mattaṣalūsh bīku. Mumkin nistaʿīr minku ʾl-kutub di? Duwal il-Khalīg bi-tistakhrig il-betrōl. ʾAna ʿaw(i)zak tistarayyaḥ! Istarayyaḥtū shwayya? Hiya khayfa ʾinnā mish ḥa-nistaḥmil il-ḥarr ish-shdīd fī shuhūr iṣ-ṣēf. Istarkhū wi ma tifakkarūsh fī ʾayyi ḥāga! Ma tistaslimsh(i)! Lāzim nistaʾzin ʿashān nilḥaʾ ʾākhir ʾaṭr. Ish-shahr kullo kānū bi-yistaḍīfūhum fī bēthum. Ḥa-tistamirrū maʿāna? Iʾfilū ʾsh-shibbāk ʿashān ma tistahwūsh! Kull is-suyyāḥ kānū mustaʿiddīn ʾuddām il-ʾotobīs. Il-mustashār it-tigārī ʿarrafna ʿala wafd il-mustasmirīn il-ʾagānib. Lē(h) mastaʿartūsh minhum kharīṭa mufaṣṣala li-Sīnā? Ma kunnāsh ʿawzīn niʿaṭṭalhum liʾinnuhum kānū mistaʿgilīn giddan.

Kammil!

1f, 2g, 3h, 4j, 5b, 6d, 7c, 8a, 9i, 10e

Lesson 17

ʾIgābāt:

1. Mrāt mandūb ish-shirka ʾl-ʾalmānīya kānit bi-tisūʾhā.
2. Il-ʿarabīya dakhalithā ʿashān is-sauwāʾa btaʿithā ma khaditsh(i) bālhā min ʿarabīya karro malyāna ʾaṣab sukkar.
3. ʾAuwilmā shāf il-ḥadsa, kān ʿāwiz yuṭlub il-ʾisʿāf.
4. ʾĀl lahā ʾinno ḥa-yīgī ʾauwilmā yikhallaṣ shughlo.
5. La, kānit bi-tākhud ʿarabīyit gōzhā marritēn talāta kull(i) shahr.
6. ʿAmalithā ʾablimā tīgī Maṣr.

7. Rāḥit ʾism il-būlīs ʿashān ʾaurāʾahā ḍāʿit minhā fī makān il-ḥadsa.
8. ʾĀl lahā ʾinn lāzim yiʿmil lahā maḥḍar gdīd.
9. Hiya muḥtāgāh ʿashān tiʾdar titḥarrak bīh li-ghāyit mā titḥall mushkilithā.
10. Ḥa-yittiṣil bihā ʾauwilmā yiruddū ʿalēh mi ʾl-ʾIsmāʿīlīya.

Targama:
Zurtū ʾl-matḥaf da kam marra? Zurnāh ḥawālī taman marrāt. Kullimā ʾasmaʿ il-mūsīqā di, ʾaftikir ʾagāzitna ʾl-gamīla. Kullimā nitkallim ʾuddāmhā ʿan is-safar, bi-tiʿayyaṭ. Di tālit marra tiḥṣal lina ʾl-mushkilā di. ʾAblimā niʿmil maḥḍar, lāzim nisʾalku ʿala kaza ḥāga. ʾAblimā tidauwar il-ʿarabīya, ʾis iz-zēt! Baʿdimā ṭallaʿū ʾt-timsāl mi ʾl-maqbara, waddūh yitrammim. Mish ʿawzīn titmashshū shwayya, baʿdimā tishrabū ʾsh-shāy? Lammā ʾāl lī ʾinno nigiḥ fi ʾl-imtiḥān, f(i)riḥt ʾawi. Lammā kunna fi Maṣr ʾauwil marra, ma kunnāsh fahmīn kalām ktīr. Baʿdimā tikhallaṣū shughluku, lāzim tistarayyaḥū. Ḥaḍretak maulūd ʾemta wi fēn? ʾAna maulūd sabʿa yūniyū sanit ʾalf tusʿumīya itnēn ʾu sabʿīn fī Brāg, bas ʾukhtī maulūda wāḥid september sanit ʾalf tusʿumīya sitta ʾu sabʿīn fi ʾl-Qāhira. Il-muntagāt di bi-tīgī mi ʾl-maṣāniʿ fi ʾl-madīntēn il-ʿĀshir min ramaḍān wi Sitta ʾOktōber. Gawāz safarī ṣadar min ʾism ig-gawazāt khamastāshar dīsember sanit ʾalf tusʿumīya tamanya ʾu tisʿīn. Lammā bi-yibʾa fāḍī, bi-yirūḥ il-ʾIskindirīya il-gumʿa wi ʾs-sabt. ʾAuwilmā ḥagazū tazākir iṭ-ṭayarān, rāḥū ʾs-sifāra ʿashān yakhdū ʾl-fīza. ʾAuwilmā tikhiffī, ḥa-n(i)rūḥ il-baḥr. Istannū hena li-ghāyit mā yīgī ʾl-otobīs! Ḥastanna ḥaḍretak fi ʾl-maktaba li-ghāyit mā tirgaʿ. ʾAuwilmā ʾaʿraf ḥāga, ḥaʾūl lak. Kullimā niʿūz nukhrug, id-dinya timaṭṭar. Lāzim yuʾʿud fi ʾl-mustashfa li-ghāyit mā ṣiḥḥito titḥassin. ʾAblimā tiftaḥī ʾl-ʾizāza, ruggīha kwayyis. ʾAblimā t(i)rūḥ ʾism ig-gawazāt, ʾiʿmil ṣuwar min ʾaurāʾak ir-rasmīya.

Kammil!
is-sāʿa:
a) sitta ʾu tisʿa (tisʿ daʾāʾy), b) itnāshar ʾillā tilt, c) tamanya ʾillā ʾarbaʿa (ʾarbaʿ daʾāʾy), d) ḥedāshar ʾillā ʿashara (ʿashar daʾāʾy), e) talāta ʾu wāhid ʾu ʿishrīn (diʾīʾa), f) itnēn ʾu talāta ʾu ʾarbaʿīn (diʾīʾa), g) ʾarbaʿa ʾu nuṣṣ ʾillā diʾīʾa, h) itnāshar ʾu nuṣṣ ʾu khamsa (khamas daʾāʾy), i) khamsa ʾu tamantāshar diʾīʾa, j) tisʿa ʾu nuṣṣ ʾu diʾītēn

Lesson 18
ʾIgābāt:
1. Mutargim il-biʿsa kallim il-ʾustāz Raʾūf fi ʾl-mauḍūʿ da.
2. La, ish-shaʾʾa bi nafs il-muwāṣafāt wi nafs il-manṭiʾa bi-titʾaggar ʾaghla bi-ktīr.
3. Sumʿit il-maʿhad it-tshīkī ʾṭ-ṭayyiba wi ʾsh-shughl ʾilli bi-yiʿmilo, yikhallū ʾl-ʾaulawīya li ʾaʿḍāʾ il-biʿsa ʾt-tshīkīya.
4. Rufūf il-khashab itshālit mi ʾl-makhzan ʿashān yitʿimil ʾoḍt in-nōm.
5. In-nās dōl ḥa-yuʾʿudū kull(i) marra mudda basīṭa.
6. Il-mutargim mish ʿārif, in-nās ḥa-yutbukhū bi-nafsuhum walla laʾ.
7. Mrāt il-bauwāb hiya li-mumkin yittif(i)ʾū maʿāh ʿala tanḍīf ish-shaʾʾa.
8. ʿAmmit il-ʾustāz Raʾūf kānit ʿāy(i)sha fīhā ʾs-sinīn li-fātit li-waḥdahā.
9. Il-ḥanafīya wi ʾl-ballāʿa wi ʾl-ḥōḍ, hiya di ʾl-ḥāgāt ʾilli kān mafrūḍ titṣallaḥ.
10. ʿAyzīn yiʾaggarūhā li ʾn-nās ʾilli tiʾaddar ʾīmithā wi fī nafs il-waʾt tiḥāfiẓ ʿalēhā.

Targama:

Di ṣūr(i)t il-fundu' 'illi kuntū sāk(i)nīn fīh? Il-mashākil 'illi kallimtū ʿanhā, itḥallit. Mīn ir-rāgel 'illi sallim ʿalayya bi-ḥafāwa shdīda? ʿAraḍ ʿalēna nafs is-siʿr 'illi 'aʿlanū ʿanno fi 'g-gurnān. Itʿarraftū ʿala 'l-iktishāfāt 'illi ʿamalhā 'aʿḍā' il-Maʿhad it-tshīkī li 'l-'āsār il-maṣrīya 'l-'adīma? 'Entū ʿār(i)fīn in-nās 'illi ḥa-yiskunū fi 'sh-sha''a di? Ish-shuwak wi 'l-maʿāli' wi 's-sakakīn 'illi ḥaḍretik lammaʿtīhā, ḥuṭṭīhā, min faḍlik, ʿa 't-tarabēza! Fēn il-'aghiza li bi-ti'īsū bihā mawāqiʿ il-ḥafrīyāt? Is-sana li fātit ruḥna 'l-'agāza maʿa nafs il-maktab li 's-siyāḥa. Mīn li mumkin nittifi' maʿāh ʿala tanḍīf ish-sha''a? 'Ē(h) li 'entū bi-tidauwarū ʿalēh? Mīn li kallimak fi 'l-mauḍūʿ da? Il-ʿummāl 'illi bi-yinazzilū hena 'ṭ-ṭūb, min 'Abū Ṣīr. Il-gawāmiʿ 'illi ṣauwarnāhā, mi 'l-ʿaṣr il-fāṭimī. Il-kutub 'illi ṭalabūhā mi 'l-khārig, gat bi-surʿa 'awi. Il-kharīṭa li sa'alt ʿalēhā, khilṣit. 'Illi ḥassēna bīh, huwa 'innuhum bi-yiḥibbūna fiʿlan. 'Illi fihimto min kalāmo, huwa 'inno ḥa-yikūn il-'ayyām 'illi gayya mashghūl giddan. 'Illi humma fāk(i)rīno, huwa 'inn id-dinya kānit ḥarr 'u fī nafs il-wa't ir-ruṭūba ʿāl(i)ya. 'Illi ṭalabo minku mudīr ish-shirka, iltizām bi 'l-mawāʿīd. Min faḍlik, mumkin 'astaʿīr minnik il-'alam; 'illi khadto maʿaya, ma ba'āsh yiktib. Mafīsh ʿand ḥaḍretak ḥassāsīya mi 'd-dawa li katabtuhū lak? Il-'aflām 'illi shufnāhā fi' sh-shuhūr 'illi fātit ʿagabitna 'awi. Da mabna Kullīy(i)t il-'ādāb 'illi itkharragt fīhā min 'arbaʿtāshar sana. Humma dōl iṭ-ṭalaba 'illi 'aṣḥābhum il-maṣrīyīn kallimūna 'embāreḥ fi 't-telefōn. Zurtū 'l-matḥaf da 'illi maʿrūḍāto mumkin titshāf fi 'l-maʿāriḍ bi-Maṣr wi 'l-khārig barḍo? 'Aftikir 'innuhum darasū nafs it-takhaṣṣuṣ. Hiya mish ʿayza tu''ud hena li-waḥdahā. Humma bi-nafsuhum gābu 'l-minaḥ li 'l-gamʿa di. 'Eḥna nafsina mish ʿār(i)fīn, mīn ḥa-yikūn mukallaf bi 'l-muhimma di.

Kammil!

1j, 2e, 3b, 4a, 5i, 6h, 7g, 8c, 9f, 10d

Lesson 19

'Igābāt:

1. 'Iza gum, mish ḥa-yi'dar yiḥḍar il-faraḥ.
2. 'Iza ge fi 'ṣ-ṣabāḥīya, ḥa-yi'ūl luhum: "Ṣabāḥīya mubār(a)ka!"
3. Fi 'l-ḥāla di ḥa-yiruddū: "ʿO'bāl ʿanduku!"
4. Lau kān ʿārif il-ḥa'ī'a di, kān gāb maʿāh ḥad.
5. 'Iza kān fāḍī, mumkin yiʿaddi ʿalēh.
6. Lau la'a nafso fāḍī, kān ḥa-yittisil bi-ṣaḥbo 'l-maṣrī.
7. Lau iṭ-ṭālib radd: "Shukran!", ḥa-yibān 'inno 'agnabī.
8. 'Iza kān ʿāwiz yistakhdim ʿibāra kamān, mumkin yi'ūl: "Shidd(i) ḥēlak!"
9. Lau ruḥt 'abārik li 'akhūya ʿashān ṭifl gdīd, kunt ḥa'ūl lo: "'Alf mabrūk!"
10. Lau ruḥna niʿazzi, ḥa-ni'ūl li 'aṣḥāb il-ʿaza "Il-ba'īya fī ḥayātku!"

Targama:

'Iza kān ʿanduku 'ayy(i) su'āl, ilga'ū li 'l-murshid bitāʿuku. Lau la'ēt iṣ-ṣūra, sibhā lī ʿala 'l-maktab. 'Iza rigiʿt 'abl il-ghada, ḥa-nilḥa' nikammil it-targama. 'Iza ma khaffish il-'alam, ḥa-yiʿmilu lo 'l-ʿamalīya. 'Iza kuntū ʿayzīn t(i)zūrū maʿbad il-Karnak, lāzim takhdū ḥanṭūr yā taks(i). ʾIza ma kānitsh(i) ish-shaʾʾa di ʿagbāhum, ḥa-n(i)shūf luhum gherhā. ʾIza ʾtghayyar barnāmig ir-riḥla, ḥa-niddī l(u)ku khabar. ʾIza ma kānsh(i) ʾl-maʿād yinās(i)bak, ʾul lī! Lau itʾakhkhart, ḥattiṣil bīku. Lau kuntū gaʿānīn, fī ʾakl gāhiz fi ʾt-tallāga. Lau fī ʿaṣīr lamūn, ḥashrab, ʿashānnī ʿaṭshān ʾawi. Lau kunti bardāna, khudī baṭanīya mi ʾd-dolāb! Lau fātnī ʾl-ʾotobīs, mumkin ʾarkab il-ʾaṭr. ʾIza ʿagabku ʾl-makān da, mumkin tuʾʿudū hena. Lau kunna ʿār(i)fīn, ḥa-tiwṣalū ʾemta, kunna ḥa-nistannāku fi ʾl-maṭār. ʾIza kānū shay(i)fīn is-siʿr da ʿālī ʾawi, mumkin yitnāz(i)lū ʿan is-safqa. Lau kānit ʿār(i)fa ʾinglīzī barḍo, kān mumkin tishtaghal fi ʾs-siyāḥa. ʾŪlī lī, lau laʾēti ʾl-kitāb da! Lau laʾēt nafsak fāḍī, ʿaddi ʿalayya! ʾIza kān fī ḍalma fi ʾl-maqbara, shaghghalū ʾl-kashshāf! Lau kuntū ḥarrānīn, shaghghalū ʾt-takyīf! ʾIza ma liḥiʾnāsh nitʿashsha fi ʾl-fundu', ḥa-n(i)rūḥ ʾayy(i) maṭʿam baʿd il-ḥafla ʾl-mūsīqīya. ʾIza kān il-mathaf ʾāfil, iʿmilū riḥla fi ʾn-Nīl. ʾIza ma kānsh(i) ʿanduhum daʿwa rasmīya, mish mumkin yakhdū fīza. ʾIn ruḥtū t(i)bār(i)kū li ʾl-ʿirsān, ma tinsūsh takhdū lhum ʿilbit shokolāta! ʾIza kharagt, sib miftāḥ il-ʾōḍa fī maktab il-istiʾbāl! ʾIza ma ruḥtūsh il-baḥr, mumkin nirkab khēl fī Saʾʾāra. Lau ma kānsh(i) il-mablagh da yikaffi, kān lāzim ʾarūḥ il-bank ʿashān ʾasḥab flūs tānī. ʾIza shuftuhum, sallim lina ʿalēhum! Lau ma shufnakūsh ʾabl is-safar, ḥan(i)shūfku baʿdimā tirgaʿū. ʾIn ma ʿiriftish ʾattaṣil bīk, ḥabʿat lak risāla ʿala ʾl-maḥmūl. Lau ruḥt fi ʾn-nōm, ṣaḥḥūnī is-sāʿa sabʿa! Ma ʾālit līsh, ʾiza kānit itkharragit fi ʾl-kullīya is-sana di walla ʾs-sana li fātit. Nifsī ʾaʿraf, ʾiza kānit iṣ-ṣuwar ṭiliʿit ḥelwa walla laʾ. Isʾalhum, ʾiza kānū ʿayzīn yirgaʿū Maṣr in-nahār da walla bukra. Ma ʿandināsh fikra, ʾiza kān il-barnāmig ʿagabhum walla laʾ.

Kammil!
1h, 2e, 3d, 4i, 5g, 6b, 7a, 8j, 9c, 10f

Lesson 20
Muzāk(a)rit il-ḥiwārāt min dars "Ḥa-tiwḥashīna yā Maṣr."

Lesson 21
ʾIgābāt:
1. La, lammā dakhal ir-rabīʿ, kān shakl ish-shāʿir ḥazīn.
2. Ḥaṭṭahā ganb ish-shāʿir.
3. Ish-shāʿir shābb walākinno ḥāsis ʾinno ʿagūz ʾawi.
4. Itʾāb(i)lū sāʿit misa.
5. Maḥaddish ʾāl l(u)hum il-kalām da.
6. ʾIza ma kānsh(i) fīhā ʾr-rabīʿ, kānit id-dinya ḥa-t(i)mūt.
7. Lau kānit id-dunya min ghēr ir-rabīʿ, waraʾit shagar kānit ḥa-tibʾa ḍaʿfāna wi mifatfita.
8. ʿUyūn hiya li bi-tākhudhā bi ʾl-ḥuḍn.
9. Ish-shāʿir ḥāsis fīhum kulluhum bi ʾl-ḥuzn.
10. Bi-yiʾūl lahā: "ʾĒsh tuṭlubī yā nafsī fōʾ kull(i) da, ḥaẓẓik bi-yiḍḥak wʾ enti mitnakkida?"
11. Mish ʿay(i)zāhum yibuṣṣū lhā bi-ʿuyūn ḥazīna keda.
12. Wara kull(i) shibbāk ʾalf ʿēn maftūḥīn.

13. Lau iltaṣaqū, kānū ḥa-yimūtū bi-ḍarbit ḥagar.
14. Lau iftaraqū, kānū ḥa-yimūtū mitḥassarīn.
15. Bēn ish-shāʿir wi ḥabīb(i)to dayman safar wi buḥūr.

Rakkib il-kalimāt:

مطار، تاكسى، فندق، رصيف، مطعم، شوربة، متحف، زيارة، قهوة، مدينة، سكّر، شيشة، سفارة، بوسطة، إمضاء، معهد، مسشفى، طبيب، جامعة، صيدلية، ستوديو، تليفون، دولة، جامع، فرح، ربّاعيات، بنك، جعران، مكتبة، شبّاك، محطّة، مترو، شارع، ميدان، استعلامات، استخدام

Iktib bi ʾl-khaṭṭ il-ʿarabī:

أ) الجمهوريّة التشيكيّة، مصر، أسوان، الجيزة، مع السلامة!، الأهرام، دكتور، فرصة سعيدة!، راس السنة، قرش، أوربّا، ألف مبروك!، صفقة، أهلاً وسهلاً!، الباشمهندس، برقوق، جواز سفر، مستشار، الجمعة، كلّ سنة وأنت طيّب!، مكتب الاستقبال، مكالمة، الشقة للإيجار، جدول المحاضرات، النهار ده، كمسرى، السنة اللى جيّة

ب) استلمت المبلغ، امض هنا، من فضلك!، حنستنّاكو قدّام الفندق!، متنسوش المفاتيح! متتأخريش!، اختاروا اللى أنتو عاوزينه!، سلّم لى على أولادك! لو لقيتو نفسكو فاضيين، فوتوا علينا بعد الظهر! حتشرّفونا أمتى إن شاء الله؟، مش التدخين ممنوع هنا؟ أيو، كلامك مضبوط!

Iktib bi ʾl-khaṭṭ il-lātīnī:

a) Brāg, il-ḥamdu liʾllāh, is-salāmu ʿalēku!, il-Qāhira, telefiz(i)yōn, ʾalf shukr!, qunṣul, istimāra, mursil, Saʾʾāra, bukra(h), kummitra, rummān, burtuʾān, faraula, būlīs, mudīr, ṭayyāra, muwaẓẓaf, ʾaghusṭus, yūl(i)yū, ʾoktōber, maktab is-siyāḥa, sentrāl, wizar(i)t il-khārigīya, ʾAbū Ṣīr, istismār, Dār il-ʾōberā, ʿīd il-mīlād, gihāz it-tasgīl
b) lā yughtafar; lissa ma shuftahāsh; il-ʾalam da ma bi-yiktibsh(i) kwayyis; humma bi-yirās(i)lūna min zamān; bi-tiḥ(i)bbū ʾahwa walla shāy?; itʿarraftū ʿalēhum ʾemta?; il-hāgāt ʾilli gibtūhā min is-sūʾ, ḥaṭṭētūhā fēn?; ʾiza ma gūsh, lāzim n(i)rūḥ luhum; lau fī ʾayy(i) mushkila, ittaṣ(i)lū bīna ʿala ṭūl!; nitmanna l(u)ku nagāḥ kbīr fī muzakrit il-ʿāmmīya ʾl-maṣrīya!!!

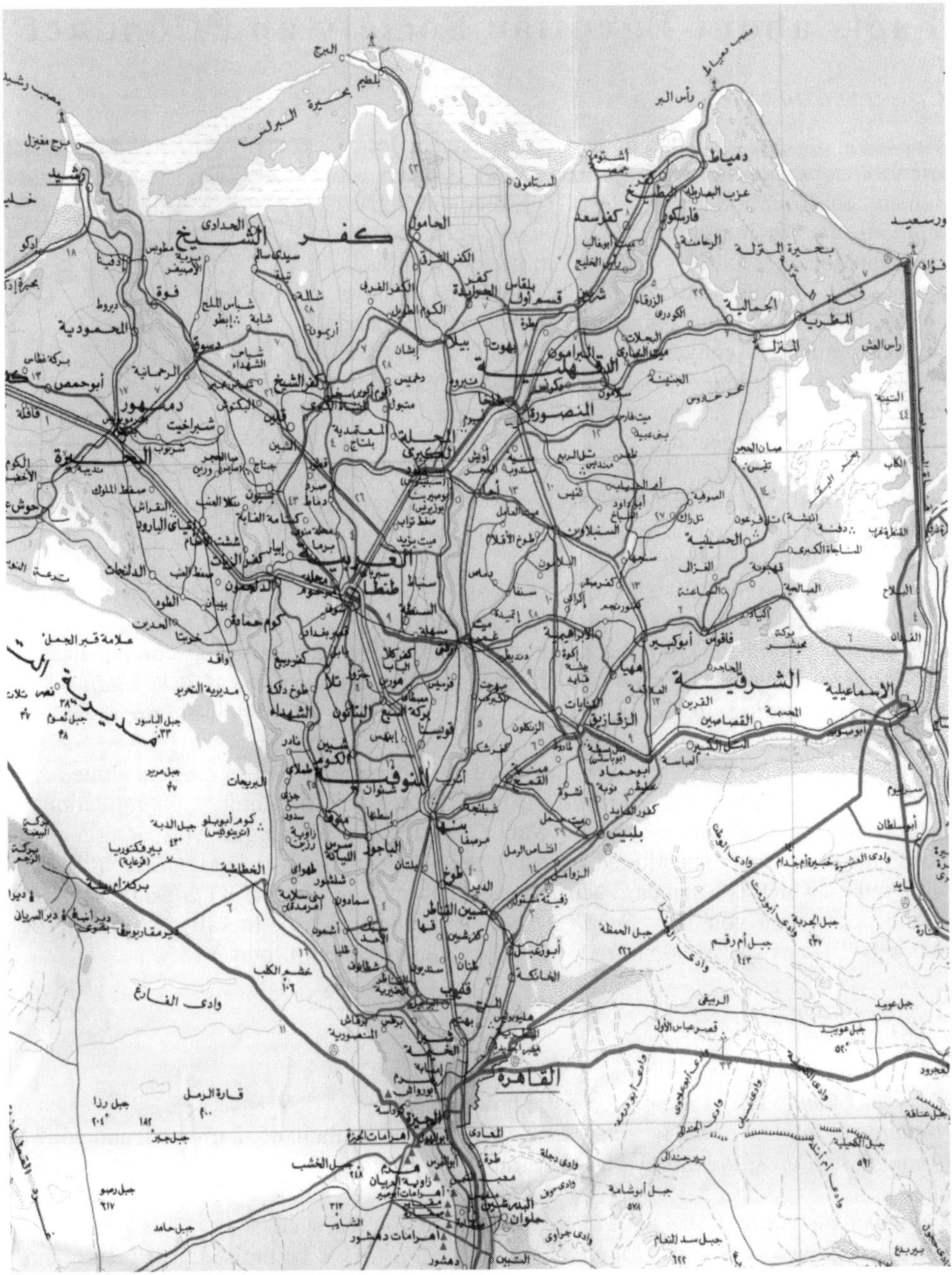

The Nile Delta

Facts about Egyptian Society and Conduct

Conversation

The common everyday use of the tongue pays a lot of attention to expressions of politeness and concern for human behaviour and relationships. The keeping of good relations among individuals is a sacred value of the Egyptian society, and it is reflected in its idiom as well. Egyptian Colloquial Arabic is remarkable for its richness in greeting and wishing phrases. Numerous are phrases related to attentive conversation about one's family and health, and no Egyptian would ever speak to his fellow without a polite inquiry about these facts, regardless the character of their meeting, be it official, unofficial or friendly. A foreigner, who is acquainted with these rules of conversation, is an esteemed and well-accepted guest, as the Egyptians are appreciative of the understanding of their language and culture, including the religious and social background of their speech.

It is useful then to master such expressions as *ʾIn shāʾallāh.* "If it be God's will" – the phrase is used to express approval, consent, wish, promise, or expectation. Or *Il-ḥamdu li ʾllāh.* – "God be thanked" – thanksgiving, praise or contentedness; *Wi ʾn-nabi.* – "By the Prophet" – an urgent wish or a surprise; *Mā shāʾallāh* – "It happened according to God's will" – an expression of appraisal, approval, or astonishment.

An important part of the speech consists of paired phrases. These are constituted by a phrase and a reply – e.g. *Mabrūk!* (literally "blessed", meaning "Congratulation") > the answer: *ʾAllāh yibārik fīk/u* ("May God give His blessing to you" – sg. / pl.). Such standard pair is constituted by every greeting, as e.g. *Is-salāmu ʿalēku* ("Peace with you" – which is a standard Muslim greeting) and the answer: *Wi ʿalēkum is-salām* ("And peace with you"); or *Ṣabāḥ il-khēr* ("Good morning", literally "Morning of goodness") – answer: *Ṣabāḥ in-nūr* (literally "The morning of light").

A conversation:

Is-salāmu ʿalēku – Hello!

Wi ʿalēkum is-salām – Hello!

ʾEzayyak, ʿāmil ʾē(h) – How do you do, how are you?

Il-ḥamdu li ʾllāh, kwayyis, w ʾenta ʿāmil ʾē(h)? – God be thanked, I am well, and you?

Il-ḥamdu li ʾllāh, kull(i) tamām wi zayy il-ʿēla – Thanks to God, I too. And how is your family?

Kulluhum kwayyisīn. Wi zayy ṣaḥḥitak – Fine. Do you feel well?

ʾAḥsan, il-ḥamdu li ʾllāh, wi shughlak ʾakhbāro ʾē(h) – God be praised, it is better, and how are you in your work?

Fataḥt maktab it-targama – I have a new translation agency.

Mā shā ʾllāh. ʾAlf mabrūk – That is great. Congratulations!

'Allāh yibārik fīk. Sallim lī 'ala madām wi wilādak – Thank you. Please greet on my behalf your wife and children.
'Allāh yisallimak – Thank you, I will.
A greeting, congratulation or leave-taking is never done without shaking hands mutually. Please note – the more you are capable of understanding and of respect for the social and cultural values and codes, the better and more friendly acceptance will you get. Albeit this may sound like a truism, many a misunderstanding can be avoided by observing this rule.

Travelling

It is quite comfortable to travel round Egypt by train. The 2nd class trains connect all the main cities of Egypt, Alexandria with Aswan, Cairo with Fayyum, Ismailiya, Suez and Port Said. Tickets can be bought in advance at the counters, which can be found at the railway station. The main station of Cairo is located on the *Ramsīs* Square (subway station *Mubārak*). The main station of Alexandria is called *Maḥaṭṭiṭ Maṣr* (The Cairo Station).
The Sinai, Mediterranean and Red sea resorts are accessible by air-conditioned buses. The tickets can be bought in travel agencies or in the offices of each transport authority. For covering shorter distances it is common to use the so-called *'arabēya bi 'n-nafar* – which is a microbus, usually for 12 persons, and runs the destinations in the environs of a city, like Cairo – southern Delta, Cairo – Fayyum or even longer routes like Cairo – Alexandria or Cairo – Zaqaziq. In the case of this shared taxi ride, it is better to fix the price in advance and pay afterwards to the driver. On the other hand, when hiring a taxi in a town, it is better to have an idea of the fare to be paid and pay afterwards without haggling over the price. The public transport is to be found in greater cities, as Alexandria or Cairo. The best to use is the Cairo subway, which is connecting the southernmost and the northernmost parts of the city (Helwan and Giza).

Shopping

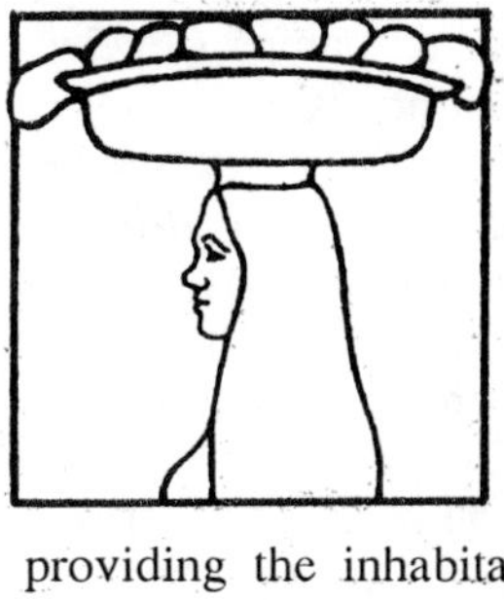

Egypt offers a lot of shopping possibilities in a wide and colourful range. The supermarkets of European style are in no way different from their European counterparts and have fixed prices. Markets (a marketplace – *sūq – sū'*) offer a complete array of goods, including jewellery, clothing, and victuals. There are a few traditional and famous markets, offering Oriental ware – Khān il-Khạlīlī in Cairo, the *sūq* of Luxor and the *sūq* of Aswan.
Every town or even every bigger quarter has its own market, providing the inhabitants with fruits, vegetables, meat, milk, bread and spices. All

prices at the markets are the result of bargaining and patient negotiations. If asking the seller for a better (lower) price, we say *Mumkin tikrimnī?* (Can you give me a discount?), trying to persuade him to sell us cheaper. If we would like to know, whether there is any further possibility, or whether the offered price is the final one, we should ask *ʾākhir kalām* (last word/speech). That is to say, if the last price said is the final one, which is not further negotiable.

The Dress

The Egyptians wear both European and traditional Arabic clothing. A lot of people prefer to use the European clothing as a formal one, worn in work and for official purposes, while at home they prefer Arabic dress.
The European visitor should note that the usual attire of a woman includes long sleeves, long skirts or trousers (not too tight), and a headscarf. European female travellers should not forget that without respecting this dress code, they would raise unnecessary comments and even provoke disrespectful behaviour, especially when travelling in the country or visiting less touristy places in towns. Moreover they are not allowed to enter any mosque in shorts or without headgear.
Modesty in dress is requested for men as well – shorts are not considered an acceptable wear, except for beach or sport resorts. If the visitors respect the basic rules of the Egyptian dress code – i. e. modest and decent clothes, they should move freely around even off the beaten track. The same rule applies here as with the language – be respectful and you will be accepted well.
In Egypt – and in the Arab world in general, it is necessary to understand that the dress is an important fact, saying a lot about its possessor – when going out or to any office (as an employee or a client) one has to dress carefully and pay attention to one's shoes as well. To put on sport shoes or sandals is unacceptable.

Mail and Phone

Postcards (*kurūt*) are sold in bookshops, stationery shops, souvenir and newspaper stalls. Postage stamps (*ṭawābiʿ*) can be bought at posts, bookshops, in hotels and in every shop marked with the sign of a stamp (usually smaller groceries or variety stores). Mailboxes (*ṣanadīʾ il-barīd*) are placed on the streets of towns and villages, as often as not in the centre or downtown (*wusṭ il-balad*). They are of two kinds. The red ones are used for ordinary mail, the blue ones are for airmail. The fastest mail is that put at the main post offices, like GPO in Cairo at the *al-ʿAtaba* Square – the central offices are at *Ramsīs* Square, next to the Main

station (*Bāb il-ḥadīd*). Fee stamps (*damgha* = fee stamp) are also available at the post offices.
Telephone boxes are usually for telephone cards, which are available in shops everywhere, where the logo of a particular communication company is fixed. The cards for mobile phones are usually equally common.

Food

Egyptian cuisine uses as basic staples the rich sources of vegetables. Dishes with vegetable components are the main part of the Egyptian diet. There is no dinner or lunch that would not be accompanied by a salad made of fresh vegetables (*salaṭa khaḍra*). There are dishes like *ṭaʿmēya* (rissoles made of beans, vegetable and spices); *fūl midammis* (cooked beans), *kosharī* (pasta, rice and lentils mixed together with a spicy sauce and fried onions) and many more. The queen of Egyptian cuisine is undoubtedly *maḥshī* (stuffed leaves of cabbage, grapevine, stuffed peppers, aubergines or courgettes). A table has to include a wide array of cold and hot dishes, and it is the rich variety, which makes every course virtually into a banquet.
Folk restaurants offer traditional dishes accompanied by country bread (*ʿēsh baladī*). Egyptian cuisine also prefers fish and seafood. In more touristy places the restaurants offer, besides typical Egyptian staples, also Mediterranean, especially Lebanese, Turkish, Greek and Italian, cuisine.

Health Care

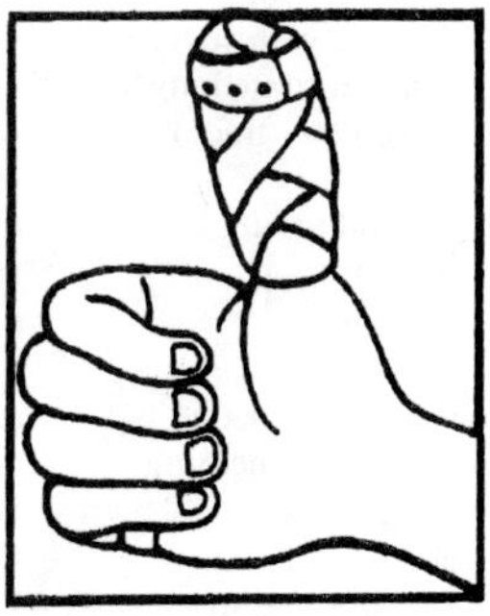

The character of Egyptian health care has, generally speaking, many different levels. While state-managed hospitals are usually fighting to fit into their budgets, private clinics have at their disposal the most advanced technologies and systems. It is quite usual, that a physician is employed in a public hospital, where he fulfills his duties at the morning, and in the afternoon and in the evening he works in his private surgery. A sign on the house, giving the name of the physician, his specialization, and the institution where he obtained his degree or where he is employed, always marks the consulting room. It is better to arrange a visit to a private surgery in advance.
Pharmacies (*ṣaydalīya* = pharmacy) in Egypt are plentiful and offer a standard variety of pharmaceutical goods of Egyptian and foreign produce. A large amount of pharmaceutical production in Egypt is manufactured in license given by great pharmaceutical companies abroad. A pharmacist (*ṣaydalānī*) has somewhat a function of a general practitioner, especially in poorer suburbs or in the country and is always of help, when an injection, a blood pressure measurement or so is needed.

Muʿgam ʾinglīzī ʿarabī

A	
to be able, can, may	ʾidir (a)
about	ʿan
above	fōʾ
abroad	il-khārig
to accept something	ʾibil (a)
accident	ḥadsa
accommodate oneself	nizil (i)
according to	ḥasab
to be acquired	itgāb VII
action	ʿamalīya
to add, complete	ʾaḍāf IV
address	ʿunwān (ʿanawīn)
addressee	mursal ʾilēh
administration	maṣlaḥa (maṣāliḥ)
advance, rise	taqaddum
advertisement	ʾiʿlān, -āt
aeroplane	ṭayyāra
affair	masʾala (masāʾil)
affair, event	kalām
to be afraid of	khāf (ā) *(min) / (ʿala)*
Africa	ʾIfrīqiyā
after	baʿd
after, afterwards	baʿdi mā
after, in	baʿd
after, then	baʿdēn
afternoon	baʿd iḍ-ḍuhr
again, once again, second, another	tānī
age, lifetime	ʿumr (ʾaʿmār)
to agree with	wāfiʾ III *(ʿala)*
to agree with someone about something	ittafaʿ VIII *(maʿa) (ʿala)*
agreement (trade)	ṣafqa (ṣafqāt)
air	hawa
airconditioning	takyīf
airport	maṭār
Alexandria	il-ʾIskindirēya
allergy	ḥassāsīya
to allow someone to do something	samaḥ (a) *(li) (bi)*
allright, ok	tamām, kull(i) tamām
also	wi, ʾu
also, further, too	kamān
also, too	barḍo
although	maʿa ʾinn
always	dayman
ambassador	safīr (sufara)
American Indian	hindī ʾaḥmar (hunūd ḥumr)
American	ʾamrīkī (ʾamrīkān)
and	wi, ʾu
angry with someone, about something	zaʿlān *(min)*
to be angry with someone	ziʿil (a) *(min)*
to be angry with someone; because of	itḍāyiʾ VI *(min)*
aniseed	yansūn
to answer to	gāwib III *(ʿala)*
to apologise to sb. for something	itʾassif V *(li) (ʿan)*
to apologise for something	iʿtazar VIII *(li) (ʿan)*
to appear that	bān (ā) *(ʾinn)*
to appear, seem to someone	ithayyaʾ V *(li)*
apples	tuffāḥ
approximately, maybe, perhaps	taʾrīban
area, region	manṭiʾa (manāṭiʾ)
area, sphere, field (abstract)	magāl
archaeologist, historical	ʾasarī
arm, plantation	mazraʿa (mazāriʿ)
around, ca., approximately	ḥawālī
to arrange	dabbar II
arrival	wuṣūl
to arrive at	wiṣil (a)
artistic, art, of art,	fannī
to be ashamed	itkasaf VII
as soon as, when	ʾawwil mā
to ask	saʾal (a) *(ʿala)*
to ask for	ṭalab (u)
to ask for permission	istaʿzin X
to ask somebody for something	waṣṣa II *(ʿala)*
assortment, range	tashkīla
to assure someone (of goods)	ʾakkid II *(li)*
Aswan	ʾAswān
at first	il-ʾawwil
at most, at the latest	bi ʾl-ktīr
at, by	ʿand
attaché	mulḥaq
attempt	tagriba (tagārib)
auntie (a familiar address of a female relative or a close acquaintance)	tanṭ

B

back, reverse, reverse side	ḍahr
background	khalfīya
bad, ugly	wiḥish
bag	shanṭa (shunaṭ)
to bake	khabaz (i)
balcony	balakōna
ball, football	kura (kuwar)
bananas	mōz
bandage	lāziʾ
bandage	shāsh
to be bandaged	itrabaṭ VII
to be brought away, taken away, removed	itshāl VII
bank	bank (bunūk)
bank	shāṭiʾ (shawāṭiʾ)
to bargain with	fāṣil III (without preposition)
to bargain with someone about	itfāṣil VI *(maʿa) (fī)*
basic (school), initial	ibtidāʾī
bath	ḥammām
to be	kān
beach	blāje (blājāt)
beans	fūl
to bear, to endure	istaḥmil X
beard	daʾn (duʾūn)
bearer	shayyāl
beautiful	gamīl (gumāl)
beautiful	ḥelu
beauty	gamāl
because of, for	ʿashān
because, because of	liʾinn
because, for, originally	ʾaṣlan
to become	baʾa (a)
bed	srīr (sarāyir)
bedroom	ʾoḍt in-nōm
beetle	khunfisa (khanāfis)
to begin with	badaʿ (a) *(bi / fī)*
to begin	ibtada VIII
beginner	mubtadiʾ
beginning	bidāya
to behave, to manage something	itṣarraf V*(fī)*
behaviour, conduct, treating somebody	muʿamla
behind	wara
belly	baṭn
beloved	ḥabīb (ḥabāyib)
to benefit from, to make use of	istafād X *(min)*
the best (elative)	ʾafḍal
the best (elative)	ʾaḥsan
to bet with	itrāhin VI *(maʿa) (ʿala)*
to bet with	rāhin III (without preposition)
better (elative)	ʾafḍal
better (elative)	ʾaḥsan
between, among	bēn
to bind, to tie	rabaṭ (u)
bill	ḥisāb, -āt
birth	mīlād
birth	wilāda
to give birth	wilid (i)
birthday	ʿīd il-mīlād
black	ʾiswid (sūd)
to turn black	iswadd IX
blacks, African Americans	sūd
blanket	liḥāf (ʾalḥifa)
to bless somone	bārik III *(li)*
blessed	mabrūk
blessed	mubārak
blind	ʾaʿma (ʿumy)
blue	ʾazraʾ (zurʾ)
to turn blue	izraʾʾ IX
boat, ship	markib (marākib)
to boast	itʿāla VI *(ʿala)*
book	kitāb (kutub)
bored, annoyed, frustrated	zahʾān
to be bored, annoyed, to have enough of something / somebody	zihiʾ (a)
born	mawlūd (mawālīd)
to borrow from	istaʿār X *(min)*
to borrow	istalaf VIII
bottle	ʾizāza (ʾazāyiz)
bowtie	bibyōna
box of chocolates	ʿilbit shokolāta
box	ṣandūʾ (ṣanadīʾ)
box, chest	ʿilba (ʿilab)
boy (plural: children)	walad (ʾawlād)
boy, apprentice	ṣabī (ṣubyān)
bread	ʿēsh
to break (into pieces)	kasar (a)
to break (oneself)	itkasar VII
breakfast	fiṭār
bricks	ṭūb
bride	ʿarūsa (ʿarāyis)
bridegroom	ʿarīs (ʿirsān)
to bring	wadda II
to bring, obtain	gāb (ī)
bring to a happy end	tammim II
bringing	gāyib
British	brīṭānī
to be broad, to broaden	wisiʿ (a)
broadcast	ʾirsāl
broom	maʾashsha
brother	ʾakh (before the genitive and pronominal suffixes ʾakhū) (ʾikhwa)

to be brought up	itrabba V
bucket	gardal (garādil)
buffet, canteen	kafeteriya
building	mabna (mabānī)
to be built	itbana VII
bus	ʾotobīs
busy	mashghūl
but	bas
but	lākin
butcher	gazzār
to buy	ishtara VIII
Byzantine	bīzanṭī

C

cabbage	kurumb
café	ʾahwa (ʾahāwī)
Cairo	il-Qāhira
cake, slice (of bread)	rghīf (ʾarghifa)
to call to someone	nadah (a) *(li)*
to calm down	haddaʿII
camera	kamera
camomille	bābung
canvas (painting)	lōḥa
capital	ʿāṣima (ʿawāṣim)
car	ʿarabīya
to be overly careful, pedantic	ḥaswik (yiḥaswik)
card, business card, postcard	kart (kurūt)
to care for someone,	rāʿa III
carriage	ḥanṭūr (ḥanaṭīr)
to carry	ḥamal (i)
to carry, carry away, remove	shāl (ī)
cartouche	kharṭūsh (kharaṭīsh)
case	dolāb (dawālīb)
case	ḥāla
in any case, at any rate	keda keda
cassette, tape	shrīṭ it-tasgīl
to catch cold	istahwa X
to catch, to be in time	liḥiʾ (a)
to cause	sabbib II
to celebrate something	iḥtafal VIII *(bi)*
celebration of the birth of a child (a week of its life)	subūʿ
celebration	ḥafla
cellular phone	maḥmūl
cement	ʾismant
center, middle	wusṭ
centimetre	santi
century	ʾarn (ʾurūn)
ceramics	fukhār
ceremony, protocol (diplomatic)	marāsim
certain, certainly	ʾakīd
chair	kursī (karāsī)
change (money)	fakka
to change	ghayyar II
to change oneself	itghayyar V
to charge someone with	kallif II *(bi)*
cheap	rkhīṣ (rukhāṣ)
cheese	gibna (giban)
chicken, poultry	farkha (frākh)
child	ṭifl (ʾaṭfāl)
chilli peppers	shaṭṭa
chocolate	shokolāta
to choose	ikhtār VIII
Christian year	sana mīlādīya
cigarette	sīgāra (sagāyir)
cinnamon	ʾirfa
city, town	madīna (mudun)
to clean	naḍḍaf II
clerk	muwaẓẓaf
client	zbūn (zabāyin)
close	ʾurayyib
close to	ʾurayyib *min*
close, conclude	ʾaffil II
to close oneself	itʿafal VII
to close, shut	ʾafal (i)
closed	maʾfūl
being closed (institution)	ʾāfil
cloth, textile	ʾumāsh
club	nādī (ʾandiya)
coat	balṭo (balṭohāt)
to coax / induce / help someone to sleep	nayyim II
code, country code	kōd, -āt
coffee, café	ʾahwa
coffin, sarcophagus	tābūt (tawabīt)
cold, cooled	sāʾiʿ
colleague	zmīl (zamāyil)
colleague, co-worker	zmīl (zamāyil)
to collect, assemble, put together	lamm (i)
collection	magmūʿa
colloquial Arabic	ʿāmmīya
colour	lōn (ʾalwān)
comb	mishṭ (ʾamshāṭ)
to come out that	bān (ā) *(ʾinn)*
to come to a place (with out preposition), to a person *(li)*	ge (yigī)
to command someone something	ʾamar (u) (without do preposition) *(bi)*
to comment	ʿallaʾ II *(ʿala)*
commentary	taʿlīʾ, -āt
commercial	tigārī
committee	lagna (ligān)
common	mushtarak
common, normal	ʿādī

company	shirka (shirkāt)
to be a competition for somebody, to compete with somebody	sābiʾ III
completely, totally, absolutely	ʿa(la) ʾl-ʾākhir
to compensate something *(ʿan)* to someone (without preposition)	ʿawwaḍ II
to compete with	itnāfis VI *(maʿa)*
to compete with	itsābiʾ VI *(maʿa)*
to compete with	sābiʾ III (without preposition)
to complain about	ishtaka VIII *(min)*
to complain, file a complaint against	shaka (i) *(min)*
to compose	rakkib II
compromise	tanāzul, -āt
concert	ḥafla mūsīqīya
condition	sharṭ (shurūṭ)
to condole someone	ʿazza II (without preposition)
condolence	ʿaza
the one who accepts condolence	ṣāḥib il-ʿaza
conductor	kumsarī, -ya
conference, congress	muʾtamar
to confess something	iʿtaraf VIII *(bi)*
to congratulate someone	bārik III *(li)*
to be connected with	irtabaṭVIII *(bi)*
consider somebody/something as	iʿtabar VIII
to consider something as a great amount	istaktar X
to consider something as a loss, damage	istakhsar X
to consider something very cheap	istarkhaṣ X
consul	qunṣul (qanaṣla)
to be in contact with	ittaṣal VIII *(bi)*
contest	musabʾa
to continue (uninterruptedly)	istamarr X
to control, to check	fattish II
conversation	muḥadsa
cook	ṭabbākh
to cook, prepare a meal	ṭabakh (u)
cool, cold	bārid
to cooperate with	itʿāwin VI *(maʿa)*
cooperation	taʿāwun
cooperation, contact	taʿāmul
to cooperate, to be in contact with	itʿāmil VI *(maʿa)*
copper	nuḥās
Coptic	ʾibṭī (ʾaʾbāṭ)
copy, printout, specimen	nuskha (nusakh)
corner	naṣya
correct, faultless	salim (sulām)
correspondence	murasla
corsair, pirate	qurṣān (qaraṣna)
to cost someone (a sum)	kallif II
to cough	kaḥḥ (u)
councillor, consultant, chancellor	mustashār
counsel	naṣīḥa (naṣāyiḥ)
to counsel	naṣaḥ (a) (without preposition) something *(bi)* someone
to take counsel with someone about	istashār X (without preposition) *(fī)*
to count	ʿadd (i)
country, village, countryside	balad (bilād)
course (language)	kurs, -āt
in the course of (the whole time), for (the whole time)	ṭūl (il-waʾt)
in the course of, while	khilāl
cover, case	grāb, -āt
to cover (a debt)	sadd (i)
crowd, (traffic) jam	zaḥma
crown (money)	kurōna
to cry	ʿayyaṭ II
cucumbers	khiyār
cultural	saqāfī
culture	saqāfa
culture, civilisation	ḥaḍāra
cup, mug	fingān (fanagīn)
to cure, treat sb.	ʿālig III
current, present	ḥāḍir
customer	zbūn (zabāyin)
customs	gumruk
to cut (with scissors)	ʾaṣṣ (u)
to cut	ʾaṭaʿ (a)
to be torn, cut	itʾaṭṭaʿ V
Czech	tshīkī (tshīk)

D

daddy	bāba
damage, loss	kh(u)sāra (khasāyir)
dark	ghāmiʾ
to turn dark	ighmaʾʾ IX
darkness	ḍalma
daughter	bint (banāt)
day	yōm (ʾiyyām)
the day after tomorrow	baʿd(i) bukra
daytime, day (from sunrise to sunset)	nahār
deaf	ʾaṣamm (ṣumm)
deaf	ʾaṭrash (ṭursh)
death	wafā (wafayāt)
to declare, proclaim, advertise something	ʾaʿlan IV *(ʿan)*

declaration, proclamation	ʾiʿlān, -āt
to deduce something, to infer something from	istantig X *(min)*
to defend something	dāfiʿ III *(ʿan)*
delegate, representative	mandūb
delegation	wafd (wufūd)
deliver, announce	ballagh II
deliver, convey	waṣṣal II
department	qism (ʾaqsām)
deposit	ʿarbūn
descend	nizil (i)
desk lamp	ʾabazhōra
desk, blackboard	lōḥa
despite	maʿa ʾinn
dessert, sweet	ḥelu
detailed	mufaṣṣal
to develop a film	ḥammaḍ II
dialogue	ḥiwār
dictionary	muʿgam (maʿāgim)
to die	māt (ū)
different, various	mukhtalif
to dine	itʿashsha V
dinner	ʿasha
diplomatic, diplomat	diblūmāsī
direction (film)	ʾikhrāg
director	mudīr (mudara)
directorate, administration	ʾidāra
discount	takhfīḍ, -āt
to discover	iktashaf VIII
to discuss with sb. about something	itnāʾish VI *(maʿa) (fī)*
to discuss, argue with	nāʾish III (without preposition) *(fī)* someone about something
discussion, defense (of a masters, doctors thesis)	munaʾsha
dishcloth	fūṭit maṭbach
distance	masāfa
to distract someone, to coax /induce someone into good mood	farfish (yifarfish)
to be distracted (from work)	itʿaṭṭal V
to distribute	nashar (u)
to dive	ghāṣ (u)
divided by (:)	ʿala
to do	ʿamal (i)
doctor	doktōr (dakatra)
doctor's thesis	risal(i)t id-doktorāh
door, gate	bāb (ʾabwāb / bībān)
doorkeeper, housekeeper	bawwāb
dough	ʿagīna (ʿagāyin)
downbeat	shidda
drawer (of a desk), shelf	durg (ʾadrāg)
drawing	rasm (rusūm)
drawn	marsūm
dress (ladies')	fustān (fasatīn)
drink made form hibiscus flowers	karkadē(h)
drink	mashrūb, -āt
to drink	shirib (a)
to drip	naʾʾaṭ II
to drive	sāʾ (ū)
driver	sawwāʾ
driver's license	rukhṣa (rukhaṣ)
to become dry	nishif (a)
to be drunk (of a drink)	itsharab VII
dumb	ʾabkam
to dusk, to get dark	ḍallim II
duty, obligation	iltizām, -āt
duty, task	wāgib, -āt

E

ear	widn (widān)
early, soon	badri
eastern, Oriental	sharʾī
easy	sahl
to eat	kal (yākul)
to be eaten	ittākil VIII
eating	wākil
to educate someone	ʿallim II
to educate, to keep, to grow a beard	rabba II
educating, educational	taʿlīmī
education	taʿlīm
effervescent	fawwār
effort	maghūd
eggs	bēḍ
eggwhite	bayāḍ
Egypt	Maṣr
Egyptian	maṣrī
either… or…	yā ... yā ...
electricity	kahraba
electronic	ʾilīktrūnī
to embarass, shame	ʾaḥrag IV
to embarrass	ḥayyar II
to be embarassed, to get embarassed	irtabak VIII
embassy	sifāra
to employ someone, to give work to someone	waẓẓaf II
to employ, to make busy	shaghal (i)
to be employed, busy	itshaghal VII
empty	fāḍī
encyclopaedia	mausūʿa
end	nihāya
end, finished	khalās
to end, finish	khiliṣ (a)

engagement	khuṭūba
engine	gihāz ('aghiza)
engineer	muhandis
English	'inglīzī ('inglīz)
enchanted, fascinated, possessed by something	maḥwūs
to increase, enlarge	kabbar II
to be enlightened	fattaḥ II
to enter	dakhal (u)
to enter, come in	khashsh (u)
to entertain someone	salla II
entirely, exactly, so	tamām
entrance	madkhal (madākhil)
to equal one another	itsāwa VI *(ma'a)*
to equal something (without preposition)	sāwa III
to equip, decorate an apartment	farash (i)
Europe	'Ūrubbā
even	ḥattā
every time, whenever	kullimā
every, any, all, entire, whole	kull
evident, visible	bāyin
exaggerated (m./f.)	mubālagh fīh / fīhā
to examine someone in	imtaḥan VIII *(fī)*
to excavate, to conduct (archaeological) excavations	ḥafar (u)
excavations (archaeological)	ḥaf(a)rīyāt
excellent	mumtāz
to exchange letters with	itrāsil VI *(ma'a)*
to exchange letters with	rāsil III (without preposition)
to excuse someone, to forgive someone	'azar (u)
executive, responsible, respresentative	mas'ūl
to exhibit	'araḍ (i)
exhibition	ma'raḍ (ma'āriḍ)
to expect	faraḍ (i)
to expect	iftaraḍ VIII
expedition, mission	bi'sa
expensive, dear, costly	ghālī
experience	khibra
to be expert in, to be good at	itmakkin V *(min)*
to explain something (without preposition) to someone (without preposition)	fahhim II
to export	ṣaddar II
express, fast	mista'gil
expression	ta'bīr, -āt
expression, word	'ibāra
to extend	madd (i)
external	khārigī
eye	'ēn ('uyūn)

F

face	wishsh (wushūsh)
factory	maṣna' (maṣāni')
Faculty of Archaeology	kullīy(i)t il-'āsār
faculty of arts	kullīyit il-'ādāb
faculty	kullīya
to fade	dibil (a)
fair (book)	ma'raḍ (ma'āriḍ)
to fall	wi'i'(a)
family	'usra ('usar)
family (closest family circle)	'ēla
family	'ahl ('ahālī)
famous	mashhūr
to become famous through	ishtahar VIII *(bi)*
to make someone or something famous	shahar (i)
far from	bi'īd min
far, distant	bi'īd
farmstead, farm, holding	'izba ('izab)
fast	sarī'
father	wālid ('ābā')
father	'ab (before the genitive and pronominal suffixes 'abū) ('ābā')
Fatimid	fāṭimī
fax	faks, -āt
fear	khōf
feast	walīma (walāyim)
to feel something	ḥass (i) *(bi)*
feeling cold	bardān
feeling warm, hot	ḥarrān
festive day, festival	'īd ('a'yād)
field, arable land	ghēṭ (ghīṭān)
field, specialisation	takhaṣṣuṣ, -āt
file	milaff, -āt
to fill	mala (a)
to be filled	itḥasha VII
film development	taḥmīḍ
film	film ('aflām)
finances, financial means	māl ('amwāl)
to find	la'a (yilā'ī)
finger	ṣubā' (sawābi')
to finish something	kammil II
to finish, end something	khallaṣ II
fire	nār (nīrān)
firm	shirka (sharikāt)
first help, ambulance	'is'āf
the first time	'awwil marra
fish	samak
flat	sha''a (shu'a')
flatter, compliment	mugamla

to flatter sb.	gāmil III (without preposition)
flight ticket	tazkarit ṭayarān (tazākir)
flour	diʾīʾ
flower	warda
to follow something, to hold to (a method)	itmassik V *(bi)*
food, meal	ʾakl (ʾakalāt)
for example	masalan
to forbid someone	manaʿ (a) (without preposition) *(min)* to do something
force, energy	ḥēl
foreign	khārigī
foreign, foreigner	ʾagnabī (ʾagānib)
foreign (particularly when referring to breads and pastries)	ʾafrangī
to forget	nisi (a)
forgetting	nāsī
fork	shōka (showak)
form, shape	shakl (ʾashkāl)
to be founded, to have good foundations	itʾassis V
four-verse poem	rubāʿīyāt
France	Faransā
free	fāḍī
fresh	ṭāze
fried burgers of beans, vegetables and spices (vegetable patties)	ṭaʿmēya
fried	maʾlī
friend	ṣāḥib (ʾaṣḥāb)
friend (an expression of the standard language, which expresses respect, esteem and deep feeling for the person in question)	ṣadīq (ʾaṣdiqāʾ)
from	min (shortened to *mi-* before the definite article: *mi ʾl- ...*)
frontier	ḥadd (ḥudūd)
frozen, chilled	mitallig
fruit salad	salaṭit fawākih
fruit	fakha (fawākih)
frying pan	ṭāsa
full	malyān
to be full, to eat to the full	shibiʿ (a)
to have fun, be entertained	itsalla V
G	
garbage	z(i)bāla
garden	gnēna (ganāyin)
garlic	tōm
gas	ghāz, -āt
generous, honoured, respected	karīm (kirām / kurama)
German	ʾalmānī (ʾalmān)
Germany	ʾAlmāniyā
to get off	nizil (i)
gift	hadīya (hadāyā)
girl	bint (banāt)
give! pass!	hāt! / hātī! / hātū!
to give	ʾidda (yiddi)
to give over something	sallim II *(li)*
to give up, capitulate	istaslim X
to give up something, to refrain from something	itnāzil VI *(ʿan)*
glass	ʾizāz
glass	kubbāya
glasses	naḍḍāra
to go (concerning a means of transporation)	rāḥ (ū)
to go around, to stop by	ʿadda II
to go by, take something	rikib (a)
to go for a walk	itmashsha V
to go home	rawwaḥ II
to go out, to go for a walk, trip	itfassaḥ V
to go up, climb, ascend	ṭiliʿ (a)
to go / come before, to make something before someone else	sabaʿ (a) (without preposition)
God, Lord, lord (landlord)	rabb
going, leaving	rāyiḥ – without preposition = to a place – with the preposition li = to a person
gold	dahab
good health, recovery, safe return, peace	salāma
good	kwayyis
good, kind	ṭayyib
grade	daraga
graduate, alumnus	khirrīg
to graduate	itkharrag V *(fī)*
granddad, grandparent	gidd (ʾagdād)
grapes	ʿinab
grateful	mamnūn
grave, tomb	maqbara (maqābir)
great, big, large	kbīr
great, excellent,	ʿaẓīm
marvellous great,	hāyil
wonderful, excellent great, wonderful, excellent; dangerous	khaṭīr
green	ʾakhḍar
to turn green	ikhḍarr IX

to greet someone from someone	sallim II *(ʿala) (li)*
greeting	salām (salamāt)
group	magmūʿa
to guarantee	ḍaman (a)
guaranteed, safe, sure	maḍmūn
guest	ḍēf (ḍuyūf)
guide, list	dalīl (ʾadilla)
guilt	zanb (zunūb)
gulf (the Gulf)	khalīg (il-Khalīg)

H

hair	shaʿr
half	nuṣṣ (ʾanṣāṣ)
hall	ṣāla
hall, audition hall	qāʿa
hand	ʾīd (ʾayādī)
handkerchief, scarf	mandīl (manadīl)
handmade goods	mashghūlāt
to hang (laundry)	nashar (u)
to hang	ʾallaʿII
to happen	gara (a)
to happen	ḥaṣal (a)
happy	saʿīd
to be happy	firiḥ (a)
being happy	farḥān
to make someone happy	farraḥ II (without preposition)
hard, difficult	ṣaʿb
head	rās (ruʾūs)
head, brain	dimāgh (ʾadmigha)
health, correctness	ṣiḥḥa
to hear, listen	simiʿ (a)
to be heard	itsamaʾ VII
hearing	sāmiʿ
heart	ʾalb (ʾulūb)
heat	ḥarr
heaven	sama (samawāt)
heavy	tiʾīl
hello! (on the phone)	ʾalō!
help	musāʿada
to help someone with something	sāʿid III (without preposition) *(fī)*
Helwan	Ḥelwān
hepatitis	ṣafra
herb	ʿushb ṭibbī (ʾaʿshāb ṭibbīya)
here	hena
here, look!	ʾaho
high	ʿālī
historical	tārīkhī
history	tārīkh
hole	khurm (khurūm)
holiday	ʾagāza
home	bēt
home, local	baladī
honestly	bi-ṣarāḥa
honour, dignity	sharaf
to honour someone with something	sharraf II (without preposition) *(bi)*
to be honoured by	itsharraf V*(bi)*
horses	khēl (khuyūl)
hospital	mustashfa, -yāt
to host, to have guests	istaḍāf X
hotel	funduʾ (fanādiʾ)
hour, watch	sāʿa
house	bēt (buyūt)
house (above all specialised for a certain activity)	dār (dūr)
housewife	rabbit manzil
how many, some, a few	kam
how? like, as	zāy? / ʾezzāy?
human (human beings)	ʾinsān (nās).

The noun *nās* is either feminine singular or plural.

humidity	ruṭūba
hundred	mīya (miʾāt)
hunchbacked	ʾaḥdab
to be hunchbacked	iḥdabb IX
being hungry	gaʿān
hunt, fish	iṣṭād VIII
Hurghada	il-Ghardaʾa
to hurry	istaʿgil X
to hurry	madd (i)
husband	gōz (ʾagwāz)

I

ice-cream	jelatti
ID card	karnē(h)
ID card	biṭāʾa
ID papers, documents	ʾawrāʾ (rasmīya)
i.e., that means	yaʿnī
if	ʾiza
if	ʾin
if, when	lau
to ignite, to turn on the light	wallaʿ II
illness, sickness	maraḍ (ʾamrāḍ)
to imagine, to be photographed	itṣawwar V
immediately	ʿala ṭūl
immediately	ḥālan
important	muhimm
the most important	ʿahamm
to improve	itḥassin V
in front of	ʾuddām
in, on, at	fī
to increase the amount, to make more numerous	kattar II

Indian	hindī (hunūd)
industrial	sināʿī
information	maʿlūma
information, questions	istiʿlāmāt
to inherit	wiris (i)
inside	gouwa
to insist on someone	itḥāyil VI *(ʿala)*
inspector	mufattish
institute	maʿhad (maʿāhid)
insurance	taʾmīn, -āt
intending	nāwī
intensive	mukassaf
intercity or international phone call	trank
to interest someone	hamm (i)
to be interested in	ihtamm VIII *(bi)*
to be invited	itʾazam VII
to be ironed	itkawa VII
to be issued by/at	ṣadar (a) *(min)*
to interrupt someone, to distract someone from something	ʿaṭṭal II *(ʿan)*
international	daulī
to introduce someone to someone / something	ʿarraf II (without preposition) *(ʿala / bi)*
to introduce someone/something to someone *(li)*	ʾaddim II
to invent	ibtakar VIII
to invite	ʿazam (i)
invention	ibtikār, -āt
to invest	istasmir X
investment	istismār, -āt
investor	mustasmir
invitation	daʿwa
iron	ḥadīd
Islamic, Muslim	ʾislāmī
is-Sayyida Zēnab, Lady Zēnab's mosque	is-Sayyida
it is necessary	mafrūḍ
it is possible	mumkin
it seems that	bāyin ʾinn

J

jacket	jakēt (jawākit)
job, office	waẓīfa (waẓāyif)
to join someone	ittaṣal VIII *(bi)*
joint	mifṣal (mafāṣil)
journalist	ṣaḥafī
journey, departure	safar
journey, trip, flight	riḥla (raḥalāt)
juice	ʿaṣīr (ʿaṣāyir)
just	lissa

K

to keep up with	kaffa II (without preposition)
keeping of something	iltizām, -āt *(bi)*
key	miftāḥ (mafatīḥ)
Khephren	Khafraʿ
Khufu (Greek Kheops)	Khūfū
to kill / slaughter (an animal)	dabaḥ (a)
kilogram, kilometre	kīlo
kind, nice	laṭīf (luṭāf)
kind, nice, pleasant	ẓarīf (ẓurāf)
kind, sort, type	nauʿīya
kind, type	nōʿ (ʾanwāʿ)
kiosk, stand	kushk (ʾakshāk)
to kiss	bās (ū)
kitchen	maṭbakh (maṭābikh)
knee	rukba (rukab)
knife	sikkīna (sakakīn)
to know	ʿirif (a)
knowing	ʿārif
knowledge	maʿrifa (maʿārif)
to be known (get known)	itʿaraf VII

L

lake	buḥēyra
language	lugha
to be late, to have a delay	itʾakhkhar V
the last	ʾakhīr
the last time	ʾākhir marra
Latin	lātīnī
to laugh	ḍiḥik (a)
laundry	ghasīl
law	ḥaʾʾ (ḥuʾūʾ)
law, truth	haʾʾ
leader, inspector, overseer	mushrif
lear, evident	wāḍiḥ
leather (adjective)	gildī
leather, skin	gild (gulūd)
to leave, let, let go	sāb (ī)
leaving, descending, accommodating	nāzil
leaving, sorting	khārig
Lebanese	libnānī, -īyīn
Lebanon	Libnān
lecture	muḥaḍra
left	shimāl
to be left, to be left behind	itsāb VII
leg	rigl
lemon	lamūn
to lend someone something	sallif II (li) (without preposition)

length	ṭūl (ʾaṭwāl)
lentils	ʿads
lesson	dars (durūs)
to let someone (do), to make someone (do)	khalla II
letter	gawāb
letter, master's or doctor's thesis	risāla (rasāyil)
level	mustawa, -yāt
library	maktaba
The National Library	Dār il-kutub
lid, cap, stopper	ghaṭa (ghuṭyān)
life	ḥayā
lift	ʾasansēr
light (colour)	fātiḥ
light	khafīf (khufāf)
light	nūr (ʾanwār)
to make light, to enlighten	fattaḥ II
lighting	m(i)nawwar
to like, to love, to wish, to like to do something	ḥabb (i)
to be liked by someone	ʿagab (i)
being liked (by someone) followed by a pronominal suffix or noun without preposition	ʿāgib
limit	ḥadd (ḥudūd)
limping, lame	ʾaʿrag
line, writing, script	khaṭṭ (khuṭūṭ)
liqorice	ʿarʾisūs
list, schedule	gadwal (gadāwil)
literature	ʾadab (ʾādāb)
a little	shwayya
a little, a bit	sinna
to live	sakan (u)
to live	ʿāsh (ī)
living	sākin
local	maḥallī
long	ṭwīl (ṭuwāl)
long, loose shirt-like dress	gallābīya (galalīb)
look (at / into)	baṣṣa
to look at something	itfarrag V *(ʿala)*
to look at, to diagnose someone	kashaf (i) *(ʿala)*
to look at, to look into	baṣṣ (u) *(fī)*
to look like, to be seen somewhere, on someone / something	bān (ā) *(ʿala)*
to get lost	ḍāʿ (ī)
to get lost	tāh (ū)
a lot, much	ktīr
luck	ḥaẓẓ (ḥuẓūẓ)
lunch	ghada
to lunch	itghadda V
Luxor	il-ʾUʾṣur

M

madam (friendly address)	sitt, -āt
to be made	itʾamal VII
magazine	makhzan (makhāzin)
magazine	magalla
main	rāʾīsī
majority	muʿẓam
man	rāgel (riggāla)
man, someone, one	il-wāḥid
mandarins	yūs(t) ʾeffendi
mango	manga
manuscript	makhṭūṭa
map	kharīṭa (kharāyiṭ)
marble	marmar
market, marketplace	sūʾ (ʾaswāʾ)
to marry someone	itgawwiz V
Master, chief (to address artisans, taxi drivers, etc.)	ʾusṭa (ʾusṭawāt)
master, mister, Sir	sayyid (sāda)
material	māddī
material	khāma
may God bless you	bārik III *(fī)*
maybe, perhaps	gāyiz
measure	ʾās (ī)
to be measured	itʾās VII
meat	laḥma (luḥūm)
medical	ṭibbī
medical	ṣiḥḥī
medicine	dawa (ʾadwiya)
meeting (one another), getting to know one another	taʿāruf
to meet sb.	ʾābil III (without preposition)
to meet someone	itʾābil VI *(maʿa)*
to meet, to be introduced to	itʿarraf V *(ʿala / bi)*
meeting	maʿād (mawaʿīd)
meeting, interview	muʾabla
melon	baṭṭīkh
member	ʿuḍw (ʾaʿḍāʾ)
Menkaura (Greek Mycerinus)	Menkaraʿ
message, news	khabar (ʾakhbār)
meter (electrometer, water meter, taxameter)	ʿaddād, -āt
method	manhag (manāhig)
milk	laban (ʾalbān)
million	milyōn (malayīn)
minaret	madna (midan)
mind	bāl
to mine, quarry	istakhrag X

mineral	maʿdanī
minister	wazīr (wuzara)
ministry of foreign affairs	wizart il-khārigīya
ministry of higher education	wizart it-taʿlīm il-ʿālī
ministry	wizāra
minus (-)	nāʾiṣ
minute	diʾīʾa (daʾāʾy)
to miss somebody / something	waḥash (a)
missing, incomplete	nāʾiṣ
to be missing	ghāb (ī)
mixer	khallāṭ, -āt
moment	laḥẓa
monastery	dēr (ʾadyira)
money	flūs
month	shahr (shuhūr / ʾashhur)
monument	ʾasar (ʾāsār)
monument, antiquity	tuḥfa (tuḥaf)
moon	ʾamar (ʾaʾmār)
more important (elative)	ʾahamm
morning	ṣubḥ
Morocco	il-Maghrib
mosque	gāmiʿ (gawāmiʿ)
mosque	masgid (masāgid)
mother	ʾumm (ʾummahāt)
mother-of-pearl	ṣadaf
mountain	gabal (gibāl)
to move	itḥarrak V
Mr. (intellectual)	ʾustāz (ʾasatza)
Mr.	bāsha (bashawāt)
Mrs. (in the city, office and intellectual environment)	madām
mum	māma
mummy	mūmiyā
museum	matḥaf (matāḥif)
music	mūsīqa
Muslim year	sana higrīya
to become a muslim, to give oneself into God's will	ʾaslam IV

N

nail	ḍāfir (ḍawāfir)
name	ʾism (ʾasmāʾ)
name, reputation	sumʿa
national	waṭanī
native speaker	nāṭiq ʾaṣlī
nature	ṭabīʿa
natural	ṭabīʿī
necessary, inevitable, it is necessary	ḍarūrī
to need something	iḥtāg VIII *(li)* or (without preposition)
negative	ʿafrīta
neighbour	gār (gīrān)
never	ʾabadan
New Year	Rās is-sana
New Year's Eve	lēlit Rās is-sana
new	gdīd (gudād)
newlyweds	ʿirsān
newspaper	gurnān (garanīn)
next to	ganb
nice	ḥelu (ḥelwīn)
night	lēl (layālī)
the Nile	in-Nīl
no	la, laʾ
nobody	maḥaddish
noodles	shiʿrīya
noon	ḍuhr
nor	walā
nose	manakhīr
not at all	ʾabadan
note, objection	mulaḥẓa
notice, sign	yafṭa (yufaṭ)
novel	riwāya
now	di ʾl-waʾti
Nubia	in-Nūba
number	nimra (nimar)
number	ʿadad (ʾaʿdād)

O

oasis	wāḥa
objection	iʿtirāḍ, -āt
to have objections to	iʿtaraḍ VIII *(ʿala)*
objects on exhibition	maʿrūḍāt
to oblige to someone	rayyaḥ II (without preposition)
occasion	munasba
occasion, chance	furṣa (furaṣ)
of course	ṭabʿan
offer, make an offer	ʿaraḍ (i)
office, writing table	maktab (makātib)
officer	ẓābiṭ (ẓubbāt)
official	rasmī
often	ktīr
oil	betrōl
oil	zēt (zuyūt)
ointment	marham (marāhim)
old	ʾadīm (ʾudām)
old, old man	ʿagūz (ʿawagīz)
on, at	ʿala (shortened to ʿa- before the definite article)
one	wāḥid, wāḥ(i)da
one, unique, the only	waḥīd
one-eyed	ʾaʿwar
onion	baṣal
only	bas

to open	fataḥ (a)
to open oneself	itfataḥ VII
opening	fātiḥ
opera	ʾōbera
operation (medical, military)	ʿamalīya
opinion	raʾy (ʾārāʾ)
opposite	ʾuṣād
opposite	ḍidd
or	walla
or	yā
oranges	burtuʾāl
order some thing	ṭalab (u)
to organize, arrange	rattib II
to organize a trip, walk for someone	fassaḥ II (without preposition)
outlet (in the bathroom)	ballāʿa
outside, but for, besides, except for	ghēr
outside, out, abroad	barra
oven, bakery	furn (ʾafrān)
to oversee something, to direct, lead something	ʾashraf IV *(ʿala)*

P

to pack	laff (i)
packet	ṭard (ṭurūd)
page	ṣafḥa
to be paid	itṣaraf VII
pain	ʾalam (ʾālām)
to give pain, ache someone	wagaʿ (a)
pair	gōz (ʾagwāz)
palms	nakhīl
paper, cardboard box	kartōna
papers, documents, ID cards	ʾaurāʾ
papyrus	bardī, -yāt
to be parallel, equivalent something, to correspond to a sum (without prep.)	wāza III
parameters, characteristics	muwāṣafāt
parasol, umbrella	shamsīya (shamāsī)
parent	wālid (pl. ʾābāʾ)
Paris	Bārīs
parked, left behind	markūn
parking	rākin
participant	mushārik, -īn
participant	mushtarik, -īn
participation	ḥuḍūr
party	ḥafla, -āt
party, celebration	iḥtifāl
to pass something to somebody	nāwil III (without preposition) *(li)*
to pass, to stop by, come by, come by (for) someone	fāt (ū)
passport	basbōr, -āt
passport	gawāz (gawazāt) safar
passport department	ʾism ig-gawazāt
patient, sick one	marīḍ (marḍa)
pavement, isle	raṣīf (ʾarṣifa)
to pay	dafaʿ (a)
peace, rest	rāḥa
peaches	khōkh
pears	kummitra
peasant, farmer	fallāḥ
pen, pencil	ʾalam (ʾiʾlām)
pepper	filfil rūmī
performance	ḥafla, -āt
perfume, scent	ʿiṭr (ʿuṭūr)
permission	ʾizn
person	shakhṣ (ʾashkhāṣ)
personal	shakhṣī
personally	shakhṣīyan
pharaonic	firʿaunī
pharmacy	ṣaydalīya
phone book	dalīl it-telefōnāt
phone	telefōnī
phone	telefōn, - āt
phonecall, talk	mukalma
photograph	ṣūra (ṣuwar)
to photograph, to film	ṣawwar II
photographer	muṣawwir
photographic studio	studiyo ʾt-taṣwīr
photography, filming	taṣwīr
physician, doctor	ṭabīb (ʾaṭibbāʾ)
piaster	ʾirsh (ʾurūsh)
picture	ṣūra (ṣuwar)
piece (of food, cloth)	ḥiṭṭa (ḥiṭaṭ)
pill	ḥabbāya
pill	ʾurṣ (ʾaʾrāṣ)
pipe, pipeline	ʾunbūba (ʾanabīb)
place	makān (ʾamākin)
to place, put something somewhere	ḥaṭṭ (u) *(fī)*
by airmail, by air, by plain	bi ʾl-barīd il-gawwī
plant	ʿushb (ʾaʿshāb)
plate	ṭabaʾ (ʾaṭbāʾ)
to play (theatre)	massil II
to play	liʿib (a)
plums	barʾūʾ
plus (+)	zāyid
pocket	gēb (guyūb)
poetry	shiʿr (ʾshʿār)
to point to	ʾashār IV *(ʾila)*
police	būlīs
police	shurṭa

to polish	lammaʿ II
pomegranate	rummān
Port Said	Būr Saʿīd
possible, rational, reasonable	maʿʾūl
post card	kart (kurūt)
post office	bosṭa
post	barīd
pot	ḥalla (ḥilal)
potatoes	baṭāṭis
pound	ginē(h), -āt
to pour	ṣabb (u)
to practice, train something	itdarrab V *(ʿala / fī)*
Prague	Brāg
precise, precisely	maẓbūṭ
precisely	bi ʾt-tamām
to prepare, to make ready	gahhiz II
to prepare, to make, to create	ḥaḍḍar II
present, occurring	mawgūd
pressure	ḍaghṭ (ḍughūṭ)
price	siʿr (ʾasʿār)
priority, preference	ʾaulawīya
problem	masʾala (masāʾil)
problem	mushkila (mashākil)
producer	muntig, -īn
product	muntag, -āt
to produce	ʿantag IV
production	ʾintāg
production, industry	ṣināʿa
to be a professional	iḥtaraf VIII
professor	ʾustāz (ʾasatza)
programme	barnāmig (barāmig)
to make progress, to proceed in	itʾaddim V *(fī)*
project, plan	mashrūʿ (mashārīʿ)
promise	waʿd (wuʿūd)
to promise something *(bi)* to someone (without preposition)	waʿad (i)
protest	iḥtigāg, -āt
to protest against	iḥtagg VIII *(ʿala)*
to provoke	istafazz X
provoking, inciting	mustafizz
to publish (a book)	nashar (u)
punctuality (keeping the terms)	iltizām bi ʿl-mawāʿīd
pure	nḍīf (nuḍāf)
purse	maḥfaẓa
to put down, to bring down	nazzil II
to put inside	dakhkhal II *(fī)*
to be put aside	itrakan VII
to put on	libis (i)
to be put, placed	itḥaṭṭ VII
pyramid	haram (ʾahrām/ ʾahrāmāt)

Q

quarter	ḥayy (ʾaḥyāʾ)
quarter	rubʿ (ʾarbāʿ)
to quench	ṭafa (i)
question	masʾala (masāʾil)
question	suʾāl (ʾasʾila)
questionnaire, document, form	istimāra
queue, line	ṭābūr (ṭawabīr)

R

radio	rad(i)yō
to rain	maṭṭar II
to read	ʾara (a)
to be read	itʿaraʿ VII
ready, prepared	gāhiz
to get ready for	istaʿadd X *(li)*
real	ḥaʾīʾī
really, indeed	fiʿlan
reason, cause	sabab (ʾasbāb)
to receive, to take over	istalam VIII
reception	maktab il-istiʾbāl
recipe	roshetta
recommend somebody (no preposition like in English) something	waṣṣa II (ʿala)
record	tasgīl
to recover, be cured	khaff (i)
recreation site, seaside center	maṣyaf (maṣāyif)
red	ʾaḥmar
to turn red	iḥmarr IX
reflector	kashshāf, -āt
refrigerator	tallāga
to refuse	rafaḍ (u)
regard somebody /something as ...	iʿtabar VIII
to regularly take part in	intaẓam VIII *(fī)*
relationship, intercourse	ʿalāqa, - āt
relative	ʾarīb (ʾarāyib)
to relax	istarkha X
relief	naqsh bāriz (nuqūsh barza)
remaining money, change	il-bāʾī
remaining	bāʾī
remarkable, noteworthy, conspicuous	mumayaz
remembering	fākir
rent	ʾīgār, -āt
rent	taʾgīr
to rent, to lease	ʾaggar II
to be rented	itʾaggar V
to repair	ṣallaḥ II

to be repaired	itṣallah V
representative	mandūb
republic	gumhūrīya
request	ṭalab, -āt
requested, wanted	maṭlūb
research, term paper, contribution (at a conference)	baḥs (ʾabḥās)
to reserve, book, order	ḥagaz (i)
rest, remain	baʾīya (bawāʾī)
to rest, to have a rest	istarayyaḥ X
restaurant	maṭʿam (maṭāʿim)
to be restored, reconstructed	itrammim V
result	natīga (natāyig)
to return something to someone	raggaʿ II *(li)*
to return	rigiʿ (a)
to return, to answer to	radd (u) *(ʿala)*
returning	rāgiʿ
to reveal something	ʾāl (u) *(ʿala)*
to revise, to make corrections, control something, to review (study materials)	rāgiʿ III
reward (financial), bonus	ḥawāfiz
rib	ḍilʿ (ḍulūʿ)
rice	ruzz
right	yimīn
to the right	ʿa ʾl-yimīn
right, correct	ṣaḥḥ
right, straight	ʿala-ṭūl
rise, bonus, addition	ziyāda
rising	ṭāliʿ
river	nahr (ʾanhār / ʾanhur)
road, journey	ṭarīʾ (ṭuruʾ)
road, way, path	sikka (sikak)
roast (meat)	mashwī
role, part	dōr (ʾadwār)
room	ʾōḍa
room	ʾōḍa (ʾuwaḍ)
rope	ḥabl (ḥibāl)
rope, string	dubāra
rose	warda
roses	ward
to run, flow, pass	giri (i)
rush, hurry	ʿagala

S

sad	ḥazīn
salad	salaṭa, -āt
salesman	bayyāʿ, -īn
sand	raml (rimāl)
sandwich	sandawīch, -āt
Saqqara	Saʾʾāra
sarcophagus	nāwūs (nawawīs)
satisfied	mabsūṭ
to be satisfied with	inbasaṭ VII *(min)*
to save, keep	ḥāfiẓ III *(ʿala)*
to say something	ʾāl (u)
scarab beetle	guʿrān (gaʿārīn)
scent, smell	rīḥa (rawāyiḥ)
to screen someone, to examine something	ikhtabar VIII
sea	baḥr (buḥūr)
to seal, to stamp	khatam (i)
to search for something	dawwar II *(ʿala)*
season	mōsim (mawāsim)
second, moment	sanya (sawānī)
security guards	ḥaras
to see	shāf (u)
seeing	shāyif
to sell	bāʿ (ī)
to send	baʿat (a)
sender	mursil
sensitivity	ḥassāsīya
to be sent	itbaʾat VII
sentence	gumla (gumal)
to serve someone or something	khadam (i) (without preposition)
service	khidma (khadamāt)
to set, lay the table	farash (i)
to be set, determined	itḥaddid V
to settle (financially) with someone	ḥāsib III (without preposition)
to settle (financially) with someone, to balance accounts with	itḥāsib VI *(maʿa)*
to shake, shake something	ragg (u) (without preposition)
sheep	ghanam
sheet, cover	baṭanīya
shelf	raff (rufūf)
shirt	ʾamīṣ (ʾumṣān)
shoe seller, shoemaker	gazmagī, -ya
shoes	gazma (gizam)
shop	dukkān (dakakīn)
shop	maḥall, -āt
shore, bank	kornīsh
short	ʾuṣayyar
shovel	garūf (gawarīf)
to show something to someone	warra II (without preposition) *(li)*
to show something *(ʿala)* to someone (without preposition)	farrag II (ʿala)
siblings	ʾikhwāt
side, look	naḥya (nawāḥī)
to sign	maḍa (i)
to sign something	maḍa (i) *(ʿala)*

signal, traffic light	'ishāra
signature	'imḍā'
silver	faḍḍa
simple	sahl
simple, common	basīṭ (busaṭa)
Sinai	Sīnā
since, for, because	'aṣl (+ pronominal suffix) ('aṣlo, 'aṣlī, 'aṣluku)
singer	muṭrib
sink	ḥōḍ ('aḥwāḍ)
sir (title, address)	bē(h)
sirloin	mōza
sister	'ukht ('akhawāt)
to sit, sit down	'a'ad (u)
site, position (geographical)	mauqi' (mawāqi')
sitting	'ā'id
situation, conditions	ẓarf (ẓurūf)
situation, state, condition	ḥāl (aḥwāl)
sky	sama (samawāt)
sleep	nōm
to sleep	nām (ā)
to sleep, spend the night	bāt (ā)
sleeping car	'arabīyit in-nōm
sleeping	nāyim
small piece of paper	wara'a
small	'ulayyil
small	ṣ(u)ghayyar
to make smaller, reduce	ṣaghghar I
to smear	dahan (i)
to be smeared	itdahan VII
to smell	shamm (i)
smoking	tadkhīn
snow	talg
social	igtimā'ī
socks	sharāb, -āt
solution	ḥall (ḥulūl)
to solve	ḥall (i)
to be solved	itḥall V
some	ba'ḍ
some, several	kaza
some, several, a few	shwayya
someone	ḥad
song	ghinwa ('ghānī)
soon	'urayyib
sorry	'āsif
sorry, sad about someone, something, worried about	za'lān ('ashān)
to be sorry, sad about someone, something, worried about	zi'il (a) ('ashān)
to sort	kharag (u)
soul	nafs (nufūs)
sound	ṣōt ('aṣwāt)
soup	shurba
source (in research, primary source)	margi' (marāgi')
south	ganūb
to speak	itkallim V
special	makhṣūs
specialist, expert, physician	'akhiṣṣā'ī
speed	sur'a
speech, utterance	kalām
spirit, soul	rūḥ ('arwāḥ)
spoon	ma'la'a (ma'āli')
sport	riyāḍa
spring	rabī'
square	mīdān (mayadīn)
squinting	'aḥwal
to be squinting, to squint	iḥwall IX
to stand, to stand up	wi'if (a)
to start (a car)	dawwar II (without preposition)
station, (police) station	'ism ('a'sām)
to stay, to remain	fiḍil (a)
St. Catherine	Sant Katrīn
stamp (postal)	ṭābi' (tawābi')
stamp, seal	khitm ('akhtām)
to be stamped, sealed	itkhatam VII
stand, stand up, start	'ām (u)
standard Arabic	fuṣḥa
state	daula (duwal)
state, condition	ḥāla
state, country	daula (duwal)
station	maḥaṭṭa
statue	timsāl (tamasīl)
stay	'iqāma
to step, step on	dās (ū)
to stick to something	itlaza' VII
to stick, to stick to to stick on	laza' (a)
stipend, scholarship, financial contribution	minḥa (minaḥ)
stomach, belly pain	maghaṣ
stone	ḥagar ('aḥgār)
stopper (gas, water)	maḥbas (maḥābis)
storey	dōr ('adwār)
storm	'āṣifa ('awāṣif)
stove (gas)	butagāz, -āt
street	shāri' (shawāri')
strength, force	shidda
strengthen	shadd (i)
striding, going	māshī
to strike, to beat	ḍarab (a)
stripe, belt, girdle	shrīṭ ('ashriṭa)
stroke	ḍarba
strong (drink)	ti'īl (tu'āl)
strong, relentless, strict	shdīd (shudād)
strong, sturdy, tough, hard	gāmid

strongly	gāmid
student	ṭālib (ṭalaba / ṭullāb)
studied	madrūs
to study, learn something	zākir III
to study, to be a student	daras (i)
to study, to learn	itʿallim V
to stuff, to plug	sadd (i)
study	dirāsa
to be stuffed, jammed, blocked	itsadd VII
subway, tube	metro
to succeed, to be successful at	nagaḥ (a) *(fī)*
success	nagāḥ
successful	nāgiḥ
suddenly	fagʾa
sugar cane	ʾaṣab sukkar
sugar	sukkar
to suggest something to someone *(ʿala)*	iqtaraḥ VIII (without preposition)
suit	badla (bidal)
to suit someone	nāsib III (without preposition)
to suit somebody or something	nifiʿ (a) (without preposition)
sum (financial)	mablagh (mabāligh)
summer	ṣēf
sun	shams
sunset	maghrib
sure, certainly	bi ʾt-taʾkīd
to make sure about, to make sure about something	itʾakkid V *(min)* ṭammin II *(ʿala)*
surgery	ʿayyāda
surprise	mufagʾa
to surprise someone	fāgiʾ III
to be surprised by	itfāgiʾ VI *(bi)*
to be swallowed	itbalaʿ VII
Sweden	is-Swīd
Swedish	swīdī
sweets	ḥalawīyāt
to swell	wirim (a)
swollen	wārim
syrup	dawa shurb

T

table (dining), dining room	sofra
table	tarabēza
tahīna (sesame paste)	ṭ(i)ḥīna
to take	khad (yākhud)
to take, to grasp	misik (i)
to take (active) part in	shārik VIII *(fī)*
to take (active) part in	ishtarak VIII *(fī)*
to take (passive) part in	ḥaḍar (a)
to take out, to take up, to lift, to make photos	ṭallaʿ II
to be taken, accepted	ittākhid VIII
taking	wākhid
tale, fairy tale	ḥaddūta (ḥawadīt)
tale, story	ḥikāya
to talk to, to speak with	kallim II (without preposition)
to talk, chat with	dardish (yidardish) *(maʿa)*
tall	ʿālī
tamarisk	tamr hindī
to get tanned, to become tanned	ismarr IX
tarsus, toe	mishṭ(i) rigl
task, duty	muhimma (mahāmm)
to taste	dāʾ (ū)
taxi	taks(i)
tea	shāy
to teach someone something	darris II *(li)* (without preposition)
teacher	mudarris
teflon	tīfāl
telephone exchange	sentrāl, -āt
tell, retell	ḥaka (i)
temperature	ḥarāra
temple	maʿbad (maʿābid)
term	maʿād (mawāʿīd)
terrace	shurfa (shuraf)
test, exam in	imtiḥān, -āt *(fī)*
text	naṣṣ (nuṣūṣ)
to thank someone for something	shakar (u) (without preposition) *(ʿala)*
thanking	mutashakkir
thanks to	bi-faḍl
thanks	shukr
that	ʾinn
theatre	masraḥ (masāriḥ)
theme, problem, affair	mauḍūʿ (mawaḍīʿ)
then, on that day	ʾayyāmīhā
there	hnāk
thereafter	baʿdi keda
therefore	ʿashān keda
thing, something, anything	ḥāga
to think of	fakkar II *(fī)*
to think, to opine	iftakar VIII
thinking, thoughtful, contemplating something	sarḥān *(fī)*
third	tilt
thirsty	ʿaṭshān
thought, idea	fikra (ʾafkār)
thousand	ʾalf (ʾālāf)
throat, neck	zōr
to throw, throw away	rama (i)
to be thrown away	itrama VII

ticket	tazkara (tazākir)
tie	krafatta
to tighten	shadd (i)
time	wa’t (’aw’āt)
time, era	‘aṣr (‘uṣūr)
time, era	fatra (fatarāt)
time, period	mudda (mudad)
time, period	zamān
times (x)	fī
tired	ta‘bān
to get tired, to be tired	ti‘ib (a)
to make someone tired, to bother someone	ta‘ab (a)
to, for (dative)	li
tobacco for the water pipe (usually scented)	mi‘assil
today	in-nahār da
toilet	ḥammām, -āt
tolerance	tasāmuḥ
tolerant to	mutasāmiḥ *(ma‘a)*
tomatoes	ṭamāṭim
tomorrow	bukra
tool, device	’adā (’adawāt)
totally, completely, absolutely	khāliṣ
tourism	siyāḥa
tourist	sāyiḥ (suyyāḥ)
tourist group	fōg
tourist guide	murshid
touristic	siyāḥī
towel	fūṭa (fuwaṭ)
town	madīna (mudun)
traffic	murūr
train	’aṭr (’uṭurāt)
trainer	mudarrib
training, practice	tadrībī
translation	targama (tarāgim)
to train, practice	darrab II
to translate	targim
to travel to a place (without preposition), to go to a person *(li)*	sāfir III
traveling	rākib (rukkāb)
tray	ṣīnīya (ṣawānī)
treasure	kinz (kunūz)
to treat somebody, to get along with somebody	‘āmil III (without preposition)
trees	shagar
trolley, carriage	karro
trousers	banṭalōn, -āt
truck, lorry	‘arabīyt in-na’l
to try something, to attempt something	garrab II
to try, to attempt	ḥāwil III
T-shirt	T-shirt, -āt
to turn on, launch	shaghghal II
to turn to someone	ittaṣal VIII *(bi)*
to turn to someone, something	laga’ (a) *(li)*
TV set	telefiz(i)yōn

U

uncle (father’s brother)	‘amm (’a‘mām)
uncle (mother’s brother)	khāl (khīlān)
under, below	taḥt
to understand	fihim (a)
to understand one another	itfāhim VI *(ma‘a)*
understanding (mutual)	tafāhum
understanding	fāhim
to undress, to take off	’ala‘ (a)
unforgivable	lā yughtafar
unit, unity	waḥda
university	gam‘a (gāmi‘āt)
university college	madīna gam‘īya
until	li-ghāyit mā
until, toward	li-ghāyit
Upper Egypt (southern Egypt)	iṣ-Ṣa‘īd
to use	istakhdim X
to use something	ista‘mil X
to use up, to consume	istahlik X
use, benefit	maṣlaḥa (maṣāliḥ)
to be used to	wākhid *(‘ala)*
useful, beneficient	mufīd
to be useful, beneficient to somebody (without preposition)	’afād IV

V

value	’/qīma (’/qiyam)
to value	’addar II
veal	bitello
vegetables	khuḍār
very	giddan
very, too (much)	’awi
via, by way of	‘an ṭarī’
video	fīdyo
view, scenery	manẓar (manāẓir)
visa	fīza
visit	ziyāra
to visit	zār (ū)
visitor	zāyir (zuwwār)
vitamin	fītāmīn, -āt
vocative particle “o”	yā
voice	ṣōt

W

waist, belt	ḥizām (’aḥzima)
to wait someone, something	intaẓar VIII (without preposition)

to wait, wait for someone, something	istanna X (without preposition)
waiter	garson
to wake up someone	ṣaḥḥa II
walk	mashy
to walk around	laff (i)
to walk, to go, go away, to stride	mishi (i)
wall	ḥēṭa (ḥīṭān)
wall, fence	sūr (ʾaswār)
wanting	ʿāwiz / ʿāyiz
war	ḥarb (ḥurūb)
warm	sokhn
to wash	ghasal (i)
to wash oneself, to be washed	itghasal VII
water tap	ḥanafīya
water	mayya
water-heater	sakhkhān, -āt
waterpipe	shīsha (shiyash)
to watch something	tābiʿ III
way, method	ṭarīʾa (ṭuruʾ)
we	ʾeḥna
weather, atmosphere	gauw
wedding night, wedding ritual celebrating the marriage	dukhla
wedding ritual after the first waking (the first morning) as a married couple	ṣabāḥīya
wedding	faraḥ (ʾafrāḥ)
week	ʾusbūʿ (ʾasabīʿ)
weigh	wazan (i)
weird, special	gharīb
well, shaft	bīr (ʾābār)
wellcome	ʾahlan
to welcome someone, something	raḥḥab II *(bi)*
western, European	gharbī
whatever, whichever	ʾayy(i)
when	lammā
when?	ʾemta
where from?	mnēn
where?; where to?	fēn?
which? (interrogative pronoun)	ʾanho / ʾanhi / ʾanhum?
in a while	baʿd(i) shwayya
white colour	bayāḍ
white	ʾabyad
to become white	ibyaḍḍ IX
whites (Caucasians)	bīḍ
who?	mīn
why?	lē(h)?
wide, broad, spacious, extensive	wāsiʿ
wife	ḥaram
to win something (in a contest)	fāz (u) *(bi)*
window	shibbāk (shababīk)
to wish	shāʾ (a)
to wish, to hope	itmanna V
to wish, to want	ʿāz (ū)
with	bi
with, together with	maʿa
with, together	wayya
to withdraw	saḥab (a)
without doing	min ghēr ma
without	min ghēr
woman, Mrs.	sitt, -āt
woman, wife (before a pronoun, pronominal suffix or the first component of a genitival phrase)	mrāt
to wonder at	istaghrab X *(min)*
wood	khashab
wooden	khashabī
word	kilma (kalimāt)
word, pl. vocabulary	mufrad, -āt
work	shughl (ʾashghāl)
work	ʿamal (ʾaʿmāl)
to work, to be employed	ishtaghal VIII
workers (manual)	ʿummāl
workers, employees	ʿāmilīn
working, worker	ʿāmil
workshop, workroom	warsha (wirash)
the world	dinya / dunya
worry, concern	hamm (humūm)
to write	katab (i)
writing	kātib
written	maktūb
written, noted, recommended	musaggal
to be written	itkatab VII

Y

year	sana (sinīn, sanawāt)
year	ʿām (ʾaʿwām)
yearning, longing, craving, memory	shōq (ashwāq)
yeast	khamīra
yellow colour	il-ʾaṣfar
yellow	ʾaṣfar
to turn yellow	iṣfarr IX
yes	ʾaywa
yes, sure, right	ṣaḥīḥ
yes; but yes; of course	ʾā(h)
yesterday	ʾembāreh
yet, (not) yet	lissa
yolk	ṣafār

Muʿgam ʿarabī ʾinglīzī

A

ʾab (ʾābāʾ)	father
ʾabadan	not at all, never
ʾabazhōra	desk lamp
ʾabkam (bukm)	dumb
ʾabyaḍ (bīḍ)	white
ʾadā (ʾadawāt)	tool, device
ʾadab (ʾādāb)	literature
ʿadad (ʾaʿdād)	number
ʿadd (i)	to count
ʿadda II	to go around, to stop byʿ
addād, -āt	meter (electrometer, water meter, taxameter)
ʿads	lentils
ʾafḍal	better, the best (elative)
ʿafrīta	negative
ʿagab (i)	to be liked by someone
ʾagāza	holiday
ʾaggar	to rent, to lease
ʿāgib	being liked (by someone - followed by a pronominal suffix or noun without preposition)
ʿagīna (ʿagāyin)	dough
ʾagnabī (ʾagānib)	foreign, foreigner
ʿagūz (ʿawagīz)	old, old man
ʾā(h)	yes; but yes; of course
ʾahamm	more important, the most important (elative)
ʾaḥdab	hunchbacked
ʾahlan	wellcome
ʾaḥmar (ḥumr)	red
ʾaḥsan	better, the best (elative)
ʾaho	here, look!
ʾaḥrag IV	to embarass, shame
il-ʾAhrām	name of the most famous Egyptian newspaper, the Pyramids
ʾaḥwal	squinting
ʾakh (ʾikhwa)	brother
ʾakhḍar (khuḍr)	green
ʾakhīr	the last
ʾākhir marra	the last time
ʾakhiṣāʾī	specialist, expert physician
ʾakhras (khurs)	dumb
ʾakīd	certain, certainly
ʾakkid II	to assure someone *(li)*
ʾakl (ʾakalāt)	food, meal
ʿala	on, at (shortened to ʿa- before the definite article)
ʿa(la) ʾl-ʾākhir	completely, totally, absolutely
ʿala ṭūl	right, straight, immediately
ʾalam (ʾālām)	pain
ʿalāqa	relationship, intercourse
ʾalf (ʾālāf / ʾulūfāt)	thousand
ʿālī	tall, high
ʿallaʾ II	to hang
ʿallim II	to educate someone
ʾalmānī	German
ʾAlmāniyā	Germany
ʾalō!	hello! (on the phone)
ʿām (ʾaʿwām)	year
ʾaʿma (ʿumy)	blind
ʿamal (ʾaʿmāl)	work
ʿamal (i)	to do
ʿamalīya	operation (medical, military), action
ʾamar (u)	to command someone (without preposition) to do something *(bi)*
ʿāmil	working, worker
ʿāmilīn	workers, employees
ʿamm (ʾaʿmām)	uncle (father´s brother)
ʿāmmīya	colloquial Arabic
ʾamrīkī (ʾamrīkān)	American
ʿan	about
ʿand	at, by
ʿan ṭarīʾ	via, by way of
ʾanho / ʾanhi / ʾanhum?	which? (interrogative pronoun)
ʿarabīya	car
ʿarabīyit in-nōm	sleeping car
ʿarabīyt in-naʾl	truck, lorry
ʿaraḍ (i)	to exhibit, offer, make an offer
ʾaʿrag	limping, lame
ʿarbūn	deposit
ʿārif	knowing
ʿarīs (ʿirsān)	bridegroom
ʿarʾisūs	liqorice
ʿarraf II	to introduce someone (without preposition) to someone/something *(ʿala / bi)*
ʿarūsa (ʿarāyis)	bride
ʾasarī	archaeologist, historical
ʾaṣamm (ṣumm)	deaf

ʾasansēr, -āt	lift
ʾasar (ʾāsār)	monument
ʾaṣfar (ṣufr)	yellow
il-ʾaṣfar	yellow colour
ʿāsh (ī)	to live
ʿasha	dinner
ʿashān	because of, for
ʿashān keda	therefore
ʾāsif	sorry
ʿāṣifa (ʿawāṣif)	storm
ʿāṣima (ʿawāṣim)	capital
ʿaṣīr (ʿaṣāyir)	juice
ʾaṣl (+ pronominal suffix)	since, for, because
ʾaṣlan	because, for, originally
ʿaṣr (ʿuṣūr)	time, era
ʾAswān	Aswan
ʿaṭshān	thirsty
ʾaṭrash (ṭursh)	deaf
ʿaṭṭal II	to interrupt someone, to distract someone from something *(ʿan)*
ʾaulawīya	priority, preference
ʾaurāʾ	papers, documents, ID cards
ʾaʿwar	one-eyed
ʿāwiz / ʿāyiz	wanting
ʾawrāʾ (rasmīya)	ID papers, documents
ʿawwaḍ II	to compensate some thing *(ʿan)* to someone (without preposition)
il-ʾawwil	at first
ʾawwil mā	as soon as, when
ʾawwil marra	the first time
ʿayyāda	surgery
ʾaywa	yes
ʾayy(i)	whatever, whichever
ʾayyāmīhā	then, on that day
ʿayyaṭ II	to cry
ʿāz (ū)	to wish, to want
ʿaza	condolence
ʿazam (i)	to invite
ʿazar (u)	to excuse someone, to forgive someone
ʿaẓīm (ʿuẓama)	great, excellent, marvellous
ʾazraʾ	blue
ʿazza II	to condole someone (without preposition)

B

bāʿ (ī)	to sell
baʿat (a)	to send
bāb (ʾabwāb / bībān)	door, gate
bābung	camomille
baʿd	in, after
baʿd iḍ-ḍuhr	afternoon
baʿd(i) bukra	the day after tomorrow
baʿdi keda	thereafter
baʿdi mā	after, afterwards
baʿdi shwayya	in a while
baʿḍ	some
badaʾ (a)	to begin with (fī)
baʿdēn	after, then
badla (bidal)	suit
badri	early, soon
baḥr (buḥūr)	sea
balad (bilād)	country, village, countryside
baladī	home, local
balakōna	balcony
ballagh II	deliver, announce
ballāʿa	outlet (in the bathroom)
balṭo (balṭohāt)	coat
bān (ā)	to look like, to be seen somewhere, on someone / something *(ʿala)*
banṭalōn, -āt	trousers
baʾa (a)	to become
bāʾī	remaining
il-bāʾī	remaining money, change
baʾīya (bawāʾī)	rest, remain
barḍo	also, too
bardān	feeling cold
bardī, -yāt	papyrus
bārid	cool, cold
Bārīs	Paris
barʾūʾ	plums
barra	outside, out, abroad
bas	only; but
bās (ū)	to kiss
baṣal	onion
basbōr	passport
bāsha, -wāt	Mr.
basīṭ (busaṭa)	simple, common
basīṭa (= ḥāga basīṭa)	no problem, that is easy
baṣṣ (u)	to look at, to look into *(fī)*
baṣṣa	look (at / into)
bāt (ā)	to sleep, spend the night
baṭanīya	sheet, cover
baṭāṭis	potatoes
baṭn	belly
baṭṭīkh	melon
bawwāb, -īn	doorkeeper, housekeeper
bayāḍ	1. white colour 2. eggwhite
bāyin	evident, visible
bāyin ʾinn	it seems that

bayyāʿ, -īn	salesman
bārik III	to congratulate someone *(li)*, to bless somene *(li)*, may God bless you *(fī)*
bē(h) (bahawāt)	sir (title, address)
bēḍ	eggs
bēn	between, among
bēt (buyūt)	house, home
bi	with
bi-faḍl	thanks to
bi ʾl-ktīr	at most, at the latest
bi ʾt-taʾkīd	sure, certainly
bi-ṣarāḥa	honestly
bibyōna	bowtie
bīḍ	whites (Caucasians)
bidāya	beginning
biʿīd (buʿād)	far, distant
biʿīd min	far from
bint (banāt)	girl, daughter
bīr (ʾābār)	well, shaft
biʿsa	expedition, mission
biṭāʾa	ID card
bitello	veal
bīzanṭī	Byzantine
blāge, -āāt	beach
Brāg	Prague
brīṭānī	British
buhēyra	lake
bukra	tomorrow
būlīs	police
Būr Saʿīd	Port Said
burtuʾāl	oranges
butagāz, -āt	stove (gas)

D

ḍāʿ (ī)	to get lost
dabaḥ	to kill/slaughter (an animal)
dabbar II	to arrange
dafaʿ (a)	to pay
ḍāfir (ḍawāfir)	nail
ḍaghṭ (ḍughūṭ)	pressure
dahab	gold
dahan (i)	to smear
dakhal (u)	to enter
dakhkhal II	to put inside *(fī)*
ḍallim II	to dusk, to get dark
ḍalma	darkness
ḍaman (a)	to guarantee
dāʾ (ū)	to taste
daʾn (duʾūn)	beard
dār (dūr)	house (above all specialised for a certain activity)
Dār il-kutub	The National Library
ḍarab (a)	to strike, to beat
daraga	grade
daras (i)	to study, to be a student
ḍarba	a stroke
dardish (yidardish)	to talk, chat with *(maʿa)*
dars (durūs)	lesson
ḍarūrī	necessary, inevitable, it is necessary
darrab II	to train, practice
darris II	to teach someone *(li)* something (without preposition)
dās (ū)	to step, step on
daula (duwal)	to stand
daulī	international
dawa (ʾadwiya)	medicine
dawa shurb	syrup
daʿwa	invitation
dawwar II	to search for something *(ʿala)*
dawwar II	to start (a car) (without preposition)
dayman	always
ḍēf (ḍuyūf)	guest
dēr (ʾadyira)	monastery
ḍidd	opposite
ḍiḥik (a)	to laugh
ḍilʿ (ḍulūʿ)	rib
diʾīʾ	flour
di ʾl-waʾt(i)	now
dibil (a)	to fade
diblūmāsī	diplomatic, diplomat
dimāgh	head, brain
dinya /dunya	the world
diʾīʾa	minute
dirāsa	study
doktōr (dakatra)	doctor
dolāb	case
dōr (ʾadwār)	storey; role, part
ḍuhr	noon
dukhla	wedding night, wedding ritual celebrating the marriage
durg (ʾadrāg)	drawer (of a desk), shelf

E

ʾeḥna	we
ʿēla	family (closest family circle)
ʾembāreḥ	yesterday
ʾemta	when?
ʿēn (ʿuyūn)	eye
ʿēsh	bread

F

faḍḍa	silver
fag'a	suddenly
fahhim II	to explain something without preposition) to someone (without preposition)
fakha	fruit
fakka	change (money)
fakkar II	to think of (fī)
fallāḥ, -īn	peasant, farmer
fannīy	artistic, art, of art
faraḍ (i)	to expect
faraḥ ('afrāḥ)	wedding
Faransā	France
farash (i)	to equip, decorate an apartment; to set lay the table
farfish (yifarfish)	to distract someone,
farḥān	being happy
farkha (frākh)	chicken, poultry
farrag II	to show something (ʿala) to someone (without preposition)
farraḥ II	to make someone (without preposition) happy
fassaḥ II	to organize a trip, walk for someone (without preposition)
fataḥ (a)	to open
fatra (fatarāt)	time, era
fattaḥ II	1. to make light, to enlighten
fattish II	to control, to check
fāḍī	free, empty
fāgi' III	to surprise someone
fāhim	understanding
fākir	remembering
fāṣil III	to bargain with (without preposition)
fāt (ū)	to pass
fāṭimī	Fatimid
fātiḥ	opening
fātiḥ	light
fawwār	effervescent
fāz (u)	to win something *(bi)*
fēn?	where?; where to?
fī	in, on, at
fiʿlan	really, indeed
fiḍil (a)	to stay, to remain
fīdyo	video
fihim	to understand
fikra	thought, idea
filfil rūmī	pepper
film ('aflām)	film
fingān (fanagīn)	cup, mug
firʿaunī	pharaonic
firiḥ (a)	to be happy
fītāmīn, -āt	vitamin
fiṭār	breakfast
fīza	visa
flūs	money
fō'	above
fōg ('afwāg)	tourist group
fukhār	ceramics
fundu' (fanādi')	hotel
furṣa (furaṣ)	occasion, chance
fuṣḥa	standard Arabic
fustān (fasatīn)	dress (ladies)
fūl	beans
fūṭa (fuwaṭ)	towel
fūtit maṭbach	dishcloth

G

gaʿān	being hungry
gāb (ī)	to bring, obtain
gabal (gibāl)	mountain
gadwal (gadāwil)	list, schedule
gahhiz II	to prepare, to make ready
gāhiz	ready, prepared
gallābīya (galālīb)	long, loose shirt-like dress
gamʿa (gāmiʿāt)	university
gamāl	beauty
gāmiʿ (gawāmiʿ)	mosque
gāmid	strong, sturdy, tough, hard; strongly
gamīl	beautiful
ganb	next to
ganūb	south
gara (a)	to happen
gardal (garādil)	bucket
garrab II	to try something, to attempt something
garson	waiter
garūf (gawarīf)	shovel
gauw	weather, atmosphere
gawāb, -āt	letter
gawāz (gawāzāt) safar	passport
gazma (gizam)	shoes
gazmagī, -ya	shoe seller, shoemaker
gazzār, -īn	butcher
gāyib	bringing
gāyiz	maybe, perhaps
gdīd (gudād)	new
ge (yīgī)	to come to a place (with out preposition), to a person *(li)*
gēb (guyūb)	pocket

ghāb (ī)	to be missing
ghada	lunch
ghālī	expensive, dear, costly
ghāmi'	dark
ghanam	sheep
gharbī	western, European
il-Gharda'a	Hurghada
gharīb	weird, special
ghāṣ (u)	to dive
ghasal (i)	to wash
ghasīl	laundry
ghaṭa (ghuṭyān)	lid, cap, stopper
ghayyar II	to change
ghāz, -āt	gas
ghēr	outside, but for, besides, except for
min ghēr	without
min ghēr mā	without doing
ghēṭ (ghīṭān)	field, arable land
ghinwa ('aghānī)	song
gibna (giban)	cheese
gidd ('agdād)	granddad, grandparent
giddan	very
gild (gulūd)	leather, skin
gildī	leather (adjective)
ginē(h), -āt	pound
giri (i)	to run, flow, pass
gnēna (ganāyin)	garden
gouwa	inside
gōz ('agwāz)	husband, pair
grāb, -āt	cover, case
gu'rān (ga'ārīn)	scarab beetle
gumhūrīya	republic
gumruk (gamārik)	customs
gurnān (garanīn)	newspaper

H

ḥabb (i)	to like, to love, to wish, to like to do something
ḥabbāya	pill
ḥabīb (ḥabāyib)	beloved
ḥabl (ḥibāl)	rope
ḥad	someone
ḥaḍar (a)	to take (passive) part in
ḥaḍāra	culture, civilisation
ḥaḍḍar II	to prepare, to make, to create
ḥadd (ḥudūd)	frontier, limit
hadda' II	to calm down, to reduce (speed)
ḥaddūta (ḥawadīt)	tale, fairy tale
ḥadīd	iron
ḥāḍir	current, present
hadīya (hadāyā)	gift
ḥadsa	accident
ḥaf(a)rīyāt	excavations, archaeological excavations
ḥafar (u)	to excavate, to conduct (archaeological) excavations
ḥāfiẓ III	to save, keep *('ala)*
ḥafla (-āt)	party, celebration, concert, performance
ḥafla mūsīqīya	concert
ḥāga	thing, something, any thing
ḥagar ('aḥgār)	stone
ḥagaz (i)	to reserve, book, order
ḥaka (i)	tell, retell
ḥalawīyāt	sweets
ḥāl ('aḥwāl)	situation, state, condition
ḥāla	state, condition, case
ḥālan	immediately
ḥall (i)	to solve
hamm (humūm)	worry, concern
ma tiḥmilsh(i) hamm	do not worry
hamm (i)	to interest someone
ḥammaḍ II	to develop a film
ḥammām	bath, toilet
ḥanafīya	water tap
ḥanafīya	pot
ḥanṭūr (ḥanaṭīr)	carriage
ḥa'' (ḥu'ū')	law, truth
ḥa'ī'ī	real
ḥaram	husband, wife
haram ('ahrām / 'ahrāmāt)	pyramid
ḥarāra	temperature
ḥaras	security guards
ḥarb (ḥurūb)	war
ḥarrān	feeling warm, hot
ḥaṣal	to happen
ḥasab	according to
ḥāsib III	to settle (financially) with someone (without preposition)
ḥass (i)	to feel something *(bi)*
ḥassāsīya	allergy, sensitivity
ḥaswik (yiḥaswik)	to be overly careful,
hāt! / hātī! / hātū!	give! pass!
ḥaṭṭ (u)	to place, put something somewhere *(fī)*
ḥawāfiz	reward (financial), bonus
ḥawālī	around, ca., approximately
ḥayā	life
hāyil	great, wonderful,
ḥayy ('aḥyā')	quarter
ḥayyar II	to embarrass
ḥazīn	sad

ḥaẓẓ (ḥuẓūẓ)	luck
ḥattā	even
ḥāwil III	to try, to attempt
ḥēl	force, energy
ḥelu	beautiful, nice, excellent
ḥelu	dessert, sweet
Ḥelwān	Helwan
hena	here
ḥēṭa (ḥīṭān)	wall
ḥikāya	tale, story
hindī	Indian
hindī ʾaḥmar (hunūd ḥumr)	American Indian
ḥisāb, -āt	bill
ḥitta (ḥitat)	piece (of food, cloth)
ḥizām (ʾaḥzima)	waist, belt
hnāk	there
ḥōḍ (ʾaḥwāḍ)	sink
ḥuḍūr	participation
il-Ḥusēn	the Mosque of Sayyidna il-Huseyn in Cairo

I

ʿibāra	expression, word
ibtada VIII	to begin
ibtakar VIII	to invent
ibtidāʾī	basic (school), initial
ibtikār, -āt	invention
ibyaḍḍ IX	to become white
ʾīd (ʾayādī)	hand
ʿīd (ʾaʿyād)	festive day, festival
ʿīd il-mīlād	birthday
ʾidāra	directorate, administration
ʾidda (yiddi)	to give
ʾIfrīqiyā	Africa
iftakar VIII	to think, to opine
iftaraḍ VIII	to expect
ʾīgār, -āt	rent
ighmaʾʾ IX	to turn dark
igtimāʿī	social
iḥdabb IX	to be hunchbacked
iḥmarr IX	to turn red
ihtamm VIII	to be intersted in *(bi)*
iḥtafal VIII	to celebrate something *(bi)*
iḥtāg VIII	to need something *(li)* or (without preposition)
iḥtagg VIII	to protest against *(ʿala)*
iḥtaraf VIII	to be a professional
iḥtifāl	party, celebration
iḥtigāg, -āt	protest
iḥwall IX	to be squinting, to squint
ikhḍarr IX	to turn green
ikhtabar VIII	to screen someone, to examine something
ikhtār VIII	to choose
ʾikhwāt	siblings
iktashaf VIII	to discover
ʿilba (ʿilab)	box, chest
ʿilbit shokolāta	box of chocolates
iltizām, -āt	keeping of something *(bi)*, duty, obligation
iltizām bi ʾl-mawāʿīd	punctuality (keeping the terms)
imtaḥan VIII	to examine someone in *(fī)*
imtiḥān, -āt	test, exam in *(fī)*
ʾin	if
ʿinab	grapes
inbasaṭ VII	to be satisfied with *(min)*
ʾinn	that
ʾinsān (nās)	human (human beings) The noun *nās* is either feminine singular or plural.
ʾintāg	production
intaẓam VIII	to regularly take part in *(fī)*
intaẓar VIII	to wait someone, some thing
ʾiqāma	stay
iqtaraḥ VIII	to suggest something to someone *(ʿala)*
ʾirfa	cinnamon
ʿirif (a)	to know
ʿirsān	newlyweds
irtabak VIII	to be embarassed, to get embarassed
irtabaṭVIII	to be connected with *(bi)*
ʾisʿāf	first help, ambulance
iṣfarr IX	to turn yellow
ishtaghal VIII	to work, to be employed
ishtahar VIII	to become famous through (bi)
ishtaka VIII	to complain about *(min)*
ishtara VIII	to buy
ishtarak VIII	to take (active) part in *(fī)*
il-ʾIskindirēya	Alexandria
ʾislāmī	Islamic, Muslim
ʾism (ʾasmāʾ)	name
ʾismant	cement
ismarr IX	to get tanned, to become tanned
iṣṭād VIII	to hunt, fish
istalaf VIII	to borrow
istalam VIII	to receive, to take over

isti'lāmāt	information, questions
iswadd IX	to turn black
'iswid (sūd)	black
i'tabar VIII	regard somebody / something as, consider somebody something as
it'aggar V	to be rented
it'akhkhar V	to be late, to have a delay
it'akkid V	to make sure about *(min)*
it'āla VI	to boast *('ala)*
it'ālig VI	to be treated, cured
it'allim V	to study, to learn
it'amal VII	to be made
it'āmil VI	to cooperate, to be in contact with *(ma'a)*
i'tarad VIII	to have objections to *('ala)*
i'taraf VIII	to confess something *(bi)*
it'araf VII	to be known (get known)
it'arraf V	to meet, to be introduced to *('ala / bi)*
it'ashsha V	to dine
it'assif V	to apologise to sb. *(li)* for something *('an)*
it'assis V	to be founded, to have good foundations
it'aṯṯal V	to be distracted (from work)
it'āwin VI	to cooperate with *(ma'a)*
it'azam VII	to be invited
i'tazar VIII	to apologise to someone *(li)* for something *('an)*
itbala' VII	to be swallowed
itbana VII	to be built
itba'at VII	to be sent
itdahan VII	to be smeared
itdarrab V	to practice, train something *('ala / fī)*
itḍāyi'VI	to be angry with some one; because of *(min)*
itfāgi' VI	to be surprised by *(bi)*
itfāhim VI	to understand one an other *(ma'a)*
itfarrag V	to look at something *('ala)*
itfāṣil VI	to bargain with someone *(ma'a)* about *(fī)*
itfassaḥ V	to go out, to go for a walk, trip
itfataḥ VII	to open oneself
itgāb VII	to be acquired
itgawwiz V	to marry someone
itghadda V	to lunch
itghasal VII	to wash oneself, to be washed
itghayyar V	to change oneself
itḥaddid V	to be set, determined
itḥall V	to be solved
itḥarrak V	to move
itḥassin V	to improve
itḥāsib VI	to settle (financially) with someone, to balance
itḥasha VII	to be filled
itḥaṭṭVII	to be put, placed
itḥāyil VI	to insist on someone *('ala)*
ithayya' V	to appear, seem to some one *(li)*
i'tirāḍ, -āt	objection
itkallim V	to speak
itkasaf VII	to be ashamed
itkasar VII	to break (oneself)
itkatab VII	to be written
itkawa VII	to be ironed
itkharrag V	to graduate *(fī)*
itkhatam VII	to be stamped, sealed
itlaza' VII	to stick to something
itmakkin V	to be expert in, to be good at *(min)*
itmanna V	to wish, to hope
itmashsha V	to go for a walk
itmassik V	to follow something, to hold to (a method) *(bi)*
itnāfis VI	to compete with *(ma'a)*
itnā'ish VI	to discuss with sb. *(ma'a)* about something *(fī)*
itnāzil VI	to give up something, to refrain from some thing *('an)*
it'ābil VI	to meet someone *(ma'a)*
it'addim V	to make progress, to proceed in *(fī)*
it'afal VII	to close oneself
it'ara' VII	to be read
it'ās VII	to be measured
it'aṭṭa' V	to be torn, cut
'iṭr ('uṭūr)	perfume, scent
itrabaṭ VII	to be bandaged
itrabba V	to be brought up
itrāhin VI	to bet with *(ma'a) ('ala)*
itrakan VII	to be put aside
itrama VII	to be thrown away
itrammim V	to be restored, reconstructed

itrāsil VI	to exchange letters with *(ma'a)*
itsāb VII	to be left, to be left behind
itsābi' VI	to compete with *(ma'a)*
itsadd VII	to be stuffed, jammed, blocked
itsalla V	to have fun, be entertained
itṣallah V	to be repaired
itsama' VII	to be heard
itṣaraf VII	to be paid
itṣarraf V	to behave, to manage something *(fī)*
itsāwa VI	to equal one another *(ma'a)*
itṣawwar V	to imagine, to be photo graphed
itshaghal VII	to be employed, busy
itshāl VII	to be brought away, taken away, removed
itsharab VII	to be drunk (of a drink)
itsharraf V	to be honoured by (bi)
ittafa' VIII	to agree with someone *(ma'a)* about something *('ala)*
ittākhid VIII	to be taken, accepted
ittākil VIII	to be eaten
ittaṣal VIII	to be in contact with, to turn to *(bi)*, to join someone *(bi)*
'iza	if
'izba ('izab)	farmstead, farm, holding
izra'' IX	to turn blue

J

jakēt (jawākit)	jacket
jelatti	ice-cream

K

kafeteriya	buffet, canteen
kaḥḥ (u)	to cough
kahraba	electricity
kal (yākul)	to eat
kalām	speech, utterance
kalām	affair, event
kallif II	to charge someone with *(bi)*, to cost someone (a sum)
kam	how many, some, a few
kamān	also, further, too
kamera	camera
karīm (kirām / kurama)	generous, honoured, respected
karkadē(h)	drink made form hibis cus flowers
karnē(h)	ID card
karro	trolley, carriage
kart (kurūt)	card, business card, postcard
kasar (a)	to break (into pieces)
kashaf (i)	to look at, to diagnose someone *('ala)*
kashshāf, -āt	reflector
katab (i)	to write
kattar II	to increase the amount, to make more numerous
kaza	some, several
kān	to be
kātib	writing
kbīr, kbīra	great, big, large
keda keda	in any case, at any rate
khabar ('akhbār)	message, news
khabaz (i)	to bake
khad (yākhud)	to take
khāf (ā)	to be afraid / *min* of something / *'ala* for
khaff (i)	to recover, be cured
khafīf, khafīfa	light
Khafra'	Khephren
khāl (khīlān)	uncle (mother´s brother)
khalās	end, finished
khalfīya	background
khāliṣ	totally, completely, absolutely
khallāt, -āt	mixer
khāma	material
khamīra	yeast
Khān il-Khalīlī	name of a Cairo Oriental market
kharag (u)	to sort
kharīṭa	map
kharṭūsh (kharaṭīsh)	cartouche
khashab	wood
khashabī	wooden
khashsh (u)	to enter, come in
khatam (i)	to seal, to stamp
khaṭīr	great, wonderful, excel len; dangerous
khaṭṭ (khuṭūṭ)	line, writing, script
khārig	leaving, sorting
khēl (khuyūl)	horses
khidma (khadamāt)	service
khiliṣ (a)	to end, finish
khirrīg	graduate, alumnus
khitm ('akhtām)	stamp, seal
khiyār	cucumbers
khōf	fear
khōkh	peaches

khuḍār	vegetables
Khūfū	Khufu (Greek Kheops)
khunfisa (khanāfis)	beetle
khurm (khurūm)	hole
kh(u)sāra (khasāyir)	damage, loss
khuṭūba	engagement
kilma (kalimāt)	word
kinz (kunūz)	treasure
kitāb	book
kīlo	kilogram, kilometre
kornīsh	shore, bank
ktīr	a lot, much, often
kubbāya	glass
kull	every, any, all, entire, whole
kull it-tamām	allright, ok
kullimā	every time, whenever
kullīy(i)t il-ʾāsār	Faculty of Archaeology
kummitra	pears
kumsarī, -ya	conductor
kura (kuwar)	ball, football
kurs, -āt	course (language)
kursī (karāsī)	chair
kurumb	cabbage
kushk (ʾakshāk)	kiosk, stand
kwayyis	good

L

la, laʾ	no
laban	milk
laff (i)	to walk around, to pack
lagaʾ (a)	to turn to someone, something *(li)*
lagna (ligān)	committee
laḥma (luḥūm)	meat
laḥza	moment
lamm (i)	to collect, assemble, put together
lammā	when
lamūn	lemon
laʾa (yilāʾī)	to find
laṭīf (luṭāf)	kind, nice
lātīnī	Latin
lau	if, when
lazaʿ (a)	to stick, to stick to, to stick on
lāziʾ, -āt	bandage
lē(h)?	why?
lēl (layālī)	night
lēlit Rās is-sana	New Year´s Eve
li	to, for (dative)
li-ghāyit	until, toward
li-ghāyit mā	until
libis (i)	to put on
Libnān	Lebanon
libnānī, -īyīn	Lebanese
liʿib (a)	to play
liḥāf (ʾalḥifa)	blanket
liḥiʾ (a)	to catch, to be in time
lissa	(not) yet, just
lōḥa	desk, blackboard, canvas (painting)
lōn (ʾalwān)	colour
lugha	language

M

maʿa	with, together with
maʿa ʾinn	although, despite
maʿād (mawāʿīd)	term, meeting
maʿbad (maʿābid)	temple
maʿdanī	mineral
mafrūḍ	it is necessary
maghaṣ	stomach, belly pain
maghrib	sunset
il-Maghrib	Morocco
maʿhad (maʿāhid)	institute
maʿlaʾa (maʿāliʾ)	spoon
maʿlūmāt	information
maʿraḍ (maʿāriḍ)	exhibition, fair (book)
maʿrifa (maʿārif)	knowledge
maʿrūḍāt	objects on exhibition
mablagh (mabāligh)	sum (financial)
mabna (mabānī)	building
mabrūk	blessed
mabsūṭ	satisfied
makhṣūṣ	special
maḍa (i)	to sign
madd (i)	to extend, to hurry
māddī	material
madīna (mudun)	town, city
madīna gamʿīya	university college
madna (midan)	minaret
madrūs	studied
magalla	magazine
magāl , -āt	area, sphere, field (abstract)
maghūd	effort
magmūʿa	group, collection
maḥaddish	nobody
maḥall, -āt	shop
maḥallī	local
maḥaṭṭa	station
maḥbas (maḥābis)	stopper (gas, water)
maḥfaẓa	purse
maḥmūl	cellular phone
mahwūs	enchanted, fascinated, possessed by some thing
makān (ʾamākin)	place
makhṭūṭa	manuscript
makhzan (makhāzin)	magazine

maktab (makātib)	office, writing table
maktab il-istiʾbāl	reception
maktaba	library
maktūb	written
mala (a)	to fill
malyān	full
mamnūn	grateful
manaʿ (a)	to forbid someone (without preposition) to do something *(min)*
manakhīr	nose
mandīl (manadīl)	handkerchief, scarf
mandūb	representative
manga	mango
manhag (manāhig)	method
manṭiʾa (manāṭiʾ)	area, region
manẓar (manāẓir)	view, scenery
maʾashsha	broom
maqbara (maqābir)	grave, tomb
maʾfūl	closed
maʾlī	fried
maʿʾūl	possible, rational, reasonable
maraḍ (ʾamrāḍ)	illness, sickness
margiʿ (marāgiʿ)	source (in research, primary source)
marham (marāhim)	ointment
marīḍ (marḍa)	patient, sick one
markib (marākib)	boat, ship
markūn	parked, left behind
marmar	marble
marsūm	drawn
masāfa	distance
masʾala (masāʾil)	question, problem, affair
masalan	for example
masgid (masāgid)	mosque
mashghulāt	handmade goods
mashghūl	busy
māshī	striding, going
mashrūb, -āt	drink
mashūr	famous
mashwī	roast (meat)
maṣlaḥa (maṣāliḥ)	use, benefit; administration
maṣnaʿ (maṣāniʿ)	factory
Maṣr	Egypt
maṣrī	Egyptian
masraḥ (masāriḥ)	theatre
massil II	to play (theatre)
maṣyaf (maṣāyif)	recreation site, seaside center
māt (ū)	to die
maṭʿam (maṭāʿim)	restaurant
maṭār	airport
maṭbakh (maṭābikh)	kitchen
maṭlūb	requested, wanted
matḥaf (matāāḥif)	museum
mattar II	to rain
mauḍūʿ (mawaḍīʿ)	theme, problem, affair
mauqiʿ (mawāqiʿ)	site, position (geographical)
mausūʿa	encyclopaedia
mawgūd	present, occurring
mawlūd (mawāālīd)	born
mayya	water
maẓbūṭ	precise, precisely
mazraʿa (mazāriʿ)	arm, plantation
Menkaraʿ	Menkaura (Greek Mycerinus)
metro	subway, tube
miʿassil	tobacco for the water pipe (usually scented)
mīdān (mayadīn)	square
mifṣal (mafāṣil)	joint
miftāḥ	key
mīlād	birth
milaff, -āt	file
milyōn (malayīn)	million
min	from (shortened to *mi-* before the definite article: *mi ʾl- ...*)
mīn	who?
minḥa (minaḥ)	stipend, scholarship, financial contribution
mishi (i)	to walk, to go, go away, to stride
misik (i)	to take, to grasp
mishṭ (ʾamshāṭ)	comb
mishṭ(i) rigl	tarsus, toe
mīya (miʾāt)	hundred
mnēn	where from?
mōsim (mawāsim)	season
mōz	bananas
mōza	sirloin
mrāt	wife (before a pronoun, pronominal suffix or the first component of a genitival phrase)
muʾtamar, -āt	conference, congress
muʿgam (maʿāgim)	dictionary
mubālagh fīh/fīhā	exaggerated (m./f.)
mubārak	blessed
mubtadiʾ	beginner
mudarris	teacher
mudda	time, period
mudīr (mudara)	director
mufagʾa	surprise
mufīd	useful, beneficient
mufrad, -āt	word, pl. vocabulary
muḥadsa	conversation
muhandis	engineer
muhimm	important

muhimma (mahāmm)	task, duty
mukassaf	intensive
mukhtalif	different, various
mulaḥẓa	note, objection
mumayaz	remarkable, noteworthy, conspicuous
mumkin	it is possible
mūmiyā, - āt	mummy
mumtāz	excellent
munasba, -āt	occasion
muntig, -īn	producer
murshid	tourist guide
murūr	traffic
musab'a	contest
musā'ada	help
mushkila (mashākil)	problem
mushtarak	common
mushtarik, -īn	participant
mūsīqā	music
mustashfa, -yāt	hospital
mustawa, -yāt	level
mutasāmiḥ	tolerant to (ma'a)
mutashakkir	thanking
muṭrib	singer
muwaẓẓaf	clerk
muwāṣafāt	parameters, characteristics

N

nadah (a)	to call to someone *(li)*
naḍḍaf II	to clean
naḍḍāra	glasses
nādī ('andiya)	club
nāfis III	to be a competition for sb., to compete with sb. (without preposition)
nagāḥ	success
nagaḥ (a)	to succeed, to be successful at *(fī)*
nāgiḥ	successful
in-nahār da	today
naḥya (nawāḥī)	side, look
nahr ('anhār / 'anhur)	river
nakhīl	palms
nām (ā)	to sleep
na''aṭ II	to drip
naqsh bāriz (nuqūsh barza)	relief
nār (nīrān)	fire
naṣaḥ (a)	to counsel someone something *(bi)*
nāsī	forgetting
nāsib III	to suit someone
naṣīḥa (naṣāyiḥ)	counsel
naṣṣ (nuṣūṣ)	text
naṣya	corner
natīga (natāyig)	result
nāṭiq 'aṣlī	native speaker
nau'īya	kind, sort, type
nāwī	intending
nāwūs (nawawīs)	sarcophagus
nāyim	sleeping
nāzil	leaving, accommodating, descending
nḍīf (nuḍāf)	pure
in-Nīl	the Nile
nishif (a)	to become dry
nisi (a)	to forget
nizil	to get off, descend, accommodate oneself
nōm	sleep
in-Nūba	Nubia
nuḥās	copper
nuṣṣ ('anṣāṣ)	half
nūr ('anwār)	light

O

'oberā	opera
'ōḍa ('uwaḍ)	room
'oḍt in-nōm	bedroom
'otobīs, -āt	bus

Q

qā'a	hall, audition hall
'a'ad (u)	to sit, sit down
'abl	before
'abl(i) keda	before (adverb)
'abli mā	before
'ablina, 'abl(i) sā'a	before us, an hour ago
'addar II	to value
'adīm	old
'afal (i)	to close, shut
'affil II	close, conclude
'āfil	being closed
il-Qāhira	Cairo
'ahwa	coffee, café
'ahwa ('ahāwī)	café
'ā'id	sitting
'āl (u)	to say, reveal
'ala' (a)	to undress, to take off
'alb ('ulūb)	heart
'ām (u)	stand, stand up, start
'amar ('a'mār)	moon
'amīṣ ('umṣān)	shirt
'ara (a)	to read
'arīb ('arāyib)	relative
'arn ('urūn)	century

ʾās (ī)	measure (concerning a means of transporation)
ʾaṣab sukkar	sugar cane
ʾaṣṣ (u)	to cut (with scissors)
ʾaṭaʿ (a)	to cut
ʾaṭr (ʾuṭurāt)	train
ʾawi	very, too (much)
ʾibṭī (ʾaʾbāṭ)	Coptic
ʾidir (a)	to be able, can, may
ʾ/qīma (qiyam)	value
ʾ/qism (ʾaqsām)	department, (police) station
ʾism ig-gawazāt	passport department
ʾizāz	glass
ʾizāza (ʾazāyiz)	bottle
ʾuddām	in front of
ʾulayyil, -īn	small
ʾurayyib	close, soon
ʾurayyib min	close to
ʾurṣ (ʾaʾrās)	pill
ʾuṣād	opposite
ʾuṣṣayyar	short

R

rabb	God, Lord, lord (landlord)
rabbit manzil	housewife
rad(i)yō	radio
radd (u)	to return, to answer to *(ʿala)*
rafaḍ (u)	to refuse
raff (rufūf)	shelf
ragg (u)	to shake, shake something (without preposition)
rakkib II	to compose
rama (i)	to throw, throw away
raṣīf (ʾarṣifa)	pavement, isle
rasm (rusūm)	drawing
rasmī	official
rattib II	to organize
rāʾīsī	main
rāgel (riggāla)	man
rāgiʿ	returning
rāḥ (ū)	to go
rāḥa	peace, rest
rāhin III	to bet with (without preposition)
rākib	traveling
rākin	parking
raml (rimāl)	sand
rās	head
raʾy (ʾārāʾ)	opinion
rāyiḥ	going, leaving respect, esteem and
rghīf (ʾarghifa)	cake, slice (of bread)
rigiʿ(a)	to return
rigl	leg
rīḥa (rawāyiḥ)	scent, smell
riḥla (raḥalāt)	journey, trip, flight
rikib (a)	to go by, take something
risāla (rasāyil)	letter, master's or doctor's thesis
riwāya	novel
riyāḍa	sport
rkhīṣ (rukhāṣ)	cheap
roshetta	recipe
rubʿ (ʾarbāʿ)	quarter
rubāʿīyāt	four-verse poem
rūḥ (ʾarwāḥ)	spirit, soul
rukba (rukab)	knee
rukhṣa (rukhaṣ)	driver's license
ruṭūba	humidity
ruzz	rice

S

sāʿa	hour, watch
saʾal (a)	to ask
sāb (ī)	to leave, let, let go
ṣaʿb	hard, difficult
sabab (ʾasbāb)	reason, cause
ṣabāḥīya	wedding ritual after the first waking (the first morning)
sabaʾ (a)	to go / come before, to make something before someone else (without preposition)
ṣabb (u)	to pour
sabbib II	to cause
ṣabī (ṣubyāān)	boy, apprentice
sābiʾ III	to compete with (without preposition)
ṣadaf	mother-of-pearl
ṣadar (a)	to be issued by / at *(min)*
sadd (i)	to stuff, to plug; to cover (a debt)
ṣaddar II	to export
ṣadīq (ʾaṣdiqāʾ)	friend (an expression of the standard language, which expresses respect, esteem and deep feeling for the person in question)
safar	journey, departure
ṣafḥa, -āt	page
safīr (sufara)	ambassador
ṣafqa (ṣafqāt)	agreement (trade)
saḥab (a)	to withdraw
ṣaḥḥ	right, correct

ṣaḥḥa II — to wake up someone
ṣāḥib (ʾaṣḥāb) — friend
ṣāḥib il-ʿaza — the one who accepts condolence
ṣaḥīḥ — yes, sure, right
sahl — easy, simple
saʿīd (suʿada) — happy
sakan (u) — to live
sakhkhān, -āt — water-heater
sākin — living
ṣāla — hall
salām (salamāt) — greeting
salāma — good health, recovery, safe return, peace
salaṭa, -āt — salad
salīm (sulām) — correct, faultless
ṣallaḥ II — to repair
sallif II — to lend someone *(li)* something (without preposition)
sama (samawāt) — heaven, sky
samaḥ (a) — to allow someone *(li)* to do something *(bi)*
samak (ʾasmāk) — fish
sāmiʿ — hearing
sana (sinīn, sanawāt) — year
sana higrīya — Muslim year
sana mīlādīya — Christian year
sandawīch, -āt — sandwich
ṣandūʾ (ṣanadīʾ) — box
Sant Katrīn — St. Catherine
santi — centimetre
sāʾ (ū) — to drive
saqāfa — culture
sāʾiʿ — cold, cooled
Saʾʾāra — Saqqara
sarḥān — thinking, thoughtful, contemplating something *(fī)*
sawwāʾ — driver
ṣaydalīya — pharmacy
sāyiḥ (suyyāḥ) — tourist
sayyid (sāda) — master, mister, Sir
is-Sayyida — is-Sayyida Zēnab, Lady Zēnab´s mosque
shāʾ (a) — to wish
shaʿr — hair
shadd (i) — to tighten, strengthen
shāf (u) — to see
shaghal (i) — to employ, to make busy
shaghghal II — to turn on, launch
shahar (i) — to make someone or something famous
shahr (shuhūr / ʾashhur) — month
shaka (i) — to complain, file a complaint against *(min)*
shakar (u) — to thank someone (without preposition) for something *(ʿala)*
shakhṣ (ʾashkhāṣ) — person
shakhṣī — personal
shakhṣīyan — personally
shakl (ʾashkāl) — form, shape
shāl (ī) — to carry, carry away, remove
shamm (i) — to smell
shams — sun
shamsīya (shamāsī) — parasol, umbrella
shanṭa (shunaṭ) — bag
shaʾʾa (shuʾaʾ) — flat
sharāb, -āt — socks
sharʾī — eastern, Oriental
shāriʿ (shawāriʿ) — street
sharṭ (shurūṭ) — condition
shāsh — bandage
shāṭiʾ (shawāṭiʾ) — bank
shaṭṭa — chilli peppers
shāy — tea
shāyif — seeing
shayyāl, -īn — bearer
shibbāk (shababīk) — window
shibiʿ (a) — to be full, to eat to the full
shidda — strength, force; downbeat
shimāl — left
shiʿrīya — noodles
shirib (a) — to drink
shirka (sharikāt) — firm, company
shīsha — waterpipe
shōka (shuwak) — fork
shokolāta — chocolate
shōq (ʾashwāq) — yearning, longing, thanks
shukr — thanks
shurba — soup
shurṭa — police
shwayya — some, several, a few
shwayya — little
sifāra — embassy
sīgāra (sagāyir) — cigarette
ṣiḥḥa — health, correctness
ṣiḥḥī — medical
sikka (sikak) — road, way, path
sikkīna (sakakīn) — knife
simiʿ (a) — to hear, listen
Sīnā — Sinai
sināʿa — production, industry
sināʿī — industrial
ṣīnīya (ṣawānī) — tray
siʿr (ʾasʿār) — price
sitt, -āt — woman, Mrs., madam (friendly address)

is-Sitt	epithet of the Egyptian singer ʾUmm Kulsūm
siyāḥa	tourism
siyāḥī	touristic
sofra	table (dining), dining room
sokhn	warm
ṣōt (ʾaṣwāt)	voice, sound
srīr (sarāyir)	bed
studiyo ʾt-taṣwīr	photographic studio
suʾāl (ʾasʾila)	question
ṣubḥ	morning
ṣūra (ṣuwar)	picture, photograph
subūʿ	celebration of the birth of a child (a week of its life)
ṣ(u)ghayyar	small
sukkar	sugar
surʿa	speed
sūʾ (ʾaswāʾ)	market, marketplace
sūr (ʾaswār)	wall, fence
is-Swīd	Sweden
swīdī	Swedish

T

taʿab (a)	to make someone tired, to bother someone
taʿāmul	cooperation, contact
taʿāruf	meeting (one another), getting to know one another
taʿāwun	cooperation
ṭabakh (u)	to cook, prepare a meal
ṭabʿan	of course
taʿbān, -īn	tired
ṭabbākh, -īn	cook
ṭābiʿ (ṭawābiʿ)	stamp (postal)
ṭabīb (ʾaṭibbāʾ)	physician, doctor
ṭabīʿī	natural
taʿbīr, -āt	expression
ṭābūr (ṭawabīr)	queue, line
tābūt (tawabīt)	coffin, sarcophagus
tadkhīn	smoking
tadrībī	training, practice
tafāhum	(mutual) understanding
taʾgīr	rent
taḥt	under, below
tāh (ū)	to get lost
it-Taḥrīr	Tahrir (main Cairo square)
takhaṣṣuṣ, -āt	field, specialisation
takhfīḍ	discount
taks(i)	taxi
takyīf	airconditioning
ṭalab (u)	to ask for, order something
ṭalab, -āt	request
talg	snow
ṭāliʿ	rising
ṭālib (ṭalaba / ṭullāb)	student
taʿlīmī	educating, educational
tallāga	refrigerator
tamām	entirely, exactly, so
bi ʾt-tamām	precisely
ṭamāṭim	tomatoes
ṭaʿmēya	fried burgers of beans, vegetables and spices
taʾmīn, -āt	insurance
tammim II	to bring to a happy end
tamr hindī	tamarisk
tanāzul, -āt	compromise
tant	auntie (a familiar address of a female relative or a close acquaintance)
taqaddum	advance, rise
taʾrīban	approximately, maybe, perhaps
tarabēza	table
tārīkh	history
tārīkhī	historical
ṭarīʾ (ṭuruʾ)	road, journey
ṭarīʾa (ṭuruʾ)	way, method
ṭāsa	frying pan
tasāmuḥ	tolerance
tashkīla	assortment, range (of goods)
ṭayyāra	aeroplane
ṭayyib	good, kind
ṭāze	fresh
tazkara (tazākir)	ticket
tazkarit ṭayarān	flight ticket
telefiz(i)yōn, -āt	TV set
telefōn, - āt	phone
telefōnī	phone
ṭifl (ʾaṭfāl)	child
tiʿib (a)	to get tired, to be tired
ṭiliʿ (a)	to go up, climb, ascend
tiʾīl (tuʾāl)	heavy, strong (drink)
ṭibbī	medical
tīfāl	teflon
tigārī	commercial
ṭ(i)ḥīna	tahina (sesame paste)
tilt	a third
timsāl (tamasīl)	statue
trank	intercity or international phone call
tshīkī (tshīk)	Czech
T-shirt, -āt	T-shirt
ṭūb	bricks

tuffāḥ	apples
tuḥfa (tuḥaf)	monument, antiquity
ṭūl (ʾaṭwāl)	length
ṭwīl (ṭuwāl)	long

U

ʾukht (ʾakhawāt)	sister
ʾumm (ʾummahāt)	mother
ʿummāl	workers (manual)
ʿumr (ʾaʿmār)	age, lifetime
ʾunbūba (ʾanabīb)	pipe, pipeline
ʿunwān (ʿanawīn)	address
il-ʾUʾṣur	Luxor
ʿushb (ʾaʿshāb)	plant
ʿushb ṭibbī	herb
ʾusbūʿ (ʾasabīʿ)	week
ʾusra (ʾusar)	family
ʾusṭa (ʾusṭawāt)	Master, chief (to address artisans)
ʾustāz (ʾasatza)	Mr. (intellectual); professor

W

waʿad (i)	to promise something *(bi)* to someone (without preposition)
waʿd (wuʿūd)	promise
wāḍiḥ	lear, evident
wafā (wafayāt)	death
wafd (wufūd)	delegation
wagaʿ (a)	to give pain, ache someone
wāgib, -āt	duty, task
wāḥa, -āt	oasis
waḥda	unit, unity
wāḥid	one
waḥīd	one, unique, the only
wākhid	taking
wākhid	to be used to *(ʿala)*
wākil	eating
waḥash (a)	miss somebody /some thing
il-wāḥid	man, someone, one
walā	nor
wālid (ʾābāʾ)	father, parent
walīma (walāyim)	feast
walla	or
wallaʿ II	to turn on the light, to ignite
waʾt (ʾawʾāt)	time
wara	behind
waraʾa	small piece of paper
warda	rose, flower
wārim	swollen
warsha (wirash)	workshop, shop,
wāsiʿ	wide, broad, spacious, extensive
waṣṣa II	recommend somebody (no preposition) something *(ʿala)*
waṣṣal II	deliver, convey
wayya	with, together
wazan (i)	weigh
wazīr (wuzara)	minister
wi, ʾu	and, also
widn (widān)	ear
wiḥish	bad, ugly
wilāda	birth
wilid (i)	to give birth
wiʾiʿ (a)	to fall
wiʾif (a)	to stand, to stand up
wirim (a)	to swell
wiris (i)	to inherit
wishsh (wushūsh)	face
wiṣil (a)	to arrive at
wisiʿ (a)	to be broad, to broaden
wizāra	ministry
wuṣūl	arrival
wusṭ	center, middle

Y

yā	or
yā	vocative particle "o"
yā ... yā ...	either or
yaʿnī	i.e., that means
yansūn	aniseed
yimīn	right
ʿa ʾl-yimīn	to the right
yōm (ʾiyyām)	day
lā yughtafar	unforgivable
yūs(t) ʾeffendi	mandarins

Z

ẓābiṭ (ẓubbāṭ)	officer
zahʾān	bored, annoyed, frustrated
zaḥma	(traffic) jam, crowd
zākir III	to study, learn something
zaʿlān	angry with someone
zamān	time, period
zanb (zunūb)	guilt
zār (ū)	to visit
ẓarf (ẓurūf)	situation, conditions
ẓarīf (ẓurāf)	kind, nice, pleasant
zāy? (ʾezzāy?)	how? like, as
zāyid	plus (+)
zāyir (zuwwār)	visitor

zbūn (zabāyin)	customer, client
zēt (zuyūt)	oil
z(i)bāla	garbage
zihiʾ (a)	to be bored, annoyed, to have enough of something
ziʿil (a)	to be angry with someone, about something *(min)* to be sorry, sad about someone, something, worried about
ziyāda	rise, bonus, addition
ziyāra	visit
zmīl (zamāyil)	colleague, co-worker
zōr	throat, neck

FRANTIŠEK ONDRÁŠ

Egyptian Colloquial Arabic

Published by Set Out – Roman Míšek
Tyršova 11, 120 00 Prague, Czech Republic
with the support of the Czech Institute of Egyptology, Charles University in Prague,
Celetná 20, 110 00 Prague, Czech Republic
Prague 2005

Editor Hana Navrátilová
Printed by ÚJI Zbraslav, Prague
Printed in Czech Republic